T0202919

Communications
in Computer and Information Science   1543

More information about this series at https://link.springer.com/bookseries/7899

Chawki Djeddi · Imran Siddiqi · Akhtar Jamil ·
Alaa Ali Hameed · İsmail Kucuk (Eds.)

Pattern Recognition and Artificial Intelligence

5th Mediterranean Conference, MedPRAI 2021
Istanbul, Turkey, December 17–18, 2021
Proceedings

Editors
Chawki Djeddi 🆔
Larbi Tebessi University
Tebessa, Algeria

Imran Siddiqi 🆔
Bahria University
Islamabad, Pakistan

Akhtar Jamil 🆔
FAST National University
Islamabad, Pakistan

Alaa Ali Hameed 🆔
Istanbul Sabahattin Zaim University
Istanbul, Turkey

İsmail Kucuk 🆔
Istanbul Sabahattin Zaim University
Istanbul, Turkey

ISSN 1865-0929   ISSN 1865-0937 (electronic)
Communications in Computer and Information Science
ISBN 978-3-031-04111-2   ISBN 978-3-031-04112-9 (eBook)
https://doi.org/10.1007/978-3-031-04112-9

This Springer imprint is published by the registered company Springer Nature Switzerland AG
The registered company address is: Gewerbestrasse 11, 6330 Cham, Switzerland

Preface

It gives us immense pleasure to introduce this volume of proceedings for the 5th Mediterranean Conference on Pattern Recognition and Artificial Intelligence (MedPRAI 2021). The conference was organized by the Department of Computer Engineering, Istanbul Sabahattin Zaim University, Istanbul, Turkey, during December 17–18, 2021. The conference aimed at providing researchers and practitioners from academia and industry with a forum to share the latest developments in pattern recognition and artificial intelligence.

We are pleased to announce that the response to the Call for Papers for MedPRAI 2021 was very encouraging. A total of 72 papers covering different themes in pattern recognition and artificial intelligence were submitted to the conference. These papers were reviewed by renowned researchers in the respective fields from all over the world. After a thorough and competitive paper review and selection process, 28 high-quality papers were accepted for presentation at the conference yielding an acceptance rate of 39%. This volume comprises the 28 papers which eventually qualified for presentation at the conference.

We would like to take this opportunity to thank the reviewers for their time and efforts in reviewing the papers and providing constructive feedback to the authors. We are also thankful to the keynote speakers and all the authors who submitted papers to the conference. We would also like to extend our cordial appreciation to all members of the organizing committees for their untiring efforts in making this event a success.

We thank all the attendees for participation in the conference and hope that the event provided valuable knowledge sharing and networking opportunities.

December 2021

Chawki Djeddi
Imran Siddiqi
Akhtar Jamil
Alaa Ali Hameed
İsmail Kucuk

Organization

General Chairs

Akhtar Jamil   FAST National University, Pakistan
Ismail Kucuk   Istanbul Sabahattin Zaim University, Turkey

Program Committee Chairs

Alaa Ali Hameed   Istanbul Sabahattin Zaim University, Turkey
Chawki Djeddi   Larbi Tebessi University, Algeria
Imran Siddiqi   Bahria University, Pakistan

Steering Committee

Abdel Ennaji   University of Rouen, France
Ameur Bensefia   Higher Colleges of Technology, Abu Dhabi, UAE
Chang Choi   Chosun University, South Korea
Haikal El Abed   Deutsche Gesellschaft für Internationale
                              Zusammenarbeit (GIZ) GmbH, Jordan
Haoxiang Wang   Cornell University, USA
Javad Sadri   Concordia University, Canada

Organizing Committee

Amani Yahiaoui   Istanbul Sabahattin Zaim University, Turkey
Jawad Rasheed   Istanbul Aydin University, Turkey
Moises Diaz   Universidad de Las Palmas de Gran Canaria,
                              Spain
Muhammad Davud   Istanbul Sabahattin Zaim University, Turkey
Zehra Ilmi Cogalmis   Istanbul Sabahattin Zaim University, Turkey

Program Committee

Abbas Cheddad   Blekinge Institute of Technology, Sweden
Abdel Ennaji   University of Rouen, France
Abdelhakim Hannousse   Guelma University, Algeria
Abdeljalil Gattal   Larbi Tebessi University, Algeria
Ahmad Bouridane   Northumbria University, UK
Akhtar Jamil   FAST National University, Pakistan

Tayeb Benzanati   Digital Research Center of Sfax, Tunisia
Vincent Christlein   University of Erlangen-Nuremberg, Germany
Virendra Kumar   All India Institute of Medical Sciences, India
Yassine Benayed   ISIMS Sfax, Tunisia

Contents

Document Analysis and Understanding

Artificial Intelligence and Intelligent Systems

Computer Vision and Image Processing

Human Action Recognition Using Attention Mechanism and Gaze Information

Reyhaneh MohebAli, Rahil Mahdian Toroghi[✉], and Hassan Zareian

Iran Broadcasting University (IRIBU), Tehran, Iran
{mahdian,zareian}@iribu.ac.ir

Abstract. Recent advances in deep neural networks have achieved significant progress in detecting individual objects from an image. However, object detection is not sufficient to fully understand a visual scene. Towards a deeper visual understanding, the interactions between objects, especially humans and objects are essential. Recognizing human object interactions (HOI) is an important part of distinguishing the rich variety of human action in the visual world. Since the interaction of humans and objects is complex and no temporal information is available, it is not possible to detect the interaction accurately just by extracting the appearance features of the image. In this work, we use human gaze to identify informative regions of images for the interaction. Experimental results on V-COCO dataset clearly represents the efficacy of our proposed model and validates our hypotheses about extra cues being integrated into the base model.

Keywords: Human-Object Interaction (HOI) · Human gaze · Activity understanding · Attention mechanism

1 Introduction

Scene recognition entails not only to recognize humans, but also the objects and further details included in a scene such as the interaction among those entities. Since human plays the key role in most images, understanding the inter-relations among humans and the objects around them significantly elucidates the semantic content of a specific scene. This well-known problem of Human-Object Interaction (HOI), addresses the question about positioning of the humans and objects in a given scene, as well as their interactions. The input to the HOI detection model is a still image and the output is all possible triplets $<human, interaction, object>$.

In a typical HOI problem, a stationary image is given to the system in order to extract three required information types; namely humans, objects, and their interactions. HOI is widely used in human action recognition, human-machine interactions, intelligent control, activity-based image retrieval, video summarization, activity-based image/video search in large data archives, sport analysis, and many other useful applications.

© Springer Nature Switzerland AG 2022
C. Djeddi et al. (Eds.): MedPRAI 2021, CCIS 1543, pp. 3–17, 2022.
https://doi.org/10.1007/978-3-031-04112-9_1

Recognizing the interaction type between human and objects from merely the outward features of a single image is very difficult, since there is no temporal information of the interactions available. Therefore, other features and a more complicated mechanism is required to recognize the interaction type [28]. Typical features used in the literature are, outward features, geometrical relative positions between human and objects, human body state, human gaze directions, image background scene, and so on.

In [28], gaze direction of a human is used as the key feature to recognize the human-object interaction. In our paper, in line with [28], gaze direction and distance is used to improve the attention map in the human branch of the process.

2   Related Works

In recent years, due to the large progress in deep learning and gathering large datasets for many applications, understanding the activity based on an image or a video has been significantly improved. These activities, based upon their duration and complexity, could be divided into four cases: gesture, action, interaction (human-object, and human-human), and group activity types [21], as depicted in Fig. 1.

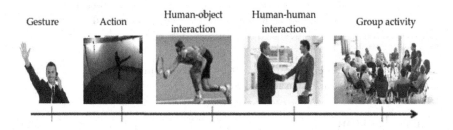

Fig. 1. Categorization of different levels of activities

Since most human activities are of the type of human-object interaction, current research has addressed this issue as a separate topic.

The present work focuses on action recognition from a stationary image. However, there are a plethora of works in which recognizing actions from video files are addressed [10,18,22].

2.1   HOI Detection

In order to identify the triplet elements of human, object, and the interaction between them some research works have used the multi-branch networks, in which the associated features of each are extracted in each individual branch and processed separately. Then, the results are combined to make the final decision

[3,6,8,13,17,28]. Combining the features are normally performed in an early fusion, or a late fusion regime [6]. In an early fusion, all the features from individual branches are concatenated first and then passed through two fully connected layers to produce the final prediction, whereas in a late fusion the action scores are first independently predicted from individual branches and then summed to produce the output prediction.

Another approach employs attention mechanism in order to more accurately recognize the human body-parts or image patches associated to a specific activity [3,23,24,26].

In another approach, graph-based models are involved to determine the interaction types, which are mainly divided into two categories: 1) approaches that consider the human and objects as nodes of the graph, and their interaction as the edges [5,12,19,23]; 2) approaches that utilize the knowledge graph to obtain the semantic relation between activities and associated objects [11,25]. There are also approaches, in which the human-object interaction is modeled as a point in the space, and the HOI detection problem is cast as a key-point estimation problem in that space [15,27].

2.2 Gaze Following

Gaze-following addresses the problem of determining the human gaze direction and detecting the looking target zone. Being so close to the eye-tracking problem, knowing the gaze direction greatly affects the understanding of what a subject human thinks about and what activity he is doing or deciding to do next. This is a highly demanding process for computer vision tasks that aim at scene understanding applications. For example, one may have a book at hand but busy watching TV. This might further assist predicting the next activity one may decide to do, since before acting on an object one should first look at that object [20].

3 The Proposed Idea

3.1 The Basic Model

The proposed model follows the structure in [6], in which three stream paths are considered. One for the human-related features, one for the object-related features and the third one to predict the interaction based on the relative position of human and the object instances. The basic model in [6], and its associated **iCAN** (Instance Centric Attention Network) module is depicted in Figs. 2a and 2b, respectively.

In the first two streams (i.e., human and object streams) of Fig. 2a, the iCAN module has been employed in order to extract the important outward features of the space around human/object using the attention mechanism in addition to the human/object appearance features. The appearance features for the regions of interest (ROI) are extracted in a standard procedure of *ROI pooling* −> *Residual block* −> *Global Average Pooling* (GAP).

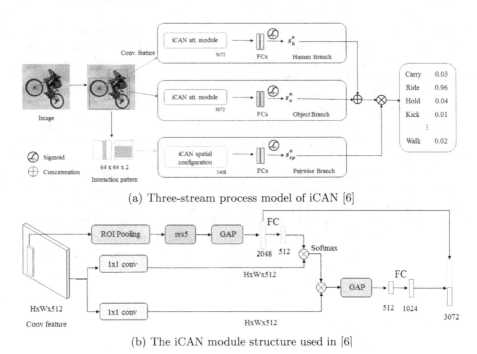

(a) Three-stream process model of iCAN [6]

(b) The iCAN module structure used in [6]

Fig. 2. Overview of the basic model structure using iCAN module for HOI-detection, as in [6]

The attention map highlights relevant regions in an image that might be helpful for recognizing HOI associated with the given human/object instance. The human-centric attention map often focuses on the surrounding objects that help disambiguate action prediction for the detected person. The object-centric attention map, on the other hand, highlights the informative human body part.

The iCAN module in [6], does not consider the fact that in a normal human-object interaction the human entity normally looks directly to that object. This direction could be extracted from the human gaze information. On the other hand, the distance between human and the object instance to have interaction with should be reasonable. These two important cues are not included in the vanilla iCAN module. Our hypothesis is that through incorporating the human gaze information using the gaze heatmap, and by calculating the gaze distance between human and the object instance to be integrated in the processing pipeline, we could be able to achieve a better result. The procedure of how to integrate these novel features in the basic architecture of iCAN module will be explained in the sequel.

3.2   The Proposed Structure

Given an input image and the detected object instances in the image, our method aims at recognizing the interactions (if any) between all pairs of person and object instances. For a human-object candidate box pair (b_h, b_o) as in Fig. 3, regions inside the candidate bounding boxes are cropped and fed into the human and object branches of the processing structure in Fig. 4a respectively, along with the input image. In addition, the two-channel binary image which encodes the spatial relation between the human and object is given to the input of the pairwise branch, as mentioned originally in [1]. First channel has the value 1 at pixels enclosed by the human bounding box, and 0 elsewhere; Second channel has the value 1 at pixels enclosed by the object bounding box, and 0 anywhere else. The dimensions of each channel are considered to be 64×64.

Fig. 3. Human-object candidate box pair (b_h, b_o)

Our novelties are two-fold and belongs to the following contributions: 1) Improving the iCAN module to account for the gaze attention of the human with respect to the object instance; 2) Considering the gaze distance between the human and the associated object, since the act upon an object requires a certain distance between these two elements.

3.3   Gaze Heatmap and the Improved iCAN Module

The proposed model along with the improved iCAN module are depicted in Fig. 4. Getting the boundary boxes of human and object as a pair, as depicted in Fig. 3, the regions belonging to the human or object are cropped and then the three images: human, object, and the pair are given to the model input streams, as in Fig. 4a. The input of the pairwise branch is the common two-channel binary image, as in [1]. In this representation the pixels of human boundary box in the

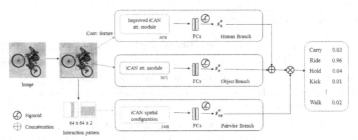

(a) The proposed 3-branch stream model, containing the improved iCAN module

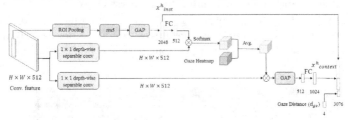

(b) Improved iCAN module using depth-wise separable convolution and integrated gaze heatmap

Fig. 4. The proposed model, as a modification to the base model [6], by adding cues (gaze heatmap and distance) and depth-wise separable convolution blocks

first channel are all ones while the other pixels are zeros. On the other hand, for the second channel all the pixels for the object boundary box are ones, and the rest are zeros. Each channel is assumed to be 64×64. The boundary box format is assumed to be $b = [x_1, y_1, x_2, y_2]$.

After detecting the human body-parts, the normalized coordinates of the eyes are given to the *Gaze-Following model* [14], so that the heatmap and the gaze direction are calculated and then incorporated in the improved iCAN module, depicted in Fig. 4b.

Similar to [6], the HOI score for a pair of human-object (b_h, b_o) is computed as,

$$S_{h,o}^a = S_h.S_o(S_h^a + S_o^a).S_{sp}^a \tag{1}$$

where S_h, S_o are the confidence scores of human and object obtained through the object detector model, respectively; S_h^a, S_o^a are the interaction scores of human and object, respectively, and S_{sp}^a is the interaction score obtained through the pairwise branch of the model. For the activities without an object (e.g., walk, and smile), the final score is computed as

$$S^a = S_h.S_h^a \tag{2}$$

There are blocks added to the standard iCAN module in our proposed model, which are described in more details, in the sequel.

Fig. 5. Gaze heatmap visualization

Gaze Heatmap. Since in many applications such as reading a book a person looks at the object, human gaze can be crucial in identifying important regions of the image associated with the interaction. Following [28], we have leveraged the gaze direction in order to extract the informative regions for HOI detection. In [28], a different processing pipeline has been considered for the gaze and determining the activity based on that. The way we incorporate it is slightly different. Based on the fact that in many applications the eye direction might be unclear or it might be occluded by a hat or eye-glasses, we use the detected gaze heatmap to improve the attention in human streaming branch of our proposed model. In the proposed method, we first obtain the gaze heatmap for each individual eye using the gaze following model [14], and take the average. Then, this average heatmap of size 56×56 is resized to $H \times W$ using nearest neighbor method, where W, H are the width and height of the image, respectively. Then stack it to make a $W \times H \times 512$ heatmap. Then we take the average of gaze heatmap and attention map calculated in the iCAN module and use it as the attention map in the improved iCAN module. Figure 5, illustrates the average gaze heatmap of the eyes of the specified human in the image. The bright part of the image is the gaze region of that person.

If one eye from the specified human in the image is invisible, the gaze heatmap of another eye would be considered as the gaze heatmap and if both eyes are occluded then the gaze heatmap would be ignored (i.e., equal to zero) and the attention map calculated in the iCAN module is the only information considered. Some real-world cases in which the gaze of one or both eyes are zero, are shown in Fig. 6.

Fig. 6. Sample images with zero gaze of one or both eyes

Gaze Distance. There are applications such as reading a book, in which the distance between the eyes and the specified object being gazed is so close. In contrast, there are cases such as watching TV in which the distance is large. That is why, considering the normalized distance between the eyes and the gazing point is a logical decision to make in order to incorporate both cases. This distance vector named $d_{gz} = [d_x^L, d_y^L, d_x^R, d_y^R]$ and is calculated as,

$$d_x = \frac{x_e - x_g}{W} \tag{3}$$

$$d_y = \frac{y_e - y_g}{H} \tag{4}$$

where d^L, d^R are the distances of the left and right eyes from the gaze region, respectively. Moreover, (x_e, y_e) and (x_g, y_g) are the positions of eye and the gazing point, as well. If any of the eyes belonging to the human is not visible in the image, the corresponding d^L or d^R information will be considered as zero.

3.4 Depth-Wise Separable Convolution

Having so much parameters in a standard convolution increases the chance of overfitting. To address this issue the depth-wise and depth-wise separable convolutions have been proposed, as introduced in Xception CNN architecture [2], and furthermore illustrated in Fig. 7. As shown in Fig. 7, a depth-wise convolution is performed for each separate channel and then followed by a 1×1 point-wise convolution. In order to enhance the attention mechanism in iCAN module we have replaced the normal convolution with this *depth-wise separable convolution* architecture.

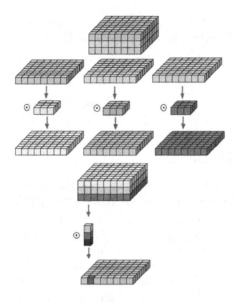

Fig. 7. Depth-wise separable convolution

4   Experimental Results

4.1   Dataset

The V-COCO dataset [9], has been used to apply the proposed algorithm for human activity recognition. This dataset contains 10346 images (including 2533 training images, 2867 validation images, and 4946 test images) along with boundary boxes around the instances inside these images, which has been prepared in 2015, and contains 29 different activity classes. Four of the classes are without any objects, including: walking, jogging, smiling and standing. This dataset is a subset of MS-COCO prepared in 2014 [16]. There are 80 different types of classes for the objects. The training and validation data samples of V-COCO are taken from the training samples of MS-COCO 2014 and the test samples are taken form the validation data samples of it. In this dataset, any human instance can be simultaneously busy with multiple activities, such as sitting on a chair and working with a laptop at the same time.

4.2   Evaluation Metrics

A common metric to evaluate the HOI detection performance is *role mean average precision* (**role mAP**), [9]. This metric could be computed by calculating the average precision (AP) of each of the HOI classes, and then taking the average over all classes. AP could be computed through measuring the surface under the curve of **precision-recall**. The True-Positive (TP) condition will occur whenever the boundary box obtained for the human and object instances of an image achieves an $IoU \geq 0.5$ with respect to its ground truth annotations and the HOI class is recognized correctly. The IoU is measured, as

$$IoU = \frac{\text{AREA OF OVERLAP}}{\text{AREA OF UNION}} \tag{5}$$

Activities which do not involve any objects are not considered in the role mAP calculation.

4.3 Implementation Details

In order to perform a fair comparison we used the same object detector (i.e., Faster R-CNN with a feature backbone of ResNet-50-FPN, Detectron implementation [7]) and feature backbone (ResNet-50) similar to the base model [6].

Analogous to the base model [6], we keep human boxes with scores s_h higher than 0.8 and object boxes with scores s_o higher than 0.4. We use the model in [4], to extract the human eyes coordinates and the model in [14], to detect the human gaze and its associated heatmap.

Training of the network has been performed using $20K$ iterations over the V-COCO train-validation dataset, the learning rate of .001, the weight decay of 0.0001 and the momentum of 0.9. The weights of the basic model in [6] are used as the initial weights of the common layers. Duration of training has been two hours over the T4 Nvidia GPU.

4.4 Quantitative Evaluation

The overall quantitative results in terms of AP_{role} on V-COCO dataset is presented in Table 1. As it is demonstrated, our proposed method outperforms the base model [6], as well as another competitive algorithm, namely Interact-Net [8]. In order to study the effectiveness of our method on various interaction classes, we analyzed the mAP for each action-target type defined in V-COCO dataset. Figure 8, shows the detailed results of InteractNet [8], the base framework iCAN [6] and our proposed model. We observe consistent actions with leading mAP, such as kick, and hit. Comparing the proposed model with the iCAN model shows that our proposed model can achieve an overall better performance on most action-target categories than the others, while showing slight worse performance on categories such as jump-istr and throw-obj.

Table 1. Performance comparison with the state-of-the-art on V-COCO test set

Method	Feature backbone	External resources	Attention mechanism	AP_{role}
InteractNet [8]	ResNet-50-FPN	No	No	40.00
iCAN (late fusion) [6]	ResNet-50	No	Yes	44.70
Proposed (late fusion)	ResNet-50	Gaze	Yes	**45.37**

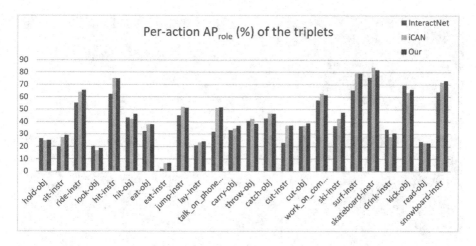

Fig. 8. AP_{role} for each activity class on InteractNet, iCAN model and the proposed model using V-COCO test data.

4.5 Qualitative Evaluation

1) HOI Detection Results. Here we show sample HOI detection results on the V-COCO dataset. We highlighted the detected human and object with blue and red bounding boxes, respectively. Figure 9 shows that our model is capable of predicting different actions.

Fig. 9. Sample HOI detections on the V-COCO test set

Fig. 10. Comparison of human-centric attention maps obtained by our method vs. iCAN [6], on example images from the V-COCO dataset. The first row contains images with the bounding boxes of the candidate human-object pairs, the second row contains the attention map obtained from the iCAN module, and the third row contains the attention map obtained from the improved iCAN module

2) Attention Map Visualization. The human-centric attention map as in the base iCAN model [6], focuses on the surrounding objects that assist disambiguate action prediction for the detected person. Figure 10, shows a comparison between the attention maps obtained using our approach versus iCAN base model on example images from the V-COCO dataset. The highlighted regions roughly correspond to the objects they are interacting with. Our model's attention maps focus on relevant regions in the human branch that are likely to contain human-object interactions.

4.6   Ablation Study

Now, we examine the impact of each proposed component with respect to the base model iCAN [6]. The results are shown in Table 2. In Table 2, B denotes the basic iCAN model proposed in [6]. Depth-wise Separable Convolution (DSC) is the one used in the iCAN module of both human and object branches. Gaze heatmap (GH) is used in the iCAN module of the human branch to improve its

Table 2. Ablation study on the V-COCO test dataset

Model	AP-role
B	44.70
B+DSC	45.06
B+GH	45.08
B+DSC+GH	45.14
B+DSC+GH+GD (final model)	45.38

attention map. Depth-wise Separable Convolution is used in the iCAN module of both human and object branches and gaze heatmap is used in the iCAN module of the human branch (DSC+GH). In addition to (DSC+GH), normalized distances from human eyes to his gaze points are also concatenated into the features extracted from the human branch (DSC+GH+GD). This table clearly shows that using the depth-wise separable convolution, gaze heatmap and the gaze distance cues to the basic model, can significantly improve the performance of the model.

5 Conclusion

In this work, we introduce a new method to improve attention modules used in existing Human-Object Interaction (HOI) detection models. We performed extensive experiments on a benchmark dataset, and validated the efficacy of our proposed components along with the extra integrated cues to the basic model in order to make it an improved attention-based module. Experimental results shows the improvement achieved through adding extra cues (gaze direction and gaze distance), as well as modifying the structure by using the depth-wise separable convolution block, in lieu of the standard block determined in the basic model.

References

1. Chao, Y.W., Liu, Y., Liu, X., Zeng, H., Deng, J.: Learning to detect human-object interactions. In: 2018 IEEE Winter Conference on Applications of Computer Vision (WACV), pp. 381–389. IEEE (2018)
2. Chollet, F.: Xception: deep learning with depthwise separable convolutions. In: Proceedings of the IEEE Conference on Computer Vision and Pattern Recognition, pp. 1251–1258 (2017)
3. Fang, H.-S., Cao, J., Tai, Y.-W., Lu, C.: Pairwise body-part attention for recognizing human-object interactions. In: Ferrari, V., Hebert, M., Sminchisescu, C., Weiss, Y. (eds.) ECCV 2018. LNCS, vol. 11214, pp. 52–68. Springer, Cham (2018). https://doi.org/10.1007/978-3-030-01249-6_4
4. Fang, H.S., Xie, S., Tai, Y.W., Lu, C.: RMPE: regional multi-person pose estimation. In: Proceedings of the IEEE International Conference on Computer Vision, pp. 2334–2343 (2017)

5. Gao, C., Xu, J., Zou, Y., Huang, J.-B.: DRG: dual relation graph for human-object interaction detection. In: Vedaldi, A., Bischof, H., Brox, T., Frahm, J.-M. (eds.) ECCV 2020. LNCS, vol. 12357, pp. 696–712. Springer, Cham (2020). https://doi.org/10.1007/978-3-030-58610-2_41

6. Gao, C., Zou, Y., Huang, J.B.: iCAN: instance-centric attention network for human-object interaction detection. arXiv preprint arXiv:1808.10437 (2018)

7. Girshick, R., Radosavovic, I., Gkioxari, G., Dollar, P., He, K.: Detectron (2018). https://github.com/facebookresearch/detectron

8. Gkioxari, G., Girshick, R., Dollár, P., He, K.: Detecting and recognizing human-object interactions. In: Proceedings of the IEEE Conference on Computer Vision and Pattern Recognition, pp. 8359–8367 (2018)

9. Gupta, S., Malik, J.: Visual semantic role labeling. arXiv preprint arXiv:1505.04474 (2015)

10. Habashi, P., Boufama, B., Ahmad, I.S.: Disparity-augmented trajectories for human activity recognition. Evol. Intell. 1–11 (2021). https://doi.org/10.1007/s12065-020-00553-y

11. Kato, K., Li, Y., Gupta, A.: Compositional learning for human object interaction. In: Ferrari, V., Hebert, M., Sminchisescu, C., Weiss, Y. (eds.) Computer Vision – ECCV 2018. LNCS, vol. 11218, pp. 247–264. Springer, Cham (2018). https://doi.org/10.1007/978-3-030-01264-9_15

12. Li, Y.L., et al.: PaStaNet: toward human activity knowledge engine. In: Proceedings of the IEEE/CVF Conference on Computer Vision and Pattern Recognition, pp. 382–391 (2020)

13. Li, Y.L., et al.: Transferable interactiveness knowledge for human-object interaction detection. In: Proceedings of the IEEE/CVF Conference on Computer Vision and Pattern Recognition, pp. 3585–3594 (2019)

14. Lian, D., Yu, Z., Gao, S.: Believe it or not, we know what you are looking at! In: Jawahar, C.V., Li, H., Mori, G., Schindler, K. (eds.) ACCV 2018. LNCS, vol. 11363, pp. 35–50. Springer, Cham (2019). https://doi.org/10.1007/978-3-030-20893-6_3

15. Liao, Y., Liu, S., Wang, F., Chen, Y., Qian, C., Feng, J.: PPDM: parallel point detection and matching for real-time human-object interaction detection. In: Proceedings of the IEEE/CVF Conference on Computer Vision and Pattern Recognition, pp. 482–490 (2020)

16. Lin, T.-Y., et al.: Microsoft COCO: common objects in context. In: Fleet, D., Pajdla, T., Schiele, B., Tuytelaars, T. (eds.) ECCV 2014. LNCS, vol. 8693, pp. 740–755. Springer, Cham (2014). https://doi.org/10.1007/978-3-319-10602-1_48

17. Liu, Y., Chen, Q., Zisserman, A.: Amplifying key cues for human-object-interaction detection. In: Vedaldi, A., Bischof, H., Brox, T., Frahm, J.-M. (eds.) ECCV 2020. LNCS, vol. 12359, pp. 248–265. Springer, Cham (2020). https://doi.org/10.1007/978-3-030-58568-6_15

18. Lorre, G., Rabarisoa, J., Orcesi, A., Ainouz, S., Canu, S.: Temporal contrastive pretraining for video action recognition. In: Proceedings of the IEEE/CVF Winter Conference on Applications of Computer Vision, pp. 662–670 (2020)

19. Qi, S., Wang, W., Jia, B., Shen, J., Zhu, S.-C.: Learning human-object interactions by graph parsing neural networks. In: Ferrari, V., Hebert, M., Sminchisescu, C., Weiss, Y. (eds.) ECCV 2018. LNCS, vol. 11213, pp. 407–423. Springer, Cham (2018). https://doi.org/10.1007/978-3-030-01240-3_25

20. Recasens, A., Khosla, A., Vondrick, C., Torralba, A.: Where are they looking? In: Proceedings of the 28th International Conference on Neural Information Processing Systems-Volume 1, pp. 199–207 (2015)

21. Sargano, A.B., Angelov, P., Habib, Z.: A comprehensive review on handcrafted and learning-based action representation approaches for human activity recognition. Appl. Sci. **7**(1), 110 (2017)
22. Sudhakaran, S., Escalera, S., Lanz, O.: Gate-shift networks for video action recognition. In: Proceedings of the IEEE/CVF Conference on Computer Vision and Pattern Recognition, pp. 1102–1111 (2020)
23. Ulutan, O., Iftekhar, A., Manjunath, B.S.: VSGNet: spatial attention network for detecting human object interactions using graph convolutions. In: Proceedings of the IEEE/CVF Conference on Computer Vision and Pattern Recognition, pp. 13617–13626 (2020)
24. Wan, B., Zhou, D., Liu, Y., Li, R., He, X.: Pose-aware multi-level feature network for human object interaction detection. In: Proceedings of the IEEE/CVF International Conference on Computer Vision, pp. 9469–9478 (2019)
25. Wang, H., Zheng, W., Yingbiao, L.: Contextual heterogeneous graph network for human-object interaction detection. In: Vedaldi, A., Bischof, H., Brox, T., Frahm, J.-M. (eds.) ECCV 2020. LNCS, vol. 12362, pp. 248–264. Springer, Cham (2020). https://doi.org/10.1007/978-3-030-58520-4_15
26. Wang, T., et al.: Deep contextual attention for human-object interaction detection. In: Proceedings of the IEEE/CVF International Conference on Computer Vision, pp. 5694–5702 (2019)
27. Wang, T., Yang, T., Danelljan, M., Khan, F.S., Zhang, X., Sun, J.: Learning human-object interaction detection using interaction points. In: Proceedings of the IEEE/CVF Conference on Computer Vision and Pattern Recognition, pp. 4116–4125 (2020)
28. Xu, B., Li, J., Wong, Y., Zhao, Q., Kankanhalli, M.S.: Interact as you intend: intention-driven human-object interaction detection. IEEE Trans. Multimedia **22**(6), 1423–1432 (2019)

Face Recognition Under Partial Occlusion: A Detection and Exclusion of Occluded Face Regions Approach

Judith Abiero$^{(\boxtimes)}$, Michael Kimwele, and Geoffrey Chemwa

Jomo Kenyatta University of Agriculture and Technology, Nairobi, Kenya
abierojudith@gmail.com, mkimwele@jkuat.ac.ke,
chemwex@icsit.jkuat.ac.ke

Abstract. Partial face occlusions such as scarfs, masks and sunglasses compromise face recognition accuracy. Therefore, this paper presents a face recognition approach robust to partial occlusions. The approach is based on the assumption that the human visual system ignores occlusion and solely focuses on the non-occluded sections for recognition. Four sections derived from a whole/un-occluded image and the whole face are used to train a classifier for recognition. For testing, an occluded face image is also divided into the four sections above from which, the non-occluded or the least occluded section is selected for recognition. Two strategies were used for occlusion detection; skin detection and the use of haar cascade classifiers. This paper mitigated weaknesses from literature review such as use of datasets that simulate real world occlusion scenarios, use of less data in training and not requiring any type of occlusion variation in training data. Additionally, the classifier performed relatively well in the classification task with an accuracy of 92% on the Webface-OCC dataset and 96% on the Pubfig dataset.

Keywords: Face recognition · Partial occlusion · Occlusion detection

1 Introduction

Face recognition is the ability to recognize human faces, this can be done by humans and advancements in computing have enabled similar recognitions to be done automatically by machines. The face recognition process involves three stages; face detection, feature extraction and classification and face recognition. Face detection determines whether a human face appears in a given image or not and where the faces are located. In feature extraction the human face patches are extracted from images [1] whereas the face recognition phase involves determining the identities of the faces from which facial features had been extracted. A face database is required and, for each individual, several images are taken and their features extracted and stored in the database [1].

One of the challenges that face recognition systems face is partial occlusion; caused when some parts of the target image are not being obtained. This poses a challenge because facial recognition methods require the availability of a whole input face, in the

C. Djeddi et al. (Eds.): MedPRAI 2021, CCIS 1543, pp. 18–32, 2022.
https://doi.org/10.1007/978-3-031-04112-9_2

lack of the above it may lead to wrong grouping [2] or lead to a drop in recognition accuracy [3]. Some of the occlusion robust approaches that have been used to counter the challenge are; extraction of local descriptors from the non-occluded facial areas. Methods used in this approach are based on patch engineered features and learned features. The former involve hand crafted features like local binary patterns (LBP) or Gabor features, the latter include methods such as subspace learning, statistical learning sparse representation classifier and deep learning [4]. These methods have issues while using shallow features such as LGBP only in the hand-craft features [5]. Additionally, the need for face images to be aligned well so that features can be extracted hinders their application in real life [4] (Figs. 1 and 2).

Fig. 1. Example of an un-occluded face image from the WebFace-OCC dataset [3]

Fig. 2. Examples of partially occluded face images from the WebFace-OCC dataset [3]

The second approach achieves this by recovering clean faces from the occluded faces. These methods use techniques such as reconstruction for face recognition or inpainting which considers the occluded face as a repair problem. This is done by sparse representation classification that makes use of dictionaries and sparse representations for classification. This approach's generalization is compromised because it requires identical samples of the testing and training sets. One of the most recent approaches is the use of convolutional neural networks [5]. The convolution neural networks (CNNs) have problems such as need of huge dataset for training, translation invariance and loss of valuable information through pooling layers [6].

Occlusion aware face recognition methods assume that visible parts of the face are ready; therefore during face recognition occluded parts are excluded. The methods used under this approach are either occlusion detection based face recognition or partial face recognition. The former performs the occlusion detection first before obtaining a representation for face recognition from the un-occluded face parts only. The latter ignores the occlusion detection phase. Additionally, it is based on the assumption that a partial face is available and it is used for face recognition [4].

Therefore, this paper assumes that a partial face can be recognized from a set of both occluded faces with masks, sunglasses or other accessories and un-occluded faces by focusing on the un-occluded face features shown on the provided face. In the training phase, a whole/un-occluded face images are divided into four sections; vertically to produce the right and left sections of the face and horizontally to provide the upper and lower sections of the face. All this sections in combination with whole faces are used to retrieve feature vectors from a pre-trained convolutional neural network (CNN) model that are used to train a classifier for face recognition. In the testing phase; the occluded face is divided into four sections as described above. Thereafter, occlusion detection is done on all the four regions and the least occluded region is selected and used for recognition.

2 Literature Review

Some approaches have been developed in an effort to counter the problems caused by occluded faces. [7], classified these approaches into three categories. The first category is the occlusion robust feature extraction. This category focuses on the feature space that is not affected largely by face occlusions. For the cross-occlusion strategy learning-based and patch-based engineered features are utilized. The second category is the occlusion aware face recognition. Approaches in this category assume that visible parts are ready; therefore during face recognition occluded parts are excluded. The third category is the occlusion recovery based face recognition. Occlusion recovery is used as the cross-occlusion strategy in that the occlusion-free face is recovered from an occluded face.

These approaches work on the principle of recovering whole faces from the occluded faces hence, use face recognition algorithms directly. These methods use techniques such as reconstruction for face recognition or inpainting which considers the occluded face as a repair problem [8], proposed an approach to enable face recognition in both the training and test sets. By allowing occlusions in both the training and testing sets, they estimated the occluded test image as linear combination of the training samples of all classes. For reconstruction, non-occluded parts were used because the distinct face areas were weighted differently. In other words, they based their reconstruction on the visible data on the training and testing sets compared to previous works that focused on the testing sets. Their approach performed well on the AR dataset.

A robust and low rank representation for fast face identification with occlusions was proposed by [9]. In their proposed framework, they wanted to solve the block occlusion problems by utilizing a robust representation that was based on two features because they wanted to model the contiguous errors. The first feature used a loss function to fit the errors of Laplacian sparse error distribution, whereas the second described the error image or modelled it as low rank structural by obtaining the difference between a test face that is occluded and the training sample of the same identity that is un-occluded. Their approach was efficient in computational time and identification rates.

An occlusion detecting and image recovering algorithm was proposed by [10]. Occlusion detecting involved occlusion detection and elimination whereas the image recovery involved recovery of occluded parts and reservation of un-occluded parts. They used genuine and synthetically occluded face images. This approach produced global features that were better and beneficial to classification.

Away to recognize face with partial occlusions using In-painting was proposed by [11]. A partial differential equation method together with modified exemplar in-painting was used to remark the face region that was occluded. Despite the approach achieving recognition rate increases it had a limitation in that the image data used for the work was not representative of a real world scenario.

These approaches use methods such as handcrafted features which include; local binary patterns (LBP), scale-invariant feature transform (SIFT) and histogram of oriented gradients (HOG) descriptors. One of the advantages of such methods is the easiness that comes with extraction of features from raw images. Additionally, their discriminative and tolerance to large variability and also being computationally efficient since they lie low in the feature space constitutes to more advantages [7]. On the other hand they have limitation in that for face recognition, integration of the decision from local patches is required and also for frontal faces, alignment based on eye coordinates contributing to precise registration. In other words, the need for face images to be aligned well so that features can be extracted hinders its application in real life [7].

Learning based features methods such use learning-based approaches to extract features have been proposed. These methods include linear subspace, sparse representation classification and non-linear deep learning methods. These methods have succeeded because of the characteristics such as smooth surface and regular texture that face images have in common compared to regular images. For discrimination among features, subspace learning preserves variation in faces [7]. This has been applied by Eigenfaces using principal component analysis (PCA). Eigenface designed by [12] is a simple method that is less sensitive to pose variation and it also has better performance when small databases and training sets are used. It uses features such as eyes, mouth and nose on a face and relative distances between these features. In facial field these features are known as Eigen faces. It uses PCA a mathematical tool to extract facial features. The Eigen faces when combined can reconstruct an image from the training set [13].

Another method that has been used is Fisherface using linear discriminant analysis (LDA) [7]. Fisher face was first introduced by [14]. It works by learning a class specific transformation matrix. Its performance depends heavily on the input data. It is a supervised dimension reduction algorithm. It allows reconstruction of an image but a nice reconstruction is impossible because, the features had already been discriminated before. It is also an enhanced Eigen face method that for dimensionality reduction, it uses Fisher's Linear Discriminant Analysis (LDA) whereby, the LDA works better in discrimination than PCA in that the ration between a class scatter to within a class scatter is maximized. It's better when the face images have illumination and facial expression variations [13]. The Eigenface and Fisherface methods have a disadvantage in that there's a need for the eye location to be aligned properly. This is not the case in real world data.

For the occlusion possibility to be accounted for, statistical learning methods are used as pointed out by [7] in their survey. Methods such as self-organizing maps projections, take into account that probability of occlusions occurring is different dependent on the occlusion. Another approach is the sparse representation classifier. With the goal that a representation that accounts for occlusion and corruption is generated, training samples and sparse errors are combined linearly.

A low-rank regression with generalized gradient direction was proposed by [15] to suit occluded face recognition. Dictionary learning sparse representation was used in combination with low rank representation on the error term leading to a low rank optimization problem. Their approach had robustness to any size, type and kind of occlusion like shadows, objects on the face and achieved better performance compared to the state-of-art frameworks at the time.

A joint and collaborative representation was proposed by [16] with local adaptive convolution feature. With their aim being able to achieve robust face recognition under occlusions, they used convolutional neural networks (CNNs) to learn convolution features extracted from local regions that were discriminative to the face identity. Their approach exploited the uniqueness and commonness of the different local regions. Their experiments showed that varying local regions have varying discrimination, furthermore, some local regions never contribute to and sometimes they may even mislead the face recognition.

Another approach in this category is deep learning. If a massive training dataset having enough occluded faces is provided for a deep network then occlusion robust face recognition is achieved [17]. One of the milestones in deep learning is the FaceNet model. FaceNet was developed by google researchers [18]. It was a data driven system in that they used a large dataset of labelled faces which enabled them attain pose, illuminations and other variations and it attained advanced results with benchmark datasets. The limitation was that it was data driven and this is not always the case in practical scenarios.

A deep dictionary representation based classification (DDRC) that was proposed by [19] to improve robustness in face recognition with occluded faces. They used an already trained convolutional neural network (CNN) for feature extraction, whereby, they performed a nonlinear mapping from the image space to the deep feature space. By defining the deep feature vector of a subject having a small error, as a linear combination of the column vectors of the matrix defining all the deep feature vectors of the same subject in the training samples, a dictionary representation was achieved. This approach had a limitation in that it assumed the test faces occlusion patterns were included in the auxiliary dictionary, hence limiting its usage.

One of the approaches in this category is the occlusion detection based face recognition. To tackle the occlusion problem, these methods first perform occlusion detection and later a representation is obtained from the non-occluded parts [7]. The other approach is the partial face recognition, based on the assumption of the availability of a partial face and uses it for face recognition and the occlusion detection stage is not considered. In other words, this approach focuses on the face recognition stage and avoids the face occlusion detection stage. Partial faces can often be found in real world data such as in mobile devices or surveillance cameras [20].

For occlusion detection, items such as sunglasses and scarves are used as a representation of occlusion because of their frequent appearance in the real world. For the visible parts selection, it is done through the assumption that previous knowledge of occlusion is known hence, skipping the face occlusion detection phase. [5], proposed a pairwise differential Siamese network (PDSN) that was to capture the relationship between the occluded facial block and corrupted feature elements, thereafter, establish a mask generator. The mask generator was to be used to create a combination of the feature discarding mask of random partial occlusions. This combination created could later be multiplied with the original feature to eliminate the effect of partial occlusion from recognition. It showed significant improvement in the performance on face recognition on both the real and synthesized face datasets.

For partial face recognition, [20], proposed an alignment-free approach in partial face recognition. Their proposed method did not require any alignment of the face's focal points. For the representation of a partial face with variable length, they employed multi-key point descriptors. A dictionary was constructed from the descriptors from a gallery that was large; hence, the descriptors of the probe image were represented sparsely and inferred the identity of the probe image. It had a limitation in practical application because; the number of faces required by SRC to cover all variations is quite high.

3   The Proposed Framework

In the proposed framework, a trained model or classifier would be derived from whole/un-occluded face images. Therafter, the trained model would be used to identify or classify occluded face images. Figures 3 and 4 show the principal steps in the training and testing phases respectively.

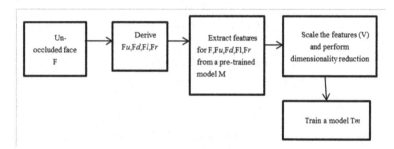

Fig. 3. Training phase flowchart

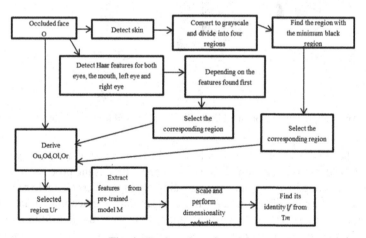

Fig. 4. Testing phase flowchart

3.1 Training Phase

The whole/un-occluded face images from the training set of each dataset were used for training. An aligned and cropped face image was denoted as a Cartesian plane; the height of the image as the y-axis and the width as the x-axis. Using these axes; dividing the image equally along the y-axis (height)/horizontally produced the upper section F_u and the lower section F_d of the face whereas dividing it equally along the x-axis (width)/vertically produced the left section F_l and right sections right section F_r of the face. The height of the F is denoted as H and the width of F was denoted as W. Given the origin of F as (0, 0) (Fig. 5):

$$Fu = \left(0, \frac{H}{2}\right), (W, H) \qquad (1)$$

$$Fd = (0, 0), \left(W, \frac{H}{2}\right) \qquad (2)$$

$$Fl = (0, 0), (\frac{W}{2}, H) \qquad (3)$$

$$Fr = \left(\frac{W}{2}, 0\right), (W, H) \qquad (4)$$

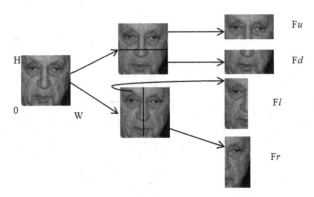

Fig. 5. An example image from the Pubfig dataset [28] used to demonstrate Eq. (1) to (4)

Due to the small size of data that was used for training per class, there was a need to augment the data to create more data. Data augmentation is the process of artificially creating new training images from existing training images. This can help reduce over-fitting and improve generalization [24]. In this paper, data augmentation functions with corruptions such as noise, Gaussian blur, zoom blur were used. Additionally, other functions such as image sharpening, image multi hue saturation, adding canny edges, embossing and blend alpha were also used. To find out how many images are required to learn a class; 5, 10 and 15 augmentations were added to each image. In other words, 500%, 1000% and 1500% of images were added. Therefore, for each of the five images derived in Eq. (1) to (4) and the original image, it was augmented to create more samples.

For F_i from Eq. (1) to (4) and the original image

$$F_{i1}, F_{i2} \ldots F_{in} = \text{augment\_data}(F_i) \tag{5}$$

Whereby; augment_data represents the data augmentation algorithm [29].

Given the pre-trained model as M, a feature vector V is derived by passing the original and all other augmented face images through it. Representing each face image as from Eq. (5) as F_m

$$V = M \rightarrow F_m \tag{6}$$

The feature vectors (V) were scaled using the min max scaler from [27]. The method was fit with the features and the derived scaler fit was used to transform the train and test data into normalized data. Thereafter, dimensionality reduction was performed using linear discriminant analysis (LDA) to extract the most relevant features for training a classifier. The scaled features were projected to the LDA space and depending on the classes used, the features retrieved equaled to the total number of classes minus 1. Dimensionality reduction is important because it helps remove random noise that is independent, that is, it's not correlated with the input and the label. It also removes unwanted degrees of freedom in that the input can change without the label changing [25]. Given V_s as the scaled data and V_d as the dimensionally reduced feature vector, a classifier C is trained hence generating a trained model T_m.

$$V_s = \text{scaling}(V) \tag{7}$$

$$V_d = \text{dim\_reduce}(V_s) \tag{8}$$

$$T_m = C \rightarrow V_d \tag{9}$$

3.2 Testing Phase

The occluded face images from the testing sets were used for testing the trained classifier/model derived from Eq. (9) above. The occluded face O, is divided into four sections as in Eq. (1) to (4) above to generate; O_u for the upper section, O_d for the lower section, O_r for the right section and O_l for the left section of the face. The O was used to detect the non-occluded section of the face, so that it can be used for the identification of the face. Two strategies were used to detect the non-occluded section; skin detection and haar cascade classifiers.

Skin detection can be defined as a way of finding the skin-colored regions and pixels in an image whereby the skin color is the primary identifier of the skin [21]. Skin color can be segmented using HSV and YCbCr color spaces. In this paper a combination of the watershed algorithm and the two color spaces was used [22]. After skin detection and segmentation the image was converted to grayscale. The grayscale image was divided into the four regions as discussed above and each region was converted to an array and its black or the 0 values elements were summed up. The least occluded region was selected by identifying the minimum value of the four summed up elements' values from the four regions.

On the other hand, haar cascade classifier is an object detection algorithm [23]. Some of the objects or regions that were detected were both eyes, to detect visibility of the upper section of the face, the mouth, to detect visibility of the lower section of the face, the right eye, to detect the visibility of the right section of the face and the left eye to detect the visibility of the left section of the face.

Depending on the region that was non-occluded or least occluded U_r, its corresponding section from the divided face sections was selected as the input to generate a feature vector from the pre-trained model. For example if both eyes are detected; O_u is selected or if lower section has a lot of skin than other regions O_d is selected.

$$U_r = \min \left(O_u, O_d, O_r, O_l \right) \tag{10}$$

After deriving the feature vector from Eq. (6), the test sample feature vector was scaled as in Eq. (7) and the result projectedto the dimension space of Eq. (8) to generate the final feature vector V_{ur} that would be used to predict the identity of the face I_f.

$$I_f = T_m \rightarrow V_{ur} \tag{11}$$

4 Experiments

4.1 Implementation Details

The publicly available datasets that were collected were the Webface-OCC [3] and Public Figures Face Dataset (Pubfig) [28] that was later modified to be used in this paper and a custom dataset. The Webface-OCC dataset contains images with simulated or synthesized occlusions. It has 804,704 face images of 10,575 subjects [3]. Images from the Pubfig dataset have large variations in parameters, scene, lighting, pose and imaging conditions they were taken from uncontrolled environment and the subjects were not cooperative.

The Webface-OCC dataset has both the occluded and un-occluded faces. 20 classes were selected for this research. For the 20 classes, at most 20 whole face images were used per class for training, 10 occluded face images for testing the model. The Pubfig dataset did not have occluded faces. This meant that some of the faces therein had to be synthetically occluded for this research. 20 classes from the Pubfig dataset were selected for this research. For the training data, at most 20 face images were set aside for it, at most 10 face images for testing the approach.

For feature extraction the Inception Resnet (V1) model from [26] pre-trained on the VGGFace2 dataset was used as feature extractor. A square face image of dimensions 160 * 160 was used as input to the pre-trained model from which, a 512 feature vector was retrieved.

A supervised learning approach was used to train the models. The process followed the stages outlined in Sect. 3. Three classifiers were chosen for training. The Linear discriminant analysis (LDA) and multi-layer perceptron (MLP) classifiers from the scikit-learn library [27] and a custom multi-layer perceptron (Custom MLP) built from scratch for performance comparison with the scikit-learn classifiers.

A linear discriminant analysis classifier finds a linear combination of features that separate classes of objects. It is based on the assumption that each class's Gaussians share the same covariance matrix. In this research it was used as both a dimensionality reduction algorithm and a classifier. On the other hand, a multi-layer perceptron is an algorithm that can learn a non-linear function approximate for classification provided a set of features and targets.

The experiments were implemented on a virtual machine with Intel Xeon 5118 2.3 GHz CPU, 8 GB RAM, and an Ubuntu operating system.

4.2 Evaluation Metrics

To evaluate the model, performance measures such as accuracy, precision, recall and F1 score were used. Accuracy measures the percentage of correct classifications given test data.

$$Accuracy = \frac{True\,Positive + True\,Negative}{True\,Positive + False\,Positive + False\,Negative + True\,Negative}$$

Precision measures the ratio between the true positives and all positives. It is used to measure all relevant data points and is also referred to as specificity of the model.

$$Precision = \frac{True\,Positive}{True\,Positive + False\,Positive}$$

Recall measures the ability of a classification model to correctly identify true positives and ability to identify relevant data. It is also referred to as the true positive rate or sensitivity.

$$Recall = \frac{True\,Positive}{True\,positive + False\,Negative}$$

F1 score used to show how precise and robust the classification model is and is based on the precision and recall metrics. The best value of an F1 score is 1 and the worst value is 0.

$$F1\,score = 2 * \frac{Precision * Recall}{Precision + Recall}$$

4.3 Non-occluded Region Retrieval Using Skin Detection

For this experiment, training of the models/classifiers was done as described in Sect. 3. For the testing phase, the skin detection algorithm that used a watershed algorithm and a combination of hue, saturation and value (HSV) and luma component, blue component and red component (YCbCr) color spaces was used.

Table 1. Webface-OCC dataset results using skin detection

Model	Accuracy	Precision	Recall	F1 score
LDA	87%	90%	87%	87%
MLP	85%	89%	85%	85%
Custom MLP	82%	88%	82%	83%

Table 1 above shows results that were obtained from the Webface-OCC dataset. 20 classes were selected randomly for this experiment. At most 20 images from each class were used for training whereas at most 10 images were set aside for testing. From the results above it's very clear that the model performed well on the testing set. The varying scores of precision, recall and F1 score in the test set shows that the model performed lower compared to the results in Table 3. The results were lower because some of the synthetically occluded images in the test sets had been occluded by objects colored in the same color space as human skin. Therefore, the detection of the non-occluded section or human skin failed for some images leading to wrong classification.

Table 2. Pubfig dataset results using skin detection

Model	Accuracy	Precision	Recall	F1 score
LDA	97%	97%	97%	97%
MLP	95%	96%	95%	95%
Custom MLP	96%	97%	96%	96%

Table 2 shows results from the Pubfig dataset. 20 classes each having 20 images for training and at most 10 images for the test set were used. The values of accuracy, precision, recall and F1 score were almost similar and close to 100%, which shows that the models did not over-fit nor under-fit. The results were better in this dataset because the colored masks that were used to occlude the face images did not belong to same color space as human skin.

4.4 Non-occluded Region Retrieval Using Haar Cascade Classifiers

The training phase was conducted as described in Sect. 3. For the testing phase haar cascade classifiers were used to detect the non-occluded region/section of the occluded face. Haar cascade classifiers are algorithms used to classify objects. In this paper pre-trained haar cascade classifiers for the eyes, right eye, left eye and mouth were used. They were used to detect the existence of the named regions. If a region was detected, the corresponding region from the original divided occluded face image was selected for testing the trained classifier/model.

Using the haar cascade classifiers showed improved results as shown in Table 3 compared to the results in Table 1 on the same dataset. The haar cascade classifiers

Table 3. Webface-OCC dataset results using haar cascade classifiers

Model	Accuracy	Precision	Recall	F1 score
LDA	92%	93%	92%	92%
MLP	90%	93%	90%	90%
Custom MLP	90%	93%	90%	90%

depend on the objects being detected and not the human skin. Therefore, the color of the objects used for occlusion did not affect the performance of the cascade classifier. On the other hand, the results are a bit lower than the state of art because haar cascade classifiers misclassify objects from time to time. The values of accuracy, precision, recall and F1 score show that the classifiers/models trained well.

Table 4. Pubfig dataset results using haar cascade classifiers

Model	Accuracy	Precision	Recall	F1 score
LDA	96%	97%	96%	96%
MLP	94%	94%	94%	94%
Custom MLP	96%	96%	96%	96%

There was a slight decrease in performance of the model when using haar cascade classifiers as compared to using skin detection for non-occluded region retrieval as shown in Table 4. This could be attributed to the failure of the haar cascade classifiers to classify the face regions correctly. The classifiers generally learnt well.

For all the experiments that were run on the different datasets, the accuracy, precision, recall and F1 score had high values, close to 100% and the values were almost similar. This meant that the classifiers learnt well and performed well in the classification task.

4.5   Effect of the Number of Images in Learning a Class

To study the number of images required to learning a class effectively; experiments were run on a subset of the Pubfig dataset. The experiments involved running it non augmented data 0, data that had 5, 10 and 15 augmentations. A slight improvement in the recognition rate was observed as the number of images increased as shown in Fig. 6 below.

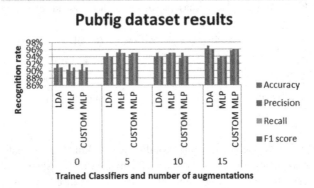

Fig. 6. Chart showing the effect of number of images on recognition rate

5 Conclusion

In this paper a face recognition approach that is robust to partial occlusions was developed. The approach mitigated some of the state of the art weaknesses such use of large volumes of data, where our approach only required at most 20 samples from each class from the Webface-OCC and Pubfig datasets for training. Secondly, other frameworks did not use datasets that reflected real world occlusion scenarios, our approach used the new synthetically occluded Webface-OCC dataset and an algorithm was used to synthetically occlude the Pubfig dataset by drawing masks on the face images to reflect the real world scenario.

Finally, the problem that all types of occlusion variations are required for better performance was mitigated as the approach did not require occluded faces for training; it used non-occluded/whole face images. Additionally, such an algorithm can be used in criminal identification systems because; criminals have a tendency to hide part of their faces when committing crimes.

For future work, we plan to investigate if the proposed method is robust to scaling in terms of increasing the number of classes or faces. We will perform an analysis on its computational complexity.

References

1. Bansal, A.: A study of factors affecting face recognition systems. Int. J. Manage. Eng. **8**, 669–672 (2018)
2. Santonkar, S., Kurhe, B., Khanale, B.: Challenges in face recognition: a review. Int. J. Adv. Res. Comput. Sci. **2**(4), 82–85 (2011)
3. Huang, B., et al.: When face recognition meets occlusion: a new benchmark. In: ICASSP, IEEE International Conference on Acoustics, Speech and Signal Processing - Proceedings, June 2021, pp. 4240–4244 (2021)
4. Mao, L., Sheng, F., Zhang, T.: Face occlusion recognition with deep learning in security framework for the IoT. IEEE Access **7**, 174531–174540 (2019)

5. Song, L., Gong, Di., Li, Z., Liu, C., Liu, W.: Occlusion robust face recognition based on mask learning with pairwise differential siamese network. In: Proceedings of the IEEE International Conference on Computer Vision, October 2019, pp. 773–782 (2019)
6. Tarrase, M.: What is wrong with Convolutional neural networks? https://towardsdatascience.com/what-is-wrong-with-convolutional-neural-networks-75c2ba8fbd6f. Accessed 10 Sept 2021
7. Zeng, D., Veldhuis, R., Spreeuwers, L.: A survey of face recognition techniques under occlusion. IET Biometrics **10**, 581–606 (2021)
8. Jia, H., Martinez, A.M.: Face recognition with occlusions in the training and testing sets. In: 2008 8th IEEE International Conference on Automatic Face and Gesture Recognition, FG 2008 (2008)
9. Iliadis, M., Wang, H., Molina, R., Katsaggelos, A.K.: Robust and low-rank representation for fast face identification with occlusions. IEEE Trans. Image Process. **26**(5), 2203–2218 (2017)
10. Wang, M., Hu, Z., Sun, Z., Zhao, S., Sun, M.: Varying face occlusion detection and iterative recovery for face recognition. J. Electron. Imaging **26**(3), 033009 (2017)
11. Vijayalakshmi, A.: Recognizing faces with partial occlusion using inpainting. Int. J. Comput. Appl. **168**(13), 20–24 (2017)
12. Turk, M., Pentland, A.: Face Recognition Using Eigenfaces. Vision of Modelling Group, The Media Laboratory MIT (1991)
13. Ismail, N., Sabri, M.I.M.: Review of existing algorithms for face detection and recognition. In: Proceedings of the 8th WSEAS International …, September, pp. 30–39 (2009)
14. Etemad, K., Chellappa, R.: Discriminant analysis for recognition of human face images. In: Bigün, J., Chollet, G., Borgefors, G. (eds.) AVBPA 1997. LNCS, vol. 1206, pp. 125–142. Springer, Heidelberg (1997). https://doi.org/10.1007/BFb0015988
15. Wu, C.Y., Ding, J.J.: Occluded face recognition using low-rank regression with generalized gradient direction. Pattern Recogn. **80**, 256–268 (2018)
16. Yang, M., Wang, X., Zeng, G., Shen, L.: Joint and collaborative representation with local adaptive convolution feature for face recognition with single sample per person. Pattern Recogn. **66**, 117–128 (2017)
17. Zhou, E., Cao, Z., Yin, Q.: Naive-Deep Face Recognition: Touching the Limit of LFW Benchmark or Not? (2015)
18. Schroff, F., Kalenichenko, D., Philbin, J.: FaceNet: a unified embedding for face recognition and clustering. In: Proceedings of the IEEE Computer Society Conference on Computer Vision and Pattern Recognition, 07–12 June 2015, pp. 815–823 (2015)
19. Cen, F., Wang, G.: Dictionary representation of deep features for occlusion-robust face recognition. IEEE Access **7**, 26595–26605 (2019)
20. Liao, S., Jain, A.K., Li, S.Z.: Partial face recognition: alignment-free approach. IEEE Trans. Pattern Anal. Mach. Intell. **35**(5), 1193–1205 (2013)
21. Kolkur, S., Kalbande, D., Shimpi, P., Bapat, C., Jatakia, J.: Human skin detection using RGB. HSV YCbCr Color Models **137**, 324–332 (2017)
22. Jean, Skin Detection Algorithm. https://github.com/Jeanvit/PySkinDetection. Accessed 10 Sept 2021
23. Mittal, A.: Haar Cascades, Explained. https://medium.com/analytics-vidhya/haar-cascades-explained-38210e57970d. Accessed 10 Sept 2021
24. Dvornik, N., Mairal, J., Schmid, C.: On the importance of visual context for data augmentation in scene understanding. IEEE Trans. Pattern Anal. Mach. Intell. **43**(6), 2014–2028 (2021)
25. Wang, W., Carreira-Perpiñán, M.: The role of dimensionality reduction in classification. Proc. Natl. Conf. Artif. Intell. **3**(2), 2128–2134 (2014)
26. Esler, T.: FacenetPytorch: Pretrained Pytorch face detection and recognition models. https://pypi.org/project/facenet-pytorch/. Accessed 10 Sept 2021

27. Pedregosa, F., et al.: Scikit-learn: machine learning in Python. JMLR **12**, 2825–2830 (2011)
28. Kumar, N., Berg, A., Belhumeur, P., Nayar, S.: Attribute and simile classifiers for face verification. In: International Conference on Computer Vision (ICCV) (2009)
29. Jung, A.: Imgaug. https://imgaug.readthedocs.io/en/latest/. Accessed 10 Sept 2021

Color Vision Deficiency and Live Recoloring

Imran Shafiq Ahmad$^{(\boxtimes)}$ and Sami Ali Choudhry

School of Computer Science, University of Windsor, Windsor, ON N9B 3P4, Canada
{imran,choud116}@uwindsor.ca

Abstract. Color information is an essential part of our daily life. Color Vision Deficiency (CVD), commonly known as color blindness, is a significant cause of concern for a fairly large number of people in the world. In general, such people lack the ability to differentiate and recognize certain colors. CVD is classified into several different categories such as monochromacy, dichromacy and anomalous trichromacy and have been sub-categorized further. This paper provides a novel scheme to address CVD by employing variations of colors during pixel plotting to capture color disparities and resolve through color compensation. The proposed scheme is capable of identifying type of CVD and then based on that specific type of CVD, provides color contrast variation. The proposed scheme is capable of handling both stored and live transmission of visual information (both static and continuous). The type of CVD can be determined by identifying the particular color deficiency associated with it. The proposed scheme involves color transformation from RGB (Red, Green, and Blue) scheme to LMS (Long, Medium, and Short) scheme. This transformation not only helps in identifying the specific color deficiency but also in adjustments of color contrasts. The efficient processing and rendering of recolored video and/or images, allows the affected CVD patients to observe affected shades in the recolored frames of video or images.

Keywords: CVD · Color Vision Deficiency · Color blindness · Monochromacy · Dichromacy · Trichromacy · Anomalous trichromacy · Color compensation

1 Introduction

World is full of colors and colors are an essential part of our daily life. All of the objects around us have specific and distinguishable colors. It is important to distinguish between perceived colors not only for aesthetic purposes but also to carry out our daily lives and make important decision such as stopping at a traffic sign/light and choosing appropriate clothing. However, substantial world population is devoid of this capability. This lack of ability to distinguish between colors is called *Color Vision Deficiency* (CVD) or more commonly *color blindness.* For their daily activities, people with normal vision tend to differentiate

© Springer Nature Switzerland AG 2022
C. Djeddi et al. (Eds.): MedPRAI 2021, CCIS 1543, pp. 33–46, 2022.
https://doi.org/10.1007/978-3-031-04112-9_3

between colors quite easily whereas those suffering from CVD, the ability to distinguish between colors is compromised and that makes it quite challenging for them to perform even the basic chores such as choosing appropriate clothing. This makes their lives quite uncomfortable. For majority of people suffering from CVD, the primary underlying reason is genetics and family traits. CVD is more dominant in men then women [7]. Most people with CVD can see colors but differently. The most common type of CVD results in lack of ability to distinguish between red and green. It is important to note that pure red and pure green are not the only hues responsible for this issue but any color with components of red and green can result in uncertainty. In another type of CVD, it is difficult to differentiate between blue and yellow. It is also possible that some CVD patients may not be able to see colors at all. This condition is also known as monochromacy but is not very common [7]. It is important to note that regardless of the type, color blindness is not curable [6] and colorblindness is not total loss of color vision but only a lack of ability to recognize wide range of colors.

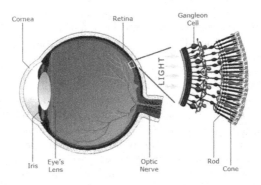

Fig. 1. Simple anatomy of the human eye [10] (Color figure online)

Retina in human eyes contains millions of tightly packed photoreceptors. These photoreceptors are responsible for not only capturing colors but also translating them into electrical signals which are then carried to the brain through the optic nerve. There are two different types of photoreceptors: cones and rods. Human eye contains approximately 5 million cones. These cones are responsible of providing sharp, detailed central vision and color vision. There are separate cones for light with low frequencies (red tones), medium frequencies (green tones) and high frequencies (blue tones). Therefore, one can consider the human eye to have a design of the RGB color model. Along with cones, human eye also contains about 120 million rods. These rods are responsible for not only clarity of vision but also for night and peripheral vision. Rods are very important for seeing any type of movement, but the information transmitted to the brain is only in black and white. To perceive colors, sufficient amount of light is required. If there is not enough light, one may not be able to perceive colors but will still be able to observe silhouettes and figures in the dark. This is simply because of the high density of rods (about 24 times more than number of cones). CVD occurs when light-sensitive cells in the retina fail to appropriately respond to the variations in wavelengths of light which is necessary to see the range of colors. However, every individual's impairment may differ since it depends on the amount of shift in wavelength (20 nm is the maximum limit of shift) [7]. Any shift of wavelength or deformity in cones produces some degree of color blindness. Figure 1 shows basic anatomy of eye, including rods and cones [10].

CVD is passed on through inheritance. Men are more likely to be color blind than women. In terms of genetics, the X chromosomes carry traits related to color blindness. The X and the Y chromosomes, known as the sex chromosomes, determine whether a person born is a female (XX) or a male (XY) and also carry other essential traits that are not related to gender. Since a female has two X chromosomes, there is less chance for a female to have color blindness and that is why, less number of women suffer from CVD. Accordingly, the color blindness based on genetics give rise to following two cases [16]:

- Case 1: **Autosomal Recessive Inheritance:** It takes two copies of the mutant gene to give rise to the disease.
- Case 2: **Autosomal Dominance Inheritance:** It takes just one copy of the mutant gene to bring about the disease.

Color vision deficiency can be detected through many different types of vision tests. However, the most common and well-know among them is the Ishihara test [17]. Figure 2 is an example of Ishihara test plate images. This test is named after its developer, Shinobu Ishihara and has been around since 1917. It is commonly used for routine color vision screening in schools, driving examination centers, etc. It can simply determine if an individual is color deficient. However, it cannot determine if an individual is suffering from partial color blindness or a specific type of color blindness that may involve more advance and sophisticated tests.

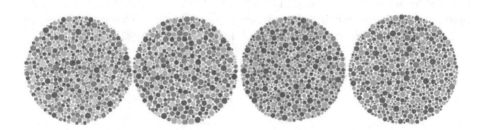

Fig. 2. Ishihara plates. From top left: 7, 10, 4, 2 [17] (Color figure online)

In this paper, we propose a system that is capable of re-coloring both images and video (both live and stored) for color vision deficient patients. Many of the earlier proposed systems require multiple passes on each frame, have ad hoc design and implementations and are not capable of supporting live applications. For processing of video applications, previously proposed systems required multiple passes on each frame, thus, resulting in slower overall processing and making them unsuitable for live applications. However, the proposed system requires only a single pass on each frame of a video (or image) and, hence, is capable of supporting live applications with minimal to no loss of frame data (i.e., missing frames) for all types of color vision deficiencies. The proposed system is flexible and can accommodate different types of color spaces and can modify the underlying color space based on its requirements. The suggested video quality enhancement techniques also use minimal computational resources.

In rest of the paper, Sect. 2 provides necessary background about color vision deficiency and reviews some of the existing techniques. In Sect. 3, we discuss the proposed system and implementation details. Section 4 provides some experimental results as well as evaluation and analysis of the results. Finally, Sect. 5 provides some concluding remarks.

2   Background and Related Work

A normal human eye contains three different types of cone cells: (i) red cone cells, (ii) blue cone cells and (iii) green cone cells. Each of these cell types is responsible of detecting specific range of wavelengths. Table 1 provides a summary of different types and subtypes of CVD and their prevalence. **Anomalous trichromacy** is the most common type of inherited CVD [22]. In anomalous trichromacy, the values to which anomalous cones are sensitive are shifted to different bands of the spectrum as shown in Fig. 3 [13]. In **protanomaly**, sensitivity values of **L** cones become quite similar to those of the **M** cones, i.e., shift towards shorter wavelength bands, thus, resulting in poor red–green hue discrimination. In **deuteranomaly**, the green-sensitive cones malfunction. As a result, the sensitivity functions are mapped onto the spectrum of the L type cones, i.e., towards the longer wavelengths. It is the most common type of CVD and results in affecting red-green hue discrimination. **Tritanomaly** is quite rare but equally affects both males and females [2,20]. In this condition, **S** cones malfunction resulting in shifting of sensitive values of **S** cones to longer wavelengths and affecting blue-green and yellow-red hue discrimination [22].

Table 1. Types of color vision deficiencies [15]

Type	Name	Cause of defect	Prevalence
Anomalous trichromacy	Protanomaly	L-cone defect	1.3%
	Deuteranomaly	M-cone defect	4.9%
	Tritanomaly	S-cone defect	0.01%
Dichromacy	Protanopia	L-cone absent	1.0%
	Deuteranopia	M-cone absent	1.1%
	Tritanopia	S-cone absent	0.02%
Monochromacy	Protanopia	Rod Monochromacy	Rare

People suffering from **dichromacy** are devoid of one of the three types of cones, making them perceive colors with only two remaining types of cones [22]. For individuals suffering from **protanopia**, red cones are missing and, hence, they cannot distinguish between blue and green or between red and green colors. People suffering from **deuteranopia** cannot perceive green color. Those suffering from **tritanopia** are devoid of blue cones. As a result, blues appear greenish, yellows and oranges appear pinkish, and purple colors appear deep red. However, this condition is very rare [20].

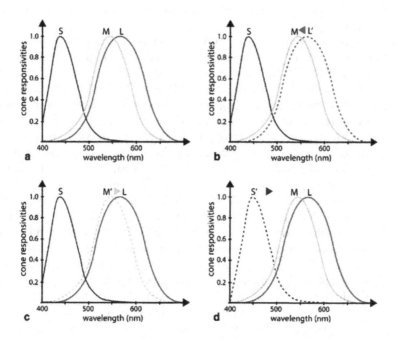

Fig. 3. LMS cones shift for CVD (a) Normal Trichromacy (b) Protanomaly (anomalous L cone type) (c) Deuteranomaly (anomalous M cone type) (d) Tritanomaly (anomalous S cone type) [13] (Color figure online)

Existing schemes to deal with CVD can be generally divided into two main categories: (i) hardware solutions and (ii) self-regulating or software-based solutions. Primary focus of hardware solutions is to alter enigmatic groups of colors through special set of glasses or contact lenses and tend to work only on limited set of colors and lighting conditions [6,9]. However, since nature and, thereby, visual information contain moderate color differences or many varying colors, these solutions are not useful for everyday life.

Therefore, self-regulating or software-based solutions provide a better alternative, especially in the realm of digital media. Wakita and Shimamura [21] describe the most fundamental color effects and relatively rigid approaches to re-color the visual information and suggested a repainting approach while focusing on the intentions of the content developers. They proposed a color mapping framework such that the mapping error has three different components. The first one measures the squared difference between the color differences among the colors. The second provides a measure of error between the colors differences among the original image and the mapped versions of these colors that are maximally different. The third component is the "punishment for mapping certain special colors to new positions" [8]. However, the optimization requires complex computation [8] and the proposed approach fails to always provide an optimized response on a global platform. In addition, the mathematical complexity tends to be more exorbitant.

For computer users suffering from CVD, Jefferson and Harvey [8] proposed an adaptation algorithm. The proposed algorithm is claimed to increase accessibility and also provide a basis for adaptive technology via simple interface. The authors evaluated the proposed algorithm using Ishihara color plate test. However, in their own words, the proposed algorithm is "successful, at least in terms of a restricted task and a relatively small number of viewers" [8].

Rasche et al. [18] proposed an approach to transform color components in an image to an equivalent gray-scale image. In order to transform or re-color images for people affected by dichromacy, Kuhn et al. [11] developed a mass-spring system technique that is said to conserve the legitimate original colors. The proposed algorithm is claimed to be deterministic while satisfying global consistency issues. The proposed scheme attempts to maintain color contrast even after re-coloring and re-mapping process. To properly handle and preserve important colors and for their remodeling, authors proposed an allotment technique in which middle point of every allotment group is considered an important key component color. By employing an objective function, Ichikawa et al. [7], proposed a technique to recolor web pages for anomalous trichromats. Optimization of the objective function is achieved through genetic algorithm.

Generally speaking, a survey of literature [3–5,12–15,17] indicates a number of attempts to overcome problems faced by people suffering from CVD. Most of these algorithms are designed for static visual information. To the best of our knowledge, none of the existing algorithms support live re-coloring of visual information. In some cases, the proposed schemes are specific only to a particular type of CVDs discussed earlier and tend to be more effective. Hardware solutions can provide support for live information but are limited due to their support for only specific types of CVDs and specific colors. Therefore, regardless of the type of CVD, there is a need for a software-based solution for live re-coloring of visual information.

3   Proposed System

$$\begin{bmatrix} L \\ M \\ S \end{bmatrix} = \begin{bmatrix} 17.8824 & 43.5161 & 4.11935 \\ 3.45565 & 27.1554 & 3.86714 \\ 0.0299566 & 0.184309 & 1.46709 \end{bmatrix} \begin{bmatrix} R \\ G \\ B \end{bmatrix} \tag{1}$$

For normal life activities, sense of colors and color perception is very important. An understanding of various CVD types and the resulting problems, can allow one to devise techniques and possible solutions. As stated earlier, existing research work has resulted in a number of different implementations. However, none has yielded perennial results, or the results are limited to only a specific type of CVD and do not support live-information. The proposed solution primarily focusses on all types of anomalous trichromacy and dichromacy and live visual information.

"Daltonization is a process performed by the computer that allows people with color vision deficiencies to distinguish a range of detail they are otherwise excluded from perceiving. For instance, in the daltonization of an Ishihara test plate (a popular test of color vision) numbers emerge from a pattern that were once invisible to the color blind person" [1]. In other words, in daltonization process, a range of colors which are harder to distinguish are replaced by colors that are easier to differentiate. This method is employed to re-color images by multiplying each pixel's RGB value by a 3×3 matrix depicting spectral sensitivity values as given in Eq. 1 [19]. It is an important part of the proposed technique. Following is a complete algorithm of our proposed technique:

Input: Live Video
Output: Live video

1. Capture video
   while(True(video))
2.   For each frame, obtain RGB values;
3.   Convert frame from RGB to LMS color space using Eq. 1;
4.   Based on the type of CVD, obtain modified LMS values, LMS';
5.   Convert LMS' to $(RGB)'$ such that: $(RGB)' = RGB_{Matrix} * (LMS)'$;
6.   Calculate any error: Error $= RGB_{diff} = (RGB)' - RGB$;
7.   Update RGB values in conjunction with the $Error\_Matrix$;
8.   Remove any noise;
9.   Smooth video;
10.   Display video by playing frames in a sequence.

Return: Re-colored Video;

In the first stage, we simulate the original frame or image (since a frame of a video is nothing but an image, the terms image and frame are interchanged but depending on the context, could also mean a frame). This allows us to obtain a representation of an image that is visible to a CVD patient. This representation is then subjected to the daltonization algorithm. As a first step, the RGB color space is converted to a LMS color space according to Eq. 1 [19]. LMS color space is the most commonly used color space for hues transformation since it provides robust results under varied illumination conditions [11]. The numbers indicated are fixed values to get appropriate values for large (L), medium (M) or small (S) cones.

$$RGB_{Matrix} = \begin{bmatrix} 0.0809444479 & -0.130504409 & 0.116721066 \\ -0.0102485335 & 0.0540193266 & -0.113614708 \\ -0.000365296938 & -0.00412161469 & 0.693511405 \end{bmatrix} \quad (2)$$

The proposed system addresses CVD issues by variations in pixel plotting process while capturing colors. Actual conversion of captured image is performed in the next step which involves changing the appropriate LMS color space values based on the type of sensitivity or the type of affected cones (either missing or misaligned) using the relationship:

$$(LMS)' = (CVD_{matrix}) * (LMS) \quad (3)$$

where CVD_{matrix} is one of the matrices given in Eq. 4, 5 and 6 to address specific types of CVD [19].

$$Protanopia = \begin{bmatrix} 0.0 & 2.02344 & -2.52581 \\ 0.0 & 1. & 0.0 \\ 0.0 & 0.0 & 1.0 \end{bmatrix} \quad (4)$$

$$Deuteranopia = \begin{bmatrix} 1.0 & 0.0 & 0.0 \\ 0.494207 & 0.0 & 1.24827 \\ 0.0 & 0.0 & 1.0 \end{bmatrix} \quad (5)$$

$$Tritanopia = \begin{bmatrix} 1.0 & 0.0 & 0.0 \\ 0.0 & 1.0 & 0.0 \\ -0.395913 & 0.801109 & 0.0 \end{bmatrix} \quad (6)$$

Therefore, depending on the type of CVD, the LMS values get modified. As an example, if the type of CVD indicates missing L cones, the updated LMS values accommodate the corresponding type of CVD. The resultant matrix is then used for further computation in subsequent steps.

Now that we have modified LMS values $(LMS)'$, these values are then further used to obtain updated RGB values, $(RGB)'$, to reflect accommodation of the appropriate type of CVD. At this point, we can compute the difference between the original RGB values and the updated RGB values. These differences serve to isolate those colors that are difficult to observe by the CVD patients and are defined as: $RGB_{diff} = (RGB)' - RGB$. By multiply RGB_{diff} in conjunction with those given in Eq. 7 [19], the color values are shifted towards those spectrum values that are visible to the CVD patients.

$$Error\_Matrix = \begin{bmatrix} 0.0 & 0.0 & 0.0 \\ -0.7 & 1.0 & 0.0 \\ -0.7 & 0.0 & 1.0 \end{bmatrix} \quad (7)$$

Once obtained, we add these difference values to the original RGB values to shift the entire image towards the visible spectrum of the domain. As a result, some of the color values in the original image will remain while some other will change and will result in colors that previously were not discerned by individuals with CVD.

For smoothening and to improve the quality of a video frame (or an image), a two steps process is employed. In first step, we apply Gaussian Blurring [24] to remove any Gaussian noise from the frame/image. In the second step, alpha blending [23] is used to amalgamate the updated (colored) pixels with original pixels which tend to serve as background to create appropriate appearance of the image contents.

4   Experiments and Results

An application based on the proposed scheme is developed in python using OpenCV-Python version 3.7 on a PC equipped with 2.8 GHz Intel® Core i7™ processor, 16 GB RAM, build-in GPU, and running Microsoft Windows 10®.

Fig. 4. A video frame with red object (left) and after recoloring (right) (Color figure online)

Table 2. Results of lag time for different video

Parameters	Video 1	Video 2	Video 3
Video duration	2 s	2 min	5 min
Lag time	0.29 s	1.59 s	2.38 s

For experimental evaluation of the proposed scheme, we ran a series of experiments using multiple live video of various durations and resolution while keeping the playback rate fixed at 50 frames per second. Figure 4 is an image (frame 1) of a video whereas Fig. 5 is the graphical representations of the RGB values of the first frame of the video in which only the red component changes as per

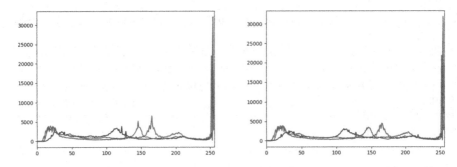

Fig. 5. Graphical result for red anomaly (Color figure online)

red anomaly CVD. The individual in this video is holding a bottle with red hue (left). This frame has been re-colored with respect to red anomaly through the proposed system and appears on the right. During processing, rest of the component colors remained unchanged, with a smooth video playback. We tested out system on video with length between 1000 to 15000 frames and evaluated the frames dropped and the total time for evaluation for all red, blue, and green hues. It was observed that no frame drop occurred and the playback time including processing time remained almost the same as the duration of the original video or increased minimally as evident from Table 2.

Fig. 6. Recoloring of video with green object (Color figure online)

Likewise, Figs. 6, and 8 are examples of the first frame of video for blue and green hues respectively whereas Figs. 7 and 9 are the graphical representations of the RGB values of the first frame of the video in which only the green component changes as per the green anomaly CVD as well as for blue component and blue anomaly CVD respectively for the corresponding wavelengths of the respective hues. It should be noted that the images in Figs. 4 and 6 represent daytime lighting condition whereas the image in Fig. 8 represents the night light scenario.

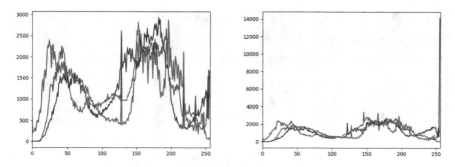

Fig. 7. Graphical result for green anomaly (note a difference in scale) (Color figure online)

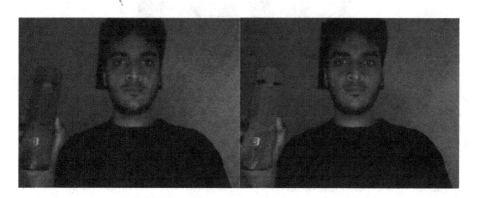

Fig. 8. Recoloring of video with blue object (Color figure online)

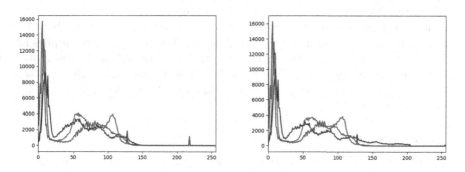

Fig. 9. Graphical result for blue anomaly (Color figure online)

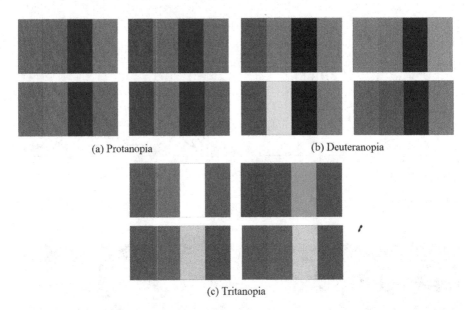

(a) Protanopia   (b) Deuteranopia

(c) Tritanopia

Fig. 10. Re-coloring of images. Top left: original image, top right: simulated image as observed by the CVD patiend, bottom left: re-colored image as a CVD patient is expected to see, bottom-right: re-colored image that a CVD individual will perceive for (a) Protanopia, (b) Deuteranopia, (c) Tritanopia (Color figure online)

Figure 10 is an example of images processed through the proposed system for all three cases, viz., (a) protanopia, (b) deuteranopia, and (c) tritanopia. Image in each of these three categories has four sub-images such that top-left image is the original image with variations in colors. For demonstration, each of this original image is re-colored three times such that the top-right sub-image constitutes stimulated image, bottom-left sub-image is re-colored image and the bottom-right sub-image is the simulated recolored image. A simulated image implies an image that CVD person may perceives rather than the original image. Re-colored image implies an image that a CVD individual is expected to perceive whereas a simulated re-colored image implies the one that a CVD individual may perceive after it has been re-colored.

5   Conclusion

Our life is full of colors. Visual media such as images, video, online learning media are part of our daily lives. However, individuals suffering from color vision deficiency fail to enjoy and take full advantage of visual information. Therefore, there is a need to device a system that could enable them to distinguish between colors so that they could also as much enjoy the visual media as rest of the population. This paper provides a new scheme to re-color visual media (both stored and live) and, hence, enables individuals suffering from CVD to enjoy both static as well as sequential media such as images and video respectively, even when the information is streamed. Obviously, no system could provide a complete satisfaction to such individuals since they won't be able to see the actual colors but at least by enabling them to distinguish between colors, it can remove confusion and ambiguity and enjoy much of the visual media. As it stands, the proposed system can be used for both stored and live streaming of continuous media from popular forums such as YouTube®, Netflix®, Amazon Prime Video®, etc. A possible future extension of this work could potentially allow a user to be able to specify their own specific type of CVD and select their own color choices. Further, current implementation does not rely in anyway on GPU processing capabilities. Therefore, there is a need to explore the impact of GPU for processing of both static images as well as video, especially in application involving live streaming of visual information.

References

1. Daltonize. http://www.daltonize.org/p/about.html. Accessed 07 Aug 2021
2. Deeb, S.S.: Molecular genetics of colour vision deficiencies. Clin. Exp. Optom. **87**(4–5), 224–229 (2004)
3. Flatla, D.R.: Accessibility for individuals with color vision deficiency. In: Proceedings of 24th ACM Symposium Adjunct on User Interface software and Technology, pp. 31–34 (2011)
4. Gupta, A., Laxmi, G., Nittala, M., Raman, R.: Structural and functional correlates in color vision deficiency. Eye **25**(7), 909–917 (2011)
5. Han, D., Yoo, S.J., Kim, B.: A novel confusion-line separation algorithm based on color segmentation for color vision deficiency. J. Imaging Sci. Technol. **56**(3), 30501-1 (2012)
6. Everyday Health. https://www.everydayhealth.com/color-blindness/guide/treatment/. Accessed 06 Aug 2021
7. Ichikawa, M., et al.: Preliminary study on color modification for still images to realize barrier-free color vision. In: 2004 IEEE International Conference on Systems, Man and Cybernetics, vol. 1, pp. 36–41 (2004)
8. Jefferson, L., Harvey, R.: An interface to support color blind computer users. In: Proceedings of the SIGCHI Conference on Human Factors in Computing Systems, pp. 1535–1538 (2007)
9. Karepov, S., Ellenbogen, T.: Metasurface-based contact lenses for color vision deficiency. Opt. Lett. **45**(6), 1379–1382 (2020)
10. Kolb, H.: Simple anatomy of the retina. In: Webvision: The Organization of the Retina and Visual System, pp. 11–34. University of Utah Health Sciences Center, Salt Lake City (2021)
11. Kuhn, G.R., Oliveira, M.M., Fernandes, L.A.: An efficient naturalness-preserving image-recoloring method for dichromats. IEEE Trans. Visual Comput. Graphics **14**(6), 1747–1754 (2008)
12. Lin, H.Y., Chen, L.Q., Wang, M.L.: Improving discrimination in color vision deficiency by image re-coloring. Sensors **19**(10), 2250 (2019)
13. Milić, N., Novaković, D., Milosavljević, B.: Enhancement of image content for observers with colour vision deficiencies. In: Color Image and Video Enhancement, pp. 315–343 (2015)

14. El Moussawi, Z., Boueiri, M., Al-Haddad, C.: Gene therapy in color vision deficiency: a review. Int. Ophthalmol. **41**(5), 1917–1927 (2021). https://doi.org/10.1007/s10792-021-01717-0

15. Nigamand, P.K., Bhattacharya, M.: Colour vision deficiency correction in image processing. In: 2013 IEEE International Conference on Bioinformatics and Biomedicine, p. 79 (2013)

16. Ostergaard, E., Batbayli, M., Duno, M., Vilhelmsen, K., Rosenberg, T.: Mutations in PCDH21 cause autosomal recessive cone-rod dystrophy. J. Med. Genet. **47**(10), 665–669 (2010)

17. Poret, S., Dony, R., Gregori, S.: Image processing for colour blindness correction. In: 2009 IEEE Toronto International Conference Science and Technology for Humanity (TIC-STH), pp. 539–544 (2009)

18. Rasche, K., Geist, R., Westall, J.: Detail preserving reproduction of color images for monochromats and dichromats. IEEE Comput. Graphics Appl. **25**(3), 22–30 (2005)

19. Tecson, G.R., Calanda, F.B., Cayabyab, G.T., Reyes, F.C., Jr.: Covisance: a real time mobile recolorization tool for aiding color vision deficient users utilizing D-15 color arrangement test. In: Proceedings of the 2017 International Conference on Computer Science and Artificial Intelligence, pp. 95–99 (2017)

20. Tovee, M.J.: An Introduction to the Visual System. Cambridge University Press, Cambridge (2008)

21. Wakita, K., Shimamura, K.: Smartcolor: disambiguation framework for the colorblind. In: Proceedings of the 7th International ACM SIGACCESS Conference on Computers and Accessibility, pp. 158–165 (2005)

22. Wong, B.: Color blindness. Nat. Methods **8**(6), 441 (2011)

23. Yu, T., Song, K., Miao, P., Yang, G., Yang, H., Chen, C.: Nighttime single image dehazing via pixel-wise alpha blending. IEEE Access **7**, 114619–114630 (2019)

24. Zhang, Z., Klassen, E., Srivastava, A.: Gaussian blurring-invariant comparison of signals and images. IEEE Trans. Image Process. **22**(8), 3145–3157 (2013)

Real Time Handling Occlusion in Augmented Reality Based on Photogrammetry

Bekiri Roumaissa$^{(\boxtimes)}$ and Babahenini Mohamed Chaouki

LESIA Laboratory, Mohamed Khider University, Biskra, Algeria
{roumaissa.bekiri,mc.babahenini}@univ-biskra.dz

Abstract. Augmented Reality (AR) technology has become an effective tool in many domains as visualization, planning, operations design in construction, manufacturing, surgery, and other applications. Incorporating virtual objects in a physical world to obtain a realistic augmentation requires correct relationships between real and virtual objects. The traditional static vision of AR consists of interaction and navigation through human beings using computer screens. However, the new technology based on photogrammetry and AR allows strengthening the possibilities in 3D data visualization, navigation, and interaction. This paper proposes a close-range photogrammetry method for 3D reconstruction based on imagery acquisition to get a highly accurate 3D model. The proposed method will deal with real-time orientation and tracking, merging close-range photogrammetry and AR. We validated our approach on data sets representing realistic scenes. Obtained results show the proposed approach's efficiency and accuracy for solving the occlusion problem in AR systems.

Keywords: Augmented Reality (AR) · Close-range photogrammetry · Real-time realistic occlusion · 3D model · Augmentation · Tracking

1 Introduction

Nowadays, Augmented reality (AR) technology has become a more attractive and widely popular topic in many mobile applications such as entertainment, education, clinical psychology, medicine, robotic-assisted-surgery, tourism, and machine manufacturing. This technology superimposes computer-generated graphics (visual, sound, or haptic) in image or video sequences captured by a camera in real-time [10]. More specifically, it lets users merge and interact with the existing scene. To achieve an accurate AR application, the real and virtual objects must be seamlessly integrated into the user's environment. Three main types of problems occur when we try to release this effect:(i) Illumination problems must be handled considering conditions of rendering the same lighting in both virtual and real environments. (ii) Estimation parameters of a camera arise

© Springer Nature Switzerland AG 2022
C. Djeddi et al. (Eds.): MedPRAI 2021, CCIS 1543, pp. 47–62, 2022.
https://doi.org/10.1007/978-3-031-04112-9_4

when we want to align the actual camera with the virtual objects. In this context, a registration problem that arises when we want to align virtual objects with the real objects in the scene. (iii) The occlusion problem must be managed correctly so that users can look at the natural scene. Much research on solving this problem has come up with three different approaches: Contour based, depth-based and 3D reconstruction-based [12].

Recently, Estimating the correct relationships between virtual and real objects has become a crucial topic. The occlusion problem is received considerable attention in the field of AR research. However, displaying the correct occlusion between the virtual and real objects has a significant impact on the user's understanding, feeling that the virtual objects genuinely exist in the physical world and get accurate augmented reality systems [19]. Therefore, an AR application must automatically judge and display the occlusion between virtual and real objects.

This paper is set up for handling occlusion problems in AR; our method classifies into a model-based approach that provides an accurate (offline) 3D model of the real environment objects. The proposed system presented is fictional, but it points out the power of combining two different purpose technologies, AR and photogrammetry. Firstly, AR is more concerned with real-time processing, high speed, and continuous visualization over rough models. Secondly, the photogrammetry technique contributes the visual reality environment to the augmented 3D world, which is currently an effective tool to get geometrical information from digital imagery geometry and match 3D models and imagery quickly, efficiently, and in an accurate manner.

The rest of the paper is structured as follows: Sect. 2 presents existing proposals for handling occlusion methods. Section 3 details our system overview and its various components. Section 4 presents the implementation of our approach as well as some results obtained. Finally, Sect. 5 concludes the paper and presents some perspectives.

2 Related Work

In the literature, several researchers proposed to handle mutual occlusion in real-time in augmented reality. According to Yuan Tian et al., many methods are provided to resolve the occlusion problem; there are three categories: contour-based methods, depth-based methods, 3D reconstruction-based methods.

2.1 Contour-Based Methods

Tian et al. [16] proposed in their work a segmentation method to obtain the contour of the real objects. Then they tracked the contour objects in a subsequent frame to get an augmented image by redrawing all pixels to display the correct spatial relationships. Thus, they optimized the previous architecture by proposing [15] an automatic occlusion handling method based on computing the disparity map of real objects in the first frame. However, this handling occlusion is affected by extracting contour results in the first frame. **Fuckiage et al.** [3] offered an alternative solution to the occlusion problem that does not require a precise foreground-background segmentation method and takes considers characteristics of human transparency perception in a psychophysical experiment which provides accurate results in real-time even with in complicated scenes. **Sanches et al.** [13] presented, in their paper, a method that enables AR environments based on fiducial markers to support mutual occlusion between a real element and many virtual ones using fiducial markers, according to the element's position (depth) in the environment.

2.2 Depth-Based Method

To highlight the second work that aims to compare each pixels value of real objects with that of virtual objects and display unoccluded parts of the virtual objects to obtain correct occlusion. In this context, we chose the work of **Schmidt et al.** [8] that addresses calculating dense disparity maps in the stereo images for detecting and handling mutual occlusion in augmented reality. Where **Hayashi et al.** [4] used a contour-based stereo matching approach to acquire an accurate depth of the real object for detection occlusion. The main idea is to resolve problem of user's hands when occluded by virtual objects in a tabletop of the AR system. This method does not give accurate occlusion results between real and virtual objects. **Setohara et al.** [14] the authors proposed a method to detect moving objects in front of a set marker pattern, using the marker pattern as a background image. However, if the depth value of moving objects in a real environment is not acquired, it is impossible to resolve occlusion. In this context, **Kim et al.** [5] used the same approach stereo matching to estimate the depth of the real environment to get correct occlusion between the real and virtual object. However, this technique is computationally expensive and it is difficult to process in real time. **Ohta et al.** [9] proposed an approach called "client-servers" depth sensing, clients can obtain depth information of real environment from the server. These depth sensing devices provide an accurate depth in real-time. Therefore, if the viewpoint of both clients and servers is not the same, the error appears from depth sensing from the client viewpoint because not acquired well. **Yokoya et al.** [18] used stereo matching to acquire depth information of real objects. However, using stereo matching is limited in the region where virtual objects should be rendered to decrease cost. The main problem of this method is that it is not accurate, so the boundary between the virtual and real environment does not provide a model correctly. **Fuhramann et al.** [17]proposed an approach using the 3D models of real objects called "phantoms" to obtain a model with the same properties of real objects exits. The specialist in this method will work when the object is rigid to handling the problem of occlusion. **Lu and Smith** [8] their method aims to segment objects and calculate the depths of the area covered by the virtual object and they used(GPU) based method for computing occlusion between real and virtual objects in real-time. However, to obtain information from the captured stereo image to get a depth of real objects, and used GPU-based segmentation to accelerate processing speed to segment the occlusion. This method is used when virtual objects and real objects move independently. **Dong and Kamat** [17] proposed a framework consisting of two stages, in the first stage rendering using the TOF (Time of flight) camera giving depth buffer and color buffer of real objects by redrawing, as usual, the background scene. In the second stage, they are redrawing the virtual object with depth buffer testing enabled. Therefore, the part included of the virtual object, either hidden by another part of the virtual object or by real objects, will be handling occlusion.

2.3   3D Reconstruction Based Method

The main idea of this method is to create the 3D model of real objects and compare each depth pixel of the real objects with that of virtual to resolve occlusion. Therefore, 3D reconstruction consumes much time to build a 3D model for complicated and huge scenes. **Fuhraman et al.** [17] Their method is specially used for a static scene to model the users representation as a kinematic chain of articulated solids to simulate the occlusion of a virtual object. **Ong et al.** [17] proposed a new framework to derive a 3D model about the real scene based on recovered geometry information and user segmented object silhouettes to solve occlusion. This method is so easy to implement, and no expensive tool is required. **Lepetit et al.** [7] the proposed method permits the user in each key view to outline the boundary of the occluding objects. The 3D occluding boundary was obtained according to the two key views based on re-projecting and refined in inter-mediate frames, and the correct occlusion was achieved. The disadvantage of this method the inaccurate occlusion handling, especially when the user changes the viewpoints. **Yuan Tian** [17] proposed an approach divided into two stages: In the offline stage: using an RGB-D camera to obtain the depth map of a real scene then reduce noises of the depth values. In the Online stage: compare each pixel's Z coordinate of real objects with virtual objects to reduce the consuming time and achieve a good performance in real-time. Finally, the synthetic image with correct occlusion is shown in real-time. **Portales et al.** [10] proposed a method based on photogrammetry and augmented reality by using close-range photogrammetry to build high-accuracy 3D photos-models integrated into the real world. Then, they used a see-through video head-mounted (HMD) to obtain an augmented environment, whereas the user's merged into a real world. **Carrion-Ruiz et al.** [2] presented an architecture based on reconstructing the 3D model of the Queen Victoria sculpture using the photogrammetric method and looking through a window in an AR application. In general, the key of the depth-based method is to compute the depth information of the real scene in real-time. However, the drawback is that more than two cameras are required to calculate the depth and due to their expensive cost which is provides for static scene and viewpoint. In contrast, the cost of the contour-based method is less than the depth method and cannot handle mutual occlusion. The 3D reconstruction-based method provided good performance and efficiency for large-angle viewing with handling mutual occlusion.

This paper engaging in a new approach that can be classified into a 3D reconstruction-based method. It uses two main techniques, the first photogrammetry technology to obtain 3D photos-models in high accuracy and efficiency, this latter AR technology that used the previous to improve the augmented scene in real-time and high speed.

3 System Overview

This paper proposes a new technique to resolve the occlusion problem in real-time using two leading technologies, photogrammetric and Augmented Reality. The main goal is to resolve the problem of virtual objects that occurs in front in real scene in AR system. Our process consists of two stages (Fig. 1):

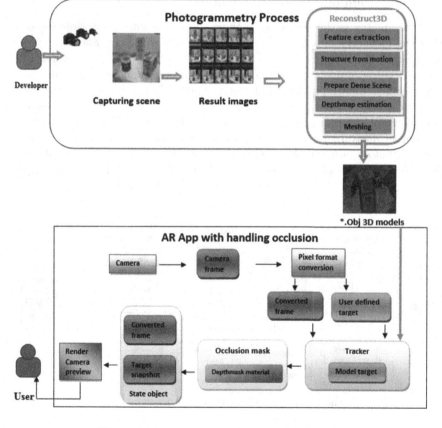

Fig. 1. System overview of proposed approach.

- **Photogrammertic 3D modeling:** We used a close-range photogrammetry method to build the 3D model of a real scene followed by the pipeline defined by the Alicevision meshroom's, which is composed of 12 nodes.
- **AR application development with handling occlusion:** Our approach is based on a marker-less tracking solution to extract the main features points which is means to merge digital data with input from real-time, real-environment input registered to physical space. We used software Vuforia SDK for tracking our model target as obtained from the photogrammetry process, which is fulfills the primary condition to get a good disparity and high complexity. Thus, we created our AR application by augmenting our scene with a 3D virtual object which is similar to the proposed scene. In this case, by applying a Depth mask material provided by software unity3D, we can view realistic results to hides objects behind a model target.

3.1   Photogrammertic 3D Modeling

Photogrammetry is the science of making measurements from photographs. It infers the geometry of a scene from a set of unordered photographs or videos. Photography is the projection of a 3D scene into a 2D plane, losing depth information. Photogrammetry aims to create three-dimensional models from a set of images using a known pipeline of photogrammetry. It is classified into three categories: far-range, close-range, very close-range. In this paper, we are interested in Close range photogrammetry generally applied for industrial applications where non-contact measurements have to be done with a range vary between (1 cm^2 to 1 mm^2). In close range photogrammetry, we need to capture photographs using digital cameras/cell phones with 300 m of test objects. As follows, we explain these default nodes of the photogrammetry algorithm one by one (Fig. 2).

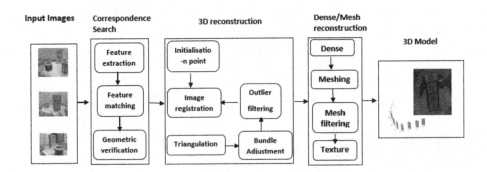

Fig. 2. The flow diagram of photogrammetric.

CameraInit
CameraInit is the first node in the default pipeline of photogrammetry. The input of this step is photographs from different view points and the output is generated

as(.sfm) files. Each image is attaches with camera/sensors. Every camera has parameters like the size of the image captured, local length, parameter intrinsic and extrinsic, bundle point, distortion coefficient, and camera/sensor type. These parameters are stored all data of cameras in a file that recommended for custom calibration cameras in the later stage [11].

Feature Extraction

The main objective of this node is to extract feature sets of pixels that are, to some level, unaffected by view-points changes of cameras throughout image capturing. Therefore, the characteristic of the image scene should contain the same features as all images. In this stage, the most popular and efficient method that allows detecting features from images is the SIFT (Scale-invariant features transform) system. In general, SIFT algorithm can be decomposed into four steps: firstly, the scale space of an image is produced from the convolution of a Gaussian kernel (Blurring) at different scales with the input image. Using Difference of Gaussian to generate sets of images from blurred images. Secondly, finding accurate localization of each Keypoint. Then, we assign an orientation to key points. At this point, each key point has a location, scale, orientation. The next step is to compute a descriptor for the local image region about each key point as highly distinctive and invariant as possible to variations such as changes in viewpoint and illumination. This descriptor is stored in 128 bits [11].

Image Matching

This stage aims to match images that contains similar parts from the scene. They use image recovery method to find pair images that share nearly the same information without resolving each feature in details. The objective is to restructure the image in a dense image descriptor, which calculates the distance between all dense image descriptors. To get this descriptor using the vocabulary of tree approach, which is the most popular method, once all features descriptors are extracted, it decomposes their descriptors after comparison to the ones on every node of these trees. Each leaf of the trees is associated with one feature descriptor. In order to obtain an accurate and efficient 3D model from image reconstruction, we should be collect a high number of images capturing [11].

Feature Matching

The main objective is to match features between accurate and adequate image pairs. Firstly, this node achieved photometric matches between sets of descriptors using two input images. For every feature in the first image, a list of rival features in the second image are retrieval on another side to delete a lousy matching candidate. Meshroom assume that there is one suitable feature in the other image. Also, the output of this node is a list of feature matching contenders validated by only photometric criteria. Using the brute force method to identify two closet descriptors from the 2nd image for every feature. This node uses epipolar geometry to make geometric filtering from the feature position in the image in an outlier detection framework called RANSAC (RANdomSAmple Consensus).

Structure from Motion

This node aims to introduce the relationship between different observations from input images and extract the structure scene with 3D points, their position, their orientation, and the internal parameter of every camera. This pipeline allows to reconstruct scene by choosing firstly the best initial image pair. It should provide robust matching initial features to get an efficient reconstruction of objects and iterative process by introducing other views. Also, it joint for all feature matches between image pair into a tracks. Each track is considered a point in space remarkable from a different camera with many outliers, but this node removes the dis-joined track throughout the process of matches. We calculate the essential matrix between two images and the first one is supposed to be the origin of the coordinate system. Meshroom registers the position and orientation of the second photo and triangulates the corresponding of 2D features into 3D points. It completes the resectioning for every new camera using the PnP (perspective-n-Point) algorithm in a RANSAC framework to identify the position and orientation of the camera device. This validates most feature relationships after this node initiates a group adjustment to get all cameras' extrinsic and intrinsic parameters and the position of all points. After the triangulation of the new points, there are more candidate points to pass in the next selection.

Prepare Dense Scene

The principal goal of this node is to obtain undistorted images with eliminating re-projection errors and compute a depth from distortion function.

Depth Map Estimation

This node allows us to retrieve the depth value of each pixel using numerous methods like Block Matching, Semi-Global Matching, or ADCensus. This node-based on Semi-Global Matching running in Alice vision meshroom pipeline. Generally, it selects the Nbest/closet camera nearby of each image with a selection of front parallel planes obtained by the intersection of the optical axis with the pixel selection of the neighboring cameras. It generates a volume W, H, Z with several of the contender's depths of each pixel of the image by applying a Zero Mean Normalized Cross-Correlation (ZNCC) to estimate the similarity for each one of the pixels. This node provides for every photo a volume of resemblances with noise, then it applies a filtering step to X and Y axes that groups local cost, which reduces the score of outlier's value. Later, this node selects the local minima and replaces the plane index with the value of depth map volume where is saved, using a refining step to calculate depth values with sub-pixel accuracy. Also, the depth maps value autonomously computing as a parallel process and apply filtering to get more uniformity between numerous cameras. Generally, this node takes a long time, but a parameter allows running different cameras as different standalone commands [1].

Depth Map Filter

The depth map values obtained from the previous node is not wholly consistent, so this node filters some areas that are occluded by other depth maps.

Meshing
The output of this node is to construct a dense geometric surface of the image scene. At this stage, it fuses each depth map value into an octree. Besides, this node achieves a 3D Delaunay tetrahedralization and calculates weights on cells and facets by applying a complicated voting method. This node implement Graph Cut Max-Flow to cut the volume in the best way. Later, by filtering the terrible cells on the surface obtained simplified mesh to decrease the redundant vertices [1].

Mesh Filtering
This node is considered post-processing of the previous node with some refinement, applying some filtering operations as smoothing the mesh, ignoring the large triangles, maintaining the largest mesh, and removing the small mesh.

3.2 AR Application Development with Handling Occlusion

Computer vision renders 3D virtual objects from the same viewpoint in which the images of the real scene are being taken by tracking cameras. Augmented reality image registration uses a different method of computer vision, mostly related to video tracking. These methods are usually consisting of two stages: tracking and reconstructing/recognizing. In this paper, we are interested in Vuforia, which is means an augmented reality software development kit (SDK) for mobile devices that helps providing in augmented reality applications. It aims to recognize and track planar images and 3D objects in real-time. This image registration capability enables developers to position and orient virtual objects, such as 3D models and other media, with real-world objects when viewed through a mobile device's camera. The virtual object then tracks the position and orientation of the image in real-time so that the viewer's perspective on the object corresponds with the target's perspective. It thus appears that the virtual object is a part of the real-world scene.

In this context, we use vuforia SDK to create a model with features to know the location of a similar shape in reality. We create a virtual environment similar to the real scene in all the details by adding virtual objects that match this environment to study occlusion. This environment has a virtual camera that moves in all directions to capture all the scenes. Thus, we receive real-time video camera recordings of the real scene. For every frame, we project the 3D model into the 2D frame with the help of the coordinates transformation calculation software (Vuforia). Then, we estimate the pose of cameras by aligning the actual camera coordinates with the virtual camera coordinates and see the virtual objects in the foreground of the physical world. We are now handling occlusion to be easier in this case.

Theoretically, the correct occlusion relationship between real and virtual object scans is obtained by comparing their Z coordinates. The usage of an occlusion mask was a crucial task to create the illusion of looking through a screen. This mask provides realistic results to hide objects backside the image target. The case study presented, adding a Depth Mask material provided by Unity3D to handle the occlusion between the objects.

4   Results and Discussion

In this section, we present the implementation of our proposed architecture and some achieved results.

4.1   Experimental Results

Data Acquisition

We are capturing multiple images of the study scene using the phone's camera. Our proposed scene contains three small objects (Refrigerator, Electric oven, Cooking pot). In close-range photogrammetry is essential to know what's needs to be measured and reconstructed to acquire images. Thus, the main condition for successful photogrammetry is that the triangulation of surface points should be considered accurately and recommend to be not high range from 60 to 110 °C (i.e., consecutive photos should have 20 to 30 °C of difference). So, the image acquisition process changes when capturing small to large scale objects for reconstruction [6].

Generally, images are captured around an object should respect the orientation in a clock-wide direction and matching different heights and view angles for each image acquisition position. That are it's defined two parameters for the location of a camera: **Tilt angle** (Ψ) denotes the tilt of the camera to the xy plane of the object and steps angle and **the step angle** (Θ) is the rotating phase of the turning table [11] (Fig. 3).

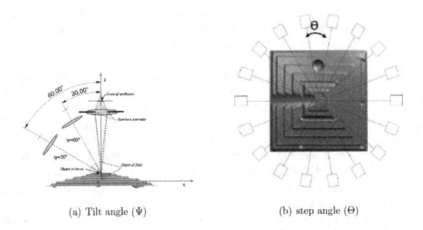

(a) Tilt angle (Ψ)   (b) step angle (Θ)

Fig. 3. Camera positions strategy.

Photogrammetry Algorithm

By applying close-range photogrammetry using Meshroom program, we construct 3D model of the real scene as shown in the Fig. 4:

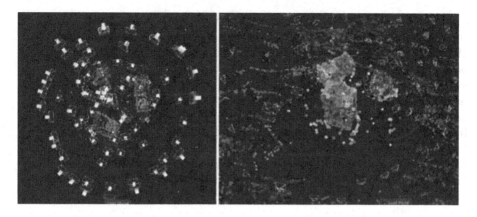

Fig. 4. The results of photogrammetry pipeline on Meshroom.

AR Application

After reconstructing the 3D model of our real scene, we filtering the 3D model using Meshlab. Next, we use the Model Target Generator (MTG), which converts an existing 3D model into a Vuforia Engine database that the Vuforia Engine can use latter for Model Target tracking. This tool confirms that the spatial features of our model will be usable, sets up the initial snapping position by defining an angle 360° from all sides of objects, and then exports the final model target.

We created our AR application which is augmenting by virtual element similar to the real scene in Unity3D software for handling mutual occlusion in real-time as shown in the figure:

Fig. 5. (a) AR image. (b) AR occlusion (c) AR handling occlusion

The occlusion problem in AR considered a crutial research domain. Occlusion commonly refers to objects blocking other objects located behind them from a given viewpoint which create a misunderstanding to users how think that the real objects are far from the viewpoint of the virtual objects. The image of Fig. 5(a) shows the result of the augmented reality application for image tracking. The image of Fig. 5(b) shows the incorrect relative relationship between the real and virtual objects without occlusion handling as it appears the virtual object is in front of the real world. The correct occlusion handling results after using our method are shown in the image of Fig. 5(c). From the results, we can see that using an occlusion mask is crucial when appearing a part of our model target hides with virtual object part. In this case, it can effectively solve the occlusion problem in real-time (Figs. 6 and 7).

Fig. 6. Resolving occlusion using Shader dapthMap material provided in Unity3D

Fig. 7. Handling occlusion in Augmented reality app with different point views in real-time using Unity3D

4.2 Discussion

This section will validate the results obtained by our proposition, which consists of achieving two main objectives, photogrammetry, and AR and managing AR occlusion in real-time. We have proved that the photogrammetric method builds a very good and accurate photorealistic 3D model of the proposed scene. We used meshroom software to implement a photogrammetry pipeline composed of 12 nodes to get high performance of the 3D model.

Many associative parameters are used in the processing to augment quality concerned the photogrammetric method. Firstly, we obtained high measurement accuracy by using a single camera position which has a good spread to achieve accuracy up to 5um. Thus, we got the high efficiency of a model by extracting more feature information from data points in a short time. Besides, when we are testing different examples with various conditions, we can obtain a stable performance. The resolution of the camera is crucial because it gives a higher resolution of images that are used as input in our software, which gives better results. The size of objects composed in our scene should be smaller to get a high reconstructed model, and the quality of this photogrammetric mesh is dependent on sets of parameters such as: number of images, the default parameters set inside photogrammetry methodology, calibration of the camera device for correct settings, image acquisition procedure. Also, there is an important parameter consist to capture consecutive photographs with an angle that doesn't measure less than 60°, taking in consideration that the ideal angle of intersection would be 90° to provide a higher accuracy of the recognition. In contrast, the photogrammetric should followed some conditions to release better results, much experience is required to capture photographs; the appropriate camera position would be the essential part; also camera calibration is necessary to define it.

As mentioned earlier, we use Vuforia to track the objects from the real scene and estimate the camera's pose to build an augmented reality application in order to solve the occlusion problem. Visualization of the 3D model with augmented reality provides good results with high accuracy of viewing. The main objective is to develop the concept of image-based 3D modeling using close-up photogrammetry to handle occlusion of objects behind the target to obtain a realistic real-time view.

To analyse the results of our approach, we proposed a comparison based on five important criteria to prove that our system is more efficient than the previous methods. First, The applicable scene is considered. In practical applications, The method proposed in **Sanches et al.** [13], **Lu and Smith.** [8] the objects are not static. However, **Lepetit et al.** [7], and this approach cannot deal with this situation. Second, the criteria regarding the viewpoint changes of the camera over a wide range of viewing angles and volumes is considered when resolving the occlusion problem. The method of **Lepetit et al.** [7] restricts the viewpoint, which largely reduces the practicability. In contrast, the viewpoint of our system and **Sanches et al.** [13], **Lu and Smith.** [8] the choice of viewpoint is arbitrary. Third, an additional condition which is the necessary equipment in the implementation of the application. In **Sanches et al.** [13] used the Fiducial markers as an efficient solution to solve the registration problem in AR which is obtained by optical tracking and each virtual object is overlaid on marker to align it with the real environment. In our work, we used the DSLR camera to acquire sets of photographs and Vuforia SDK to recognize and track planar images and 3D objects in real time and estimate the camera's pose. The last criteria is real-time which is required in all of the methods. More details are presented in Table 1.

Table 1. A comparison between the proposed method and the previous methods.

Method	Scene	Viewpoint	Equipment	Handle mutual occlusion	Real-time
Sanches et al. [13]	Dynamic	Arbitrary	Fiducial markers	Yes	Yes
Lu and Smith [8]	Dynamic	Arbitrary	No	No	Yes
Lepetit et al. [7]	Static	Restricted	No	No	Yes
Our method	Static	Arbitrary	Vuforia SDK	Yes	Yes

5 Conclusion

Augmented reality has become a destination for developers as it provides them with an enjoyable experience and interaction with virtual objects. This paper has proposed a new and effective occlusion handling method based on 3D reconstruction for AR tasks. The key concept is handling mutual occlusion using two different technologies: Augmented reality and photogrammetry. We also created an AR application using a famous SDK software called Vuforia, which allows us to extract most of the features of our scene and estimate the pose of a camera to find the right alignment of our AR systems. Thus, we managed the occlusion by comparing the third coordinate of real and virtual objects in real time using masks. We are also testing by real scene using small objects, and the results show that our method can satisfy accuracy, efficiency, and the real-time requirement in augmented reality applications. Finally, for future work, we suggest some ideas that can improve our system, such as:

- Increasing the realism of virtual objects by adding shaders.
- Applying deep learning techniques to better extract the sources of lighting in the scene.
- Studying the lighting and its positions in the scene and its effect on virtual objects.
- Merging augmented reality with virtual reality to create a mixed reality.

References

1. Bullinger, S., Bodensteiner, C., Arens, M.: A photogrammetry-based framework to facilitate image-based modeling and automatic camera tracking. arXiv preprint arXiv:2012.01044 (2020)
2. Carrión-Ruiz, B., Blanco-Pons, S., Weigert, A., Fai, S., Lerma, J.: Merging photogrammetry and augmented reality: the Canadian library of parliament. Int. Arch. Photogramm. Remote Sens. Spatial Inf. Sci. **42**(2/W11), 367–371 (2019)
3. Fukiage, T., Oishi, T., Ikeuchi, K.: Reduction of contradictory partial occlusion in mixed reality by using characteristics of transparency perception. In: 2012 IEEE International Symposium on Mixed and Augmented Reality (ISMAR), pp. 129–139. IEEE (2012)
4. Hayashi, K., Kato, H., Nishida, S.: Occlusion detection of real objects using contour based stereo matching. In: Proceedings of the 2005 International Conference on Augmented Tele-Existence, pp. 180–186 (2005)
5. Kim, H., Yang, S.j., Sohn, K.: 3D reconstruction of stereo images for interaction between real and virtual worlds. In: The Second IEEE and ACM International Symposium on Mixed and Augmented Reality 2003. Proceedings, pp. 169–176. IEEE (2003)
6. Kortaberria, G., Mutilba, U., Gomez-Acedo, E., Tellaeche, A., Minguez, R.: Accuracy evaluation of dense matching techniques for casting part dimensional verification. Sensors **18**(9), 3074 (2018)
7. Lepetit, V., Berger, M.O.: A semi-automatic method for resolving occlusion in augmented reality. In: Proceedings IEEE Conference on Computer Vision and Pattern Recognition. CVPR 2000 (Cat. No. PR00662), vol. 2, pp. 225–230. IEEE (2000)
8. Lu, Y., Smith, S.: GPU-based real-time occlusion in an immersive augmented reality environment. J. Comput. Inf. Sci. Eng. **9**(2), 024501 (2009)
9. Ohta, Y., Sugaya, Y., Igarashi, H., Ohtsuki, T., Taguchi, K.: Share-Z: client/server depth sensing for see-through head-mounted displays. Presence Teleoperators Virtual Environ. **11**(2), 176–188 (2002)
10. Portalés, C., Lerma, J.L., Navarro, S.: Augmented reality and photogrammetry: a synergy to visualize physical and virtual city environments. ISPRS J. Photogramm. Remote Sens. **65**(1), 134–142 (2010). https://doi.org/10.1016/j.isprsjprs.2009.10.001
11. Potabatti, N.S.: Photogrammetry for 3D reconstruction in SOLIDWORKS and its applications in industry. Ph.D. thesis, Purdue University Indianapolis, Indiana (2019)

12. Rabbi, I., Ullah, S.: A survey on augmented reality challenges and tracking. Acta graphica: znanstveni časopis za tiskarstvo i grafičke komunikacije **24**(1–2), 29–46 (2013)
13. Sanches, S.R., Tokunaga, D.M., Silva, V.F., Sementille, A.C., Tori, R.: Mutual occlusion between real and virtual elements in augmented reality based on fiducial markers. In: 2012 IEEE Workshop on the Applications of Computer Vision (WACV), pp. 49–54. IEEE (2012)
14. Setohara, H., Kato, H., Kawamoto, K., Tachibana, K.: A simple solution of occlusion problem in augmented reality and its application for interaction. Trans. Virtual Reality Soc. Jpn. **9**(4), 387–395 (2004)
15. Tian, Y., Guan, T., Wang, C.: An automatic occlusion handling method in augmented reality. Sens. Rev. (2010)
16. Tian, Y., Guan, T., Wang, C.: Real-time occlusion handling in augmented reality based on an object tracking approach. Sensors **10**(4), 2885–2900 (2010)
17. Tian, Y., Long, Y., Xia, D., Yao, H., Zhang, J.: Handling occlusions in augmented reality based on 3D reconstruction method. Neurocomputing **156**, 96–104 (2015)
18. Yokoya, N.: Stereo vision based video see-through mixed reality. In: Proceedings of the 1st International Symposium On Mixed Reality, Yokohama, March 1999 (1999)
19. Zhou, Y., Ma, J.-T., Hao, Q., Wang, H., Liu, X.-P.: A novel optical see-through head-mounted display with occlusion and intensity matching support. In: Hui, K., et al. (eds.) Edutainment 2007. LNCS, vol. 4469, pp. 56–62. Springer, Heidelberg (2007). https://doi.org/10.1007/978-3-540-73011-8_8

Colour Image Encryption Based on Fisher-Yates Algorithm and Chaotic Maps

Renjith V. Ravi[1](✉) , S. B. Goyal[2] , and Chawki Djeddi[3,4]

[1] Department of Electronics and Communication Engineering, M.E.A Engineering College, Kerala, India
renjithravi@meaec.edu.in
[2] City University, Petaling Jaya, Malaysia
drsbgoyal@gmail.com
[3] Department of Mathematics and Computer Science, Larbi Tebessi University, Tebessa, Algeria
c.djeddi@univ-tebessa.dz
[4] LITIS Lab, Rouen University, Rouen, France

Abstract. Due to its highly sensitive initial values and parameters and complicated features such as ergodicity and pseudorandomness, chaos-based systems are extensively used in digital image encryption. On the other hand, the authors looked at the impact of these maps on the encryption of colour images. The current research presents an image encryption using Fisher-Yates shuffling (FYS) and a 2D-LTM. FYS is a program that creates random permutations of finite sequences. At first, this FYS is used for randomly permuting the plain mage in rows and columns wise. Second, at the diffusion step, the 2D-LTM is utilized to confuse the values of pixel in the shuffled image. The suggested method is used to process a variety of images. Many tests are carried out to ensure the proposed algorithm's security and performance. Furthermore, numerical simulations and experimental findings have ensured that the suggested method can withstand various attacks.

Keywords: Image encryption · Fisher-Yates shuffling · Logistic-Tent map · Chaotic encryption

1 Introduction

In this modern era of sophisticated technology, a significant quantity of data, pictures, and video is transmitted via the channel daily. Information communication has become more susceptible as a result of technological advancements. Images and movies are saved and transferred over the channel thanks to enhanced multimedia coding technology [21]. The broadcaster must ensure that authorised users only read the material. Cryptography is one of the methods for preventing

---

Supported by City University, Petaling Jaya, MALAYSIA.

C. Djeddi et al. (Eds.): MedPRAI 2021, CCIS 1543, pp. 63–76, 2022.
https://doi.org/10.1007/978-3-031-04112-9_5

the harmful use of media [9]. It's a technique for concealing data by utilising lines of code and converting the original data into an format which is unreadable for all others those who are not having the right decryption key. Only the authorised person on the receiving end could extract the data using secret keys.

Multimedia communication, such as image, video, and audio, is becoming increasingly important and needed in today's society, due to the fast development of smartphones and other intelligent terminals [31]. However, the openness and sharing of networks expose digital communication to many security concerns. Digital images have an essential part as an essential medium of multimedia communication [29]. The digital image has a wealth of helpful information that is freely disseminated through the open Internet. Some of them, however, is confidential or contain sensitive information. As a result, protecting the security of image material is a critical job. Images contain unique features compared to conventional texts or words, such as massive data, significant redundancy, a strong connection between neighbouring pixels, and low information entropy [28]. As a result, in order to encrypt images for security reasons, people need a lengthy keystream.

Digital data may be generated and distributed across different networks due to the rapid development of information technology. Digital images are among the most frequently utilized digital data types because they provide a direct visual impact. A digital image also has much potential and can hold a lot of information [22]. A personal image, for example, may communicate not just a person's physical appearance but also other information such as their health and age. Consequently, protecting digital images in platforms such as cloud computing from unwanted access is crucial [19,20].

The highly sensitive reliance on starting circumstances and system parameters, ergodicity, and random behaviour of chaos-based systems make them fit for image encryption. Consequently, different chaos-based systems have been utilized for image encryption in many recent studies [1,8,18,27]. For example, Chai et al. [8] developed a high dimension hyperchaotic system capable of performing permutation at both pixel-level and bit-level for image encryption techniques. A 2D Hénon-Sine map-based algorithm for image encryption was described by Wu et al. [2,12]. Over a broad range of parameters, the novel map shows excellence in the case of ergodicity, pseudorandomness, and chaos. Chai et al. [23] utilized a hyperchaotic system with CA and DNA operations for image encryption. Generalized self-excited attractors produce all chaos-based algorithms in the image encryption techniques described here. It has been demonstrated that a self-excited attractor's attractive basin is linked to a point of equilibrium [30]. By finding equilibrium sites in the phase space for chaos-based systems produced by self-excited attractors, the attractors may be retrieved. Consequently, certain attackers may reconstruct chaotic sequences by recreating the original system's attractors, rendering the image encryption technique of chaotic systems' self-excited attractors insecure.

Many chaos-based encryption methods have drawbacks regarding the chaos-based systems used and their encryption procedures. In [12] Zhongyun Hua et al. created a 2D logistic-tent map (2D-LTM) to circumvent these limitations. According to performance tests, 2D-LTM has a very wide and consistent chaotic range with good chaotic behaviours. Furthermore, the 2D-trajectories LTM's may be evenly dispersed across the whole phase plane, suggesting that its outputs include a significant amount of unpredictability.

Encryption technology is a commonly used technique and approach in the digital information security system. By encrypting the original data, encryption technology may be secured. The security of digital information may be safeguarded if the encryption technique is sufficiently secure and reliable. As a result, research into digital image encryption technology and methods is essential to ensure the security of digital images. In this paper, we propose an algorithm for image encryption which uses FYS for shuffling and 2D LTM for confusing the pixel values. The organization of paper as follows, Sect. 2 discusses about the algorithms and techniques used, Sect. 3 discusses the test results of simulation and lastly Sect. 4 concludes this manuscript.

2   Materials and Methods

In this section, a detailed description of all algorithms, techniques used for encryption and the proposed methodology for encryption and decryption were carried out.

Grayscale and colour images are the two types of images that can be found. Images with only grey areas and no other colours are known as grayscale images. Grayscale images, also known as one-color images, lack colour information. The distinction between grayscale and coloured images is that grayscale images require fewer data to depict a specific pixel. The intensity in a greyscale image can be 256 values ranging from [0–255]. Colour images can be thought of as three-band monochrome image data, with each band representing a different colour. Consider the following scenario: RGB images correspond to red, green, and blue bands when broken down into their constituent parts. Figure-3 shows the famous Lena photograph as a binary image (only black and white), a grayscale image (grayscale shades ranging from [0–255], i.e. black-shades-gray-white), and an RGB coloured image (comprising three separate components R, G, and B).

2.1   2D Logistic-Tent Map

Hua et al. [12] created a 2D-LTM using two chaotic maps named logistic and tent with one dimension. Listed below are the mathematical definitions for logistical (Eq. 1) and tent map (Eq. 2) types.

$$x_{i+1} = 4rx_i (1 - x_i) \tag{1}$$

$$x_{i+1} = \begin{cases} 2rx_i & \text{for } x_i < 0.5 \\ 2r(1 - x_i) & \text{for } x_i \geq 0.5 \end{cases} \tag{2}$$

The two chaotic maps are using the same control parameter $r \in [0,1]$ 2D logistic and tent maps are used to create the 2D-LTM. This procedure folds two chaotic maps into a specified range. Afterwards, the 1D map is extended to 2D. Mathematically speaking, the 2D-LTM is expressed as in Eq. 3:

$$\begin{cases} x_{i+1} = \begin{cases} (4ax_i (1-x_i) + 2by_i) \bmod 1 & \text{for } y_i < 0.5 \\ (4ax_i (1-x_i) + 2b(1-y_i)) \bmod 1 & \text{for } y_i \geq 0.5 \end{cases} \\ y_{i+1} = \begin{cases} (4ay_i (1-y_i) + 2bx_i) \bmod 1 & \text{for } x_i < 0.5 \\ (4ay_i (1-y_i) + 2b(1-x_i)) \bmod 1 & \text{for } x_i \geq 0.5 \end{cases} \end{cases} \qquad (3)$$

It is important to note that the 2D-LTM inherits the logistic and tent maps as its two parameters (a and b). These parameters may be set to any large number in the 2D-modular LTM's operation since it is globally limited. These parameters were used to evaluate the performance of the 2D-LTM.

2.2 Fisher-Yates Algorithm

Fisher-Yates shuffle algorithm (FYS) shown in Algorithm 1 was proposed initially by Ronald A. Fisher and Frank Yates. In this algorithm, a number is randomly selected from the previous level and inserted into a new array [13,16,23–25];

The following are the specifics: To create a random number x, we utilize the

---

Algorithm 1. Fisher-Yates Algorithm

1: **function** FISHER-YATES ALGORITHM PERMUTATION
2:     Initialize both the old and new arrays. The length of the initial array is n.
3:     A number $x \in [1, k]$ is generated randomly if there are k numbers in the array.
4:     From the remaining k numbers, find the nth number. After that, put it in the new array.
5:     Steps 3 and 4 should be repeated until all of the numbers have been taken. The new sequence derived from step 4 is jumbled. This method has an $O(n \times n)$ time complexity and space complexity(n).
6: **end function**

---

logistic map with $x = 3.9985 \times x \times (1 - x)$.

2.3 Diffusion Using 2D LTM

A method for encrypting data must have some diffusion function. A predefined technique is used in the majority of image encryption algorithms to spread content. On the other hand, a fixed-order processing method may result in poor encryption performance and offer attackers a significant quantity of valuable information to do cryptanalyses. Our encryption mechanism overcomes this problem by processing pixels randomly and secretly.

Since the 2D-LTM generates a chaotic sequence, the processing order is not set. As a result, any pixel from the three colour planes R, G and B may influence a pixel. First, it is necessary to create the chaos matrix A, which follows a similar procedure to the permutation mentioned above. The diffusion process is described in detail below in Eq. 4.

$$\mathbf{C}_{i,j,k} = \begin{cases} (\mathbf{S}_{i,j,k} + \mathbf{S}_{PQ,3} + \mathbf{A}_{i,j,k}) \bmod F & \text{if } i = 1, j = 1, k = 1, \\ (\mathbf{S}_{i,jk} + \mathbf{C}_{P,Q,k-1} + \mathbf{A}_{i,jk}) \bmod F & \text{if } i = 1, j = 1, k \neq 1, \\ (\mathbf{S}_{i,jk} + \mathbf{C}_{P,j-1,k} + \mathbf{A}_{i,jk}) \bmod F & \text{if } i = 1, j \neq 1, \\ (\mathbf{S}_{i,jk} + \mathbf{C}_{i-1,j,k} + \mathbf{A}_{i,j,k}) \bmod F & \text{if } i \neq 1, \end{cases} \tag{4}$$

where F = Value of pixel in each colour plane P, and mod represents the modular arithmetic process.

Also, the inverse diffusion process for decryption is as in Eq. 5

$$\mathbf{s}_{i,jk} = \begin{cases} (\mathbf{C}_{i,jk} - \mathbf{S}_{P,Q,3} - \mathbf{A}_{i,jk}) \bmod F & \text{if } i = 1, j = 1, k = 1 \\ (\mathbf{C}_{i,jk} - \mathbf{C}_{P,Q_{k-1}} - \mathbf{A}_{i,jk}) \bmod F & \text{if } i = 1, j = 1, k \neq 1 \\ (\mathbf{C}_{i,jk} - \mathbf{C}_{P,j-1,k} - \mathbf{A}_{i,jk}) \bmod F & \text{if } i = 1, j \neq 1, \\ (\mathbf{C}_{i,jk} - \mathbf{C}_{i-1,jk} - \mathbf{A}_{i,jk}) \bmod F & \text{if } i \neq 1 \end{cases} \tag{5}$$

Changes between one pixel and all subsequent pixels may be dispersed by diffusion. After one cycle of diffusion, if the Lth ($L \leq P \times Q \times 3$) pixel in a color image of $P \times Q \times 3$ pixels is modified, the number of modified pixel is shown in Eq. 6

$$R = \frac{(P \times Q \times 3) - L}{P \times Q \times 3} \tag{6}$$

To accomplish excellent diffusion, at least two rounds of diffusion are needed. Accordingly the number of rounds n is set to two. The LTM provides excellent diffusion by combining peripheral-pixel blurring with diffusion.

2.4   Proposed Method for Encrypting Colour Image

In the proposed algorithm, the Logistic-Tent map generates the key for both shuffling and diffusion processes. At, first the plain colour image will be separated into its red, green and blue channels. Then these three channels will be processed parallelly for achieving a fast execution.

The next step is shuffling the order of pixels in these channel's separately row-wise and column-wise using FYS. Further, a diffusion using 2D LTM will be carried out to change the values of each pixel in each of the plain in an ordered manner. After the diffusion process, the three planes will be integrated to prepare the cipher image for transmission.

The suggested encryption method is shown in block diagram form in Fig. 1 and its algorithmic representation is in Algorithm 2.

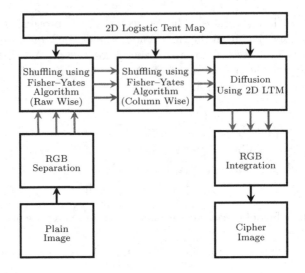

Fig. 1. Block diagram of proposed encryption algorithm

Algorithm 2. Proposed Encryption Approach

1: **procedure** ENCRYPTION(*plain_image, key*)
2:     Take the Plain image
3:     Separation of RGB components of plain image
4:     Raw Wise Permutation using FYS Algorithm
5:     Column Wise Permutation using FYS Algorithm
6:     Diffusion using 2D LTM
7:     Integration of RGB Components.
8:     Take the Encrypted image
9: **end procedure**

Decryption Process: The decryption procedure is exactly the polar opposite of encryption process, and the value of key utilized for decryption must be sent via a secure channel to the decryption side before the image can be decrypted.

In the decryption process, first, the three colour channels will be separated and processed in parallel. First, the inverse diffusion will be performed, and the inverse shuffling process. Before the decryption, the chaotic sequences were created in the same way as during encryption.

3   Results and Discussion

The objective of assessing an encryption algorithm is to assess its security. This paper's security evaluation focuses on the sequence's unpredictability and the effect of scrambling and diffusion.

The random sequences employed in digital image encryption has a significant impact on its security. The pseudorandom signal of the chaotic system has a high initial sensitivity, randomness, and unpredictability. It is ideal for use in an encryption system. As a consequence, chaotic system-based encryption is widely used in real-world applications. Encrypting data using the chaotic map's pseudorandom sequence number is highly efficient and fast. However, as information security technology has advanced, the key sequence security of a single chaotic map-based encryption scheme has grown progressively convex. Because the chaotic mapping generates the chaotic encryption sequence and there are only ten chaotic systems, the attacker may utilise the item space construction method to assess the chaotic system used in the encryption process. Unless the whole encryption process is safe, the attacker may break the chaotic sequence's parameter values and beginning values based on specific plaintext and ciphertext pairings, ruining the encryption technique.

An image encryption method must encrypt various kinds of images into unrecognizable cipher images to adapt to various application situations, with the plain image only being recoverable with the correct secret key. Figure 2 shows how the proposed algorithm's encryption and decryption operations are simulated using colour image Lena, Mandril and Peppers of size 256×256. The pixel histograms of these test images revealed that they were all-natural images with many patterns. By analyzing the histograms of the images, much information about them may be gleaned. On the other hand, the suggested method may encrypt plain images into unrecognizable images with histograms having uniform pixel distribution, which will prevent information retrieval. The suggested method can recreate the whole plain image using the right key with the same visual effects.

3.1 Statistical Attack Analysis

The three essential assessment criteria for analysis of statistical attack are the correlation coefficient, histogram analysis, and entropy, which are illustrated in the following subsections.

Histogram Analysis: An image histogram is a kind of histogram that shows the tonal dispersion of a digital image graphically. It displays the number of pixels associated with each tonal value. A viewer may analyze the full tonal distribution of an image by looking at the histogram for that image. The abscissa spans from 0 to 255 for an image size of $1024 \times 1024 \times 8$ bits, and the total number of pixels is 1024×1024. Image enhancing techniques often include the modification of original histograms.

In a statistical image, the histogram shows the number of pixels with the same value [23]. The cipher image's pixel value distribution is more uniform, as can it be seen in the findings of Fig. 3.

Adjacent Pixel Correlation: Correlation is a statistical relationship between two measured quantities. The correlation coefficient is the numerical measurement of correlation. The correlation coefficient between neighboring pixels of

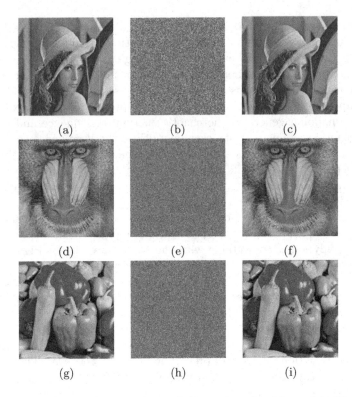

Fig. 2. Results of proposed encryption and decryption algorithms. (a), (d), (g) Plain images, (b), (c), (h) Corresponding Encrypted images, (c), (f), (i) Corresponding Decrypted images.

cipher image must be decreased to prevent others from employing statistical information assaults [5]. The pixel correlation may be calculated using the following formula shown in Eq. 7.

$$r_{ab} = \frac{\text{cov}(a,b)}{\sqrt{D(a)}\sqrt{D(b)}} \qquad (7)$$

where,

$$\begin{cases} \text{cov}(a,b) = \frac{1}{N}\sum_{i=1}^{N}(x_i - E(a))(b_i - E(b)) \\ D(a) = \frac{1}{N}\sum_{i+1}^{N}(a_i - E(a))^2 \\ E(a) = \frac{1}{N}\sum_{i=1}^{N} a_i \end{cases} \qquad (8)$$

Equation 7 and Eq. 8 are used to determine the horizontal, vertical, and diagonal correlations of plaintext and ciphertext in this work. Figure 4 depicts the statistical findings.

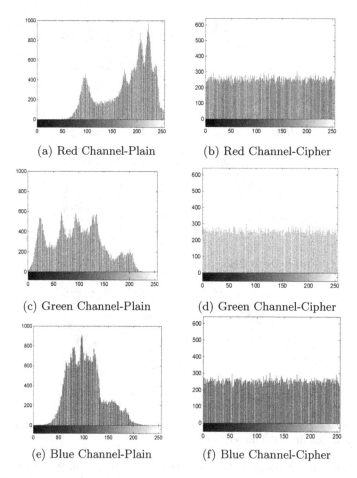

(a) Red Channel-Plain   (b) Red Channel-Cipher

(c) Green Channel-Plain   (d) Green Channel-Cipher

(e) Blue Channel-Plain   (f) Blue Channel-Cipher

Fig. 3. Comparison of histograms of plain and cipher images in R, G and B planes (Color figure online)

There is a significant connection between neighbouring pixels of the R, G, and B components in colour images. Consequently, an effective encryption method should break the correlations between neighbouring R, G, and B pixels. Figure 4 demonstrate the same position correlations and close position correlations between plain and cypher images R component. The findings indicate that correlations between neighbouring pixels are substantially decreased in encrypted images. Table 1 compares correlation coefficients using the Lena image to demonstrate the correlation coefficients between our method and other approaches, with Lena serving as the test image. According to the results, the novel approach outperforms current methods of confusion and dispersion.

Information Entropy Analysis: The term Entropy is used in cryptography to quantify the unpredictability of the ciphertext so that it does not disclose any

72   R. V. Ravi et al.

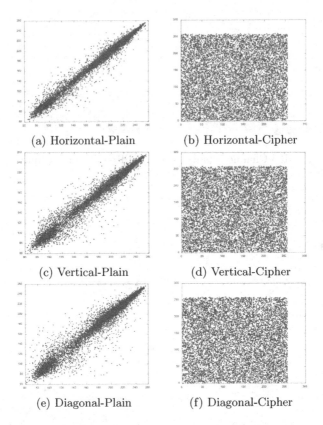

(a) Horizontal-Plain   (b) Horizontal-Cipher

(c) Vertical-Plain   (d) Vertical-Cipher

(e) Diagonal-Plain   (f) Diagonal-Cipher

Fig. 4. Correlation between plain and cipher images within the red channel in horizontal, vertical and diagonal directions

information about the plain text. The entropy of cypher images informs us how randomly the pixels are placed. The optimum entropy value for an encryption algorithm is 8. In more clear, it is used to assess the encrypted image. The encrypted image becomes increasingly chaotic as the information entropy value [26] approaches 8. The following is the information entropy calculation formula in Eq. 9:

$$H(s) = \sum_{i=0}^{2^L-1} p\left(s_i\right) \log_2 \frac{1}{p\left(s_i\right)} \tag{9}$$

where $p(s_i)$ is the probability of occurrence of s_i.

Table 2 compares this approach with other methods. The encrypted image is more chaotic and resistant to statistical assaults, as can be observed.

Differential Attack Analysis: The ability to detect small changes in plain images is a frequent feature of image encryption schemes. An attacker may use differential analysis to make minor modifications to the plain image and then re-encrypt it. Differential attacks are a kind of plaintext attack that may be used

Table 1. Correlation between two adjacent pixels for the test image *Lena*, in three directions

Image	Horizontal	Vertical	Diagonal
Plain image	0.8951	0.9650	0.9203
Proposed algorithm	−0.0012	0.0011	0.0974
Di et al. [10]	−0.0062	0.0052	0.0043
Belasi et al. [7]	−0.0318	0.0965	0.0362
Niyat et al. [17]	0.0026	−0.0012	0.0013
Belazi et al. [6]	0.0362	0.0141	0.0464
Maddodi et al. [15]	0.00046	0.0011	0.0031
Alawida et al. [4]	−0.0084	−0.0017	−0.0019
Lokesh et al. [14]	0.0340	0.0340	0.0340

Table 2. Comparison of values of information entropy for the test image *Lena*

Image	Information entropy
Lena	7.2765
Proposed Algorithm	7.9987
Di et al. [10]	7.9993
Belasi et al. [7]	7.9851
Lokesh et al. [14]	7.9969
Maddodi et al. [15]	7.9976
Alawida et al. [4]	7.9975
Niyat et al. [17]	7.9974
Belazi et al. [6]	7.9988

in different ways. When the plaintext is changed slightly, the ciphertext and the amended ciphertext are altered and examined to determine the key. To resist differential assaults, a successful image encryption system should be capable of causing large ciphertext changes from tiny changes in plaintext [3]. The UACI (Eq. 10) and the NPCR (Eq. 11) are two different metrics.

$$NPCR = \frac{\sum_{x,y} D(x,y)}{M \times N} \times 100\% \tag{10}$$

$$UACI = \frac{1}{M \times N} \left[\sum_{x,y} \frac{|C_1(x,y) - C_2(x,y)|}{255} \right] \times 100\% \tag{11}$$

In this case, M and N are the image width and height, respectively, while C_1 and C_2 are the cipher images. If C_1 and C_2 are true, then $D(x,y)$ equals 1, else $D(x, y)$ equals 0. More sensitive encryption algorithms are based on higher NPCR values, whereas larger UACI values indicate a greater average change intensity [11]. Under ideal circumstances, the NPCR is closer to 99.6049 percent and the UACI is closer to 33.4635 percent. This method is compared to other algorithms in Table 3. The table shows that, while not being particularly near to the optimum value, it can withstand differential assaults better.

Table 3. Comparison of NPCR and UCAI Results

Image	NPCR	UACI
Proposed Algorithm	99.6302	33.4521
Di et al. [10]	99.6002	33.3635
Belasi et al. [7]	99.6140	33.4828
Wei et al. [26]	99.6239	33.6623
Belazi et al. [6]	99.6143	33.6532
Niyat et al. [17]	99.6414	33.4702
Maddodi et al. [15]	99.6155	28.567
Alawida et al. [4]	99.6710	33.5050

4   Conclusion

Image encryption often employs chaotic systems. This research looked at the current chaos-based image encryption methods and discovered flaws in chaotic systems and encryption structures. The 2D-LTM is built on traditional logistic and tent maps, and it can produce better image encryption than chaotic maps. To wrap up this research, we would like to point out a few benefits of the suggested method that the experimental findings have shown. The benchmarks test, such as the correlation test, is an essential test to run when examining the algorithm, and our suggested method passes this test with flying colours. The picture pixel correlation is close to zero, which is exactly what we want. The UACI and NPCR readings, close to 33.4 and 99.6, also point to a brighter outlook. The ciphertext is having an entropy value which is close to 8, as needed. The method performs well on a variety of additional metrics and may be considered secure.

References

1. Abd-El-Atty, B., Amin, M., Abd-El-Latif, A., Ugail, H., Mehmood, I.: An efficient cryptosystem based on the logistic-chebyshev map. In: 2019 13th International Conference on Software, Knowledge, Information Management and Applications (SKIMA), pp. 1–6. IEEE (2019). https://doi.org/10.1109/skima47702.2019.8982535

2. Abu-Amara, F., Bensefia, A.: A handwriting document encryption scheme based on segmentation and chaotic logarithmic map. Int. J. Inf. Comput. Secur. **14**(3–4), 327–343 (2021)
3. Alanezi, A., et al.: Securing digital images through simple permutation-substitution mechanism in cloud-based smart city environment. In: Security and Communication Networks 2021 (2021). https://doi.org/10.1155/2021/6615512
4. Alawida, M., Samsudin, A., Teh, J.S., Alkhawaldeh, R.S.: A new hybrid digital chaotic system with applications in image encryption. Signal Process. **160**, 45–58 (2019). https://doi.org/10.1016/j.sigpro.2019.02.016
5. Behnia, S., Akhshani, A., Mahmodi, H., Akhavan, A.: A novel algorithm for image encryption based on mixture of chaotic maps. Chaos Solitons Fractals **35**(2), 408–419 (2008). https://doi.org/10.1016/j.chaos.2006.05.011
6. Belazi, A., Abd El-Latif, A.A., Belghith, S.: A novel image encryption scheme based on substitution-permutation network and chaos. Signal Process. **128**, 155–170 (2016). https://doi.org/10.1016/j.sigpro.2016.03.021
7. Belazi, A., Abd El-Latif, A.A., Diaconu, A.V., Rhouma, R., Belghith, S.: Chaos-based partial image encryption scheme based on linear fractional and lifting wavelet transforms. Opt. Lasers Eng. **88**, 37–50 (2017). https://doi.org/10.1016/j.optlaseng.2016.07.010
8. Chai, X., Gan, Z., Yang, K., Chen, Y., Liu, X.: An image encryption algorithm based on the memristive hyperchaotic system, cellular automata and DNA sequence operations. Sig. Process. Image Commun. **52**, 6–19 (2017). https://doi.org/10.1016/j.image.2016.12.007
9. Cheng, G., Wang, C., Chen, H.: A novel color image encryption algorithm based on hyperchaotic system and permutation-diffusion architecture. Int. J. Bifurcation Chaos **29**(09), 1950115 (2019). https://doi.org/10.1142/s0218127419501153
10. Di, X., Li, J., Qi, H., Cong, L., Yang, H.: A semi-symmetric image encryption scheme based on the function projective synchronization of two hyperchaotic systems. PLoS ONE **12**(9), e0184586 (2017). https://doi.org/10.1371/journal.pone.0184586
11. El-Latif, A.A.A., Abd-El-Atty, B., Belazi, A., Iliyasu, A.M.: Efficient chaos-based substitution-box and its application to image encryption. Electronics **10**(12) (2021). https://doi.org/10.3390/electronics10121392https://www.mdpi.com/2079-9292/10/12/1392
12. Hua, Z., Zhu, Z., Yi, S., Zhang, Z., Huang, H.: Cross-plane colour image encryption using a two-dimensional logistic tent modular map. Inf. Sci. **546**, 1063–1083 (2021). https://doi.org/10.1016/j.ins.2020.09.032
13. Karawia, A.: Image encryption based on fisher-yates shuffling and three dimensional chaotic economic map. IET Image Proc. **13**(12), 2086–2097 (2019). https://doi.org/10.1049/iet-ipr.2018.5142
14. Lokesh, S., Kounte, M.R.: Chaotic neural network based pseudo-random sequence generator for cryptographic applications. In: 2015 International Conference on Applied and Theoretical Computing and Communication Technology (iCATccT), pp. 1–5. IEEE (2015). https://doi.org/10.1109/icatcct.2015.7456845
15. Maddodi, G., Awad, A., Awad, D., Awad, M., Lee, B.: A new image encryption algorithm based on heterogeneous chaotic neural network generator and DNA encoding. Multimedia Tools Appl. **77**(19), 24701–24725 (2018). https://doi.org/10.1007/s11042-018-5669-2
16. Musanna, F., Kumar, S.: A novel fractional order chaos-based image encryption using Fisher Yates algorithm and 3-D cat map. Multimedia Tools Appl. **78**(11), 14867–14895 (2018). https://doi.org/10.1007/s11042-018-6827-2

76 R. V. Ravi et al.

17. Yaghouti Niyat, A., Moattar, M.H.: Color image encryption based on hybrid chaotic system and DNA sequences. Multimedia Tools Appl. (11), 1497–1518 (2019). https://doi.org/10.1007/s11042-019-08247-z
18. Pak, C., Huang, L.: A new color image encryption using combination of the 1D chaotic map. Signal Process. **138**, 129–137 (2017). https://doi.org/10.1016/j.sigpro.2017.03.011
19. Stergiou, C., Psannis, K.E.: Efficient and secure BIG data delivery in cloud computing. Multimedia Tools Appl. (11), 1–20 (2017). https://doi.org/10.1007/s11042-017-4590-4
20. Stergiou, C., Psannis, K.E., Plageras, A.P., Ishibashi, Y., Kim, B.G.: Algorithms for efficient digital media transmission over IoT and cloud networking. J. Multimedia Inf. Syst. **5**(1) (2018). https://doi.org/10.9717/JMIS.2018.5.1.27
21. Tsafack, N., et al.: A new chaotic map with dynamic analysis and encryption application in internet of health things. IEEE Access **8**, 137731–137744 (2020). https://doi.org/10.1109/access.2020.3010794
22. Wan, M., Li, M., Yang, G., Gai, S., Jin, Z.: Feature extraction using two-dimensional maximum embedding difference. Inf. Sci. **274**, 55–69 (2014). https://doi.org/10.1016/j.ins.2014.02.145
23. Wang, S., Wang, C., Xu, C.: An image encryption algorithm based on a hidden attractor chaos system and the knuth-durstenfeld algorithm. Opt. Lasers Eng. **128**, 105995 (2020). https://doi.org/10.1016/j.optlaseng.2019.105995
24. Wang, X., Gao, S.: Image encryption algorithm for synchronously updating Boolean networks based on matrix semi-tensor product theory. Inf. Sci. **507**, 16–36 (2020). https://doi.org/10.1016/j.ins.2019.08.041
25. Wang, X., Su, Y., Luo, C., Wang, C.: A novel image encryption algorithm based on fractional order 5d cellular neural network and fisher-yates scrambling. PLoS ONE **15**(7), e0236015 (2020). https://doi.org/10.1371/journal.pone.0236015
26. Wei, X., Guo, L., Zhang, Q., Zhang, J., Lian, S.: A novel color image encryption algorithm based on DNA sequence operation and hyper-chaotic system. J. Syst. Softw. **85**(2), 290–299 (2012). https://doi.org/10.1016/j.jss.2011.08.017
27. Wu, J., Liao, X., Yang, B.: Color image encryption based on chaotic systems and elliptic curve elgamal scheme. Signal Process. **141**, 109–124 (2017). https://doi.org/10.1016/j.sigpro.2017.04.006
28. Wu, J., Liao, X., Yang, B.: Image encryption using 2D hénon-sine map and DNA approach. Signal Process. **153**, 11–23 (2018). https://doi.org/10.1016/j.sigpro.2018.06.008
29. Yin, Q., Wang, C.: A new chaotic image encryption scheme using breadth-first search and dynamic diffusion. Int. J. Bifurcation Chaos **28**(04), 1850047 (2018). https://doi.org/10.1142/s0218127418500475
30. Zhang, S., Zeng, Y., Li, Z., Wang, M., Zhang, X., Chang, D.: A novel simple no-equilibrium chaotic system with complex hidden dynamics. Int. J. Dyn. Control **6**(4), 1465–1476 (2018). https://doi.org/10.1007/s40435-018-0413-3
31. Zhu, H., Zhang, X., Yu, H., Zhao, C., Zhu, Z.: An image encryption algorithm based on compound homogeneous hyper-chaotic system. Nonlinear Dyn. **89**(1), 61–79 (2017). https://doi.org/10.1007/s11071-017-3436-y

Robust SLAM System by Incorporating UWB Positioning and Landmark Localization

Ming-Chi Yeh and Huei-Yung Lin[✉]

Department of Electrical Engineering, National Chung Cheng University,
Chiayi 621, Taiwan
lin@ee.ccu.edu.tw

Abstract. In the existing SLAM techniques, the drifting errors are generally accumulated especially for the navigation in a large-scale environment. This paper presents a method for indoor localization by adding two-dimensional targets as landmarks to improve the overall robustness of the SLAM system. We split the global localization path into the frame-by-frame basis for relative pose estimation of the mobile robot. The drifting errors of the split paths are reduced using the ultra-wideband (UWB) positioning technology. By taking the advantage of the globally consistent error distribution of UWB, the inevitable local accumulation errors from SLAM computation can then be mitigated. In the experiments, different SLAM techniques are carried out in the real-world environment for performance evaluation. The results have demonstrated the feasibility of the proposed technique for the mobile robot localization in a challenging spacious indoor space.

Keywords: Mobile robot · Simultaneous localization and mapping · Robot vision · Ultra-wideband

1 Introduction

As the world is preparing to embrace the Industry 4.0 era, traditional manufacturers are gradually taking smart factories and smart robots as the development trend. For the dangerous working environments which are not suitable for manual operations, computer vision techniques are commonly used for the assistance. Therefore, the combination of industrial robots and computer vision algorithms will be the core technology for the automated factories in the future. In the past few decades, many companies have transformed the product lines to automated industrial systems. It is expected that automated industry will be able to provide the reliable products more rapidly. Since the sufficient accuracy can be achieved in current manufacturing systems, it is important for robots to perform precise positioning.

In recent years, many SLAM technologies have been developed and mature. Some available sensors include the earliest sonar, 2D and 3D lidar, monocular

© Springer Nature Switzerland AG 2022
C. Djeddi et al. (Eds.): MedPRAI 2021, CCIS 1543, pp. 77–91, 2022.
https://doi.org/10.1007/978-3-031-04112-9_6

and binocular vision system, RGB-D camera, and inertial measurement unit, etc. The fusion of different SLAM techniques generally has better performance. However, there are still many unsolvable problems. The slippery wheels of mobile robots and the influence of unknown external forces will cause some errors in the results. One important issue for the SLAM construction is the series of uncertainties in the measured distance and direction. The errors might be caused by the limited sensor accuracy as well as the environmental noise. Since every feature possesses a certain degree of uncertainty, the error of the entire SLAM system will increase with the time and location in motion. Consequently, the cumulative drifting errors cannot be ignored because of the fatal positioning for industrial robot applications.

The vision-based SLAM systems heavily rely on the feature point correspondence matching [7]. Due to the lighting condition changes, the features in the images might be disappeared and result in matching failure. This is commonly happened in some situations such as narrow tunnels or wide indoor areas. Thus, the SLAM techniques using visual information are not able to provide accurate localization results. On the other hand, the global positioning system (GPS) has achieved a certain degree of positioning accuracy in the outdoor environment. However, the GPS satellite signals cannot penetrate building materials, which makes GPS not suitable for indoor positioning. As a result, Wi-Fi, RFID, Bluetooth and UWB (ultra-wideband) have become popular localization technologies for the indoor areas.

In this paper, we propose a SLAM approach by combining different sensing and indoor positioning technologies. The drafting error is mitigated through the integration of UWB positioning with other techniques. It aims to deal with the accuracy issue of current SLAM systems operating in the space with less environmental features. The 3D based RTAB-Map (Real-Time Appearance-Based Mapping) SLAM technique and UWB localization approach are adopted. When the SLAM system starts, UWB also performs the 3D positioning simultaneously. The fusion of localization results from two methods is carried out using confidence based weighting by EKF (Extended Kalman Filter) [3]. In the proposed technique, the localization failure and drifting error are monitored continuously. UWB is used to optimize the SLAM results if the error is greater than a threshold. The experiments and performance investigated for the indoor scenes have demonstrated the feasibility of our approach.

2   Related Work

There have been a number of SLAM techniques proposed in the past few decades. In the existing literature, most classic approaches utilize lidar or camera for data acquisition. Current lidar based SLAM techniques have been thoroughly studied [1]. They are considered as the mainstream positioning method and relatively stable during the operation. In general, the 2D lidar is used for indoor robots, while the 3D lidar is adopted in the field of autonomous driving. The obstacles within a specific range are recorded as scattered point clouds with distance information. For the lidar-based SLAM systems, two point clouds acquired at different times are matched and compared to derive the relative position and orientation [8]. The transformation is then used for localization and map construction.

With the recent progress of computer vision and machine learning techniques, visual SLAM has attracted the attention of many researchers. It utilizes a large amount of image information from the environment, and possesses a strong scene recognition ability [21]. The visual SLAM developed using the depth camera is similar to the lidar-based approach, the distances to the obstacles can be directly obtained from the acquired point cloud data. For the implementation of vision-based SLAM, maplab [14] and VINS-Mono [9] are recently released with visual inertial maps. They are able to visualize the maps using only the camera and IMU. ORB-SLAM2 [11] and S-PTAM [13] are popular SLAM methods which use depth cameras for data acquisition. These methods perform loop closure through the mapped feature descriptors instead of bag-of-words. Consequently, the processing time for closed-loop detection and map optimization is significantly increased.

Different from the previous approaches, RTAB-Map [6] is also a SLAM technique using RGB-D images as input, but utilizing WM (working memory), LTM (long-term memory) and STM (short-term memory) for memory management. It is able to handle large-scale and long-term online operations without affecting the closed-loop detection. Thus, considering the cost, accuracy, computing power and ease of integration, RTAB-Map is frequently used as a basic module for advanced SLAM system development.

In addition to the vision-based SLAM techniques, there also exist many well-developed signal-based indoor positioning technologies such as Bluetooth, RFID, Wi-Fi and UWB [18]. Although the Bluetooth devices require very low power consumption, the localization accuracy is not satisfactory (1–2 m) even with a number of beacons installed in the environment. RFID is a radio frequency identification technology which utilizes electromagnetic transmission characteristics of radio frequency (RF) signals to realize data communication between RF tags and RF readers. Its advantages include high data transmission rate, high security, no non-radio frequency communication interference [20]. However, similar to Bluetooth, it requires a large number of RFID devices for indoor positioning applications.

As the most suitable technology for indoor positioning in early days, Wi-Fi adopts the nearest neighbor or cross positioning methods for the implementation. The nearest neighbor technique detects the closest hot spot or base station within a certain range for localization. If there are multiple signal sources nearby, the current location can be estimated through the triangulation cross positioning to further improve the accuracy. Since the Wi-Fi infrastructure is now widely available, there is no need to set up special devices for positioning. In recent studies, the Wi-Fi positioning technology has been integrated into the SLAM framework. Yang et al. and Kudo et al. presented the localization results of RGB-D SLAM and Lidar SLAM optimized with the Wi-Fi positioning, respectively

[4,19]. The major drawback of the technology is the high power consumption and cost of Wi-Fi hotspots. Moreover, there also exist serious co-channel interference problems.

Among the indoor positioning technologies, UWB has higher cost and power consumption compared to Wi-Fi, Bluetooth, and RFID, etc. However, it is optimized with positioning algorithms, and the maximum accuracy of 10 cm can be achieved. In the recent work, Perez-Grau *et al.* combined the results of UWB and RGB-D, and used the relationship between the UWB positioning and point clouds to form a 3D map [12]. With the fusion of UWB and RGB-D information, a robust mapping and positioning system is constructed. Alternatively, Song *et al.* combined UWB with a 2D lidar [15]. The lidar data are used to improve the UWB positioning accuracy by providing more comprehensive surrounding environment information. On the other hand, the UWB ranging can also correct the accumulated errors in the lidar-based SLAM algorithms to achieve complementary effects [16]. The localization technique based on odometry-assisted ultra-wideband ranging had demonstrated the accuracy in large-scale indoor scenes [10].

3   Proposed Approach

In this work we adopt RTAB-Map as the basic SLAM module for our development [5]. It is a typical RGB-D SLAM which is able to perform the loop closure through memory management. The core idea is to make the large-scale online closed-loop detection feasible for a long period of time. In the SLAM architecture, the frame-to-frame and frame-to-map visual odometry are processed separately. It takes the images from RGB-D or stereo camera as input, and feature detection is carried out for frame-to-map to avoid using nearest neighbor matching directly. In the case of feature loss, the matching will be performed by comparing the ratio of the first and second nearest neighbors. If the frame-to-frame method is used, the feature matching is directly computed using optical flow. Since the optical flow field is not continuous and uniform, the moving object or the movement of the camera can be detected. This approach can eliminate the requirement for the extraction of feature descriptors, and solve the motion trajectory of the camera.

When performing motion prediction, the motion model predicts the positions of the key frames and the feature map in the current frame based on the previous action. This process allows the search window for feature matching being limited to a certain range. Thus, it is able to provide a better match in the dynamic or repeated texture environments. In the motion estimation stage, PnP (perspective-n-point) and RANSAC algorithms are used to calculate the current frame, key frame and the feature transformation [2]. The local bundle adjustment is then applied on the key frames with geometric consistency constraints and update the camera pose.

When UWB is used for positioning, at least three base stations are required for two-dimensional calculation, and at least four base stations are necessary for three-dimensional computation. There are three commonly used methods: time-of-flight (TOF), time-of-arrival (TOA), and time-difference-of-arrival (TDOA). The two-way time-of-flight (TW-TOF) approach generates an independent time stamp from the start of each UWB module. Suppose the transmitter of module A transmits a request pulse signal at Ta1 on its time stamp, and the receiver of module B receives the transmitted signal at Tb1 on its time stamp. After processing the signal, module B transmits a pulse signal at time Tb2 as a responsive signal, and module A will receive it on its own time stamp Ta2. The flight time of the pulse signal between the two modules can be calculated to determine the distance by

$$S = C * [(T_{a2} - T_{a1}) - (T_{b2} - T_{b1})] \tag{1}$$

where C is the speed of light. If there are multiple modules used for positioning, the distances between the label and multiple modules are computed, and the trilateral method is used to derive the coordinates.

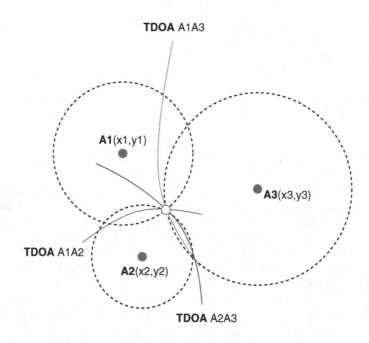

Fig. 1. The derivation of UWB positioning based on the time-difference-of-arrival (TDOA) method. It is an improved version of TOA, but with lower requirements for time synchronization.

As shown in Fig. 1, TDOA is an improved version of TOA, but with lower requirements for time synchronization. It determines the position of the mobile tag by detecting the time difference between the signals reaching two or more modules. When the tag enters the area covered by the set base station, the positioned tag will actively transmit a signal to the positioned base station. The positioning system will then calculate the dual position of the positioning tag according to the time difference of the same frame signal received by different base stations. Finally, the intersection of multiple hyperbolas is used to derive the coordinates of the label. The prerequisite of using this method is synchronizing the time between the modules. Although TDOA is more difficult to set up due to the requirement of synchronization between modules, it only needs to send out signals instead of waiting for the tag's response. Thus, this method has more free time to locate other tags.

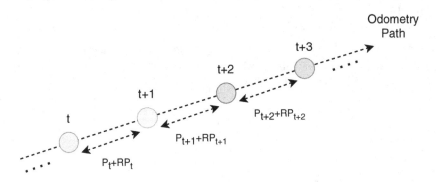

Fig. 2. The global localization path is split into the frame-by-frame basis for relative pose estimation of the mobile robot.

Since UWB utilizes TDOA for distance measurement and localization, it can be regarded as indoor GPS and does not have the drifting error problem due to the movement of mobile platforms. The error will be constrained without accumulation and the positioning result is globally closer to the ground-truth. In general, SLAM based localization techniques estimate the relative pose between multiple frames as illustrated in Fig. 2. To make the localization results obtained from the SLAM system constrained by the UWB measurements without losing short-term accuracy, we extract the relative pose estimates between the SLAM frames and split them into multiple ones. Let P_t be the coordinates accumulated at time t, and RP_t be the transformation between the times t and $t + 1$. The frame-by-frame relative position can then be derived as $(\Delta x, \Delta y)$. At the same time, UWB and SLAM are aligned in time and the positioning results are cross-referenced. If the estimation difference is greater than a threshold, the localization is restricted according to the time frame as shown in Fig. 3.

Considering the large error of UWB in the z-axis direction, the distance between the points is calculated on the xy-plane. Given two points (x_1, y_1) and (x_2, y_2), the update of new positioning result is determined by

$$\Delta_{xy} = \sqrt{(x_1 - x_2)^2 + (y_1 - y_2)^2} \tag{2}$$

The idea of overall error correction is shown in Fig. 4. If the distance between the newly created position and the current point estimated by UWB is greater

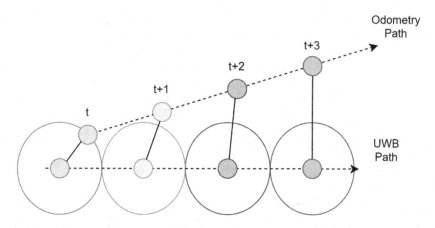

Fig. 3. The localization difference between odometry and UWB is used for correction. If it is greater than a threshold, the result is restricted according to the time frame.

than a threshold τ, the new positioning coordinates are used for update. The new localization position (x_3, y_3) has the same direction as (x_2, y_2) with an offset controlled by the threshold, and is given by

$$x_3 = \begin{cases} x_2 + \Delta x, & \text{if } \Delta_{xy} < \tau \\ x_1 + \tau cos\theta, & \text{if } \Delta_{xy} \geq \tau \end{cases} \tag{3}$$

$$y_3 = \begin{cases} y_2 + \Delta y, & \text{if } \Delta_{xy} < \tau \\ y_1 + \tau sin\theta, & \text{if } \Delta_{xy} \geq \tau \end{cases} \tag{4}$$

4   Experiments

The mobile robot system used in the experiment is shown in Fig. 5(a). It consists of a Pioneer P3-DX mobile platform with an aluminum extrusion rack . A laptop computer and an Intel Realsense D455 depth camera are placed on top for SLAM computation and image acquisition. A UWB tag is mounted below the camera to facilitate UWB positioning. The indoor positioning principle of UWB is very similar to the use of GPS satellites. Several UWB base stations are arranged with known coordinates, and the mobile platforms are equipped with positioning tags. A general configuration is illustrated in Fig. 6(a), the tags will emit pulses at a certain frequency and continuously communicate with the base stations. The base station conducts ranging and computes the location of the tag through the localization algorithm. In our experimental environment, SLAM is carried out in an indoor wide area as shown in Fig. 5(b) and the positioning effect is generally not good enough. Thus, AprilTags are added as landmarks in the space for localization assistance [17]. The current AprilTag setting is illustrated in Fig. 6(b), with 16 landmarks equally distributed on the ground.

For the mobile robot motion in an indoor spacious area, the drifting error will inevitably occur even the AprilTags are used as landmarks for localization. In

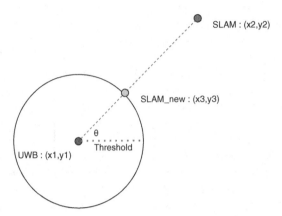

Fig. 4. The idea of UWB error correction. If the distance between the newly created position and the current point estimated by UWB is greater than a threshold, the new positioning coordinates are used for update.

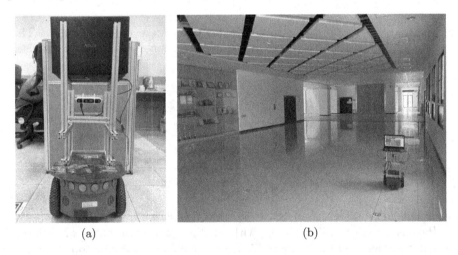

Fig. 5. (a) The mobile robot system constructed for the experiment. (b) The indoor environment used for evaluation in our experiment.

our experiment, even the robot moving against the walls with sufficient feature points detected, the localization still has a significant drifting error. As shown in Fig. 7, the trajectories derived from the UWB and SLAM positioning are marked in blue and red, respectively. The localization results obtained using the proposed method with the integration of UWB and SLAM are shown in Fig. 8. Figures 8(a) and 8(a) correspond to the trajectories calculated using the threshold settings of 2 m and 0.5 m, respectively.

Since the UWB positioning is more reliable globally but less accurate locally, its covariance matrix parameter is set to 0.5. On the other hand, the covariance matrix parameter of SLAM is set to 1 to perform the EKF for localization

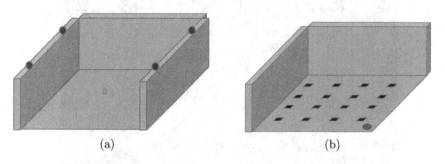

(a)   (b)

Fig. 6. (a) A general configuration of the UWB setting. (b) The current landmark setting using AprilTags.

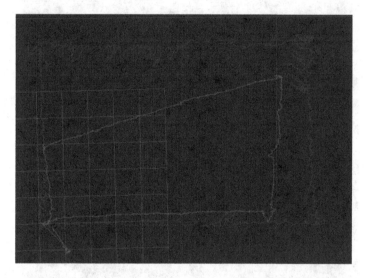

Fig. 7. The trajectories derived from the UWB positioning and SLAM using RTAB-Map are marked in blue and red, respectively. (Color figure online)

fusion. In Fig. 9(a), the localization results from SLAM, UWB and after the EKF fusion are shown in red, blue and green, respectively. It can be seen that, even the SLAM fails to track, EKF will still refer to the positioning result if the covariance matrix is not updated. Consequently, there will be large errors in the final fusion result. In our implementation, the SLAM covariance matrix parameter is changed to 999 if the SLAM tracking failure is detected. The fusion trajectories are shown in Fig. 9(b), the EKF fusion result is not affected by the SLAM failure after the modification.

For most of the RGB-D datasets which are publicly available for SLAM evaluation, their ground-truth are obtained using high-precision motion capture systems. In our experiment, the positioning results using AprilTag are adopted. The camera poses are calculated based on the coordinate origin of the AprilTag

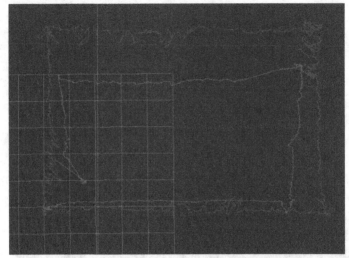

(a) The result with a threshold of 2 meters.

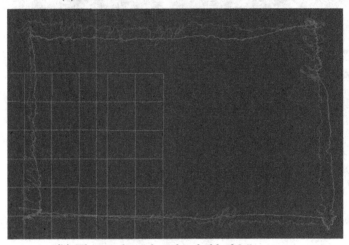

(b) The result with a threshold of 0.5 meters.

Fig. 8. The localization results obtained using the proposed method with the integration of UWB and SLAM with different threshold settings.

setting. To obtain the ground-truth through sampling, we use a method based on the absolute trajectory error to evaluate the accuracy. The relative errors of SLAM, UWB and EKF fusion results are evaluated using the following formulae

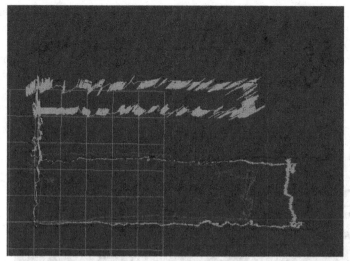

(a) The trajectories obtained with covariance set as 1.

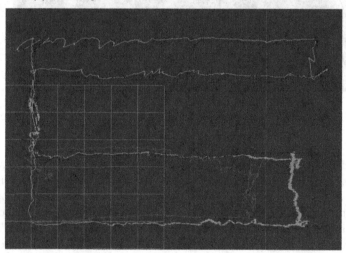

(b) The trajectories obtained with covariance set as 999.

Fig. 9. The localization results from SLAM, UWB and after the EKF fusion are shown in red, blue and green, respectively. (Color figure online)

for N sample points.

$$x_{error} = \frac{\sum_{i=1}^{N} \sqrt{(x_{est}(i) - x_{gt}(i))^2}}{N}$$

$$y_{error} = \frac{\sum_{i=1}^{N} \sqrt{(y_{est}(i) - y_{gt}(i))^2}}{N} \quad (5)$$

$$z_{error} = \frac{\sum_{i=1}^{N} \sqrt{(z_{est}(i) - z_{gt}(i))^2}}{N}$$

where x_{error}, y_{error} and z_{error} are the average absolute trajectory errors in the three axes of the translation matrix T. The points $(x_{est}(i), y_{est}(i), z_{est}(i))$ and $(x_{gt}(i), y_{gt}(i), z_{gt}(i))$ denote the estimated translation matrix and the true ground pose at the sampling point i. We perform the experiment on several paths in a spacious indoor environment, and evaluate with different methods as follows.

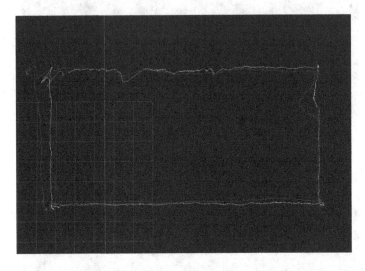

Fig. 10. The experimental result of a mobile robot moving in a rectangular path.

Figure 10 shows the experimental result of a mobile robot moving in a rectangular path. The trajectories marked in red, blue and green represent the localization from SLAM, UWB and after the EKF fusion. The translation errors are tabulated in Table 1, where SLAM' represents the drifting corrected SLAM result. It can be seen in the table that the average errors in the x and y axes are dropped from 0.647 m to 0.182 m and from 1.399 m to 0.387 m, respectively, after the drifting correction. The results have demonstrated a great improvement on drifting errors using the proposed technique. In the experiment, the EKF fusion normally suppresses the translation error. However, the performance of UWB in the y-axis is slightly better although its trajectory is noisy as shown in Fig. 10. This is because the evaluation is based on the sampled locations, which makes the UWB results closer to the ground-truth points even the overall trajectory is noisy.

Table 1. Translation error 1

	SLAM	SLAM	UWB	EKF
x ave. error	0.647 m	0.182 m	0.175 m	0.146 m
y ave. error	1.399 m	0.387 m	0.188 m	0.245 m
z ave. error	0.709 m	0.528 m	0.391 m	0.081 m
# of samples	1372	1372	1372	1372

In the second experiment, a more complicated path is used to evaluate the stability of the proposed method in a wide indoor area. The robot motion includes straight lines and curves, and some irregular paths to avoid the movement against the wall during travel. As shown in Fig. 11, the trajectory contains many harsh positioning conditions with few feature points but our method can still provide a good localization result with less drifting errors. Table 2 tabulates the evaluation of the translation errors. Although the drifting is more severe in the z-axis due to the lack of detected features for localization, we are able to suppress the errors in all directions as shown in SLAM'. The result of EKF fusion not only successfully reduces the error, but also avoids the noise of UWB. It demonstrates the feasibility of the proposed technique in some challenging conditions for practical applications.

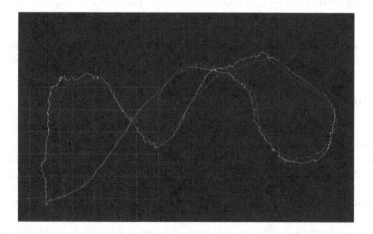

Fig. 11. A more complicated path is used for evaluation in a wide indoor area. The trajectory contains many harsh positioning conditions, and our method can still provide a good localization result with less drifting errors.

Table 2. Translation error 2

	SLAM	SLAM'	UWB	EKF
x ave. error	0.661 m	0.183 m	0.203 m	0.183 m
y ave. error	0.547 m	0.346 m	0.247 m	0.258 m
z ave. error	1.246 m	0.746 m	0.433 m	0.103 m
# of samples	1503	1503	1503	1503

5   Conclusion

In general, the positioning results become unbearable due to the lack of feature points and unreliable depth information when a robot navigates in a spacious indoor space. In this paper, a fusion method of UWB and SLAM techniques for mobile robot localization based on EKF is proposed. The idea is to use the globally consistent error distribution of UWB to mitigate the inevitable local accumulation errors from SLAM computation. By integrating various sensors and positioning technologies, our approach has successfully reduced the drifting error induced by the SLAM systems. The experiments carried out in the real-world environment have demonstrated the feasibility of the proposed indoor localization technique.

Acknowledgment. The support of this work in part by the Ministry of Science and Technology of Taiwan under Grant MOST 106-2221-E-194-004 and the Advanced Institute of Manufacturing with High-tech Innovations (AIM-HI) from The Featured Areas Research Center Program within the framework of the Higher Education Sprout Project by the Ministry of Education (MOE) in Taiwan is gratefully acknowledged.

References

1. Aulinas, J., Petillot, Y., Salvi, J., Lladó, X.: The slam problem: a survey. In: Artificial Intelligence Research and Development, pp. 363–371 (2008)
2. Chum, O., Matas, J.: Optimal randomized RANSAC. IEEE Trans. Pattern Anal. Mach. Intell. **30**(8), 1472–1482 (2008)
3. Do, C.H., Lin, H.Y.: Incorporating neuro-fuzzy with extended Kalman filter for simultaneous localization and mapping. Int. J. Adv. Rob. Syst. **16**(5), 172988141987464 (2019)
4. Kudo, T., Miura, J.: Utilizing WiFi signals for improving SLAM and person localization. In: 2017 IEEE/SICE International Symposium on System Integration (SII), pp. 487–493. IEEE (2017)
5. Labbe, M., Michaud, F.: Appearance-based loop closure detection for online large-scale and long-term operation. IEEE Trans. Rob. **29**(3), 734–745 (2013)
6. Labbé, M., Michaud, F.: RTAB-map as an open-source lidar and visual simultaneous localization and mapping library for large-scale and long-term online operation. J. Field Robot. **36**(2), 416–446 (2019)
7. Lin, H.Y., He, C.H.: Mobile robot self-localization using omnidirectional vision with feature matching from real and virtual spaces. Appl. Sci. **11**(8), 3360 (2021)

8. Lin, H.Y., Hsu, J.L.: A sparse visual odometry technique based on pose adjustment with keyframe matching. IEEE Sens. J. **21**(10), 11810–11821 (2021)
9. Lin, Y., et al.: Autonomous aerial navigation using monocular visual-inertial fusion. J. Field Robot. **35**(1), 23–51 (2018)
10. Magnago, V., Corbalán, P., Picco, G.P., Palopoli, L., Fontanelli, D.: Robot localization via odometry-assisted ultra-wideband ranging with stochastic guarantees. In: IROS, pp. 1607–1613 (2019)
11. Mur-Artal, R., Tardós, J.D.: ORB-SLAM2: an open-source slam system for monocular, stereo, and RGB-D cameras. IEEE Trans. Rob. **33**(5), 1255–1262 (2017)
12. Perez-Grau, F.J., Caballero, F., Merino, L., Viguria, A.: Multi-modal mapping and localization of unmanned aerial robots based on ultra-wideband and RGB-D sensing. In: 2017 IEEE/RSJ International Conference on Intelligent Robots and Systems (IROS), pp. 3495–3502. IEEE (2017)
13. Pire, T., Fischer, T., Castro, G., De Cristóforis, P., Civera, J., Berlles, J.J.: S-PTAM: stereo parallel tracking and mapping. Robot. Auton. Syst. **93**, 27–42 (2017)
14. Schneider, T., et al.: maplab: an open framework for research in visual-inertial mapping and localization. IEEE Robot. Autom. Lett. **3**(3), 1418–1425 (2018)
15. Song, Y., Guan, M., Tay, W.P., Law, C.L., Wen, C.: UWB/lidar fusion for cooperative range-only slam. In: 2019 International Conference on Robotics and Automation (ICRA), pp. 6568–6574. IEEE (2019)
16. Wang, C., Zhang, H., Nguyen, T.M., Xie, L.: Ultra-wideband aided fast localization and mapping system. In: 2017 IEEE/RSJ International Conference on Intelligent Robots and Systems (IROS), pp. 1602–1609. IEEE (2017)
17. Wang, J., Olson, E.: Apriltag 2: efficient and robust fiducial detection. In: 2016 IEEE/RSJ International Conference on Intelligent Robots and Systems (IROS), pp. 4193–4198 (2016)
18. Witrisal, K., Hinteregger, S., Kulmer, J., Leitinger, E., Meissner, P.: High-accuracy positioning for indoor applications: RFID, UWB, 5G, and beyond. In: 2016 IEEE International Conference on RFID (RFID), pp. 1–7 (2016)
19. Yang, S., Sun, Q., Dong, X., Yuan, J.: A novel slam method using Wi-Fi signal strength and RGB-D images. In: 2018 IEEE 8th Annual International Conference on CYBER Technology in Automation, Control, and Intelligent Systems (CYBER), pp. 540–545. IEEE (2018)
20. Yao, C.Y., Hsia, W.C.: An indoor positioning system based on the dual-channel passive RFID technology. IEEE Sens. J. **18**(11), 4654–4663 (2018)
21. Yu, C., Liu, Z., Liu, X.J., Xie, F., Yang, Y., Wei, Q., Fei, Q.: DS-SLAM: a semantic visual slam towards dynamic environments. In: 2018 IEEE/RSJ International Conference on Intelligent Robots and Systems (IROS), pp. 1168–1174 (2018)

Intelligent Systems for Medical Diagnosis

Deep Learning for Liver Disease Prediction

Ebru Nur Mutlu[1], Ayse Devim[1], Alaa Ali Hameed[3], and Akhtar Jamil[2(✉)]

[1] Istanbul Sabahattin Zaim University, 34303 Istanbul, Turkey
{ebru.mutlu,ayse.devim}@std.izu.edu.tr
[2] National University of Computer and Emerging Sciences, Islamabad, Pakistan
akhtar.jamil@nu.edu.pk
[3] Department of Computer Engineering, Istinye University, Istanbul, Turkey
alaa.hameed@istinye.edu.tr

Abstract. Mining meaningful information from huge medical datasets is a key aspect of automated disease diagnosis. In recent years, liver disease has emerged as one of the commonly occurring diseases across the world. In this paper, a Convolutional Neural Network (CNN) based model is proposed for the identification of liver disease. Furthermore, the performance of CNN was also compared with traditional machine learning approaches, which include Naive Bayes (NB), Support Vector Machine (SVM), K-nearest Neighbors (KNN), and Logistic Regression (LR). For evaluation, two datasets were used: BUPA and ILPD. The experimental results showed that CNN was effective for the classification of liver disease, which produced an accuracy of 75.55%, and 72.00% on the BUPA and ILPD datasets, respectively.

Keywords: Liver diseases classification · Convolutional Neural Networks · Machine learning · Disease classification

1 Introduction

The liver is the largest internal organ with approximately 4% body weight and has a blood flow of 1.5 L/min [1]. It plays a significant role in the circulation of blood throughout the body. The liver regulates the levels of most chemicals in our blood and helps in the metabolism of alcohol, drugs and destroys toxic substances. Due to its significant importance, medical specialists are particularly interested in the investigation of various diseases related to it.

The liver can be infected by parasites, viruses that cause inflammation and diminish its function [2]. It has the potential to maintain normal functions, even when a part of it is damaged. Recent statistics show that there has been an increasing trend in the number of liver disease cases. The main reason includes alcohol consumption, viral hepatitis, and obesity leading to nonalcoholic fatty liver disease. However, it is crucial to diagnose liver disease early that can help increase the survival rate of patients.

Generally, liver diseases can be categories into four main groups: hepatocellular (hepatitis, heart failure, and toxins), cholestatic, infiltrative diseases (tumor, sarcoid), and cirrhosis (hepatocellular loss and scarring). Expert physicians are required for various examination tests to diagnose liver disease, but they may not confirm the correct

© Springer Nature Switzerland AG 2022
C. Djeddi et al. (Eds.): MedPRAI 2021, CCIS 1543, pp. 95–107, 2022.
https://doi.org/10.1007/978-3-031-04112-9_7

diagnosis [3]. However, the recent development in diagnosis methods and machine learning techniques makes it possible to help medical specialists investigate liver diseases with higher accuracy.

Machine learning (ML) is a field of computer science that uses computer algorithms to identify patterns in extensive data and assist in predicting various outcomes based on data [4]. ML techniques have emerged as a potential tool for prediction and decision-making in many disciples [5]. Due to the availability of clinical data, ML has been playing a critical role in medical decision-making [6, 7]. In addition, deep learning models also play a critical role in disease prediction. Deep learning is a subfield of machine learning. Deep learning algorithms are complex structures created with hierarchical modules that learn by data representations. Because of their architecture and functions, they possess several advantages over traditional machine learning algorithms. As opposed to many conventional ones, these algorithms' learning complexity does not increase exponentially with the linear increase of the dimension of the data [8]. Developing deep learning and machine learning models would serve as a valuable aid in identifying disease and making a real-time effective clinical decision. It would also optimize hospital resources by classifying the right patients with several significant risk factors earlier.

In the last decade, a number of researchers have implemented different machine learning methods such as SVM, KNN, RF, Decision Tree, Neural Networks, etc., to detect liver diseases. By using machine learning techniques.

In this study, a CNN-based model is employed for the detection of liver disease. Also, a comprehensive comparison was drawn between CNN and conventional machine learning approaches. All models' performance was evaluated in terms of accuracy, precision, recall, and f-1 score.

2   Related Works

A number of research works have been dedicated to liver disease classification. For instance, authors have applied Naive Bayes, FT Trees, and Kstar algorithms to detect liver disorders [9]. These models were evaluated on the liver dataset from the UCI repository. This dataset consists of 345 instances with seven attributes. The highest accuracy (97.10%.) was obtained for the FT Tree algorithm. Similarly, in [10], authors employed Naïve Bayes, C4.5, backpropagation neural network, K-NN, SVM for liver disease classification. The results showed that 51.59% accuracy was obtained using Naïve Bayes classifier, 55.94% with C4.5 algorithm, 66.66% with BPNN, 62.6% with KNN and 62.6% accuracy using SVM classifier.

In study [11], in order to identify if the patients have the liver disease or not they applied Decision Tree, Naive Bayes and NBTree algorithms. Relevant study used data sets from the university of California Irvine (UCI) repository. The data set contains 583 patients, where 416 patients were positively affected by liver disease and as many as 167 patients do not suffer from liver disease. The result shows NBTree algorithm has the highest accuracy (66.14%), however the Naive Bayes algorithm gives the fastest computation time. This study presents promising results in giving recommendation if the patients have the disease.

Study [12] describes the categorization of liver disorder through feature selection and fuzzy K-means classification. The dataset used in this study is unique and collected in hospital in Tamil Nadu. The dataset consists of 48 attributes and 6078 instances. From the experimental results it is clear that Fuzzy based classification performs well and reached an accuracy of around 94%.

The poor performance in the training and testing of the liver disorder dataset as resulted from an insufficient in the dataset. Therefore, Sug [13], suggested a method based on oversampling in minor classes in order to compensate for the insufficiency of data effectively. The author considered two algorithms of decision tree for the research work. These algorithms are C4.5 and CART and the dataset of BUPA liver disorder was also considered for the experiments [13].

Christopher et al. [14] proposed a system to diagnose medical diseases considering 6 benchmarks which are liver disorder, heart diseases, diabetes, breast cancer, hepatitis and lymph. The authors developed two systems based on WSO and C4.5, an accuracy of 64.60% with 19 rules of liver disorder dataset and 62.89% with 43 rules which was obtained from the WSO and C4.5 respectively.

The main objective of study [15] is to predict liver diseases using classification algorithms. The algorithms used in this work are Naïve Bayes and support vector machine (SVM). These classifier algorithms are compared based on the performance factors i.e. classification accuracy and execution time. Experiments were performed on Indian Liver Patient Dataset. From the experimental results, this work concludes, the SVM classifier is considered as a best algorithm because of its highest classification accuracy. On the other hand, while comparing the execution time, the Naïve Bayes classifier needs minimum execution time.

In study [16], in order to predict liver disease, authors proposed back propagation neural network and radial basis neural network models. Following, they compare the proposed models with C4.5, CART, Naive Bayes and SVM algorithms. From the obtained results, it is concluded that the radial basis function neural network is the optimal model because it has an accuracy of 70%.

3 Materials and Methods

3.1 Datasets

Two datasets were used for this study: BUPA and ILPD. The following sections provide details about these datasets.

BUPA Liver Disorders dataset is prepared by BUPA Medical Research Company. It includes 345 samples consisting of 6 attributes and two classes. Each sample is taken from an unmarried man. 200 of these samples belong to liver patients, while the remaining 145 belong to the non-liver patient class. The first five attributes of the collected data samples are the results of blood tests, while the last attribute includes daily alcohol consumption. This dataset is taken from UCI machine learning database [17].

The Indian Liver Patient Dataset (ILPD) has been collected from northeast of Andhra Pradesh, India. This data was downloaded from the UCI repository [18]. The dataset contains 583 samples and two classes. The liver patients are labeled as 1, which includes 416 samples, while non-liver patients are represented with label 2, consisting of 167 samples. This dataset contains 441 males and 142 females. Table 1 summarizes the dataset used for this study.

Table 1. Summary of the datasets used.

Dataset	Class	Label	Samples
BUPA	Patient	1	416
	Non-Patient	2	167
ILPD	Patient	1	200
	Non-Patient	2	145

3.2 Preprocessing

Preprocessing is a crucial step to improve the quality of data for further processing. Therefore, both datasets were preprocessed before training the models. Firstly, data imputation and normalization were performed to get a high-quality dataset. Secondly, Synthetic Minority Over-Sampling Technique (SMOTE) method was applied to generate synthesis samples for the minority class and balance the positive and negative values of the training set. Finally, principal component analysis (PCA) was performed to select the features that were more relevant or meaningful to the classification task.

3.3 Model Building

The preprocessed data was then fed to the models for training. As mentioned before, five models were evaluated. This section provides a short summary of each model and its characteristics.

Convolutional Neural Networks are powerful tools for recognizing local patterns in data samples [19]. As interrelated data is present in data samples, CNNs are suitable architectures for the task. CNs detect local patterns by creating feature maps by conducting element-wise multiplication with our kernel and the slide area of the input value and then adding all the values to transfer it to a feature map. After a feature map is captured, a nonlinear function is applied, converting every negative value to 0 and maintaining all positive values as they are. The mentioned function is the Rectified Linear Unit (ReLU) function, (3). Non-linearity is utilized here as the data at hand cannot be merely described with linear functions. Therefore, non-linearity is crucial for detecting patterns in our data.

Then, pooling, which comes in variations of maximum, average and sum pooling, is applied, making the data more manageable with fewer parameters, as the dimensions are reduced.

In our architecture, max pooling is utilized as it has been found more effective in previous studies [13]. Max pooling reduces the dimensions of the feature map while maintaining the most important identity values through sliding kernels over the rectified feature map and merely capturing the highest values. For the following steps, the current output is flattened and converted to one long vector, which is crucial for the classification algorithms. After this point, a regular feedforward backpropagation neural network methodology is applied. A fully connected layer that calculates the probabilities for different classes is applied to the features detected from the prior steps. After obtaining an output, the loss function is calculated. Finally, the network is backpropagated based on the selected optimizer function for adjusting the weights.

The proposed CNN model consists of 4 layers; one input, two hidden, and one output layer with 68, 70,70,2 neurons, respectively. To eliminate the overfitting issue among all layers, Dropout layers were placed. ReLU, sigmoid and hyperbolic tangent were used as activation functions in both input and hidden layers, while softmax was used in the output layer. The learning rate was set to 0.01, 0.001. Note that all the above-mentioned hyperparameters are variants for each experiment.

Naive Bayes is a simplification of Bayes theorem, known as the theory of probability, to find the most likely of the possible classification. Naive Bayes classification provides a way to combine prior probabilities and conditional probabilities in a single formula that can calculate the probability of each class [20]. Bayesian theory is a basic statistical method that aims to minimize the probability of making wrong decisions or expected risk. There are some reasons why naive Bayes is widely used in classification, including Naive Bayes classification is very easy to understand and build [21]. Naive Bayes algorithm can deal with noise data and missing values. Naive Bayes works extremely effectively when tested on real datasets, especially when combined with several attribute selection procedures [22], is easy to construct, and often is surprisingly effective in real practical application [23]. Naive Bayes classifier has also been successfully used in the classification problem where the class variable is a discrete value. The general form of Bayes theorem, which has been simplified as:

$$P(H|E) = P(E|H) \times \frac{P(H)}{P(E)}$$

where E represents the data with an unknown class, H hypothesizes the data E as a specific class. $P(H|E)$ is the probability the hypothesis H based on the condition of E (posterior probability), $P(H|E)$ denote the probability of E based on the condition of the hypothesis H, and P(E) is the probability of the data E.

Naive Bayes applies principles known as the maximum a posterior hypothesis (MAP) to classify new data. MAP calculating the posterior probability P(H|E) using (3) and determine the class of the data E that produces the maximum value of P(H|E).

Support Vector Machine is a supervised learning method used for both classification and regression. A support vector machine (SVM) finds a maximum margin linear discriminant function $h(x) = w^{(T)}\phi(x) + b$ to classify the feature representation $\phi(x)$ of an example x using a weight vector w and a bias parameter b. An SVM determines the optimal values of w and b by using a training set $S = \{(x_i, y_i)|i = 1, 2, \dots N\}$ of examples with corresponding labels $y_i = +1$ for normal and abnormal cases, respectively. This is done by solving the following optimization problem:

$$\min_{w,b} \frac{1}{2}||w||^2 = c \sum_{i=1}^{N} lsvm(h, x, y_i)$$

Here, the first term $||w||^2$ is responsible for margin maximization and the second term controls the number of misclassification over training data by using a hinge loss function (lsvmh, x_i, y_i) = max$\{0, 1 - y_i h(x_i)\}$. The hinge loss function penalizes misclassifications and margin violations. The hyper-parameter is the weighting factor between these two terms and is chosen through cross-validation.

K-nearest Neighbor is one of the supervised learning algorithms that have been used in many applications in the field of data mining, statistical pattern recognition and many others. It follows a method for classifying objects based on the closest training examples in the feature space. Simple K nearest neighbor algorithm has two major steps: 1) find the K training instances which are closest to unknown instances 2) pick the most commonly occurring classification for these K instances.

There are various ways of measuring the similarity between two instances with n attribute values. Every measure has the following three requirements. Let $dist(A, B)$ be the distance between two points A, B then.

$$\text{dist}(A, B) \geq \text{ and dist}(A, B) = 0 \text{ if } A = B$$

$$\text{dist}(A, B) = \text{dist}(B, A)$$

$$\text{dist}(A, C) \leq \text{dist}(A, B) + \text{dist}(B, C)$$

The last equation is called a "Triangle inequality." It states that the shortest distance between any two points is a straight line. The most common distance measure used is Euclidean distance. For continuous variables, Z score standardization and min-max normalization are used.

Logistic Regression is one of the discrete models that belong to multivariate analysis. It is the most commonly used method of empirical analysis in sociology, biostatistics, clinical medicine, quantitative psychology, econometrics, marketing and often uses to compare with machine learning studies [24]. It has many advantages, including high power and accuracy. The equation of logistic regression:

$$y = \frac{e^{(b_0 + b_1 * x)}}{(1 - e^{(b_0 + b_1 * x)})}$$

Here y is the predicted output, b_0 is the bias or intercept term and b_1 is the coefficient for the single input value (x). Each column n the study input data is associated withthebcoefficient(aconstantrealvalue) learned from training data.

4 Experimental Results

This section presents the performance analysis of all models on both BUPA and ILPD datasets. Evaluation of the proposed CNN model is done first, followed by conventional machine learning models. 70% of the data was used for training for each experiment, while the remaining 30% was used for testing. All the experiments were performed on the standard Intel (R) Core (TM) I5-7200U CPU @ 2.50GHz computer, using Spyder as the development environment and Python (3.7) as the programming language. In addition, we used TensorFlow, Keras, and Sklearn libraries for implementation.

4.1 Model Evaluation

The performance of the classification methods was evaluated in terms of accuracy, precision, recall (or sensitivity), and f1-score and are calculated using the relations given below:

$$\text{Accuracy} = \frac{TP + TN}{TP + FP + TN + FN}$$

$$\text{Precision} = \frac{TP}{TP + FP}$$

$$\text{Recall} = \frac{TP}{TP + FN}$$

$$\text{F1score} = 2 \times \frac{\text{Recall} \times \text{Precision}}{\text{Recall} + \text{Precision}}$$

Here, True Positive (TP): The prediction result correctly identifies that a patient has liver disease. False Positive (FP): The result of prediction incorrectly identifies that a patient has liver disease. True Negative (TN): The result of prediction correctly rejects that a patient has liver disease. False Negative (FN): The result of prediction incorrectly rejects that a patient has liver disease. The precision gives the contrast between sound and patient capacity ratio utilizing the prediction model. To obtain the precision of classification, we used true positive, true negative, false positive, and false negative.

5 Results and Discussion

In the present study, experiments were performed separately on both datasets. In the first step, algorithms' performances were evaluated on the BUPA dataset, while in the second step, evaluation was done on the ILPD dataset.

5.1 Experiments on BUPA Dataset

The CNN model requires fine-tuning some important hyper-parameters for obtaining optimal results. These hyper-parameters include learning rate, number of epochs, optimizers, activation function, etc. We run the experiments several times with a varying combination of parameters to obtain the best setting. First, the proposed model was trained with Adam Optimizer, hyperbolic tangent activation function, and learning rate 0.001. The proposed model obtained 75.45% training and 71.25% testing accuracy. Another experiment was run with ReLU as activation function and learning rate to 0.01. The obtained results show that the CNN model performs better with a learning rate of 0.01 and ReLU activation function, which obtained 81.25% training and 71.25% testing accuracy. Visual results for both training and testing are shown in Fig. 1 for these two experimental setups.

The experiments were also performed with Stochastic Gradient Descent (SGD) and Adam optimizers. For this experimental setup, the learning rate was set to 0.01, and ReLU activation function was used. It was observed that the model trained with SGD yielded the worst performance (accuracy = 69%) for training and testing (accuracy = 68%). In contrast, the model trained with Adam optimizer gets the best performance with an accuracy of 81.25% for training and 75.55% for testing. Accuracy and loss of the model trained with SGD optimizer and Adam are shown in Fig. 2.

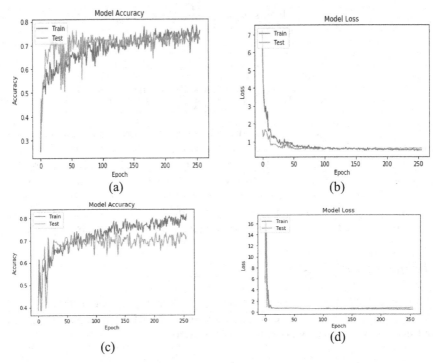

Fig. 1. (a), (b) Accuracy and loss of CNN model for training and testing phases, with learning rate 0.001 and hyperbolic tangent activation function. (c), (d) Accuracy and loss for both phases, with learning rate 0.01 and ReLU activation function.

The quantitative results obtained for all models are presented in Table 2. Among all, CNN model produced the highest F1 Score while LR produced the highest accuracy. On the other side, KNN achieved the worst accuracy (66.32%). The performance of different models was also similar, indicating that all models performed well on this dataset.

Further experiments were performed to assess the effect of PCA on the classification accuracy of the models. Table 3 summarizes the results obtained for feature selection. The response shows that selecting too small features resulted in lower accuracy, which can be attributed to the fact that important information is lost due to the selection of a small subset of features. Similarly, selecting a relatively smaller set of features using PCA helped the classifiers increase their classification accuracy.

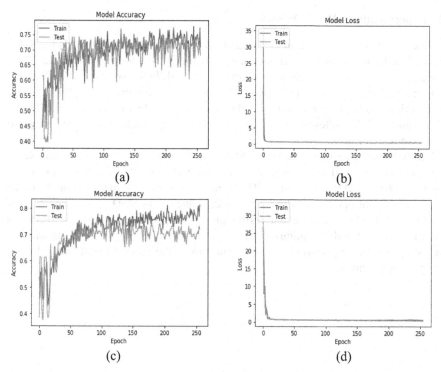

Fig. 2. (a), (b) Accuracy and loss of the proposed CNN model trained with SGD optimizer. (c), (d) Accuracy and loss of proposed CNN model trained with Adam optimizer.

Table 2. Quantitative results for CNN model and its comparison with conventional ML.

Methods	Accuracy	Precision	Recall	F1-score
LR	78.22	72.77	72.25	72.98
NB	67.75	55.45	87.54	67.82
SVM	72.45	70.65	49.46	58.50
KNN	66.32	57.52	51.66	54.06
CNN	75.55	72.08	76.64	74.30

Table 3. A comparative analysis of feature selection on the accuracy (%) of the classifiers

Methods	Features = 6	Features = 5	Features = 3	Features = 2	Features = 1
LR	78.22	77.56	79.73	73.20	48.22
NB	67.75	68.36	68.54	73.85	56.75
SVM	72.45	71.65	76.65	70.51	45.45
KNN	66.32	68.98	75.50	64.65	53.62
CNN	75.55	73.65	75.36	72.21	66.45

5.2   Experiments on ILPD Dataset

This section presents the experimental results obtained for each classifier on the ILPD dataset. Similar to the first experiment, the CNN model was trained with Adam Optimizer, sigmoid activation function, and learning rate 0.01. In this setting, the CNN model produced 95.45% training and 66.25% testing accuracy. Moreover, with ReLU activation function and learning rate to 0.001, the model achieved an accuracy of 90.25% on training and 72.25% on testing data. Training and testing results for both accuracy and loss are shown in Fig. 3.

Similarly, in the second experiment, Stochastic Gradient Descent (SGD) and Adam optimizers were used. The learning rate was set to 0.01, and ReLU activation function was used. The model trained with SGD optimizer yielded better performance than the model with Adam optimizer. The CNN model trained with SGD gets an accuracy of 71.50% and 72.00% in training and testing phases, respectively. In contrast, the CNN model trained with Adam optimizer gets an accuracy of 93.00%, 65.25% in training and testing phases, respectively. Accuracy and loss of the model trained with different hyperparameters are shown in Fig. 3.

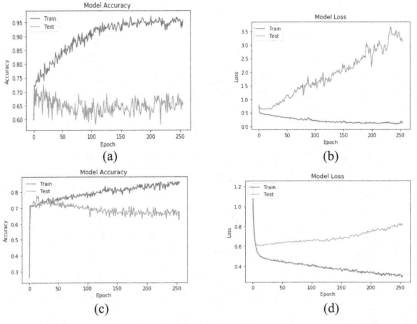

Fig. 3. (a), (b) Accuracy and loss of proposed CNN model for training and testing phases, with learning rate 0.01 and sigmoid activation function. (c), (d) Accuracy and loss for both phases, with learning rate 0.001 and ReLU activation function.

The training and testing accuracies for liver disease classification from the ILPD dataset for CNN model using SGD and Adam optimizer are shown in Fig. 4. These obtained results show that LR classification technique is more effective than the other classifiers for predicting chronic liver disease. The performance comparison of applied supervised machine learning techniques is presented in Table 4. LR achieved the highest accuracy of 71% and NB achieved the worst performance of 54%. With respect to precision, NB achieved the highest score 94% and SVM performs worst 72%. When considering the recall, SVM achieved the highest value 95% and NB obtained the worst 39%. LR was also the best performer in terms of f1 measure 83% and NB obtained the worst performance 55%. When considering training KNN achieved the highest value 80% and NB the lowest 58%. Additional experiments were performed to assess the effect of feature selection with PCA. The behavior of models was similar to the previous experiment. Selecting too few features results in lower accuracy while selection some features less than total features was effective. The results of PCA and classification are summarized in Table 5.

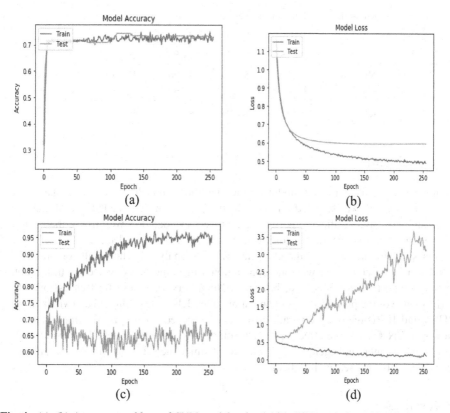

Fig. 4. (a), (b) Accuracy and loss of CNN model trained with SGD optimizer. (c), (d) Accuracy and loss of CNN model trained with Adam optimizer.

Table 4. Performance of each model for ILPD dataset.

Methods	Accuracy	Precision	Recall	F1-score
LR	71.44	77.32	88.62	82.22
NB	54.91	94.87	39.41	55.68
SVM	70.98	72.39	95.84	82.20
KNN	70.55	76.40	85.08	80.43
Proposed	72.25	73.56	75.65	74.59

Table 5. Performance comparison before and after PCA.

Methods	Number of features			
	7	5	3	1
LR	72.15	71.12	71.80	61.52
NB	58.55	54.21	58.96	45.90
SVM	73.63	70.60	75.21	60.15
KNN	79.55	70.05	80.81	58.10

6   Conclusion

In this paper, we used a CNN model for the identification of liver disease. Relatively a shallower network was selected for classification, which in turn needed a small number of parameters. Some critical hyperparameters were evaluated as well to see their effect on the classification accuracy. Moreover, the effect of feature selection using PCA on the classification accuracy of the classifier was also analyzed. The results obtained for CNN were also compared with the conventional machine learning techniques: Naive Bayes, Support Vector Machine, K-nearest Neighbors, and Logistic Regression. The performance of the proposed model and applied models were evaluated on two datasets: BUPA and ILPD datasets. Overall, all models achieved good classification accuracy. However, CNN was more effective than the other conventional models. In the future, we would like to integrate a genetic algorithm to optimize the selection of hyperparameters for CNN for liver disease classification.

References

1. Edginton, A.N., Ritter, L.: Predicting plasma concentrations of bisphenol a in children younger than 2 years of age after typical feeding schedules, using a physiologically based toxicokinetic model. Environ. Health Perspect. **117**(4), 645–652 (2009)
2. Pandey, B., Singh, A.: Intelligent techniques and applications in liver disorders. Survey, January (2014)
3. Takkar, S., Singh, A., Pandey, B.: Application of machine learning algorithms to a welldefined clinical problem: liver disease. Int. J. E-Health Med. Commun. **8**(4), 38–60 (2020)

4. Motwani, M., et al.: Machine learning for prediction of all-cause mortality in patients with suspected coronary artery disease: a 5-year multicentre prospective registry analysis. Eur. Heart J. **38**, 500–507 (2016)
5. Sani, A.: Machine Learning for Decision Making, Université de Lille 1 (2015)
6. Raghupathi, W., Raghupathi, V.: Big data analytics in healthcare: promise and potential. Health Inf. Sci. Syst. 2 (2014) https://doi.org/10.1186/2047-2501-2-3
7. Groves, P., Kayyali, B., Knott, D., Kuiken, S.V.: The' Big Data' Revolution in Healthcare: Accelerating Value and Innovation (2016)
8. Arel, I., Rose, D.C., Karnowski, T.P.: Deep machine learninga new frontier in artificial intelligence research. IEEE Comput. Intell. Mag. **5**(4), 13–18 (2010)
9. Rajeswari, P., Sophia Reena, G.: Analysis of liver disorder using data mining algorithm. Global J. Comput. Sci. Technol. **10**(14), 48–52 (2010)
10. Ramana, B.V., Surendra Prasad Babu, M., Venkateswarlu, N.B.: A critical study of selected classification algorithms for liver disease diagnosis. Int. J. Database Manage. Syst. **3**(2), 101–114 (2011)
11. Alfisahrin, S.N.N., Mantoro, T.: Data mining techniques for optimization of liver disease classification. In: 2013 International Conference on Advanced Computer Science Applications and Technologies. IEEE (2013)
12. Aneeshkumar, A.S., Jothi Venkateswaran, C.: A novel approach for Liver disorder Classification using Data Mining Techniques. Eng. Sci. Int. J. **2**(1), 15–18(2015)
13. Sug, H.: Improving the prediction accuracy of liver disorder disease with oversampling. Appl. Mat. Electr. Comput. Eng. **7**, 331–335 (2012)
14. Olaniyi, E.O., Adnan, K.: Liver disease diagnosis based on neural networks. In: Advances in Computational Intelligence, pp. 48–53 (2013)
15. Vijayarani, S., Dhayanand, S.: Liver disease prediction using SVM and Naïve Bayes algorithms. Int. J. Sci. Eng. Technol. Res. (IJSETR) **4**(4), 816–820 (2015)
16. Olaniyi, E.O., Aadnan, K.: Liver disease diagnosis based on neural networks. In: Advances in Computational Intelligence, Proceedings of the 16th International Conference on Neural Networks (NN 2015), November 7–9 (2015)
17. UCI machine learning database. ftp://ftp.ics.uci.edu/pub/machinelearning-databases. Accessed 2020
18. Lichman, M.: UCI Machine Learning Repository. http://archive.ics.uci.edu/ml/datasets.html. University of California, School of Information and Computer Science, Irvine, CA (2013)
19. Krizhevsky, A., Sutskever, I., Hinton, G.E.: Imagenet classification with deep convolutional neural networks. In: Advances in Neural Information Processing Systems, pp. 1097–1105 (2012)
20. Bramer, M.: Principles of Data Mining, 2nd edn. Springer, London (2013). https://doi.org/10.1007/978-1-4471-4884-5
21. Gorunescu, F.: Data Mining Concepts, Models and Techniques. Springer, Berlin (2011). https://doi.org/10.1007/978-3-642-19721-5
22. Witten, I.H., Frank, E., Hall, M.A.: Data Mining Practical Machine Learning Tools and Techniques, 3rd edn. Morgan Kaufmann, United States (2011)
23. Wu, X.: Top 10 algorithms in data mining. Knowl. Inf. Syst. **14**(1), 1–37 (2008)
24. Dreiseitl, S., Ohno-Machado, L.: Logistic regression and artificial neural network classification models: a methodology review. J. Biomed. Inform. **35**(5–6), 352–359 (2002)
25. Kingma, D.P., Ba, J.: Adam: a method for stochastic optimization. arXiv preprint arXiv:1412. 6980 (2014)

Pre-trained Backbones Effect on Nuclei Segmentation Performance

Chifa Maarouf[1]([✉]), Mohamed Lamine Benomar[1,2], and Nesma Settouti[1]

[1] Biomedical Engineering Laboratory, University of Tlemcen, Tlemcen, Algeria
{chifa.maarouf,mohamedamine.benomar,nesma.settouti}@univ-tlemcen.dz
[2] University of Ain-Temouchent Belhadj Bouchaib, Ain-Temouchent, Algeria

Abstract. In histopathology, nuclei segmentation is the most important step that leads to an integral diagnosis, the right nuclei localization
can help the physician's decision about the type and grade of the tumor,
but the scarcity of necessary ground truth makes it a hard task even
with the latest developed deep learning models. In this work, we aim to
respond to this problem using transfer learning by benefiting from the
extra features of a pre-trained model and using them as the backbone of
a classical Encoder-Decoder model. A comparative study is conducted
between hybrid architecture with different backbones that showed their
efficiency in nuclei segmentation with the Triple Negative Breast Cancer
dataset. Results experimentations show that the U-Net with Efficient-
Neb3 as backbone performed the best by improving the Dice score and
the Intersection over Union value.

Keywords: Nuclei segmentation · Deep learning · Transfer learning ·
Backbone · Histopathology images

1 Introduction

Histopathology is a term that combines two several terms, histology which is
the study of biological tissues and their structures, and pathology which is the
branch of medicine that deals with diseases, thus Histopathology is the study
of tissue diseases. To provide a diagnosis and therapy, cancer (or any tissue
anomaly) should be removed and analyzed, including a doctor involvement to
make a histological study of different sections of the tumor, previously stained
with specific markers (Hematoxylin stain to dye nuclei in blue-purple, and Eosin
stain to dye cytoplasm in pink (H&E)) [8,15,24].

The gold standard for cancer examination is the histological image treatment
in which the nuclei segmentation is of the utmost importance, as it can enable
extraction of high-quality features for nuclear morphometrics and other analysis
of digital microscopic tissue images in computational pathology [19].

For several years, many Deep Learning (DL)-based algorithms have been proposed for nuclei segmentation in histological images [18], and most of them was
focusing on semantic segmentation which separates foreground (nuclei) from the

C. Djeddi et al. (Eds.): MedPRAI 2021, CCIS 1543, pp. 108–118, 2022.
https://doi.org/10.1007/978-3-031-04112-9_8

background (cytoplasm and the extracellular connective tissue matrix). In nuclei segmentation, the main issue is the lack of the ground truth, due to difficulty in manual nuclei annotation and the huge time that operation consumes, that's why transfer learning is one of the recently proposed solutions to improve some-how the performance of nuclei segmentation models, for more improved results the proposed transfer learning way is using pre-trained backbones (Encoders), since the Encoder-Decoder (E-D) algorithms are the most used in biomedical image segmentation [12].

In this paper, we aim to apply a comparative study between three different backbones (VGG16 [20] - MobileNet [14] - EfficientNetb3 [2]) on two E-D models (U-Net [21] and LinkNet [6]), our main purpose is to enhance the performance of the two models using pre-trained Encoders, and then evaluate and compare the model's behavior with and without pre-trained backbones in term of execution time, and nuclei segmentation's precision based on two metrics, Intersection over Union (IoU) and F1 score.

For that, we organize the paper as follows: The first section to represent previous works, a quick reminder on used models is exposed, followed by our experiment and results, then we end up with a conclusion and perspectives.

2   Background

In digital histopathology, the nuclei segmentation is a very important first step for all researches in the domain, that's why we can find in the literature many papers that enrich this field. Starting with classical methods used to segment similar images Cuevas et al. [9] who applied a comparison between different nature inspired algorithms such as Particle Swarm Optimization, Artificial Bee Colony Optimization and Differential Evolution used to calculate parameters of the mixture of Gaussian functions to approximate the 1D histogram of a gray level image in multi threshold segmentation. In [4] color transformation and morphological operations were applied as a preprocessing step to estimate nuclei ration parameter in order to filter the healthy tissue patches according to their cell nuclei amount by assigning high cellularity to high-grade carcinoma, in [11], Flores et al. identify all the cell nuclei contained in images, they used edge detection and image filters, Convolutional Neural Network, U-Net, and Mask R-CNN. Recently, nuclei segmentation method was proposed in [15] following three steps: Pre-processing step that consists on data augmentation, color nor-malization to solve the problem of color variation in histological images, nuclear segmentation using Mask R-CNN. Vu et al. [24] proposed a deep residual aggre-gation network (DRAN) with two consecutive processing paths such as those of U-Net (E-D), using a modified ResNet-50 (with 3×3 kernel instead of 7×7 kernel) as the contraction path (Encoder), Hassan et al. [13] proposed a feasible deep learning model for nuclei segmentation by combining robust deep learn-ing architectures applied on whole slide images collected from different scanners and several organs, Zhao et al. [27] first proposed SEENS a Selective-Edge-Enhancement-based Nuclei Segmentation method applied on pap smear images, the first step is ROIs extraction then edge enhancement method based on the canny operator and mathematical morphology used to extract edge information for nuclei segmentation.

In 2017 Naylor et al. [18] first released the nuclei detection dataset Triple-Negative Breast Cancer (TNBC) which is the subject of our application, in that paper he presented a fully automated workflow to segment nuclei using Deep Neural Networks (PangNet, FCN, and DeconvNet), then one year after Naylor et al. [19] present a method of automatic nuclei segmentation using U-Net, Distance map, and Fully Convolutional Network (FCN), and he aimed to formulate the nuclei segmentation problem as a regression task of the distance map.

In the transfer learning domain using backbones, a comparison between various backbones was done as in Zhang et al. [26] which approved that Xception performed the best between other tested backbones such as ResNet34, ResNet101, and VGG. A 2-stage U-Net was proposed by Abedalla et al. [1] using ResNet34 pre-trained on ImageNet as the backbone, in the first stage the researcher trained the model on a lower resolution (256×256) and then they loaded the previous weights to retrain the network on higher resolution (512×512). Pravitasari et al. [20] conducted a study to classify the region of interest (ROI) and non-ROI using a FCN with a hybrid architecture of U-Net and VGG16 with transfer learning to simplify the U-Net, Lagree et al. [17] proposed a novel gradient boosting network (GB U-Net) which concatenate three U-Net like models using transfer learning with pre-trained (VGG19 - DenseNet-121 - ResNet-101) as encoders, and the concatenated image is passed through a final U-Net, GB U-Net demonstrated a superior performance applied on datasets exclusively containing breast tissue images, Ali et al. [3] proposed a novel light-weight alternative PPU-Net that applies skip connections between the down-sampling blocks, and deploys the pyramid pooling module between down-sampling and up-sampling paths, evaluated on histopathological datasets of eight different cell lines.

With the same objective of resolving the ground truth scarcity problem, Englbrecht et al. [10] reduced the nuclei labeling time by 99.5% with an automatic annotation process of a custom fluorescent cell nuclei image dataset, the experimental results applied on automatically annotated dataset have shown a coequal segmentation performance compared to manual data annotation. In the same field, Kurmi and churasia [16] proposed an unsupervised nuclei segmentation method for hematoxylin and eosin-stained histopathology images based on the content of images; passing through three cascaded stages; histogram equalization as pre-process, nuclei center, and region extraction, then the complete nuclei segmentation by extracting boundaries and associating them with center points.

In the literature (E-D) models achieved the best nuclei segmentations [12], and recent research are more focus on transfer learning in the contraction path to improve (E-D) performance [1,26], furthermore TNBC dataset represents a good histopathological item for nuclei segmentation [18], thereby the main idea of this work is a comparative study among different architectures chosen to be backbones for (E-D) models applied on TNBC dataset.

3   Methods

In this paper, we used two supervised deep learning models extended from FCN [1] with (E-D) architecture, Encoder (contracting path to capture content) and Decoder (Expanding path that enables precise localization) [12,21].

The first one is U-Net proposed in 2015 [21], which proved its efficiency in cell tracking challenges, and had a very good performance on many biomedical segmentation [12,21], The second one is LinkNet proposed in 2017 [6] with very similar architecture but using ResNet18 in the contracting path. The main difference between these two DL models resides in that U-Net uses a concatenation operation to attach encoding layers with decoding ones, while LinkNet uses an adding operation for that [6,21,25] as represented in Fig. 1.

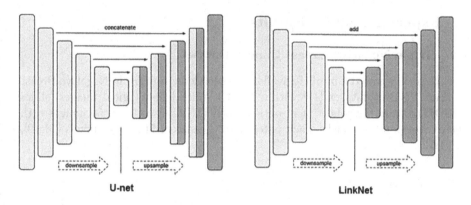

Fig. 1. Simplified architecture of U-Net and LinkNet (sourced [25]).

The strategy adopted in this work is to use backbone for one of the previous models, which means to replace the contraction path (Encoder) with a pre-trained model and adapt the Decoder to a new model, as a kind of transfer learning to improve learning in the target task by the knowledge used from the source task [20]. In this paper, we used three models pre-trained on ImageNet as backbones for U-Net and LinkNet:

3.1   VGG16

The first advantage of using backbone should be extra features brought from pre-trained model, and besides that VGG uses a small convolutional kernel (3×3) and pooling kernel (1×1), what makes the neural network deeper with less number of parameters, what improves its performance [20,26], the input image to this network is a fixed-size of (224×224) that is passed through a stack of convolutional layers [22].

3.2   MobileNet

Because complicated networks cost lots of resources and are not compatible with embedded devices [7], we're trying to pay more attention to models with fewer parameters, such as VGG and MobileNet which doesn't drop a lot in accuracy although it takes only one-eighth (1/8) of computational cost [7], MobileNet is based on depth-wise separable convolutions which applies a single filter to each input channel [14].

3.3   EfficientNet B3

It's a mobile-size baseline developed in 2019 [23], this model is a scaling method that can be scaled up very effectively, it's a method that uniformly scales all dimensions of (depth, width, resolution) using a compound coefficient, it could surpass state-of-art accuracy in transfer learning [23].

4   Experiments and Results

4.1   Triple Negative Breast Cancer Dataset

In this work, we used a publicly available nuclei detection Triple-Negative Breast Cancer (TNBC) dataset [19] within (H&E) stained histological images, slides were taken from the cohort of 11 patient with TNBC, it contains 50 images with their corresponding masks, each patch is in the size of 512×512 pixels [18,19], in Fig. 2.

4.2   Pre-processing

Since the shape of the input image was defined in all the "Segmentation Models" library presented in Sect. 2 at about 224×224. The image size of 512×512 of the TNBC dataset is too large for training our models, to resolve that issue, we sliced each image into four smaller patches in the size of 256×256 pixels, instead of resizing directly images which led to a big loss of information by causing nuclei overlapped in Ground truth and predictions as consequence. 40 images were used for the training task (160 small patches), and 10 images were reserved for testing (40 small patches).

For deep learning models, a large amount of data is required, and in histological datasets, the lack of nuclei segmentation's ground truth is the biggest snag facing researchers [12], and a few training data may lead the model to over-fitting [15]. Therefore, we extracted 1160 images with their corresponding masks from the 160 training patches, for that we applied the Albumentation PyTorch functions [5] which is a fast and flexible open-source library for image augmentation, containing various image transformations and it's easy-to-use compared to other libraries. We generated 1000 extra patches randomly by Rotation, Horizontal and Vertical flip, Grid distortion, and Transpose.

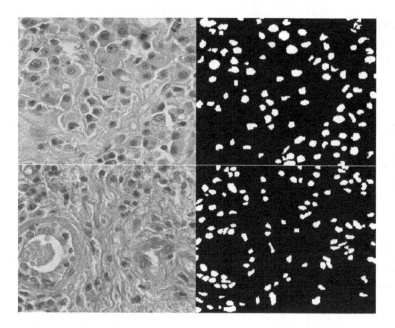

Fig. 2. Dataset, Left column 2 samples from 2 patients, right column corresponding ground truth.

4.3 Methodology

To evaluate the effect of each pre-trained backbone on U-Net and LinkNet's performance, we used different combination architectures like (Original U-Net), (VGG16 + U-Net), (MobileNet + U-Net), (EfficientNetb3 + U-Net), (Original LinkNet), (VGG16 + LinkNet), (MobilNet + LinkNet), and (EfficientNetb3 + LinkNet).

By and large, eight different models were fitted with the pre-treated dataset, the environment used for implementation was Colab[1], in which we trained each model for 50 epochs with the batch size of 16 and 10% of training data reserved for validation using the "adam" optimizer and 'binary-cross-entropy' as loss function.

We assessed our models in terms of rapidity with the execution time factor, and accuracy of nuclei prediction using IoU per object metric represented by the formula 1, where the numerator represents the area of overlap between "ground truth" represented in the formula by (G) and "prediction" represented as (Pr) and the numerator represents the area of union between (G) and (P) [11,19].

$$IoU = \frac{G \cap Pr}{G \cup Pr} \tag{1}$$

---

[1] https://colab.research.google.com/.

And we evaluate in term of precision with a per pixel metric, the F1 score which is defined as the harmonic mean between Precision (P) and Recall (R) at the pixel level, represented by the formula 2 [19]:

$$F1score = 2 * \frac{P * R}{P + R} \tag{2}$$

All the results are resumed in Table 1.

Table 1. Models comparison based on evaluation metrics (IoU and F1 score) and execution time.

Backbones	U-Net			LinkNet		
	IoU	F1score	Time/image (ms)	IoU	F1 score	Time/image (ms)
Original Backbone	0.6839	0.8123	801	0.6768	0.8072	766
VGG16	0.6987	0.8226	801	0.6964	0.8192	780
MobileNet	0.7080	0.8290	274	0.7016	0.8246	190
EfficientNetb3	0.7213	0.8381	502	0.7098	0.8303	475

As represented in Table 1 the rapidity of the model depends on the complexity of the architecture, as MobileNet backbone is the simplest with less than 5 million parameters with LinkNet and less than 9 million when linked to U-Net, it was the fastest with only 8s taken to predict the 40 test patches from the hybrid model (MobileNet + LinkNet), and 11s from the model (MobileNet + U-Net) compared to other models as VGG16 + U-Net which was the most complicated architecture with more than 23 million parameters, what makes it the slowest. We can notice either that VGG16 architecture doesn't differ a lot from the original backbones of U-Net and LinkNet what makes it take almost the same reckoning time with them, hence, we can say that reckoning time is completely depending on the complexity of the architecture of the model.

From Table 1, we can see the improvement in both models performance using backbones, and EfficientNetb3 gave the best IoU and F1 score with the two models especially with U-Net which performed the best with all backbones, the (EfficientNetb3 + U-Net) was the best-trained model among others.

Even if the enhancement was only with about 0.03 (3%) it's still considered as a good advance in histological image treatment because it improves the nuclei detection as it's shown in Fig. 3 and Fig. 4, this improvement was noteworthy when you know that the used backbones were pre-trained on ImageNet which is not a nucleus or even medical dataset.

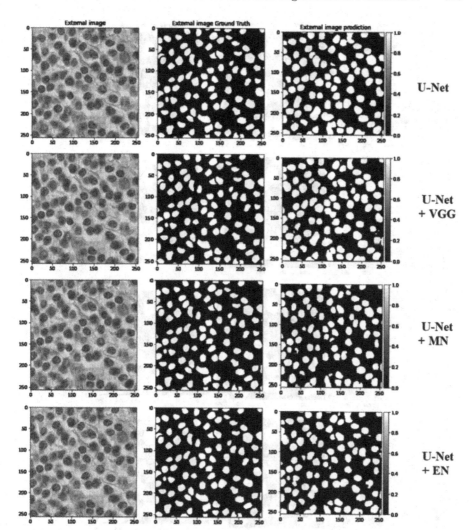

Fig. 3. Results of nuclei prediction for one of the test images: First line using U-Net, And next three lines using (VGG16, MobileNet, EfficientNet) respectively as backbones for the U-Net, in the first column on the left the original image, next to it the corresponding ground truth, and in the third column on the right the prediction.

116   C. Maarouf et al.

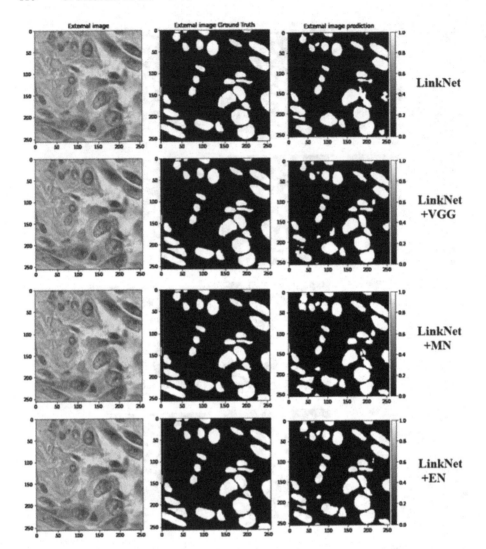

Fig. 4. Results of nuclei prediction for one of the test images: First line using LinkNet, And next three lines using (VGG16, MobileNet, EfficientNet) respectively, as backbones for the LinkNet, in the first column on the left the original image, next to it the corresponding ground truth, and in the third column on the right the prediction.

5   Conclusion

In this paper, eight models were trained on pre-processed TNBC dataset, U-Net, LinkNet, and three pre-trained backbones added to each one of them, we aimed to apply a comparative study between different backbones, and find out how does the transfer learning affect the accuracy of an E-D model, from the experimental results we could find that U-Net was the best dealing with nuclei segmentation, and the hybrid model composed of pre-trained Encoder + Decoder performed better than the original architecture, and among backbones, Efficient-Netb3 proved to be the best used pre-trained Encoder for both of the models U-Net and LinkNet.

Although our backbones were trained on ImageNet which is a dataset of natural images, the results were enhanced, therefore, we aim subsequently to apply transfer learning using models trained on histological images to get more ameliorations in terms of evaluation metrics (IoU and F1 score).

As future work, this transfer learning task can be applied on different datasets of other organs such as kidney tissue images, and the extracted features of the nucleus can be furthermore used in classification tasks to subtype tumors and even in statistical analysis of histopathological images.

Acknowledgements. The authors would like to thank the Directorate-General of Scientific Research and Technological Development (Direction Générale de la Recherche Scientifique et du Développement Technologique, DGRSDT, URL:www.dgrsdt.dz, Algeria) for the financial assistance towards this research.

References

1. Abedalla, A., Abdullah, M., Al-Ayyoub, M., Benkhelifa, E.: The 2st-UNET for pneumothorax segmentation in chest x-rays using resnet34 as a backbone for u-net. arXiv preprint arXiv:2009.02805 (2020)
2. Alhichri, H., Alswayed, A.S., Bazi, Y., Ammour, N., Alajlan, N.A.: Classification of remote sensing images using efficientnet-B3 CNN model with attention. IEEE Access **9**, 14078–14094 (2021)
3. Ali, M.A., Misko, O., Salumaa, S.O., Papkov, M., Palo, K., Fishman, D., Parts, L.: Evaluating very deep convolutional neural networks for nucleus segmentation from brightfield cell microscopy images. SLAS DISCOVERY: Adv. Sci. Drug Discov. **26**(9), 1125–1137 (2021)
4. Benomar, M.L., Settouti, N., Debreuve, E., Descombes, X., Ambrosetti, D.: Identifying regions of interest in whole slide images of renal cell carcinoma. Res. Biomed. Eng. 1–18 (2021)
5. Buslaev, A., Iglovikov, V.I., Khvedchenya, E., Parinov, A., Druzhinin, M., Kalinin, A.A.: Albumentations: fast and flexible image augmentations. Information **11**(2), 125 (2020)
6. Chaurasia, A., Culurciello, E.: LinkNet: exploiting encoder representations for efficient semantic segmentation. In: 2017 IEEE Visual Communications and Image Processing (VCIP), pp. 1–4. IEEE (2017)
7. Chen, H.Y., Su, C.Y.: An enhanced hybrid mobileNet. In: 2018 9th International Conference on Awareness Science and Technology (iCAST), pp. 308–312. IEEE (2018)
8. Chen, J.M., Li, Y., Xu, J., Gong, L., Wang, L.W., Liu, W.L., Liu, J.: Computer-aided prognosis on breast cancer with hematoxylin and eosin histopathology images: a review. Tumor Biol. **39**(3), 1010428317694550 (2017)
9. Cuevas, E., Sossa, H., et al.: A comparison of nature inspired algorithms for multi-threshold image segmentation. Expert Syst. Appl. **40**(4), 1213–1219 (2013)

10. Englbrecht, F., Ruider, I.E., Bausch, A.R.: Automatic image annotation for fluorescent cell nuclei segmentation. PLoS ONE **16**(4), e0250093 (2021)
11. Flores, J., Prasad, T., Kassof, J., Slater, R.: Automate nuclei detection using neural networks. SMU Data Sci. Rev. **2**(1), 8 (2019)
12. Ghosh, S., Das, N., Das, I., Maulik, U.: Understanding deep learning techniques for image segmentation. ACM Comput. Surv. (CSUR) **52**(4), 1–35 (2019)
13. Hassan, L., Saleh, A., Abdel-Nasser, M., Omer, O.A., Puig, D.: Promising deep semantic nuclei segmentation models for multi-institutional histopathology images of different organs. Int. J. Interact. Multimedia Artif. Intell. **6**(6) (2021)
14. Howard, A.G., Zhu, M., Chen, B., Kalenichenko, D., Wang, W., Weyand, T., Andreetto, M., Adam, H.: MobileNets: efficient convolutional neural networks for mobile vision applications. arXiv preprint arXiv:1704.04861 (2017)
15. Jung, H., Lodhi, B., Kang, J.: An automatic nuclei segmentation method based on deep convolutional neural networks for histopathology images. BMC Biomed. Eng. **1**(1), 1–12 (2019)
16. Kurmi, Y., Chaurasia, V.: Content-based image retrieval algorithm for nuclei segmentation in histopathology images. Multimedia Tools Appl. **80**(2), 3017–3037 (2020). https://doi.org/10.1007/s11042-020-09797-3
17. Lagree, A., et al.: A review and comparison of breast tumor cell nuclei segmentation performances using deep convolutional neural networks. Sci. Rep. **11**(1), 1–11 (2021)
18. Naylor, P., Laé, M., Reyal, F., Walter, T.: Nuclei segmentation in histopathology images using deep neural networks. In: 2017 IEEE 14th international symposium on biomedical imaging (ISBI 2017), pp. 933–936. IEEE (2017)
19. Naylor, P., Laé, M., Reyal, F., Walter, T.: Segmentation of nuclei in histopathology images by deep regression of the distance map. IEEE Trans. Med. Imaging **38**(2), 448–459 (2018)
20. Pravitasari, A.A., et al.: UNet-VGG16 with transfer learning for MRI-based brain tumor segmentation. Telkomnika **18**(3), 1310–1318 (2020)
21. Ronneberger, O., Fischer, P., Brox, T.: U-Net: convolutional networks for biomedical image segmentation. In: Navab, N., Hornegger, J., Wells, W.M., Frangi, A.F. (eds.) MICCAI 2015. LNCS, vol. 9351, pp. 234–241. Springer, Cham (2015). https://doi.org/10.1007/978-3-319-24574-4_28
22. Simonyan, K., Zisserman, A.: Very deep convolutional networks for large-scale image recognition. arXiv preprint arXiv:1409.1556 (2014)
23. Tan, M., Le, Q.: EfficientNet: rethinking model scaling for convolutional neural networks. In: International Conference on Machine Learning, pp. 6105–6114. PMLR (2019)
24. Vu, Q.D., et al.: Methods for segmentation and classification of digital microscopy tissue images. Front. Bioeng. Biotechnol. **7**, 53 (2019)
25. Yakubovskiy, P.: Segmentation models. GitHub repository (2019)
26. Zhang, R., Du, L., Xiao, Q., Liu, J.: Comparison of backbones for semantic segmentation network. J. Phys. Conf. Ser. **1544**, 012196 (2020)
27. Zhao, M., Wang, H., Han, Y., Wang, X., Dai, H.N., Sun, X., Zhang, J., Pedersen, M.: Seens: nuclei segmentation in pap smear images with selective edge enhancement. Future Generation Comput. Syst. **114**, 185–194 (2021)

Organ Detection in US Scanning by Non-expert Operator

François Derache[1]([✉]), Philippe Arbeille[2], Didier Chaput[1], and Nicole Vincent[3]

[1] Cadmos CNES, Avenue Edouard Belin 17, 31400 Toulouse, France
francois.derache@cnes.fr
[2] UMPS-CERCOM Faculté de Medecine - Université, Tours, France
[3] LIPADE, Université de Paris, Paris, France

Abstract. The acquisition of appropriate images for diagnosis on both superficial and deep organs requires a skilled professional sonographer, who performs the echography directly on the patient. In order to allow any distant operator novice in echography to make a volume capture covering the whole organ we developed a soft for auto-mated recognition of the organ contours.

The later analysis by a sonographer, will allow to analyze the contour and content of the organ and deliver a reliable medical diagnosis. Our method analyzes, detects and segments organs in ultrasounds scan based on the greyscale variation along a one-dimensional segment in real time. The objective of this paper is to present a method which allows anybody, anywhere, to find and scan organ regions for a later post-process analysis by remote sonographer. The soft was tested on a set of data provided by a dry immersion study of 5 days (MEDES 2019) on 18 subjects.

Keywords: Ultrasound · Automated-detection · Organ-detection · Teleoperation · Segmentation

1 Introduction

Presently, only operator with intensive practice of ultrasound on patient can provide reliable imaging of superficial and deep organs. Recently the control of both the probe orientation and the echograph set up and function have been developed and allow to perform safely an echographic investigation remotely. Such modalities have been validated on patient in rural isolated area and in astronauts onboard the Space station [4]. But even with such teleoperation, the novice by the side of the patient or the astronaut has to find the acoustic windows of the organ and needs to be guided vocally by a sonographer on ground. Thus, in case of bad or intermittent internet link or in case of long delay of transmission between a spaceship and earth it is necessary to have a system that helps the isolated operator (novice in ultrasound) to find the acoustic window that is to say to visualize at least partially the organ.

Nowadays, many segmentation methods applicable in ultrasound images are possible with satisfying results in line with medical expectations [12]. There are 3 main current

© Springer Nature Switzerland AG 2022
C. Djeddi et al. (Eds.): MedPRAI 2021, CCIS 1543, pp. 119–131, 2022.
https://doi.org/10.1007/978-3-031-04112-9_9

approaches of segmentations: active contour models (snakes) [13, 14], region based [2, 8, 10, 11] and deep leaning [9]. They are illustrated in Fig. 1. As ultra-sound scans tend to come along with significant background noise, in particular the speckle effect, the final segmentation quality is affected whatever method used. In these cases, the acquisition has included a phase during which the expert has optimized the image quality.

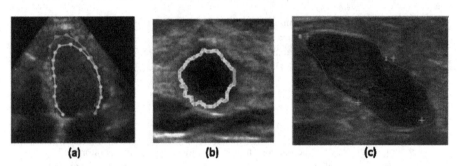

Fig. 1. Left ventricle of the heart using manifold with deep belief networks (a) [9], anatomical structure from an ultrasound breast lesion using active contour algorithm (b) [14] segmentation results for a malignant breast tumor using region-based segmentation (c) [10]

The objective of this paper is to present a method which allows anybody, anywhere, to find and scan organ regions for a later post-process analysis by remote radiologists. The method was based on the segmentation of a dedicated organ during a 2D ultrasound acquisition. The soft was tested on a set of data provided by a dry immersion study of 5 days (MEDES 2019) on 18 subjects.

2   Principle of the Method

Our approach consists in 3 steps (Fig. 2). An ultrasound scan provides a series of planar acquisitions of organ cross sections. An organ, generally, has a rather homogeneous texture of greyscale level in a distinct shape, repeated in the nearby scans of the examined volume. Fluids are anechoic, meaning they do not reflect echoes which makes gallbladder, vessel or ventricles appear dark on scans. As the brightness of both the organ and the background is not regular, the contour of the organ is not clearly delimited and it is difficult to adopt a global contrast approach, whereas a local contrast detection provides a more reliable contrast gap detection. The variety of behaviors around a point lead us to think that a directional view would be more efficient. That's why we have chosen to work in a specific 1D process. The main goal of the whole project, is to provide the expert with the section of an organ with the highest area and segmentation precision, in order to give the best 2D overview of the organ. Here, we look for best accurate segmentation on the different sections in the acquisition volume in a real time process in order to make it possible for the acquisition to be done in a better position. We developed the methods by mean of distinctive steps (Fig. 2), a global detection of an organ frame by frame that will be interpreted as a potential seed to find precisely the organ, a research of connectivity between detected potential organs in nearby frames, an accurate segmentation of the organ contour. In this paper we will focus mainly on the segmentation part (Contour detection).

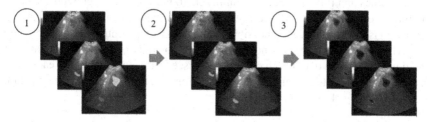

Fig. 2. Schematic of the overall steps of the approach. (1) Detection of seeds in frames independently, (2) connections of the seeds on each frame related to the same organ and (3) organ contouring (segmentation)

2.1 Detection of Seeds

The very first step of our approach concerns only one frame at a time and consists in detecting and giving a first general approximation of the organs, along with their sizes and positions in the scanned volume. This coarse vision gives what we have called seeds on every image of the acquisition set. To do so, every single image is studied separately by using a MSER method, revealing successive increasing regions. When the threshold growth leads to enough stability regarding the spatial position and growing area of the region, then the region is declared as a potential organ in the frame (Fig. 2). The region needs to have a minimum acceptable size to be considered as a potential organ. This minimum size is useful to filter out all the too small regions. To fulfill the properties of an organ compared to unstructured parts or to noise, analyzing the pixel grey levels distribution. We have introduced in the MSER method a new spatial constraint assuming that in a region of interest, the gravity center of the region is spatially stable, that is allowed when the grey level is changed, the gravity center is positioned in the neighborhood of the previous position, we assume that with the MSER method, the center of a region is stable but nevertheless allowed to move around a certain neighborhood (Fig. 3).

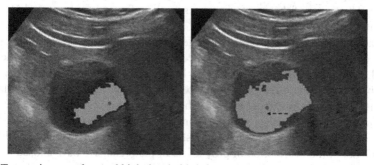

Fig. 3. Two regions at a low and high threshold (left and right), the gravity center of the region towards the scan moved slightly to the left

2.2 Connectivity of Seeds with Nearby Frames

Now we take into account the overall frames. Some tracking of the seeds is performed along the frames and if the potential organ in one frame follows the previous detection (minimum size, stability toward threshold growth and gravity center position), then an investigation is made to look for a possible connection with potential organs in previous frames. The connection is established and the two potential organs of each frame are declared to be the same one if both centers of the seeds are close enough to each other. With this method, detected organs are monitored along the frames of the scanned volume as illustrated on Fig. 4.

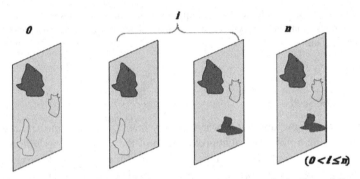

Fig. 4. For each successive frames, connections are made chronologically to follow an organ display. The blue seed is stable from 0 to n, the green seed disappears and reappears, the yellow seed disappears and never reappears and the red seed appears only later without any connection to the previous ones (e.g. yellow). (Color figure online)

2.3 Point Detection

The next step of our method focuses on the fine segmentation of the organ on each frame of the sequence. The main idea is that the organ and its surrounding have not the same texture (for instance in the bladder or vessel cases, the organ is darker than its surrounding). This can be observed on the graphs of Fig. 7 on the left quarter of the graph. The center of this region is chosen as the reference point (named O) of our segmentation method on this frame.

Instead of processing the overall 2D image as all other methods do, we are to process 1D parts of the image crossing the actual seed. More precisely, we focus on the pixel greylevel evolution along each half straight lines issued from the reference point and indexed by the angle with the horizontal direction (Fig. 6). According to the shape of the organs we are studying, these half straight lines are supposed to intersect the organ contour in one point in an orthogonal direction with respect to the contour tangent. Thus, the study of a 2D image segmentation is transformed into 1D investigation. It is difficult to get a model of the distribution of grey levels of the organ. We have chosen to adapt a model figuring on the one hand the organ and on the other hand its surrounding. The parameters of the models are set according to each straight line enabling to handle the changes in contrast along the different directions. The simplest way to approximate the evolution of a value is a constant model, for example the mean grey level within the organ. This is a too coarse approximation as evolution of the greylevels can be observed. We have chosen to build a model with several freedom degrees (Fig. 5). Two linear models will approximate the evolution of the grey levels along the straight lines starting in the core of the organ. One is supposed to model the organ where a low positive slope is expected and the second one may model the wall of the organ and tissues. The limit between the two parts will adapt itself in each half straight line as well as the two slopes defining the model and be considered as a contour point of the organ section.

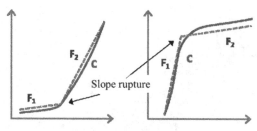

Fig. 5. Proposed model to fit to the C curve, comprising two parts that are approximated, with a minimum error, into two linear regression straight lines F1 and F2, highlighting the slope break of C.

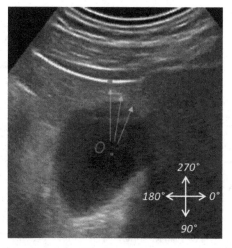

Fig. 6. Greyscale evolution along every 1° radius as above orange radii. The red point represents the center of the organ O and the blue point represents the brightest point in the radius that is **Pmax**. While we are in the organ, we expect a low greyscale level. (Color figure online)

In order to limit as much as possible, the concerned domain on the line, we define a limit of our study as the brightest point when moving away from the center (Fig. 6). The organ boundary is necessarily between the center and this brightest point we called p_{max}. As we drift away from the center and therefore, from a darkest to a brightest greylevel pixel, the greylevel profile tends to follow a specific pattern illustrated in Fig. 7.

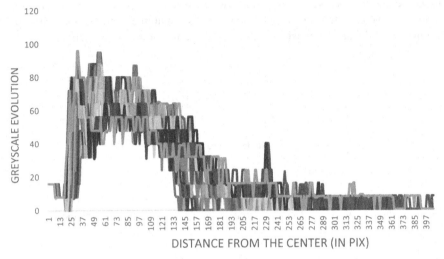

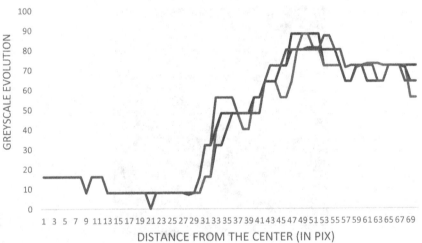

Fig. 7. On the first graph, the greyscale tendency of greyscale evolution (every 10° above and for a set of 4 different radius below). The horizontal axis represents, for every radius, the distance from the center, the first point starting from the left is the center of the organ. The second graph is scaled on the horizontal axis from the center O of the organ to p_{max}.

As the contour of an organ corresponds in fact with a fleeting change in brightness, it can be distinguished by a slope discontinuity in the curve before reaching the maximum greylevel. In order to identify the precise location of the slope rupture, which is potentially the organ contour, we opted for an exhaustive search between 0, the index of O and p_{max} the index of the brightest point. Two linear regressions are performed on the grey levels on [0, p] and [p, p_{max}] respectively. Each segment is characterized by the approximation error that is done, replacing the reality with the approximation given by the models, $\mathcal{F}_1$ and $\mathcal{F}_2$ (Fig. 8).

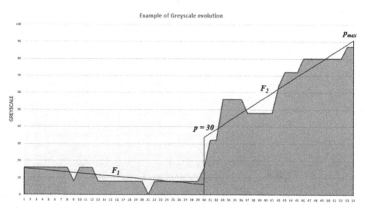

Fig. 8. The linear approximation $\mathcal{F}_1$ from the center of the organ (very left) to p then $\mathcal{F}_2$ from p to the brightest point in the radius p_{max}. Here is an example when $p = 30$

More precisely, in our method, the approximation error is computed as the sum of the approximation errors $E_1(p)$ and $E_2(p)$ on both segments. The approximation error is measured for each index as the distance between the linear regression value at index l and the real value of the pixel grey level with the same index $ri(l)$. $E_1(p)$ will be the error associated with $\mathcal{F}_1$ and $E_2(p)$ the error associated with $\mathcal{F}_2$. Obviously, we aim to get the lowest global error. We introduce $E(p)$, the total error at p:

$$E_1(p) = \sum_{l=0}^{p}(r_i(l) - \mathcal{F}_1(l))^2 \tag{1}$$

$$E_2(p) = \sum_{l=p}^{p_{max}-i}(r_i(l) - \mathcal{F}_2(l))^2 \tag{2}$$

$$E(p) = E_1(p) + E_2(p) \tag{3}$$

As a result, we get an error curve $E(p)$ representing the error of approximation by the global model for every point p of the greylevel profile along the considered radius. In our experiments we considered on each frame, 360° radii regularly dispatched around O.

The index leading to the minimum of E function, gives us the index p* of the contour point in the studied direction (Fig. 9). The left part corresponds to the interior of the organ and the right part to the outer part (Fig. 10).

Therefore, for each radius, we identify a potential contour point of the detected organ. The number of contour points is linked to the number of radii we have studied all referring to O, the center of the organ (Fig. 6).

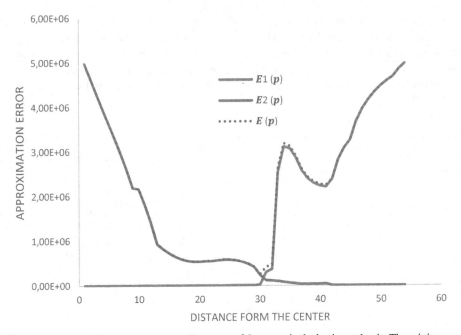

Fig. 9. Evolution of the error, based on the center of the organ in the horizontal axis. The minimum is identified at $p = 30$.

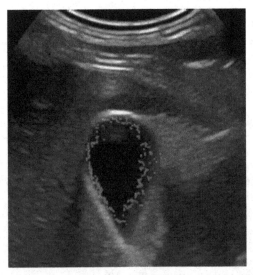

Fig. 10. Results of the regression analysis on every radius, marked in red, on a bladder. Some outliers are visible and a smoothing step is needed to refine the results. (Color figure online)

2.4 Coherence of the Contour

In this final step, once we have identified all the potential contour points, we smooth the results by studying the point density surrounding each point and close the shape. in order to obtain a final contour. To do so, the neighborhood of each point is analyzed to search for other points identified in the previous step at others radii. Then, the barycenter is deduced with a ponderation based on the proximity of the radii. After that, we close the contour by linear segments joining points ordered thanks to the angle of the straight line they belong to.

2.5 Study Population

A total of 9 subjects were included in the study (9M, age: 34 ± 7, height: 176 ± 6 cm, weight: 74 ± 7 kg). All subjects were informed about the experimental procedures and gave their written informed consent. The experimental protocol conformed to the standards set by the Declaration of Helsinki and was approved by the local Ethics Committee (CPP Est III: October 2, 2018, n° ID RCB 2018-A01470-55) and French Health Author-ities (ANSM: August 13, 2018). Clinical Trials.gov Identifier: NCT03915457.

2.6 Experimental Protocol

It included four days of ambulatory baseline measurements before immersion (DI-4d to DI-1d) five days (120 h) of dry immersion (DI-1d to DI-5d) and two days of ambulatory recovery (R0, R + 1). The DI proto-col was as previously detailed in [1]. During DI, subjects remained immersed in a semi re-cumbent position for all activities and were continuously observed by video monitoring. Due to various measurements requiring the subjects to move out of the water tank on Day 5, the final ultrasound scans in real DI were completed on day four (DI-4d). In our experiment, the data were collected during the 4 days ambulatory baseline measurement before immersion.

3   Results

We have experimented the proposed method on twenty images including different organs such as bladder, vessels and heart cavities. To evaluate the method, 2 experts have drawn ground truths of contours, manually. To evaluate the precision of the detected contours, we have dilated with different thicknesses the ground truth line and considered the ratio of detected contour points within the wide contours according to their width denoted w. The evaluation is done thanks to this ratio defined in formula (4). Considering D contour points, we note $Di(w)$ is the number of contour points within the thick ground truth and then the Ratio R according to the width w is:

$$R(w) = \frac{Di(w)}{D} * 100 \tag{4}$$

When comparing expert 1 to expert 2, ground truth evaluation $R(w)$ varies from 5% to 49% depending on the thickness and when the comparison is done considering expert 1 as a reference, variation is from 5% to 34%.

The organ segmentation is especially good for scans near the center of the organ computed in the 3D volume as the contrast of the organ is more significant. It gets less clear for the scans near the edges of the organ. The ultrasound scan quality has a significant impact on the segmentation result; brightness of the scans, for instance, can bias the returned echogenicity of the organs. We also observed some issues when the grey level evolution along a radius was too linear, indeed, the slope rupture is therefore difficult to clearly be detected, either visually or by computation. In order to solve these problems, we have improved the results by considering several nearby centers. Even though the method should be invariant towards such translation, it enables the straight lines radii to cross the contour in new directions. Besides, we can select more than one minimum and so get more contour candidates in a recursive way, the disadvantage being to introduce too many outliers.

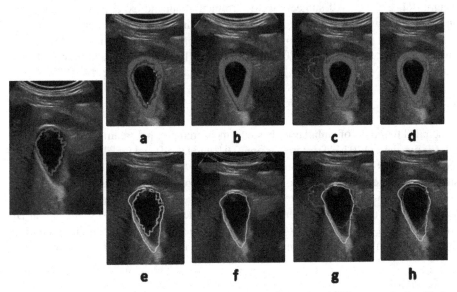

Fig. 11. On the left in red, our segmentation. From (a) to (d), results of different methods with the thickest ground truth of expert 1. From (e) to (h), we compare the same methods using the thinnest ground truth of expert 2. The methods compared are, on (a) and (e), our method, on (b) and (f), the canny method. On (c) and (g), the watershed method and on (d) and (h), a deep learning method. (Color figure online)

In Fig. 11 is compared the result of our method with other known methods against the 2 different ground truths. We here show the thickest line of expert 1 and the thinnest one of expert 2. From (a) to (h), the wrong part of a computed contour is shown in green whereas a correct one is shown in blue. When using ground truth drawn by expert 1, the accuracy of our method varies from 20% to 95% and from 5% to 34% with expert 2. This is far better than Canny or watershed methods (less than 50%) and only the deep learning methods can reach such an accuracy. Unfortunately, the deep learning method is not able to compute a segmentation in real-time. The evaluation is quite satisfactory when compared to the ratios between the two experts.

The next step is to refine the result and get rid of some outliers appearing on some images. A smoothing phase has to be added. The simplest way is to eliminate the isolated points or with too few contour points in their neighborhood. Another approach would be to attract distant points and bring them back to zones of higher density.

4 Discussion

The benefits of the presented method are twofold. Our method suggests an innovative solution to analyze, detect and segment organs in ultrasounds scan based on the greyscale study through a one-dimensional approach in real time. As the complexity of the algorithm is low, it enables a real-time segmentation of any echogenic organ including automatic initialization. The self-initialization avoids therefore any interaction to obtain a segmented organ. The results are obtained in real-time thanks to the low complexity of the model and therefore used directly by a sonographer during an organ scan. It can be implemented easily and is adaptable to any echogenic organ. Software guided sonography could be used everywhere on earth and beyond without implying significant design changes in current systems.

Compared to other methods, region based and active contours cannot provide a self-initialization of enough good quality to guarantee a good result and therefore cannot be considered as fully autonomous methods as they involve a human interaction. Region based segmentation such as local or variable thresholding technics, are not completely reliable due to the instability of the greyscale all along the edges of the organs in an ultra-sound scan. However, they present an advantage in term of speed unlike active contours. Region growing-methods appear to be effective when it comes to detect the general shape and position of the organ but the out-line is most often not accurate enough [10, 11].

Over the last few years, deep learning has been used in various application areas of medical analysis [9]. Several methods have shown an increasing performance of results, nevertheless, there is still room for improvement. As a matter of fact, this performance is clearly related to the amount of training data; in most applications they are difficult to obtain with a specific annotation due to restricted access to the data because of confidentiality barrier. Moreover, as the detection becomes more complex, the loss of transparency increases until the models get almost impossible to explain. Additionally, in order to reach real-time segmentation, computers with high level of performance are mandatory.

Until today remote ultrasound (onboard spaceship) was achieved using

- a) "Voice remote guidance" the isolated subject find the organ, tilt rotate the probe to reach the right view (long, short axis) and adjust the echograph set ups and functions (Doppler, Time motion) record the images…[7],
- b) "Teleoperated echo": the isolated subject find the organ, but both the probe movement and the echograph setup and functions are controlled from the ground [4],
- c) "3D Capture and post processing" the subject finds the organ and performs 3D capture for post processing on the ground [3].

For all these 3 methods the isolated subject needs to be guided vocally by the ground expert to find the acoustic window, (the location from where at least part of the organ can be visualized), but this requires a quite real-time audio/video link between the isolated subject and the ground expert, which is the case with astronauts onboard ISS or on the moon (delay < 5 s). In the case of higher delay or low flow rate between the expert and subject sites (Mars plan-et) the Voice remote guidance and Teleoperation methods could not be used while the method presented in the present paper will allow the isolated subject to locate the probe on top of the acoustic window by his own and perform 3D captures and send them to the ground for medical analysis. At last, the isolated subject will locate the probe using the automatic organ detection, then activate the 3D capture, both actions being non operator dependent.

4.1 Limitations

Still, the quality of the image remains an important aspect for the precision of the segmentation and the probe placement doesn't allow too much drift on the acoustic window of the targeted organ. Therefore, and just like other methods, a placement on the right acoustic window is mandatory.

5 Conclusion

Here, we have proposed a new approach to organ segmentation that does not need any human intervention and can adapt itself to different organs thanks to a model with enough degrees of freedom. We intend to adapt the method for different other kinds of organs such as kidney, heart, which, for astronauts, are important to be monitored while microgravity exposure. Besides, a smoothing of the contour has to be further performed. After a full reconstruction of the organ, the method is also able to provide the highest cross section of the scanned organ.

Acknowledgment. The authors want to acknowledge the French Space Agency (CNES) for financial support and MEDES for organizing the experiment.

References

1. De Abreu, S., et al.: Multi-system deconditioning in 3-day dry immersion without daily raise. Front. Physiol. **13**(8), 799 (2017). https://doi.org/10.3389/fphys.2017.00799.eCollection2017
2. Abdel-Dayem, A.R., El-Sakka, M.R.: Carotid artery ultrasound image segmentation using fuzzy region growing. In: Kamel, M., Campilho, A. (eds.) Image Analysis and Recognition. Lecture Notes in Computer Science, vol. 3656, pp. 869–878. Springer, Heidelberg (2005). https://doi.org/10.1007/11559573_106
3. Arbeille, P., et al.: Tele sonography: virtual image processing of remotely acquired abdominal, vascular, and fetal sonograms. J. Clin. Ultrasound **42**(2), 67–73 (2014). https://doi.org/10.1002/jcu.22093

4. Arbeille, P., et al.: Remote echography between a ground control center and the international space station ISS using tele operated echograph with motorized probe. Ultrasound Med. Biol. (2018). pii: S0301-5629(18)30267-9. https://doi.org/10.1016/j.ultrasmed bio.2018.06.012. [Epub ahead PMID:30093338]

5. Lorza, A.M.A., et al.: Carotid artery lumen segmentation in 3D free-hand ultrasound images using surface graph cuts. In: Mori, K., Sakuma, I., Sato, Y., Barillot, Christian, Navab, N. (eds.) MICCAI 2013. LNCS, vol. 8150, pp. 542–549. Springer, Heidelberg (2013). https://doi.org/10.1007/978-3-642-40763-5_67

6. Dutt, V., Greenleaf, J.F.: Statistics of the log-compressed echo envelope. J. Acoust. Soc. Am. **99**, 3817 (1996)

7. Hamilton, D.R., et al.: On-orbit prospective echocardiography on international space station crew. Echocardiography **28**, 491–501 (2011)

8. Kima, D.H., Plataniotisb, K.N., Roa, Y.M.: Level-set based free fluid segmentation with improved initialization using region growing in 3D ultrasound sonography. In: Proceedings, Medical Imaging 2014: Computer-Aided Diagnosis, vol. 9035 (2014)

9. Liu, S., et al.: Deep learning in medical ultrasound analysis: a review, Engineering **5**(2), 261–275 (2019). ISSN 2095-8099

10. Luo, Y., Liu, L., Huang, O., Li, X.: A novel segmentation approach combining region- and edge-based information for ultrasound images. Hindawi BioMed. Res. Int. Article ID 9157341, 18p (2017)

11. Mahmood, N.H., Zulkarnain, N., SaradatulAkmar Zulkifli, N.S.: Ultrasound liver image enhancement using watershed segmentation method. J. Eng. Res. Appl. (IJERA) **2**(3), 691–694 (2012)

12. Noble, J.A., Boukerroui, D.: Ultrasound image segmentation: a survey. IEEE Trans. Med. Imaging **25**(8) (2006)

13. Rabhi, A., Adel, M., Bourennane, S.: Segmentation of ultrasound images using geodesic active contours. ITBM-RBM **27**, 8–18 (2005)

14. Talebi, M., Ayatollahi, A., Kermani, A.: Medical ultrasound image segmentation using genetic active contour. J. Biomed. Sci. Eng. **4**(2) (2011)

Deep Transfer Learning Techniques for Automated Classification of Histological Childhood Medulloblastoma Images

Ghezali Waffa$^{(\boxtimes)}$ and Settouti Nesma

Biomedical Engineering Laboratory, University of Tlemcen, Tlemcen, Algeria
{waffa.ghezali,nesma.settouti}@univ-tlemcen.dz

Abstract. The automated classification invaded the world of health, but some diseases are still diagnosed manually as is the case of medulloblastoma (MB) cancer, which is a high-risk malignant tumor in the Central Nervous System (CNS). This tumor has many types and is diagnosed by biopsy when examining the histological images, which takes a lot of effort and time. In this paper, we propose to perform an automated Childhood Medulloblastoma classification based on Convolutional Neural Networks (CNN) by exploiting the knowledge learned through different datasets (medical PatchCamelyon (PCam) and ImageNet) with transfer learning. A comparative study is carried out by following two strategies: deep feature extractor and partial fine-tuning, we applied the most popular architectures namely VGG-16, VGG-19, ResNet-50, Inception-V3. Experiments prove that there is an important role of similarity when dealing with deep features extractor or partial fine-tuning. Indeed, when there is a high similarity between the scope application, the deep features extractor is the best, otherwise, partial fine-tuning is more suitable. In our case application, results demonstrate that the process of partial fine-tuning using Inception-V3 pre-trained on ImageNet achieved the best result with an accuracy of 99.16 %.

Keywords: Convolutional neural network · Partial fine-tuning · Deep features extractor · Histological images · Medulloblastoma · Classification

1 Introduction

Medulloblastoma is an embryonal cancerous primary neuroectodermal malignancy of the brain of the fourth degree

Medulloblastoma is a grade four embryonal cancerous primary neuroectodermal[1] malignancy of the brain. According to the World Health Organization (WHO) [15] it develops in the middle of the cerebellum near the fourth ventricle

---

[1] malignant tumors thought to arise from the central or peripheral nervous system.

© Springer Nature Switzerland AG 2022
C. Djeddi et al. (Eds.): MedPRAI 2021, CCIS 1543, pp. 132–144, 2022.
https://doi.org/10.1007/978-3-031-04112-9_10

at the level of the vermis, it is a rapidly growing invasive tumor and can metastasize throughout the central nervous system via the Cerebro-Spinal Fluid (CSF). It is the most common and best-known accounting for 20% of CNS tumors and half of the posterior fossa tumors [21]. It is more common in children under 16 years and can be seen in older adolescents, less often, in adults. The MB signs and symptoms are headaches, nausea, and vomiting, often worse in the morning, fatigue or changes in activity levels, dizziness, loss of balance, clumsiness, difficulty writing, vision impairment, back pain, difficulty walking, and problems with urination or changes in bowel function (the last three ones appear if the tumor has spread to the spinal cord). The risks stratification of MB are broken down into two categories, average (standard) and high-risk [32].

Medulloblastoma is classified and described based on certain characteristics such as histology, molecular features, and metastasis. The histological classification of medulloblastoma using microscopic features (size, shape, ...) shows that there are several types, some are defined by the WHO (Classic MB (CMB), Desmoplastic/Nodular MB (DN), MB with extensive nodularity (MBEN), Large cell/Anaplastic MB (LCA) and MB non-specified (NOS)) and others not (Classic biphasic MB (B-MB), Ganglioneuroblastoma (GNB), Paucinodular) [19,21].

The diagnosis of this tumor is based on medical history, neurological examinations, Magnetic Resonance Imaging (MRI), and much more on the biopsy through histological images. A biopsy is an integral part of the prognosis because it allows us to know the different characteristics of the tumor such as dimensions, location, form, etc. The treatment of this disease includes surgery, chemotherapy, and radiotherapy but long-term monitoring has shown that such treatment leads to mainly neurocognitive impairment, neuropathy, endocrinopathy, delayed bone growth, impaired motor function, hearing loss, and secondary malignancy. These effects are dose-related to radiation therapy and the age of the patient (overall survival is 5 years with a percentage of 75% but can increase with early diagnosis) [21]. However, The sensitivity of the treatment is not systematic, and the identification and diagnosis of this tumor depend on qualitative visual examination of histological slides of biopsy samples by clinical experts and requires hard and tedious work, which makes the diagnosis burdensome for experts. The solution to this problem is to propose an automated histological diagnosis of Childhood Medulloblastoma using machine learning tools. One of the new techniques of machine learning is deep learning. Lately, with the development of machine learning methods and the contribution of deep learning this has allowed great advances in computer vision, therefore, it is important to experiment and test the application of method based on Convolutional Neuronal Network (CNN). CNN is a neural network based on convolutional layers and is formed by a succession of blocks. There are several architectures with a different number of blocks that varied from one to another.

Learning CNN requires a large database with thousands and millions of data samples, but we can use it with small dataset by resorting to transfer learning. It has three approaches, two of them (partial fine-tuning and deep features extractor) are designated for the small data. These transfer learning approaches help to reuse image representations learned from a source task and a dataset with a large amount tagged into a second dataset which is small, like our case, in which we have a database (Childhood Medulloblastoma) which is relatively small (as is the case in most medical data). In this work, we investigate which approach and which architecture and knowledge (through images of nature/medical) are the most relevant for the recognition of MB. A comparative study is conducted with some of the most famous architectures like VGG-16, VGG-19, ResNet-50, Inception-V3. These models are pre-trained on ImageNet (straight-forward natural-image classification datasets) and the PCam (histological images benchmark) using partial fine-tuning and deep features extractor strategies. Through experimentations, we will demonstrate what strategy and model are the most suitable for our case application.

The rest of the paper is presented as follow: Sect. 2 reviews a few related works and studies that have been done on the automated classification of medulloblastoma, Sect. 3 introduces the dataset used as well as CNN, and the transfer learning strategies used for MB classification, the results, and its discussion are in Sect. 4, and Sect. 5 concludes this paper with perspectives.

2   Related Works

This section recognizes the studies and works that were proposed on medulloblastoma and which are represented in Table 1, all listed researches can be categorized on the data types used namely MRI and histological images.

We identify two works on medulloblastoma classification with MRI images, Grist et al. [13] separate between the brain tumors, using classical classifiers with PCA and Univariate, Quon et al. [23] use the convolutional neural network to this task with ResNet-50.

In the histological images type, all papers were focused on using features with different levels: high-level features, advanced latent features, and deep level features.

In high-level features, Das et al. [8] used different features extraction methods such as GLCM and HOG. In the advanced level features, MANOVA and PCA were used by Das et al. [3,7,10,11] for dimensionality reduction to obtain performance better than using all features with classic classifiers. For the deep level features, a hybrid approach was applied where CNNs pre-trained models were used to extract features and different classifiers to obtain tumor class. O. Attallah [4] conducted this hybrid approach with a process that goes through three stages, first, feature extraction, second, feature selection or dimension reduction step, and finally, the classification step.

In [3,4], researchers used transfer learning to extract features from pre-trained models on ImageNet. Besides, Cruz-Roa et al. [6] make a comparison between deep features extracted from pre-trained models (VGG and IBCa) on ImageNet and on histological.

Table 1. List of related works with details of features and classifiers applied.

IMG TYPE	FEATURES	CLASSIFIERS	CLASSES	ACCURACY (%)
MRI [13]	ACP, univariate with ADC, CCBV, UCBV, K2	AdaBoost, RandomForest, KNN, RN	MB, EP, Astrocytoma	86
MRI [23]	/	ResNet 50-32-4d	MB, DMC, PA, EP	92
Hist [6]	VGG-16, IBCa	softmax	anaplasic, non anaplasic	89.8
Hist [8]	GLCM, GRLN, HOG,Tamura	SVM, KNN, Trees, LR, LD, QD	Normal, CMB	100
Hist [7]	PCA with GLCM, GRLN, HOG,Tamura	SVM, KNN, Trees, LD, QD	CMB, LCA, MBEN, DN, Normal	91.3
Hist [10]	PCA with texture, color, morphology	SVM, KNN, Trees, LR, LD, QD	CMB, LCA, MBEN, DN, Normal	100
Hist [11]	with MANOVA	SVM	CMB, LCA, MBEN, DN, Normal	96.5
Hist [3]	PCA with denseNet-201, mobileNet and ResNet-50	LDA, ESD	CMB, LCA, MBEN, DN, Normal	100
Hist [4]	/	AlexNet, ResNet 50, EfficientNet,VGG 16	CMB, DN	/

Therefore, the transfer learning is used in some works to extract features in which a model that was trained on images of natures (ImageNet) which have a very low similarity with our small medulloblastoma dataset, and histological images (just in one work).

To work with CNN which is current and trending approach, we must be careful on the choice of the model and hyper-parameters. In this work for histological childhood images classification, since we have a small dataset, this leads us to two approaches of transfer learning : the partial fine-tuning or deep features extractor. The first strategy, if the models are trained on dataset not similar with our data. And the second, if we have pre-trained models on dataset very similar to our data.

The choice of the process is clear now, but there are different architectures and models that it is important to make the right choice. That what we will see in the next section.

3 Material and Methods

This section presents our study as well as the dataset and the different techniques used with parameters settings.

3.1 Childhood MB Dataset

All of Guwahati Medical College, GMCH Hospital and GNRC had been collaborating to collect the Childhood Medulloblastoma dataset. This dataset was obtained from patients under 15 years of age who were identified in GMCH. Samples were taken from tissue blocks and used as a component of the postoperative process. These blocks of tissues were stained, at Ayursundra Pvt, using H & E with the help of a local medical professional. Subsequently, a qualified pathologist at the pathology department of the GNRC observed the scans of the slide and the region of interest for ground truth. Pictures of the region of interest were captured using a Leica 1CC50 HD microscope and were saved in JPG format for the four subtypes of MB tumors. The dataset contains 204 and 258 pictures with magnification 10× and 100× from 15 patients [3,9]. The dataset distribution in our Transfer Learning comparison strategy is as follow: 240 train images split into 50 normal and 190 abnormal images. The half of training images number are used for test with 24 normal and 96 abnormal images. The validation contains two images, the first image represents normal MB, and the second represents abnormal MB.

3.2 Convolutional Neural Networks (CNN)

CNN is a type of artificial neural network with convolutional operations; it is made up of neurons whose parameters take the form of weights and biases that can be changed or adjusted during the learning operation. CNN is formed by a succession of processing blocks as represented in Fig. 1 to extract the characteristics discriminating the class of membership of the image of others [22]. A treatment block consists of one to several: convolutional layers (CONV), activation layer (ReLU), pooling layer, fully-Connected Layer, the activation function.

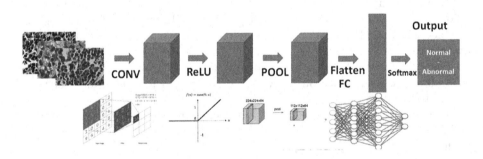

Fig. 1. CNN architecture.

The goal of a convolutional layer is to identify the presence of a set of features in the images received as input [16]. For this, convolution filtering is carried out: the principle is to "drag" a window representing the filter onto the image and to calculate the convolution product between the filter and each portion of the scanned image. The output of this operation is called a feature map or also activation map. The correction or activation layer is the application of a nonlinear function to the characteristic map's output from the convolution layer.

The ReLU function ($ReLU(x) = max(0, x)$) (Rectified Linear Units) remove every negative value from convolution results and replace it with zeros, it makes it easier to extract complex features that cannot be modeled by a linear combination or a regression algorithm. In the pooling layer, a down-sampling operation is applied after a convolutional layer, the most popular types of pooling are max and average pooling, where maximum and average values are taken, respectively [2,22]. The fully-Connected Layer is applied to a previously flattened input (It simply consists of taking all previously calculated matrices and put them into a single list or a vector, to exploit them in the input layer of a neural network) where all neurons are connected to each input. These layers are typically present at the end of CNN architectures and can be used for the optimization of goals such as class scores. The role of the activation function is the prediction and the right activation function depends on the type of classification problem, and two common functions are:

- Sigmoid is generally used for binary classification problems, as it is a logistic function.
- Softmax ensures that the sum of values in the output layer sum to 1 and can be used for both binary and multi-class classification problems.

3.3 Transfer Learning

Transfer learning is a deep learning technique that makes it possible to re-use general models already trained (a model created by someone else to solve a similar problem) to another one. Transfer learning technique makes it possible to transfer the knowledge acquired to a "source" dataset to better process a new "target" dataset, especially, when vastly bigger training sets are already used for training a source task's model. In transfer learning, the trained model is compiled as "weights" of the network, then transfers the learned features to a second network.

There are three approaches of transfer learning, which are: total fine-tuning, partial fine-tuning, and deep features extractor [31].

- Total fine-tuning is used when the data size of our task is large and its similarity with the data pre-trained is very high. We replace the last fully connected layer of the pre-trained network with a classifier adapted to the new problem (SVM, logistic regression...) and initialized randomly. All layers are then trained on the new images. It is used when the new collection of images is large: in this case, we can afford to train the whole network without running the risk of over-fitting. Moreover, since the parameters of all layers (except the last one) are initially those of the pre-trained network, the learning phase will be done faster than if the initialization had been random [34].
- Partial fine-tuning is used when the dataset size of our task is small and its similarity with the pre-trained data is very low. In this approach, we use the pre-trained model of 'n' layers with random initialization of all its weights. Have freeze a number 'k' of initial layers of the pre-trained model then we

train this model again on dataset of our task with the remaining '$n - k$' layers. More precisely, the last fully connected layer is replaced by the new randomly initialized classifier, and the parameters of some layers of the pre-trained network are fixed. Thus, in addition to the classifier, we train on the new images the non-fixed layers, which generally correspond to the highest ones of the network [34].

– Deep features extractor is used when the data size of our task is small and its similarity with the pre-trained data is very high. In this approach, we don't need to retrain the model because we have the same task. Here we remove the last fully connected layer and fix all the other parameters. This truncated network will then compute the representation of each input image from the features already learned during the pre-training. We then train a randomly initialized classifier on these representations to solve the new problem [20].

3.4   Conducted Comparative Study

The experimentation is based on a comparative study of two transfer learning strategies (partial fine-tuning and deep features extractor) with four CNN architectures : VGG-16, VGG-19 [26,33], ResNet-50 [14,18], Inception-V3 [27] which have proven themselves in science competitions and which have given a boost to the field of deep learning around the world [2]) trained on nature image classification (ImageNet) [1,25] and histological image classification (PCam) [29]. The idea behind this experimentation is to investigate which of the partial fine-tuning or deep features using pre-trained models on ImageNet or PCam dataset gives the best results on the Childhood MB Dataset our target dataset.

Medical PatchCamelyon (PCam) derived by Veeling et al. [29] from the Camelyon16 Challenge [12]. 400 H&E stained WSIs of sentinel lymph node sections are gathered in this dataset. The slides were acquired and digitized at 2 different centers using a 40× objective (resultant pixel resolution of 0.243 microns). The PCam benchmark dataset contains 327680 color histological images with a resolution of 96×96 px. This dataset consists of two classes in which each image is labeled indicating the presence of metastatic tissue. Its packs the task of metastasis detection which is clinically relevant into a straight-forward binary image classification task. It was trained and tested on CancerNet[2] architecture [17] by Soumya Ranjan Behera on Histopathologic Cancer Detection in the Kaggle Competition[3].

3.5   Classification Process

In partial fine-tuning strategy, first with ImageNet dataset, we need to freeze some layers and retrain them again with medulloblastoma dataset. In the VGG-16 and VGG-19, we had freeze the two last layers. However, in ResNet-50 and

---

[2] CancerNet was firstly used by Adrian Rosebrock on Breast cancer images [24].

[3] https://www.kaggle.com/soumya044/histopathologic-cancer-detection.

Inception-V3, we had freeze layers from the layer 171 and 305 respectively. Second, for the fine-tuning with the PCam dataset, we load all of VGG-16, VGG-19, ResNet-50, inception-v3 pre-trained models without weights. Next, we add the weights obtained after the training of CancerNet on PCam dataset available on Kaggle[4] to these models. We freeze the same layers as partial fine-tuning with the ImageNet dataset in all of the four architectures.

In the deep features extractor strategy, the models are used to extract features from the ImageNet dataset. Then transfer them to another classifier. Here, we use the SVM [28] and the Random forest [5] for the classification. For the PCam dataset, we load the models with CancerNet weights and without the top layer. We use the models to extract features and transfer them to the SVM and Random Forest classifier for performance study.

In addition to some hyper-parameters in which we set batch-size on 30 and learning rate on 0.0001 with "adam" optimizer in all models. Also we fix n-estimators on 50 in both of SVM and random-forest classifiers, and choosing 42 random-state.

4   Experiments and Results

All the experiments were performed with google colaboratory Colab[5], it is based on a Jupyter notebook environment that requires no setup to use and runs entirely in the cloud. The evaluation of models was measured by the accuracy. The accuracy was calculated as:

*Accuracy= (true positive + true negative) / samples number * 100*

The results of the two approaches using pre-trained models on ImageNet dataset are in Table 2, and pre-trained models on PCam dataset are in Table 3.

In the deep features extractor strategy, the pre-trained models on the PCam dataset give the best result compared to the pre-trained models on ImageNet. This can be explained by the fact that the PCam dataset (histological lymph node sections images) has a very high similarity with our dataset task in contrary to the ImageNet dataset (nature images) which has a poor similarity.

Nevertheless, the results of the deep features extractor with the pre-trained model on PCam must be better than that we have obtained, it needs more parametrization. To obtain the best parameters, more experimentation should have been done. The SVM and random forest classifiers are at the same level, both give a high accuracy of 92.5%.

---

[4] https://www.kaggle.com/soumya044/histopathologic-cancer-detection.
[5] https://colab.research.google.com/.

Table 2. Performances of pre-trained models on ImageNet.

MODELS	PARTIAL FINE-TUNING (%)	DEEP FEATURES EXTRACTOR	
		SVM (%)	Random Forest (%)
VGG-16	94.16	87.5	85.83
VGG-19	93.33	90.83	87.5
ResNet-50	87.50	80	75
Inception V3	99.16	88.33	86.66

Table 3. Performances of pre-trained models on PCam.

MODELS	PARTIAL FINE-TUNING (%)	DEEP FEATURES EXTRACTOR	
		SVM (%)	Random Forest (%)
VGG-16	80	90	88.33
VGG-19	81.66	92.5	92.5
ResNet-50	84.16	80	85.83
Inception V3	81.66	80	90

On the other side, in the partial fine-tuning strategy, the pre-trained models on ImageNet give the best result in comparison with pre-trained on PCam dataset. Here the notion of similarity changes, because partial fine-tuning is used when the models were trained on a dataset not similar to the MB dataset. The partial fine-tuning allows us to re-use image representations learned from a source task and a dataset with a large quantity labeled on a second dataset which is different. The partial fine-tuning is intended for databases that are different from the pre-trained databases. The Inception-V3 model outperforms the other architectures for partial fine-tuning on ImageNet. It gives the best accuracy at all (99.16%).

In comparison with related works cited, we report only O. Attallah [3] and Bengs et al. [4] works that applied deep features extracted using a pre-trained model on ImageNet, Cruz-Roa et al. [6] for their part used two different pre-trained models, one on ImageNet and the other on histological data. The comparative study conducted in this work, quest on what is the best choice of transfer learning strategy to use and if the similarity between the pre-trained data and target data is important for best performances. Experiments prove that there is an important role of similarity when dealing with deep features extractor or partial fine-tuning. We conclude that when there is a high similarity between the two data, the deep features extractor is the best, when none, partial fine-tuning is more suitable.

Our preliminary study has many limitations which we detail in this section. Regarding the classification phase, the main limitation is that we only used accuracy as a metric to assess the performance of classifiers. Recall and precision are two important measures in assessing the quality of a classifier and should be taken into consideration. Another limitation is linked to the generalization of our results. Indeed, the task is very specific to the study subject, the small datasets as well as the type of texts make it difficult to generalize our approach. Our results show a variability in the quality of classification according to the datasets. This would tend to say that the analysis is specific to them and consequently that the networks only adapt without generalizing their knowledge. However, our methodology and results can be used as a benchmark for further studies on the automatic medulloblastoma classification task.

5   Conclusion

In this paper, the objective is to answering the question *"how to avoid the hard work and to gain time for medulloblastoma classification task"* . We assumed that the solution is in machine learning approaches. We had then proposed an automated classification of the childhood medulloblastoma dataset based on CNNs. The size of our dataset task constrained us to deal with two approaches of transfer learning, partial fine-tuning or deep features extractor. The partial fine-tuning is used when we have models pre-trained on a dataset not similar to our dataset case application, the deep features extractor is used when there is a high similarity between our dataset task and the dataset on which the model is trained.

We carry out a comparative study between partial fine-tuning and deep features extractors using the most popular architectures in literature as VGG-16, VGG-19, ResNet-50, Inception-V3. The experimentation made is to evaluate the performances of the pre-trained models on both on ImageNet (straight-forward natural-image classification datasets) and the PCam dataset (histological images benchmark). The experimentations conducted show that, even on partial fine-tuning or deep features extractor, the choice of the pre-trained model is very important. In finality, we can concluded that there is a rule which is *"if the model was trained on dataset similar as our case study, the deep features extractor must be applied; If the model was trained on dataset not similar, the partial fine-tuning must be applied; and vice versa."* In our case application, the results show that the partial fine-tuning process using the Inception-V3 pre-trained model on ImageNet achieved the best accuracy with 99.16%.

In perspectives, we are working for the use of CanceNet and other architectures to reach a suitable setting. Also, new deep learning techniques are being explored to facilitate the explainability of such models [30] and might be useful in this context.

References

1. Ahmed, K.T., Irtaza, A., Iqbal, M.A.: Fusion of local and global features for effective image extraction. Appl. Intell. **47**(2), 526–543 (2017). https://doi.org/10.1007/s10489-017-0916-1
2. Alzubaidi, L., et al.: Review of deep learning: concepts, CNN architectures, challenges, applications, future directions. J. Big Data **8**(1), 1–74 (2021). https://doi.org/10.1186/s40537-021-00444-8
3. Attallah, O.: MB-AI-His: Histopathological diagnosis of pediatric medulloblastoma and its subtypes via AI. Diagnostics **11**(2), 359 (2021). https://doi.org/10.3390/diagnostics11020359
4. Bengs, M., Bockmayr, M., Schü ller, U., Schlaefer, A.: Medulloblastoma tumor classification using deep transfer learning with multi-scale EfficientNets. In: Tomaszewski, J.E., Ward, A.D. (eds.) Medical Imaging 2021: Digital Pathology, vol. 11603, pp. 70–75. International Society for Optics and Photonics, SPIE (2021). https://doi.org/10.1117/12.2580717
5. Breiman, L.: Random forests. Mach. Learn. **45**, 5–32 (2001)
6. Cruz-Roa, A., Arévalo, J., Judkins, A., Madabhushi, A., González, F.: A method for medulloblastoma tumor differentiation based on convolutional neural networks and transfer learning. In: Romero, E., Lepore, N., García-Arteaga, J.D., Brieva, J. (eds.) 11th International Symposium on Medical Information Processing and Analysis. Society of Photo-Optical Instrumentation Engineers (SPIE) Conference Series, vol. 9681, p. 968103, December 2015. https://doi.org/10.1117/12.2208825
7. Das, D., Mahanta, L.B., Ahmed, S., Baishya, B.K.: Classification of childhood medulloblastoma into who-defined multiple subtypes based on textural analysis. J. Microscopy **279**(1), 26–38 (2020). https://doi.org/10.1111/jmi.12893
8. Das, D., Mahanta, L.B., Ahmed, S., Baishya, B.K., Haque, I.: Automated classification of childhood brain tumours based on texture feature. Songklanakarin J. Sci. Technol **41**(5), 1014–1020 (2019)
9. Das, D., Mahanta, L.B.: Childhood medulloblastoma microscopic images. IEEE DataPort (2020). https://doi.org/10.21227/w0m0-mw21
10. Das, D., Mahanta, L.B., Ahmed, S., Baishya, B.K.: A study on Manova as an effective feature reduction technique in classification of childhood medulloblastoma and its subtypes. Netw. Model. Anal. Health Inform. Bioinform. **9**(1), 1–15 (2020)
11. Das, D., Mahanta, L.B., Ahmed, S., Baishya, B.K., Haque, I.: Study on contribution of biological interpretable and computer-aided features towards the classification of childhood medulloblastoma cells. J. Med. Syst. **42**(8), 1–12 (2018)
12. Ehteshami Bejnordi, B., Veta, M., Johannes van Diest, P., van Ginneken, B., Karssemeijer, N., Litjens, G., van der Laak, J.A.W.M.: The CAMELYON16 consortium: diagnostic assessment of deep learning algorithms for detection of lymph node metastases in women with breast cancer. JAMA **318**(22), 2199–2210 (2017). https://doi.org/10.1001/jama.2017.14585
13. Grist, J.T., et al.: Distinguishing between Paediatric brain Tumour types using multi-parametric magnetic resonance imaging and machine learning: A multi-site study. NeuroImage. Clin. **25**, 102172–102172 (2020)
14. He, K., Zhang, X., Ren, S., Sun, J.: Deep residual learning for image recognition. In: 2016 IEEE Conference on Computer Vision and Pattern Recognition (CVPR), pp. 770–778 (2016). https://doi.org/10.1109/CVPR.2016.90

15. Joud, A., Klein, O., Chastagner, P., Pretat, P.H., Bernier-Chastagner, V., Marchal, J.C.: Pediatric medulloblastomas. Encyclopedia Neurochirurgica, 12 May 2015, https://www.neurochirurgica.org/spip.php?article31&artpage=4-7. Accessed 04 April 2021

16. Ke, Q., Liu, J., Bennamoun, M., An, S., Sohel, F., Boussaid, F.: Chapter 5 - computer vision for human-machine interaction. In: Leo, M., Farinella, G.M. (eds.) Computer Vision for Assistive Healthcare, pp. 127–145. Computer Vision and Pattern Recognition, Academic Press (2018). https://doi.org/10.1016/B978-0-12-813445-0.00005-8

17. Khan, Z.Y., Niu, Z.: CNN with depthwise separable convolutions and combined kernels for rating prediction. Expert Syst. Appl. **170**, 114528 (2021). https://doi.org/10.1016/j.eswa.2020.114528

18. Mahmood, A., et al.: Automatic hierarchical classification of kelps using deep residual features. Sensors **20**, 447 (2020). https://doi.org/10.3390/s20020447

19. Northcott, P.A., Dubuc, A.M., Pfister, S., Taylor, M.D.: Molecular subgroups of medulloblastoma. Expert Rev. Neurotherapeutics **12**(7), 871–884 (2012)

20. Orenstein, E.C., Beijbom, O.: Transfer learning and deep feature extraction for planktonic image data sets. In: 2017 IEEE Winter Conference on Applications of Computer Vision (WACV), pp. 1082–1088 (2017). https://doi.org/10.1109/WACV.2017.125

21. Orr, B.A.: Pathology, diagnostics, and classification of medulloblastoma. Brain Pathol. **30**(3), 664–678 (2020). https://doi.org/10.1111/bpa.12837

22. O'Shea, K., Nash, R.: An introduction to convolutional neural networks. CoRR abs/1511.08458 (2015), http://arxiv.org/abs/1511.08458

23. Quon, J., et al.: Deep learning for pediatric posterior fossa tumor detection and classification: a multi-institutional study. Am. J. Neuroradiol. (2020). https://doi.org/10.3174/ajnr.A6704

24. Shahidi, F., Mohd Daud, S., Abas, H., Ahmad, N.A., Maarop, N.: Breast cancer classification using deep learning approaches and histopathology image: a comparison study. IEEE Access **8**, 187531–187552 (2020)

25. Russakovsky, O., et al.: ImageNet large scale visual recognition challenge. Int. J. Comput. Vis. **115**(3), 211–252 (2015)

26. Simonyan, K., Zisserman, A.: Very deep convolutional networks for large-scale image recognition. In: Bengio, Y., LeCun, Y. (eds.) 3rd International Conference on Learning Representations, ICLR 2015, San Diego, CA, USA, 7–9 May 2015, Conference Track Proceedings (2015)

27. Szegedy, C., Vanhoucke, V., Ioffe, S., Shlens, J., Wojna, Z.: Rethinking the inception architecture for computer vision. In: 2016 IEEE Conference on Computer Vision and Pattern Recognition (CVPR), pp. 2818–2826 (2016). https://doi.org/10.1109/CVPR.2016.308

28. Vapnik, V., Golowich, S.E., Smola, A.J.: Support vector method for function approximation, regression estimation and signal processing. In: Advances in Neural Information Processing Systems 9, NIPS, Denver, CO, USA, 2–5 December 1996, pp. 281–287 (1996)

29. Veeling, B.S., Linmans, J., Winkens, J., Cohen, T., Welling, M.: Rotation equivariant CNNS for digital pathology. CoRR abs/1806.03962 (2018)

30. Xie, N., Ras, G., van Gerven, M., Doran, D.: Explainable deep learning: a field guide for the uninitiated. CoRR abs/2004.14545 (2020), https://arxiv.org/abs/2004.14545

31. Yamada, M., Chang, Y.: Transfer learning: algorithms and applications. Elsevier Science & Technology Books (2018), https://books.google.dz/books?id=_GRlvgAACAAJ
32. Yu, J., Zhao, R., Shi, W., Li, H.: Risk factors for the prognosis of pediatric medulloblastoma: a retrospective analysis of 40 cases. Clinics (Sao Paulo, Brazil) **72**(5), 294–304 (2017)
33. Zhang, X., Zou, J., He, K., Sun, J.: Accelerating very deep convolutional networks for classification and detection. CoRR abs/1505.06798 (2015)
34. Zhiqiang, S., Zechun, L., Jie, Q., Marios, S., Kwang-Ting, C.: Partial is better than all: revisiting fine-tuning strategy for few-shot learning. arXiv preprint arXiv:2102.03983 (2021)

A New Medical Image Encryption Algorithm for IoMT Applications

Renjith V. Ravi[1]([envelope]) [iD], S. B. Goyal[2] [iD], and Chawki Djeddi[3,4] [iD]

[1] Department of Electronics and Communication Engineering,
M.E.A Engineering College, Malappuram, Kerala, India
renjithravi@meaec.edu.in
[2] City University, Petaling Jaya, Malaysia
[3] Department of Mathematics and Computer Science, Larbi Tebessi University,
Tebessa, Algeria
c.djeddi@univ-tebessa.dz
[4] LITIS Lab, Rouen University, Rouen, France

Abstract. Data security and privacy are essential for transmitting, storing, and preserving medical images. This article provides a secure chaotic framework for medical image encryption. The suggested technique has two stages: bit-level permutation and 2D SIM-based diffusion. The lossless technique is recommended for medical image encryption and decryption. It addresses the limitations of low-dimensional chaotic maps, such as small intervals and few parameters, and medical images' unique texture and form. The keyspace of the new method is sufficiently big, and the encryption and decryption procedures are key-sensitive. Simulations and testing validate the new algorithm's effectiveness and efficiency. According to security assessments, the algorithm is resistant to common attacks. A comparison of several encryption methods is performed. The proposed encryption method surpasses current encryption techniques when it comes to encrypting medical images.

Keywords: Medical image encryption · Bit-level permutation · 2D SIM

1 Introduction

Novel Internet of Things (IoT) technologies has reshaped many networking applications due to fast advancements in micro-computing, small hardware manufacturing, M2M communications etc. [20]. The Internet of Medical Things (IoMT) [13] technologies are one of the IoT branches that have modernized healthcare systems. Patients with chronic illnesses may be tracked remotely using IoMT devices. As a result, it may offer rapid diagnostics for patients, perhaps saving their lives in an emergency. Security of these essential systems, on the other hand, is a significant issue that must be addressed before they can be fully used.

Supported by City University, Petaling Jaya, MALAYSIA.

C. Djeddi et al. (Eds.): MedPRAI 2021, CCIS 1543, pp. 145–157, 2022.
https://doi.org/10.1007/978-3-031-04112-9_11

The Internet of Medical Things (IoMT) collects medical devices and applications connected to healthcare IT systems through internet computer networks [11]. Wi-Fi-enabled medical equipment enables machine-to-machine communication that serves as its basis [1]. IoMT devices communicate with cloud services such as Amazon Web Services, which store and analyse collected data. IoMT is another term for healthcare IoT.

Much medical imaging equipment is now linked and utilised to help physicians diagnose and treat patients, such as brain magnetic resonance imaging (MRI) for brain tumour identification and computed tomography (CT) of the lung for lung nodule detection, due to better in IoMT. On the other hand, these medical images include sensitive and private information about patients, and their disclosure may have privacy consequences for individuals and legal repercussions for institutions [19]. As a result, attempts have been made to develop security solutions (such as cryptographic primitives) to secure these medical images and safeguard patients' privacy [6].

Digital images, especially medical images, do not lend themselves to traditional encryption techniques because of the high degree of connectivity between image pixels, the enormous size of the images, and the redundancy of the data. Several medical image encryption techniques [2, 4, 12, 17, 18] have been proposed to reduce the amount of correlation between pixels and redundancy in medical images. According to Singh et al. [14], a medical image enciphering technique is suggested based on a newer ElGamal enciphering algorithm. The problem with expansion of data has been resolved, and improved the application's overall performance. It was shown by Hua et al. [10] that a new medical image enciphering technique can be implemented using randomized data insertion, high-speed permutation, and diffusion with pixel adaptivity. According to Chen et al. [5], a generalised optical encryption algorithm for enciphering medical images based on Shearlets and DRPE has been developed. An edge map-based medical image encryption technique has been suggested by Cao and colleagues [3]. A bit-plane decomposition algorithm, the generation of a random sequence, and permutation are the three primary components of the method.

2   Materials and Methods

2.1   Bit-level Permutation

The bit-level permutation [16] method scrambles each pixel's qubits (Y, X). The bit-planes interact with each other in our suggested bit-level permutation approach, includes cross-XOR and shifting operations to alter bit values. After this step, the gray value $|p_{ba}^7 p_{ba}^6 p_{ba}^5 p_{ba}^4 p_{ba}^3 p_{ba}^2 p_{ba}^1 p_{ba}^0\rangle$ is changed to $|p_{ba}^{7'} p_{ba}^{6'} p_{ba}^{5'} p_{ba}^{4'} p_{ba}^{3'} p_{ba}^{3'} p_{ba}^{1'} p_{ba}^{0'}\rangle$. The bit-planes that were acquired may be represented [16] as in Eq. 1:

$$\left|p_{ba}^{7'}\right\rangle = \left|p_{ba}^{0} \oplus p_{ba}^{7}\right\rangle, \left|p_{ba}^{3'}\right\rangle = \left|p_{ba}^{5} \oplus p_{ba}^{3}\right\rangle$$

$$\left|p_{ba}^{6'}\right\rangle = \left|p_{ba}^{1} \oplus p_{ba}^{6}\right\rangle, \left|p_{ba}^{2'}\right\rangle = \left|p_{ba}^{6} \oplus p_{ba}^{2}\right\rangle$$

$$\left|p_{ba}^{5'}\right\rangle = \left|p_{ba}^{2} \oplus p_{ba}^{5}\right\rangle, \left|p_{ba}^{1'}\right\rangle = \left|p_{ba}^{7} \oplus p_{ba}^{1}\right\rangle$$

$$\left|p_{ba}^{4'}\right\rangle = \left|p_{ba}^{3} \oplus p_{ba}^{4}\right\rangle, \left|p_{ba}^{0'}\right\rangle = \left|p_{ba}^{0}\right\rangle \tag{1}$$

The grey value is then subjected to a bit-plane shift operation. $|p_{ya}^{7'}p_{ba}^{6'}p_{ba}^{5'}p_{ba}^{4'}p_{ba}^{3'}p_{ba}^{2'}p_{ba}^{1'}p_{ba}^{0'}\rangle$ will rearrange the bit-planes. The sequence of bit-planes is flipped and changed, and a grey value $|p_{ba}^{2'}p_{ba}^{3'}p_{ba}^{4'}p_{ba}^{5'}p_{ba}^{6'}p_{ba}^{7'}p_{ba}^{0'}p_{ba}^{1'}\rangle$ is produced to use the quantum circuit consisting of swap gates.

For pixel (B, A), the permutation technique bit-plane may be carried out by U_{BA} formulated in the following way [16] as in Eq. 2.

$$U_{BA}\left(|P_{BA}\rangle\right) = U_{BA}\left(\left|p_{BA}^{7}p_{BA}^{6}\cdots p_{BA}^{1}p_{BA}^{0}\right\rangle\right) = \left|p_{BA}^{2'}p_{BA}^{3'}\cdots p_{BA}^{0}p_{BA}^{1'}\right\rangle \tag{2}$$

Then define the sub-operation L_{BA} by using permutation operator [16] U_{BA} as shown in Eq. 3.

$$\mathbf{L}_{BA} = \left(\mathbf{I}^{\otimes 8} \otimes \sum_{b=0}^{2^n-1}\sum_{a=0}^{2^n-1} |ba\rangle\langle ba|\right) + U_{BA} \otimes |BA\rangle\langle BA| \tag{3}$$

L_{BA} is a unitary quantum sub-operation [16]. Performing the sub operation $L_{B0,A0}$ on quantum state $|I_1\rangle$ yields the following outcome (Eq. 4 and Eq. 5) for bit-level permutation of pixel $(B0, A0)$.

$$L_{BA} = \frac{1}{2^m}\left(\sum_{b=0}^{2^m-1}\sum_{a=0}^{2^m-1}\left|P_{b'a'}|b'\right\rangle|a'\rangle + \left|p_{B_0A_0}^{2'}p_{B_0A_0}^{3'}\cdots p_{B_0A_0}^{0}p_{B_0A_0}^{1'}\right\rangle|B_0A_0\rangle\right) \tag{4}$$

$$L_{B_0A_0}\left(|I_1\rangle\right) = L_{B_0A_0}\left(\frac{1}{2^m}\sum_{b=0}^{2^m-1}\sum_{a=0}^{2^m-1}|P_{ba}\rangle|b'\rangle|a'\rangle\right)$$

$$= \frac{1}{2^m}L_{B_0A_0}\left(\sum_{b=0}^{2^m-1}\left.\sum_{a=0}^{2^m-1}\right|^{2^m}|P_{ba}\rangle|b'\rangle|a'\rangle + |P_{B_0A_0}\rangle|B_0A_0\rangle\right)$$

$$= \frac{1}{2^m}\left(\sum_{b=0}^{2^m-1}\sum_{\substack{a=0\\ba\neq B_0A_0A_0}}|P_{ba}\rangle|b'\rangle|a'\rangle + U_{BA}\left(|\,P_{B_0A_0}\rangle\right)\right)|B_0A_0\rangle$$

$$= \frac{1}{2^m}\left(\sum_{b=0}^{2^m-1}\left.\sum_{a=0}^{2^m-1}\right|^{2}|P_{b'a'}|\,||b'\rangle|a'\rangle\right.$$

$$+ \left|p_{B_0A_0}^{2'}p_{B_0A_0}^{3'}\cdots p_{B_0A_0}^{0}p_{B_0A_0}^{1'}\right\rangle|B_0A_0\rangle)$$

$$\tag{5}$$

The sub-operation will be [16] L_{B1A1} is applied on the Eq. 6 to change the gray value of the pixel $(B1, A1)$.

$$L_{B_1 A_1} L_{B_0 A_0} (|I_1\rangle) = L_{B_1 A_1} L_{B_0 A_0} \left(\frac{1}{2^m} \sum_{b=0}^{2^m-1} \sum_{a=0}^{2^m-1} |P_{ba}\rangle |b'\rangle |a'\rangle \right)$$

$$= \frac{1}{2^m} \left(\sum_{\substack{b=0 \\ ba \neq B_0 A_0, B_1 A_1}}^{2^m-1} \sum_{a=0}^{2^m-1} |P_{ba}\rangle |b'\rangle |a'\rangle + U_{BA} (|P_{B_0 A_0}|) |B_0 A_0\rangle \right.$$
$$\left. + U_{BA} (|P_{B_1 A_1}\rangle) |B_1 A_1\rangle \right)$$

$$= \frac{1}{2^m} \left(\sum_{\substack{b=0 \\ ba \neq B_0 A_0, B_1 A_1}}^{2^m-1} \sum_{a=0}^{2^m-1} |P_{ba}\rangle |b'\rangle |a'\rangle + \left| p_{B_0 A_0}^2 p_{B_0 A_0}^{3'} \cdots p_{B_0 A_0}^{0'} p_{B_0 A_0}^{1'} \right\rangle |B_0 A_0\rangle \right.$$ (6)
$$\left. + \left| p_{B_1 A_1}^{2'} p_{B_1 A_1}^{3'} \cdots p_{B_1 A_1}^{0'} p_{B_1 A_1}^{1'} \right\rangle |B_1 A_1\rangle \right)$$

To alter all of the pixel values $|I_1\rangle$, 2^{2m} sub-operations [16] must be implemented as in Eq. 7.

$$L(|I_1\rangle) = \prod_{B=0}^{2^m-1} \prod_{A=0}^{2^m-1} L_{BA} (|I_1\rangle)$$

$$= \prod_{B=0}^{2^m-1} \prod_{A=0}^{2^m-1} L_{BA} \left(\frac{1}{2^m} \sum_{B=0}^{2^m-1} \left. {}^{2^m-1} \right|_{A=0}^{m} |P_{BA}\rangle |B\rangle |A\rangle \right)$$

$$= \frac{1}{2^m} \sum_{B=0}^{2^m-1} \sum_{A=0}^{m_m} U_{BA} (|P_{BA}\rangle) |B\rangle |A\rangle$$ (7)

$$= \frac{1}{2^m} \sum_{B=0}^{2^m-1} {}^{2^m-1} \sum_{A=0}^{m} \left| p_{BA}^{2'} p_{BA}^{3'} \cdots p_{BA}'' p_{BA}^{1'} \right\rangle |BA\rangle$$

$$= \frac{1}{2^m} \sum_{B=0}^{2^m-1} \sum_{A=0}^{2^m-1} |P'_{BA}| |BA\rangle$$

$$= |I_2\rangle$$

2.2   2D SIM Model

The closed-loop linkage technique (CMC) is used to produce the 2D SIM [9,15]. Whenever the Sine map is used to modify the result of ICMIC in the CMC model, the 2D SIM is given as in Eq. 8.

$$\begin{cases} m_{i+1} = c \cdot \sin(\pi \cdot n_i) \cdot \sin\left(\frac{d}{m_i}\right), \\ n_{i+1} = c \cdot \sin(\pi \cdot m_{i+1}) \cdot \sin\left(\frac{d}{n_i}\right). \end{cases}$$ (8)

We created a two-dimensional delayed Sine ICMIC modulating map (2D SIM) by replacing the Sine map in 2D SIM with the DSM as in Eq. 9:

$$
\begin{cases}
m_{i+1} = c \cdot \sin\left(4\pi \cdot n_i \cdot (1 - n_{i-1})\right) \cdot \sin\left(\frac{d}{m_i}\right), \\
n_{i+1} = c \cdot \sin\left(4\pi \cdot m_{i+1} \cdot (1 - m_i)\right) \cdot \sin\left(\frac{d}{n_i}\right)
\end{cases}
\tag{9}
$$

Both c and d are systemic variables, and the system comprises various positive *Lyapunov exponents* $(6.0788, 5.2529)$ for $c = 0.2$ and $d = 3$. . As a result, it is hyperchaotic.

2.3 Diffusion Using 2D SIM

The plaintext responsiveness has been enhanced by the diffusion algorithm [9,15] to withstand differential assaults better. The recently enciphered pixel and indeed the total of un-enciphered pixels are introduced into the diffusion equation. The cyclic bit-shift operation is utilized to improve the algorithm's security even further. As a result, every pixel change will influence every step of iteration in the diffusion process. There's a good chance that the responsiveness will be present in the decryption process as well. In the decryption procedure, the avalanche effect does not occur. We can retain resilience when noise attacks or data loss since there is no sensitivity between the decrypted and the cipher images. There are two types of diffusion: forward diffusion and reverse diffusion. From the first to the final pixel of the image, Eq. 10 is used in the forward diffusion procedure. Equation 11 is applied from the pixels at the last position to the pixel at the first position, in backward diffusion process. During each cycle of encryption, we do diffusion forward and backward. The following is a description of the 2D SIM diffusion [9,15]:

$$
\begin{cases}
D_0(1) = U(1) \oplus S_1(1) \oplus \mathrm{mod}(\mathrm{sum}(U(2:\ \mathrm{end}\ )) + c0, F), \\
D(1) = D_0(1) \lll S_2(1), \\
D_0(i) = U(i) \oplus S_1(i) \oplus \mathrm{mod}(\mathrm{sum}(U(i+1:\ \mathrm{end}\ )) + D(i-1), F), \\
D(i) = D_0(i) \notlll S_2(i), \\
D_0(n) = U(n) \oplus S_1(n) \oplus \mathrm{mod}(D(n-1), F), \\
D(n) = D_0(n) \notlll S_2(n),
\end{cases}
\tag{10}
$$

$$
\begin{cases}
D_0^b(n) = D(n) \oplus S_1^b(n) \oplus \mathrm{mod}\left(\mathrm{sum}(D(1:n-1)) + c^b0, F\right), \\
D^b(n) = D_0^b(n) \lll S_2^b(n), \\
D_0^b(i) = D(i) \oplus S_1^b(i) \oplus \mathrm{mod}\left(\mathrm{sum}(D(1:i-1)) + D^b(i+1), F\right) \\
D^b(i) = D_0^b(i) \lll S_2^b(i), \\
D_0^b(1) = D(1) \oplus S_1^b(1) \oplus \mathrm{mod}\left(D^b(2), F\right), \\
D^b(1) = D_0^b(1) \notlll S_2^b(1),
\end{cases}
\tag{11}
$$

2.4 Proposed Encryption Algorithm

The block diagram of depiction of proposed encryption and decryption algorithms are shown in Fig. 1a and Fig. 1b respectively. Further, in algorithm form these steps are written in Algorithm 1 and Algorithm 2 respectively.

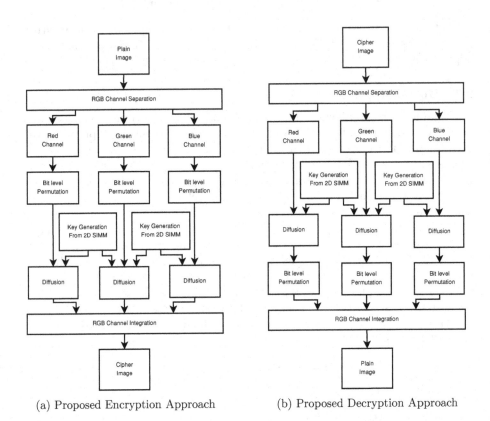

(a) Proposed Encryption Approach   (b) Proposed Decryption Approach

Fig. 1. Proposed encryption and decryption approaches

The plaintext image will first be separated into R, G, and B components in the proposed encryption algorithm. These R, G, and B components will be processed in parallel for bit-level permutation and diffusion using the key generated from 2D SIM. Finally, the encrypted versions of these three components will be integrated to create the cipher image. The entire encryption process is depicted in Fig. 1a and Algorithm 1.

In the decryption phase, the inverse processes of all the procedures done in encryption will be carried out in reverse order. The cipher image will be separated into its three components processed in parallel. First, the three components will undergo inverse diffusion and then inverse bit-level permutation using the key generated using the 2D SIM process. As the initial parameters used in encryption

---

Algorithm 1. Proposed Encryption Approach

1: **procedure** ENCRYPTION(*plain_image, key*)
2:    Take the Plain image
3:    Separation of R, G, and B Components
4:    Bit level permutation
5:    Key generation from 2D SIM
6:    Diffusion using the key
7:    R, G and B Integration
8:    Obtain Cipher image.
9: **end procedure**

---

and decryption are the same, the 2D SIM will generate the same key as generated in the encryption process. The decryption process is depicted in Fig. 1b and Algorithm 2,

---

Algorithm 2. Proposed Decryption Approach

1: **procedure** ENCRYPTION(*cipher_image, key*)
2:    Take the cipher image
3:    R, G and B Channel Separation
4:    Key Generation from 2D SIM
5:    Inverse Diffusion using the key
6:    Inverse bit level Permutation
7:    R, G and B Channel Integration
8:    Plain Image
9: **end procedure**

---

3   Results and Discussion

As the proposed algorithm is intended for secure transmission of medical images, we have used only images from medical database for simulation and performance evaluation of the algorithm. The test images used in this work are shown in Fig. 2.

3.1   Key Sensitivity Analysis

One of the criteria used to assess the effectiveness of an image encryption scheme is key sensitivity, and even a minor change in the key will fail decryption for a competent cryptosystem. The image shown in Fig. 3a is used as an example, with slightly different keys used to decode the encrypted image to demonstrate the suggested system's key sensitivity. Figure 3 shows the decryption findings. With the proper keys, the original image may be correctly decrypted. Even if all other keys are maintained the same, a minor change in the control parameter is insufficient to decode the image. As can be observed from the initial study, the suggested system is sensitive to keys.

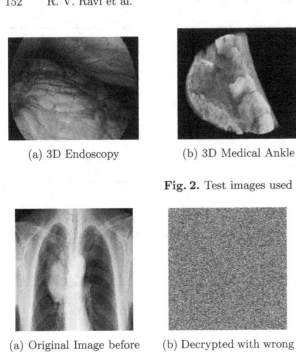

(a) 3D Endoscopy   (b) 3D Medical Ankle   (c) Chest X-Ray

Fig. 2. Test images used

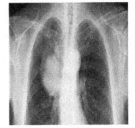

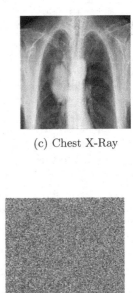

(a) Original Image before encryption

(b) Decrypted with wrong key-1

(c) Decrypted with wrong key-2

(d) Decrypted with wrong key-3

(e) Decrypted with correct key

Fig. 3. Key sensitivity test

3.2 Key-Space Analysis

The *keyspace* of a robust encryption algorithm should be big enough to withstand brute force assaults. The *keyspace* should be more than 2^{100}, based on current computing capabilities. The control parameter μ, the starting value d_0, and the iteration periods r are essential components of our suggested method.

The parameter μ has a precision of 10^{12}, and d_0 has an accuracy of 10^{14}, correspondingly. The values range belongs to $(0, +\infty)$ due to the sine logistic map's feature. As a result, the *keyspace* is theoretically limitless. The suggested method provides a big enough *keyspace* to withstand brute-force assaults since these keys are distinct.

3.3 Histogram Based Analysis

The histogram is a graphic illustration of the statistical distribution of pixels. The histogram of plain-image and the matching cipher image is shown in Fig. 4. Unlike the original image, the encrypted image's pixel dispersion is entirely consistent. As a result, extracting useful and necessary information content from the distribution pattern is challenging for an assailant.

The plaintext images, its histograms,corresponding encrypted images and its histograms are shown in Fig. 4. The Fig. 4a, Fig. 4b and Fig. 4c are the plaintext images. The Fig. 4d, Fig. 4e and Fig. 4f shows the corresponding histograms. The Fig. 4g, Fig. 4h and Fig. 4i are the encrypted versions of Fig. 4a, Fig. 4b and Fig. 4c are shown. Figure 4j, Fig. 4k and Fig. 4l shows the histograms of encrypted images are shown in Fig. 4g, Fig. 4h and Fig. 4i are depicted.

From Fig. 4j, Fig. 4k and Fig. 4l, it is clear that the histograms ar having a uniform distribution and the proposed encryption algorithm is resistant to all the attacks.

3.4 Information Entropy Analysis

Shannon brought the notion of entropy onto information theory, which relates to the measure of confusion. The information entropy (IE) of an 8-bit image with *probability distribution* P is calculated as in Eq. 12:

$$\text{IE} = -\sum_{i=0}^{2^8-1} P(i) \log_2 P(i) \tag{12}$$

where $P(i)$ represents the probability of grey value i in an image, the optimum IE value would be 8 if image pixels are perplexing sufficiently and each gray value does have the same *probability*. The IE values of plaintext and ciphertext images are listed in Table 1. The suggested method performs well since the values are more significant than 7.99 and quite near to 8. In terms of information entropy, two state-of-the-art algorithms [7] and [8] are compared in Table 2, and the values are lower than the suggested method. As a result, the suggested system is resistant to entropy-based attacks.

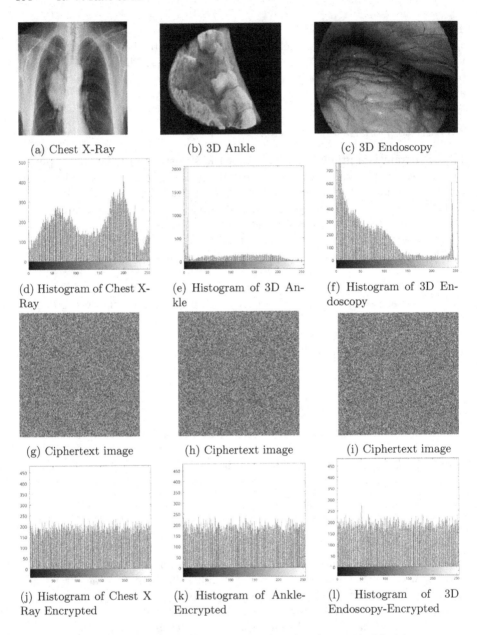

(a) Chest X-Ray

(b) 3D Ankle

(c) 3D Endoscopy

(d) Histogram of Chest X-Ray

(e) Histogram of 3D Ankle

(f) Histogram of 3D Endoscopy

(g) Ciphertext image

(h) Ciphertext image

(i) Ciphertext image

(j) Histogram of Chest X Ray Encrypted

(k) Histogram of Ankle-Encrypted

(l) Histogram of 3D Endoscopy-Encrypted

Fig. 4. Comparison of histograms of original and encrypted images

Table 1. Entropy values of plaintext and ciphertext images

Image	Entropy					
	Plaintext image			Encrypted image		
	R	G	B	R	G	B
Figure 4a	7.9002	7.7238	7.7266	7.9905	7.9916	7.9927
Figure 4b	4.8645	4.9691	5.2052	7.9942	7.9928	7.9931
Figure 4c	7.4356	6.6920	6.4108	7.9928	7.9936	7.9938

Table 2. Comparison of Entropy values for Fig. 4b with state of art algorithms

Reference	R	G	B
Proposed method	7.9942	7.9928	7.9931
Gafsi et al. [7]	7.9563	7.9559	7.9559
Hfsa et al. [8]	7.9563	7.9559	7.9559

3.5 UACI and NPCR Analysis

The *unified average changing intensity (UACI) and number of pixels change rate (NPCR)* specified as follows are used to test the proposed scheme's resilience to differential assault.

$$\text{UACI} = \frac{1}{2^{2n}} \sum_{p,q} \frac{|A_1(p,q) - A_2(p,q)|}{255} \times 100\% \tag{13}$$

$$\text{NPCR} = \frac{1}{2^{2n}} \sum_{p,q} |D(p,q)| \times 100\% \tag{14}$$

In Eq. 13, the variables $A1$ and $A2$ are the encrypted images whe using the original plaintext image and one pixel altered version of original plaintext image. If the value of pixels of $A_1(p,q)$ corresponds to $A_2(p,q)$, the value of $D(p,q)$ should be 0. If $A_1(p,q)$ and $A_2(p,q)$ do not vary, then, in Eq. 14, $D(p,q)$ is set to 1. The findings are presented in Table 3 by random changes of one pixel in the initial image and by calculation of the associated *UACI* and *NPCR*. In addition, the *UACI* and *NPCR* findings derived from Refs. [7] and [8] are compared in Table 4. The suggested technique's *UACI* result is nearer to the optimum value of 33.4635 percent, while the average *NPCR* result is closer to 99.6094 percent. The suggested algorithm's supremacy is shown by the average UACI and NPCR findings in bold, indicating that the suggested technique is more responsive to fluctuations in intensity values and can withstand differential assaults.

Table 3. NPCR and UACI values for the test images

Image	NPCR (%)			UACI(%)		
	R	G	B	R	G	B
Figure 4a	99.682	99.768	99.872	33.763	33.786	33.882
Figure 4b	99.898	99.859	99.897	34.964	34.947	34.877
Figure 4c	99.789	99.956	99.885	34.067	34.172	34.186

Table 4. Comparison of *NPCR* and *UACI* values for Fig. 4b with state of art algorithms

Image	NPCR (%)			UACI (%)		
	R	G	B	R	G	B
Figure 4b	99.898	99.859	99.897	34.964	34.947	34.877
Gafsi et al. [7]	99.89427	99.83960	99.89441	34.07125	34.08311	34.19787
Hfsa et al. [8]	99.699	99.687	99.898	33.896	33.895	33.678

4 Conclusion

Numerous networking applications have been reshaped as a result of the fast advances in micro-computing, tiny device manufacturing and machine to machine (M2M) communications. One of the IoT branches that have modernized healthcare systems is the IoMT. The IoMT devices can be used to track patients with chronic illnesses remotely. As a result, it may provide patients with rapid diagnostics, potentially saving their lives in an emergency. The security of these critical systems, on the other hand, is a significant concern that must be addressed before they can be fully utilized. Based on bit-level permutation and 2D SIM-based diffusion, this article offers an efficient and safe image encryption method. Bit-level scrambling and chaotic diffusion utilizing 2D SIM are the three phases of the proposed cryptographic method. The results demonstrate that the suggested method is both secure and quick. Statistical assaults, differential attacks, and brute-force attacks are examples of frequent attacks that they can withstand. Our method has excellent application prospects in image encryption communication in IoMT applications, according to simulation findings.

References

1. Alanezi, A., et al.: Securing digital images through simple permutation-substitution mechanism in cloud-based smart city environment. Secur. Commun. Netw. **2021** (2021). https://doi.org/10.1155/2021/6615512
2. Belazi, A., Talha, M., Kharbech, S., Xiang, W.: Novel medical image encryption scheme based on chaos and dna encoding. IEEE Access **7**, 36667–36681 (2019). https://doi.org/10.1109/access.2019.2906292

3. Cao, W., Zhou, Y., Chen, C.P., Xia, L.: Medical image encryption using edge maps. Signal Process. **132**, 96–109 (2017). https://doi.org/10.1016/j.sigpro.2016.10.003
4. Chen, J., Chen, L., Zhang, L.Y., Zhu, Z.: Medical image cipher using hierarchical diffusion and non-sequential encryption. Nonlinear Dyn. **96**(1), 301–322 (2019). https://doi.org/10.1007/s11071-019-04791-3
5. Chen, M., Ma, G., Tang, C., Lei, Z.: Generalized optical encryption framework based on shearlets for medical image. Opt. Lasers Eng. **128**, 106026 (2020). https://doi.org/10.1016/j.optlaseng.2020.106026
6. El-Latif, A.A.A., Abd-El-Atty, B., Belazi, A., Iliyasu, A.M.: Efficient chaos-based substitution-box and its application to image encryption. Electronics **10**(12), 1392 (2021)
7. Gafsi, M., Abbassi, N., Hajjaji, M.A., Malek, J., Mtibaa, A.: Improved chaos-based cryptosystem for medical image encryption and decryption. Sci. Program. **2020** (2020). https://doi.org/10.1155/2020/6612390
8. Hafsa, A., Gafsi, M., Malek, J., Machhout, M.: Fpga implementation of improved security approach for medical image encryption and decryption. Sci. Program. **2021** (2021). https://doi.org/10.1155/2021/6610655
9. He, P., Sun, K., Zhu, C.: A novel image encryption algorithm based on the delayed maps and permutation-confusion-diffusion architecture. Secur. Commun. Netw. **2021** (2021). https://doi.org/10.1155/2021/6679288
10. Hua, Z., Yi, S., Zhou, Y.: Medical image encryption using high-speed scrambling and pixel adaptive diffusion. Signal Process. **144**, 134–144 (2018). https://doi.org/10.1016/j.sigpro.2017.10.004
11. Joyia, G.J., Liaqat, R.M., Farooq, A., Rehman, S.: Internet of medical things (iomt): Applications, benefits and future challenges in healthcare domain. J. Commun. **12**(4), 240–247 (2017)
12. Ke, G., Wang, H., Zhou, S., Zhang, H.: Encryption of medical image with most significant bit and high capacity in piecewise linear chaos graphics. Measurement **135**, 385–391 (2019). https://doi.org/10.1016/j.measurement.2018.11.074
13. Koutras, D., Stergiopoulos, G., Dasaklis, T., Kotzanikolaou, P., Glynos, D., Douligeris, C.: Security in IOMT communications: a survey. Sensors **20**(17), 4828 (2020)
14. Laiphrakpam, D.S., Khumanthem, M.S.: Medical image encryption based on improved elgamal encryption technique. Optik **147**, 88–102 (2017). https://doi.org/10.1016/j.ijleo.2017.08.028
15. Liu, W., Sun, K., Zhu, C.: A fast image encryption algorithm based on chaotic map. Opt. Lasers Eng. **84**, 26–36 (2016). https://doi.org/10.1016/j.optlaseng.2016.03.019
16. Liu, X., Xiao, D., Liu, C.: Quantum image encryption algorithm based on bit-plane permutation and sine logistic map. Quantum Inf. Process. **19**(8), 1–23 (2020). https://doi.org/10.1007/s11128-020-02739-w
17. Mishra, Z., Acharya, B.: High throughput and low area architectures of secure iot algorithm for medical image encryption. J. Inf. Secur. Appl. **53**, 102533 (2020). https://doi.org/10.1016/j.jisa.2020.102533
18. Shankar, K., Elhoseny, M., Chelvi, E.D., Lakshmanaprabu, S., Wu, W.: An efficient optimal key based chaos function for medical image security. IEEE Access **6**, 77145–77154 (2018). https://doi.org/10.1109/access.2018.2874026
19. Tsafack, N., et al.: A memristive rlc oscillator dynamics applied to image encryption. J. Inf. Secur. Appl. **61**, 102944 (2021)
20. Zhang, W.Z., et al.: Secure and optimized load balancing for multitier iot and edge-cloud computing systems. IEEE Internet Things J. **8**(10), 8119–8132 (2020)

Feature Relevance Analysis for Handwriting Based Identification of Parkinson's Disease

Saman Khawar[(⊠)], Anum Kaleem, Momina Moetesum, and Imran Siddiqi

Bahria University Islamabad, Islamabad, Pakistan
samankhawar5@gmail.com,
{anumkleem.buic,momina.buic,imran.siddiqi}@bahria.edu.pk

Abstract. Handwriting has gained immense popularity amongst the relevant research community as potential biomarker for early detection of Parkinson's disease (PD). Several online and offline handwriting attributes have been proposed to characterize the presence or absence of PD. Additionally, various tasks have also been designed to capture these features. Nonetheless, it is observed that features extracted from multiple tasks can result in prediction disparities. In this context, determining feature-task relevance can facilitate by selecting the most appropriate subset of features from each task to enhance the overall prediction of an automated system. Most techniques presented in the literature advocate the dominance of either offline or online features over the other. Due to the inherent challenges of directly combining both types of features, we propose a decision fusion based alternative that takes advantage of both online and offline features and improves the overall prediction. By employing a benchmark database PaHaW, we validate the effectiveness of our approach.

Keywords: Parkinson's disease · Handwriting analysis · Feature relevance · Genetic algorithm · Convolutional Neural Networks (CNN) · Support Vector Machines (SVM)

1 Introduction

Parkinson's disease (PD) is the most prevalent neurological disorder after Alzheimer's. It is characterized by several non-motor and motor symptoms that include akinesia, bradykinesia, rigidity, tremors, postural imbalance and vocal disabilities. Traditional clinical procedures for PD detection rely on neuroimaging strategies like SPECT and CT scans. However, these are effective for advanced stages of the disease. Reliable methods for early detection of PD are required to facilitate rehabilitation and to improve patient's quality of life.

Contributing authors—A. Kaleem, M. Moetesum and I. Siddiqi.

C. Djeddi et al. (Eds.): MedPRAI 2021, CCIS 1543, pp. 158–171, 2022.
https://doi.org/10.1007/978-3-031-04112-9_12

Easy accessibility of pervasive technology with sensors has enabled the pattern recognition community to focus on finding solutions for several major societal problems; early detection of PD being one. Identification of PD through modalities like handwriting, speech and gait analysis has been thoroughly investigated in the literature [1–7]. From the perspective of handwriting analysis, a number of static (offline) [6–9] and dynamic (online) [10,11] features have been identified that can serve as effective indicators of PD. Both handcrafted feature engineering [8,12–14] and deep learning-based feature extraction [6,9,15–17] techniques have been evaluated. Multimodal feature analysis has also been investigated for the detection of PD [18,19].

An important observation made in the literature suggests that tasks and templates employed for the extraction of handwriting features have a deep impact on the predictive performance of the features [5,6,15,20]. This shifted the paradigm from combining features extracted from multiple templates to combining decisions of task-specific classifiers for the overall sample classification. Nonetheless, to the best of our knowledge, no investigations have been carried out to determine the feature-task relevance in case of PD detection using handwriting. Furthermore, there are no attempts made to analyze the combined impact of handcrafted online features and machine-learned visual features extracted from handwriting samples of PD patients on the overall prediction.

This research targets several gaps outlined earlier. The key highlights of this study are outlined in the following.

1. Task-wise feature relevance is computed to determine the most appropriate subset of features for each task. For this purpose, Genetic Algorithm (GA) is employed independently on both online and offline features.
2. A decision fusion-based approach is presented to combine the predictions of both online and offline features.
3. A comprehensive analysis is performed on a benchmark dataset to assess the impact of each step introduced in the overall pipeline. The results are also compared with the state-of-the-art to validate the effectiveness of the proposed methodology.

The rest of the paper is organized as follows. An overview of the existing techniques and methodologies relevant to our research domain are presented in Sect. 2. Section 3 discusses the proposed methodology in detail. Experimental study and results are discussed in Sect. 4. Section 5 concludes the paper by highlighting the key findings.

2   Related Work

Parkinson's disease is caused by the loss of pigmented neurons in the substantia nigra of the midbrain region, which are responsible for muscle movements. The loss of these neurons results in reduction of dopamine, a neurotransmitter involved in the control and regulation of body movements. This causes tremors, sluggish movements, hypertonia, and balance issues [21]. These symptoms also impact the hand-wrist movements that adversely affects the handwriting of an individual. Computer-aided analysis of handwriting enables the identification of potential patterns that are beneficial in the detection and classification of Parkinson's disease. Several studies [22,23] have validated that handwriting analysis is an effective tool for PD diagnosis especially during early stages. Many handwriting based techniques have been proposed for identification of PD [6,24,25]. Due to highly domain-specific nature of the problem, sample acquisition and labeling for classification is a challenging task. Like most medical domains, detection of PD from handwriting is a small-sample domain problem. Recently, there have been some interdisciplinary efforts to compile publicly available datasets that have been used by most of the studies mentioned in the literature. Popular benchmark datasets include the 'PaHaW' database proposed by Drotar et al. in [5], 'HandPD' dataset [24], and 'NewHandPD' dataset [15].

Based on the mode of sample acquisition, extracted features can be categorized as offline and online. Offline features are extracted from digitized samples of handwriting whereas online features are extracted from handwriting signals captured by electronic devices like a digitizer tablet or a smart pen. Offline features are usually static and may include various visual attributes that represent micorgraphia and tremors. Pereira et al. [24] extracted a set of nine offline features from offline images of spirals and meanders and assessed their potential by utilizing three methods: Naïve Bayes (NB), Optimum-Path Forest (OPF), and Support Vector Machines (SVM) with Radial Basis Function (rbf). In [6], Moetesum et al. employed a pretrained Convolutional Neural Network as a feature extractor to overcome the limitations of handcrafted features in this problem. Authors generated near-realistic plots from the handwriting signals presented in the PaHaW database to extract rich visual attributes. These features were then fed to a classical linear SVM that attained an accuracy of 83%. Later, Diaz et al. [7], further improved the accuracy (86.76%) by plotting in-air trajectories in addition to on-surface ones. In [26], authors proposed an evolutionary approach to discriminate between samples of PD patients and healthy controls. By employing Cartesian Genetic Programming (CPG) on features extracted in [24], the authors are able to overcome the interpretability concerns faced by most machine and deep learning approaches.

Contrary to static offline features, online features are dynamic and require special equipment for sample acquisition. Dortar et al. have contributed extensively in online feature extraction for PD detection [5,10,12,13]. The most significant contribution is the compilation of PaHaW database [5], that comprises handwriting signals of 75 subjects captured using a digitizing tablet Intuos 4M. A template of eight handwriting tasks is employed to capture different types of dynamic attributes. These include temporal, kinematic and pressure features. Classification was done using an SVM (rbf) and the best accuracy obtained by the system is 80%. In the subsequent studies [5,12], Drotar et al. analyzed the potential of various dynamic features extracted from both in-air and on-surface mode. The novel set of features attained an accuracy of 85% and 89% respectively. In another study [13], authors, used online kinematic and pressure features of handwriting to train different classifiers and achieved overall accuracies of 81.3% with SVM, 78.9% with AdaBoost classifier, and 71% with KNN, respectively.

In another study [27], Ribeiro et al. employed the Recurrent Neural Networks (RNN) on handwriting sequences achieving and accuracy of 85% on the spiral and 89% on the meander samples. In [28], Gupta et al. used offline samples of hand-drawn Archimedean spiral and presented novel features for PD prediction by extracting Fourier transform based distance attributes. Tremor estimating features are combined with distance-based features and fed to the SVM classifier achieving an accuracy of 81.66%. Authors in [11] investigate online kinematic features of handwriting to identify PD. They assess a number of classifiers including SVM (rbf/linear), KNN, LDA (Linear Discriminant Analysis), NB (Naiive Bayes), RF (Random Forest), and ADA (AdaBoost), reporting accuracies of 71%, 68%, 67.90%, 66%, 57%, 73%, 61%., respectively.

In [29], Ammour et al. worked on the Arabic Handwriting dataset and extracted a number of features of different categories like Kinematics (on-surface/in-air), Mechanical Inclination, and Pen-Up features and used the semi-supervised approach for classification (Clustering and PCA). They obtained an accuracy of 97.3% .

3   Methodology

In order to determine the impact of feature relevance and decision fusion approaches, we propose a framework illustrated in Fig. 1.

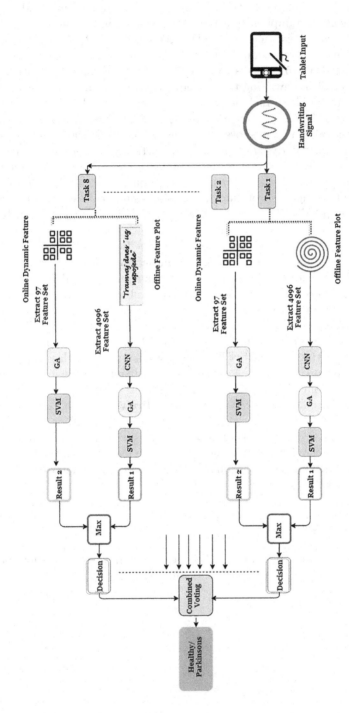

Fig. 1. Proposed methodology

3.1 Dataset

For the evaluation purposes, we employed the popular benchmark dataset PaHaW [5]. As mentioned earlier, the dataset consists of samples obtained from 37 Parkinson's patients (19 males and 18 females) and 38 healthy subjects (20 males and 18 females). Task templates are illustrated in Fig. 2 and are outlined below.

1. Sketching an Archimedian spiral
2. Inscription of the letter *l*
3. Inscription of Bigram *le*
4. Inscription of trigram *les*
5. Inscription of the following words in cursive
   (a) *lektorka*
   (b) *porovnat*
   (c) *nepopadnout*
6. Inscription in cursive sentence *Tramvaj dnes uz nepojade.*

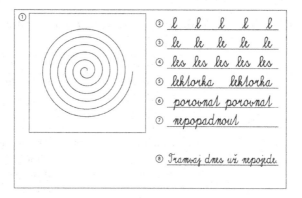

Fig. 2. PAHAW template [5]

3.2 Input

Handwriting signals in PaHaW are recorded using Wacom Intuos digitizing tablet. Raw data collected consists of pen input measures such as two dimensional coorinates (x,y), time stamp, pressure, button status, pen inclination measures like (x-tilt, y-tilt) and altitude. With the help of these raw input values, derived features such as velocity, acceleration, jerk and displacement can further be extracted.

3.3 Feature Extraction

Feature extraction is performed in two modes i.e. offline and online for each of the eight tasks respectively. The details for which are discussed in the subsequent sections.

3.3.1   Offline Features

To overcome the limitations of hand-crafted features, we employ the convolutional base of a pretrained CNN architecture, as feature extractor. Since PaHaW dataset does not contain images, therefore, our first step involves the generation of offline plots from raw signals. For this purpose, we normalize the x-, and y-coordinates corresponding to all positions where the pen tip is touching the writing surface (i.e. button status is 1). The plots are then fed to a pre-trained CNN architecture (VGG16) and a 4096-dimensional feature vector is extracted from the last fully connected layer before the softmax layer.

3.3.2   Online Features

In addition to the raw signals (x-, y- coordinates, time stamp, altitude, azimuth, and pressure), several popular dynamic features are also computed. The details of each are outlined in Table 1. For each of these, several statistical values (mode, 10th percentile, 99th percentiles, mean, standard deviations) are also computed. A feature vector comprising of 97 online features is computed for each task.

Table 1. Dynamic handwriting features. Abbreviations: r = raw feature; d = derived feature.

Feature	r/d	Description
x	r	x-coordinate of the pen position during handwriting
y	r	y-coordinate of the pen position during handwriting
Pressure	r	Pressure exerted over the writing surface
Tilt-x	r	Angle between the pen and the surface plane
Tilt-y	r	Angle between the pen and the plane vertical to the surface
Button status	r	Boolean variable indicating whether the pen is on-surface or in-air
Displacement	d	Pen trajectory during handwriting
Velocity	d	Rate of change of displacement with respect to time
Acceleration	d	Rate of change of velocity with respect to time
Jerk	d	Rate of change of acceleration with respect to time
Horizontal/vertical displacement	d	Displacement in the horizontal/vertical direction
Horizontal/vertical velocity	d	Velocity in the horizontal/vertical direction
Horizontal/vertical acceleration	d	Acceleration in the horizontal/vertical direction
Horizontal/vertical jerk	d	Jerk in the horizontal/vertical direction
First derivative of pressure	d	Rate of change of pressure with respect to time

3.4   Feature Relevance

Feature selection is the process of selecting the most relevant features with the intention to reduce the set size. The primary goal of a feature selection technique is to find the features that are useful in identification of the presence or absence of PD. The four important steps of a feature selection approach are *generation*, *evaluation, stop criterion*, and *validation*. The generation process implements a search method that produces a subset of features (typically using forward selection, backward elimination, bidirectional, etc.). The effectiveness of the resulting subset is then determined by using an evaluation criterion, which can either be independent (filter) or dependent (measurement or wrapper). A stopping condition is examined after each iteration to determine when the selection process should be stopped. Typical criteria involves achieving the optimal subset or bounds on a number of features or iterations. Once the stopping condition is met, the resultant subset of features can be confirmed [30]. For this research, we assess a wrapper (Genetic Algorithm) and a filter (Correlation) method.

3.5   Classification and Decision Fusion

For classification, we employ the traditional SVM (rbf) classifier. For each task, two SVM classifiers are trained using the online and offline features independently. Decisions from each classifier are first fused at task-level. The outcome of each type of features and the corresponding classifiers can differ due to their inherent properties. Hence, the scores from each classifier are fused to provide the final decision. Through the fusion of decision scores, online and offline features can be combined more effectively in the problem under consideration.

The second decision fusion is performed at the sample-level. The results of all task-wise classifiers are combined using majority voting to give the final sample-wise decision. As we have mentioned previously, selection of a task has a significant impact on the predictive potential of a particular feature set. Our decision-level fusion approach helps mitigate the negative impact of a particular task on the overall system performance.

4   Experimental Results and Analysis

Several experiments are carried out to assess the effectiveness of the proposed methodology. All experiments are performed using 10-fold cross validation on the samples in the PaHaW dataset and average accuracies of 10 runs are reported. The key objectives of the experimental study include the following.

- To determine the predictive performance of different features (offline/online).
- To assess the impact of different feature relevance methods employed in this study.
- To validate the effectiveness of decision fusion in comparison to feature fusion in the problem under consideration.

The results of our experiments are discussed in the subsequent sections.

4.1   Results of Offline and Online Features

Our first set of experiments was performed to establish the predictive potential of hand-crafted online dynamic features and CNN-based visual features. As
mentioned earlier, a 97-dimensional feature set of online features is used to train
an SVM with an rbf kernel and the average results of the task-wise accuracies is
outlined in Table 2. Similarly, another SVM classifier with rbf kernel is trained
using the 4096-dimensional visual feature set extracted by using a CNN. The
results are also reported in Table 2 for comparison purposes.

Table 2. Task-wise accuracies using online and offline features

Tasks	Online features (97)	Offline features (4096)
Archimedean spiral	57%	57%
Repetitive (l)	60%	43%
Repetitive (le)	62%	57%
Repetitive (les)	60%	64%
Word (lektorka)	50%	64%
Word (porovnat)	53%	50%
Word (nepopadnout)	47%	64%
Sentence	67%	64%
Overall accuracy	57%	58%

It is observed that in case of statistical online features sentence task outperforms all other including the spiral task. Sentence task is also one of the best
performing tasks in case of CNN-based visual features. By combining online features extracted from each task an overall accuracy of 57% is obtained. While in
case of offline features, it is 58%. Although, in most cases the task-wise accuracies obtained by online features are more than those achieved by CNN-based
offline features, nonetheless, due to the combination of different types of features
(pressure-based, pen-based, kinematics etc.), the overall impact can be adversely
affected. This is mostly attributed to the fact that different types of tasks are
designed to capture different graphomotor attributes.

4.2   Impact of Feature Relevance on Task-wise Accuracies

This experiment is performed to observe the impact of different feature relevance techniques on the final outcome and to select the most effective subset of
features. For this purpose, we applied both Genetic Algorithm and Correlation
techniques independently on both types of feature sets. First we built a correlation matrix, which examines the correlation of all features (for all possible
feature combinations). We identified the highly correlated features by setting

a threshold of 0.5. After removing these highly correlated features and select-ing the features which are not correlated, we fed these selected features to an SVM for training. Correlation was employed on both offline visual feature set (4096-dimensional) and online statistical feature set (97-dimensional). Task-wise performance improvement after correlation-based feature selection technique on both the feature sets (offline/online) is shown in Table 3. We then applied the Genetic Algorithm technique on each task features set and extracted the opti-mal feature subset. We performed 10 iterations to determine specific features that were selected almost every time we run the Genetic Algorithm. We fed these selected features to an SVM. The obtained results are outlined in Table 4 respectively.

Table 3. Task-wise results obtained by applying correlation

Task	No. of selected features and Accuracy (Online)	No. of selected features and Accuracy (Offline)
Archimedean Spiral	64% *with 14 features*	78% *with 2172 features*
Repetitive (l)	61% *with 17 features*	71% *with 1874 features*
Repetitive (le)	70% *with 21 features*	64% *with 1187 features*
Repetitive (les)	61% *with 17 features*	66% *with 1862 features*
Word (lektorka)	61% *with 16 features*	71% *with 1725 features*
Word (porovnat)	70% *with 20 features*	71% *with 1931 features*
Word (nepopadnout)	53% *with 19 features*	70% *with 1801 features*
Sentence	78% *with 20 features*	71% *with 1759 features*

Table 4. Task-wise results obtained by applying genetic Algorithm

Task	No. of Selected features and Accuracy (online)	No. of selected features and Accuracy (offline)
Archimedean spiral	78% *with 6 features*	86% *with 65 features*
Repetitive (l)	74% *with 8 features*	74% *with 21 features*
Repetitive (le)	75% *with 5 features*	72% *with 38 features*
Repetitive (les)	80% *with 8 features*	78% *with 33 features*
Word(lektorka)	66% *with 5 features*	75% *with 114 features*
Word (porovnat)	80% *with 5 features*	73% *with 45 features*
Word (nepopadnout)	74% *with 5 features*	71% *with 39 features*
Sentence	83% *with 6 features*	72% *with 129 features*

Significant improvement in task-wise results is observed after feature selec-tion is applied in both scenarios i.e. offline features and online features. In case of

CNN-based offline visual features, we are able to achieve performance enhancement with relatively fewer features as compared to the original 4096-dimensional feature vector. Same is obtained in online features where original feature set of 97 is reduced to less than 20 in most cases. By employing feature selection, we are able to reduce dimensionality that can cause overfitting while training a traditional machine learning classifier. As a consequence, a surge in accuracies is observed across all tasks. It was deduced that Genetic Algorithm produced more optimal results in relation to correlation, hence we employ GA in our proposed methodology as well.

4.3   Impact of Feature Fusion Versus Decision Fusion

Our last set of experiments is performed to assess the impact of feature fusion (i.e. combining both online and offline features extracted from each task and using them to train a single task-specific classifier) and decision fusion (i.e. combining the scores of two classifiers trained on online and offline features independently). As hypothesized earlier, decision fusion outperformed feature fusion in across all tasks as shown in Table 5. Furthermore, by combining decisions from each task-wise classifier using majority voting, we are able to achieve an overall accuracy of 98.25%.

Table 5. Task-wise results obtained by feature fusion and decision fusion

Task	Feature fusion Accuracy	Task-wise decision fusion Accuracy
Archimedean Spiral	80%	95.96%
Repetitive (l)	86%	97.75%
Repetitive (le)	87%	92.25%
Repetitive (les)	71%	91.11%
Word (lektorka)	84%	94.44%
Word (porovnat)	87%	92%
Word (nepopadnout)	71%	93.75%
Sentence	89%	93.17%
Sample-wise decision fusion	**92%**	**98.25%**

To further, establish the viability of the proposed model, we compare task-wise results with the popular studies employing the same dataset in Table 6. While comparing, it is ensured that same evaluation metric (mean accuracies) and experimental protocol (10-fold cross validation) are considered. Authors in [20] and [11], employed several dynamic spatio-temporal, pressure and kinematic features to train a number of machine learning-based classifiers. On the other hand, authors in [7], extracted CNN-based static features from images generated by plotting the temporal and in-air movement information provided in the PaHaW dataset. Authors in [16] rely on one-dimensional convolutions to extract meaningful patterns from handwriting samples of PD patients and then use these to train a network of stacked bidirectional Gated Recurrent Units (GPUs). Since different classifiers reported different accuracies across all tasks in each study, therefore, we selected the best task-wise results of each study for comparison. It can be seen that our proposed approach of feature relevance and decision fusion outperforms several baseline studies on this problem for each of the eight tasks in the PaHaW database.

Table 6. Performance comparison with the state-of-the-art using PaHaW

Task	Impedevo et al. [11]	Angelilo et al. [20]	Diaz et al. [7]	Moetesum et al. [16]	Diaz et al. [17]	Proposed technique
Task 1	54.67%	53.75%	75.00%	89.64%	93.75%	95.96%
Task 2	61.80%	67.08%	64.16%	75.00%	96.25%	97.75%
Task 3	72.28%	62.50%	58.33%	73.75%	88.75%	92.25%
Task 4	55.28%	57.91%	71.67%	72.32%	90.00%	91.11%
Task 5	59.80%	54.58%	75.41%	79.46%	93.75%	94.44%
Task 6	63.71%	56.75%	63.75%	74.46%	91.25%	92.00%
Task 7	60.98%	61.67%	70.00%	79.28%	92.50%	93.75%
Task 8	71.95%	70.40%	67.08%	81.42%	92.50%	93.17%

5   Conclusion

The potential for handwriting features to indicate Parkinson's disease is discussed in this study. The literature has looked at both online and offline features, however, in our study, we used a combination of online and offline features and extracted a set of features that performed better on a specific task template. This study does not deny previous research on online and offline features; rather, it enhances the expertise and demonstrated the utility of both online and offline features. We explore two popular feature relevance techniques to select the most optimal subset of offline and online features. We evaluated our proposed methodology using a benchmark dataset (PaHaW) and observed that our proposed system reports an overall accuracy of 98.25% when we combine the decisions of all task-wise classifiers. In conclusion, we have demonstrated that such a method could be beneficial to clinicians in the diagnosis of Parkinson's disease since it allows them to select the most important features for detecting and diagnosing PD and, as a result, develop a set of guidelines for defining fresh testing protocols.

References

1. Tucker, C., et al.: A data mining methodology for predicting early stage Parkinson's disease using non-invasive, high-dimensional gait sensor data. IIE Trans. Healthcare Syst. Eng. 5(4), 238–254 (2015)

2. Naranjo, L., Perez, C.J., Campos-Roca, Y., Martin, J.: Addressing voice recording replications for Parkinson's disease detection. Expert Syst. Appl. **46**, 286–292 (2016)
3. Jeancolas, L., et al.: X-vectors: new quantitative biomarkers for early Parkinson's disease detection from speech. Front. Neuroinform. **15**, 4 (2021)
4. Karaman, O., Çakın, H., Alhudhaif, A., Polat, K.: Robust automated parkinson disease detection based on voice signals with transfer learning. Expert Syst. Appl. **178**, 115013 (2021)
5. Drotár, P., Mekyska, J., Rektorová, I., Masarová, L., Smékal, Z., Faundez-Zanuy, M.: Analysis of in-air movement in handwriting: a novel marker for Parkinson's disease. Comput. Meth. Progr. Biomed. **117**(3), 405–411 (2014)
6. Moetesum, M., Siddiqi, I., Vincent, N., Cloppet, F.: Assessing visual attributes of handwriting for prediction of neurological disorders–a case study on Parkinson's disease. Pattern Recogn. Lett. **121**, 19–27 (2019)
7. Diaz, M., Ferrer, M.A., Impedovo, D., Pirlo, G., Vessio, G.: Dynamically enhanced static handwriting representation for Parkinson's disease detection. Pattern Recogn. Lett. **128**, 204–210 (2019)
8. Pereira, C.R., et al.: A step towards the automated diagnosis of Parkinson's disease: analyzing handwriting movements. In: 2015 IEEE 28th International Symposium on Computer-based Medical Systems, pp. 171–176 (2015)
9. Khatamino, P., Cantürk, İ., Özyılmaz, L.: A deep learning-CNN based system for medical diagnosis: an application on Parkinson's disease handwriting drawings. In: 2018 6th International Conference on Control Engineering & Information Technology (CEIT), pp. 1–6. IEEE (2018)
10. Drotár, P., Mekyska, J., Smékal, Z., Rektorová, I., Masarová, L., Faundez-Zanuy, M.: Contribution of different handwriting modalities to differential diagnosis of Parkinson's disease. In: Proceedings of 2015 IEEE International Symposium on Medical Measurements and Applications (MeMeA), pp. 344–348. IEEE (2015)
11. Impedovo, D., Pirlo, G., Vessio, G.: Dynamic handwriting analysis for supporting earlier Parkinson's disease diagnosis. Information **9**(10), 247 (2018)
12. Drotár, P.: Decision support framework for Parkinson's disease based on novel handwriting markers. IEEE Trans. Neural Syst. Rehabil. Eng. **23**(3), 508–516 (2014)
13. Drotár, P., Mekyska, J., Rektorová, I., Masarová, L., Smékal, Z., Faundez-Zanuy, M.: Evaluation of handwriting kinematics and pressure for differential diagnosis of Parkinson's disease. Artif. Intell. Med. **67**, 39–46 (2016)
14. Mucha, J., et al.: Identification and monitoring of Parkinson's disease dysgraphia based on fractional-order derivatives of online handwriting. Appl. Sci. **8**(12), 2566 (2018)
15. Pereira, C.R., Weber, S.A., Hook, C., Rosa, G.H., Papa, J.P.: Deep learning-aided Parkinson's disease diagnosis from handwritten dynamics. In: 2016 29th SIBGRAPI Conference on Graphics, Patterns and Images (SIBGRAPI), pp. 340–346. IEEE (2016)
16. Moetesum, M., Siddiqi, I., Javed, F., Masroor, U.: Dynamic handwriting analysis for Parkinson's disease identification using c-bigru model. In: 2020 17th International Conference on Frontiers in Handwriting Recognition (ICFHR), pp. 115–120. IEEE (2020)
17. Diaz, M., Moetesum, M., Siddiqi, I., Vessio, G.: Sequence-based dynamic handwriting analysis for Parkinson's disease detection with one-dimensional convolutions and bigrus. Expert Syst. Appl. **168**, 114405 (2021)

18. Vásquez-Correa, J.C.: Multimodal assessment of Parkinson's disease: a deep learning approach. IEEE J. Biomed. Health Inform. **23**(4), 1618–1630 (2018)

19. Pham, H.N., et al.: Multimodal detection of Parkinson disease based on vocal and improved spiral test. In: 2019 International Conference on System Science and Engineering (ICSSE), pp. 279–284. IEEE (2019)

20. Angelillo, M.T., Impedovo, D., Pirlo, G., Vessio, G.: Performance-driven handwriting task selection for Parkinson's disease classification. In: Alviano, M., Greco, G., Scarcello, F. (eds.) AI*IA 2019. LNCS (LNAI), vol. 11946, pp. 281–293. Springer, Cham (2019). https://doi.org/10.1007/978-3-030-35166-3_20

21. Man, J.H., Groenink, L., Caiazzo, M.: Cell reprogramming approaches in gene-and cell-based therapies for Parkinson's disease. J. Controlled Release **286**, 114–124 (2018)

22. Rosenblum, S., Samuel, M., Zlotnik, S., Erikh, I., Schlesinger, I.: Handwriting as an objective tool for Parkinson's disease diagnosis. J. Neurol. **260**(9), 2357–2361 (2013)

23. Rosenblum, S., Livneh-Zirinski, M.: Handwriting process and product characteristics of children diagnosed with developmental coordination disorder. Hum. Mov. Sci. **27**(2), 200–214 (2008)

24. Pereira, C.R., et al.: A new computer vision-based approach to aid the diagnosis of Parkinson's disease. Comput. Meth. Prog. Biomed. **136**, 79–88 (2016)

25. Palmerini, L., Rocchi, L., Mellone, S., Valzania, F., Chiari, L.: Feature selection for accelerometer-based posture analysis in Parkinson's disease. IEEE Trans. Inf. Technol. Biomed. **15**(3), 481–490 (2011)

26. Senatore, R., Della Cioppa, A., Marcelli, A.: Automatic diagnosis of neurodegenerative diseases: an evolutionary approach for facing the interpretability problem. Information **10**(1), 30 (2019)

27. Ribeiro, L.C., Afonso, L.C., Papa, J.P.: Bag of samplings for computer-assisted Parkinson's disease diagnosis based on recurrent neural networks. Comput. Biol. Med. **115**, 103477 (2019)

28. Gupta, J.D., Chanda, B.: Novel features for diagnosis of Parkinson's disease from off-line archimedean spiral images. In: 2019 IEEE 10th International Conference on Awareness Science and Technology (iCAST), pp. 1–6. IEEE (2019)

29. Ammour, A., Aouraghe, I., Khaissidi, G., Mrabti, M., Aboulem, G., Belahsen, F.: A new semi-supervised approach for characterizing the Arabic on-line handwriting of Parkinson's disease patients. Comput. Meth. Programs Biomed. **183**, 104979 (2020)

30. Siddiqi, I., Khurshid, K., Vincent, N.: Feature relevance analysis for writer identification. In: Document Recognition and Retrieval XVIII, vol. 7874, p. 78740 (2011). International Society for Optics and Photonics

EEG Based Major Depressive Disorder (MDD) Detection Using Machine Learning

Nayab Bashir$^{(\boxtimes)}$, Sanam Narejo, Bushra Naz, and Asif Ali

Mehran University of Engineering and Technology, Jamshoro, Pakistan
nabybashir@gmail.com

Abstract. Major Depressive Disorder (MDD), is a malady which has perturbed many around the globe. It has become a gigantic health concern for this world and economic burden globally. Traditionally, the clinicians use plethora of treatments to slow down the progression of this disease at early stage. This paper intent to better diagnose the depression; by transforming the Electroencephalogram (EEG) signals while using machine learning and deep learning technique. EEGs of 30 healthy and 34 Major Depressive Disorder (MDD) subjects were analyzed in this study. New features were generated from the preprocessed data and later various classifiers were used to predict the results. The finest accuracy of machine learning algorithm was acquired by K-nearest neighbors (KNN) which were 0.997; Decision tree (DT) acquired an accuracy of 0.984, Support vector machine (SVM) showed 0.957 accuracy while Naïve Bayes (NB) had an accuracy of 0.522. The proposed Deep Learning method which was convolutional neural network (CNN) resulted in the accuracy of 0.996. With these promising results this study proves a feasibility of EEG based Major Depressive Disorder diagnosis.

Keywords: Major depressive disorder · Electroencephalogram · Deep learning · Machine learning · K-nearest neighbors · Decision tree · Support vector machine · Naïve Bayes and Convolutional Neural Network

1 Introduction

The Major Depressive Disorder is a cognitive disorder which has become a widespread disease globally among every group of age. There are multiple symptoms which are pure depiction of MDD, including feel of being distressed, loss of intrigue, hyper insomnia or insomnia, weight gain or drop, fragile cognitive skills, being devitalized, psychomotor retardation, feeling of worthlessness and unnecessary guilt. If these symptoms persist for a longer duration and remain untreated they can disable a person mentally with severe conditions. The causes of MDD are known to be genetic, psychological factors or environmental. The risk factors which can expedite depression involve the family history, biochemical predisposition, chronic health problems and major life changes or trauma.

C. Djeddi et al. (Eds.): MedPRAI 2021, CCIS 1543, pp. 172–183, 2022.
https://doi.org/10.1007/978-3-031-04112-9_13

The mental state of human can be interpreted with the help of brain signals. These brain signals can be collected by invasive and non-invasive procedures. Proper decoding of brain signals can help to improve the lifestyle of an individual by recognizing the physiological and psychological status of brain. Multiple mental disorders such as depression, epilepsy and Alzheimer's disorder can be diagnosed by electroencephalogram (EEG) signals [1]. These brain signals enable to observe the brain activity in real time in fraction of milliseconds, is a powerful tool due to enhanced temporal resolution, noninvasive technique unlike electro-corticogram (ECoG) and deep brain stimulation (DBS), ease of set up and being affordable. The MDD subjects have shown malformed functional connections in the temporal and frontal lobes among different scalp regions when compared with healthy subjects [2]. According to the literature the analysis of connectivity between different scalp regions might be propitious marker for depression [3–5]. The diagnosis of MDD from resting state EEG signals has reached to the bottleneck, in order to cope with this limitation this study shows the diagnosis of depression from resting and non-resting EEG signals where the subjects are performing a cognitive task. The recent studies reveal that the size of specific brain regions can reduce in people who experience depression and hence affecting the brain activity of a person. The debate and research continues to know that how much shrinkage occurs due to depression [6]. In Fig. 1 and 2 it is evident from the EEG signals taken from the dataset that the depressed person has a reduced brain activity as compared to a healthy person. A bio signals viewing application SigViewer is used to observe the EEG signals of the subjects from the dataset used in this study.

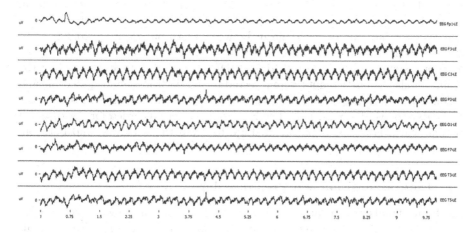

Fig. 1. Shows the EEG signals of a healthy person acquired from the 8 channels covering the frontal, central, parietal, occipital and temporal regions of brain for 10 s while performing a decision making task.

174   N. Bashir et al.

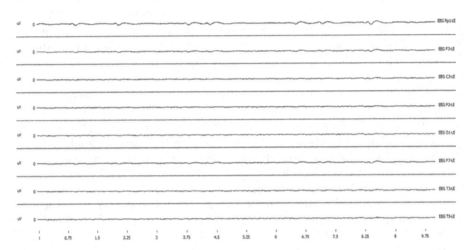

Fig. 2. Shows the EEG signals of a MDD person acquired from the 8 channels covering the frontal, central, parietal, occipital and temporal regions of brain for 10 s while performing a decision making task.

2 Material and Methods

2.1 Participants

This study is carried on the dataset which has an open access and provided by Mumtaz [7]. The committee for ethics at Hospital University Sains Malaysia accepted the procedure. EEG signals of 30 normal individuals with age in between 22 to 53 (mean = 38.3 ± 15.6) were recorded and 34 major depressive disorder individuals with age in between 27 to 53 (mean = 40.3 ± 12.9) was also achieved. The diagnostic criteria for unipolar depression without any psychotic symptoms were qualified by MDD individuals. Before recording the brain signals the participants were directed to refrain from caffeine, nicotine and alcohol. The data acquisition for each participant was performed at same time of the day to avoid any mishap. The EEG signals were recorded for a short span of time which is 5 min, which was helpful to avoid the sleepiness and boredom of the participants.

2.2 Data Acquisition and Preprocessing

The brain signals were acquired by placing an EEG cap on the scalp by following the international 10–20 standard electrode position system. The EEG signals were recorded for 5 min in different states; eyes open (EO), eyes closed (EC) and while performing a cognitive task (P300). The P300 task is basically an event related potential which is drawn out in decision making process. Its occurrence is linked to the person's response to it rather than the physical attributes of the stimulus because it is an endogenous potential. The electrodes attached to the scalp covering all four lobes comprised of Temporal (T3, T4, T5, T6), frontal

(Fp1, Fp2, F3, F4, F7, F8, Fpz), occipital (O1, O2), parietal (P3, P4, P7, P8) and central (C3, C4). A reference electrode (LE) was linked to ear and EEG data was re-referenced to infinity reference (IR) for further EEG analysis [8] . The reference electrode basically establishes the electrode potential and is used in influencing the amplitude at every EEG channel and a particular time point. The zero voltage level is defined by the reference electrode and then rest of the channels is expressed in relation to the reference electrode. EEG signals are one of the most complex and chaotic signals. The noise in these signals can be a result of muscle artifacts or EMG signals, cardiac signals or ECG, eyeball movements EOG or interference with some other device. For the achievement of accurate results in the feature generation and classification models, all the raw EEG data is to be denoised initially. A series of filters is designed to remove the noise. In order to remove these artifacts the sampling frequency of the EEG signals was adjusted 256 Hz. Later to denoise power line 50 Hz a Notch filter was applied. All the weak signals were enhanced by using an amplifier simultaneously. All the EEG signals from each channel (22 channels) and each state (EO, EC and TASK) with the cutoff frequencies of 0.1 Hz 70 Hz were band-pass filtered in order to completely preprocess them.

2.3   New Feature Generation

The EEG signals exhibit feeble, nonlinear, and characteristics sensitive to time, which display complex dynamics. The EEG features change with the state of emotional transformation. The EEG features are mainly divided into linear and non-linear features. The feature extraction and new feature formation is the crucial part of this study. In the proposed study all the 22 features (linear and non-linear) are extracted from each channel that are EEG signals recorded from the scalp. EEG signals acquired from 22 channels of 64 subjects in three different states summed up to be 4224 brain signals. In order to analyze and evaluate all these brain signals the features extracted are linear and nonlinear both. Then an extra column for Data Type is added to the features, data type represented eyes open (EO), Eyes Closed (EO) and Decision Making Task (TASK) respectively. Later, another column for class label is also added that corresponds to normal subject or Major Depressive Disorder (MDD) subject. The mentioned columns were merged with the features. Then the features received in total were high in number having approximately 18 million rows. Then the rows with nan or infinite values were removed to get the preferred features only. After removing these missing or null values from the total features there were 12.9 million rows left, these constituted our desired features. In the end standard scaling is applied to scale and prepare the signals for the application of multiple classifiers.

3   Proposed Machine Learning Methods

Figure 3 shows an overview of the proposed ML method involving EEG preprocessing, feature extraction, new feature formation and classification through various models. The Machine learning classifiers used in this study are K-Nearest

Neighbors (KNN), Decision Tree (DT), Support Vector Machine (SVM) and Naive Bayes (NB). The preprocessing leads to feature extraction and then new feature generation where the phenomenon of scaling is performed and lastly the classifiers are fed with desired features for detecting depressed and normal subjects.

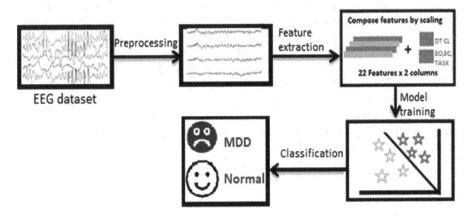

Fig. 3. Illustrates the block diagram of the proposed ML methodology summarizing the entire work.

3.1 K-Nearest Neighbors

KNN is the classifier which is robust to outliers and noisy instances as EEG signals and that is why it was used for the EEG data analysis. KNN is known to be a simple classifier and based on distance function; they utilize distances to determine similarity between two data points. The test sample found is then allocated to the most frequent particular class amongst the k nearest training data [9]. Only an integer value and a metric are required to calculate the closeness in this distance based algorithm.

3.2 Decision Tree

A supervised classification model which is tree structure based [10], described by the use of various rules and interpreting a local model, isolating and segregating a feature space, and later categorizing that feature space as clusters; binary or multiclass. Property is represented by each internal node, result is presented by edge and each leaf is a symbol of class label. The decision tree is one of the fastest classification models as compared to the rest of classification models. In the recent years classification of Alzheimer's disease has been done by DT along with depression [11].

3.3 Support Vector Machine

SVM is a supervised ML model and regression method which was proposed by Cortes and Vapnik in the year 1995. The distinctive benefits this model exhibits to cope with the matters of nonlinear data, high-dimensional pattern recognition and small sample data is exceptional [12]. A hyperplane is built on an infinite dimensional space by this machine learning model for classification and regression purpose. SVM model is being applied more often in the field of depression discrimination in the recent years [13].

3.4 Naïve Bayes

On the contrary Naive Bayes classifier (John and Langley 1995) is a maximum a posteriori classifier which assumes a powerful independence between the features. Along with that it yields the class with elevated probability with values given to the noted features. The posterior probability which is thought to be independent and also constrained by a group of features is measured using the Bayes' theorem [14]. The feature scaling is applied on the features extracted to analyze the effects of scaling on above mentioned ML classifiers.

4 Proposed Deep Learning Method

Convolutional neural networks (CNN) consist of stacked convolutional layers. Fig 4 shows the architecture of CNN used in this study. It comprises of convolutional layers, pooling layers and fully connected layers.

- In the convolutional layer a particular filter performs linear transformation on the data and important features are extracted. In the training phase, the coefficients of used filter are updated depending on the error back propagation to attain the most prominent features. Based on the input characteristics, the filters have differed length, stride, count and size of padding.
- The pooling layers reduce the dimensionality and have fixed number of kernels and stride. The overfitting is prevented by reduction of parameters.
- The fully connected layer sums up all the features by allowing the non-linear summation of features which are to be used to maximize discrimination.

The proposed model comprises of two 1D convolutional layers, one flatten layer and two dense layers. The relu activation function is used on the hidden layers whereas softmax is used on the output layer with a batch size of 32 for input and 64 for output. The filter size used for the input layer is 32, for hidden layer is 64 and output layer is 1. The CNN model was developed using Tensorflow. For enhanced accuracy and reduction of losses the optimizer opted for the proposed model is Rmsprop. As learning rate is considered to be most important hyperparameters, the optimal learning rate was achieved by Keras deep learning library. The performance improvement was calculated in multiple training epochs simultaneously inflating the learning rate by minute factor to

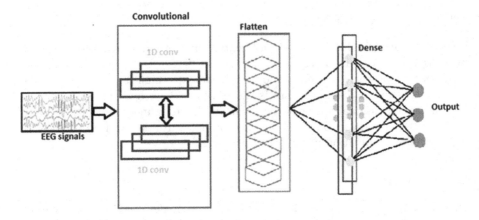

Fig. 4. Shows the block diagram of proposed deep learning method.

finally reaching the value of 0.1. The parameters which are set in the proposed model of CNN are shown in the Table 1 By applying nested cross validation on the training set these parameters were evaluated. Various techniques such as batch processing, dropout, nested cross-validation and balanced training were applied to optimize the model and prevent the phenomenon of overfitting. The number of 80% and 20% of the data were set for the training and validation of the classifier. Figure 5 a and b exhibits the loss and accuracy for the proposed model. It is evident from the figure that training loss and training accuracy continue to improve illustrating less training error versus more accuracy, on the contrary the validation loss and validation accuracy impedes after few iterations.

5   Validation of Classification Models

The confusion matrix which calculated the performance metrics are elaborated by Eqs. 1–3. The percentage of true negative cases (tn) which are rightly classified as negative cases denotes the specificity of a classification model as described by Eq. 1. The percentage of true positive cases (tp) which are accurately sorted as cases defined by Eq. 2 correlates to the sensitivity of a classification model. The percentage of precisely sorted positive cases and negative cases refers to the accuracy of classification model as illustrated in Eq. 3. While both the fp and fn in the confusion matrix, are supposed to be type-1 and type-2 errors. Specifically, the fp abbreviates for false positive, which means a MDD subject is erroneously identified as a healthy subject. Whereas fn identifies a healthy person as depressed subject. Displayed equations are centered and set on a separate line.

$$specificity = tn/(tn + fp) \qquad (1)$$

$$sensitivity = tp/(tp + fn) \qquad (2)$$

$$accuracy = (tp + tn)/(tp + tn + fp + fn) \qquad (3)$$

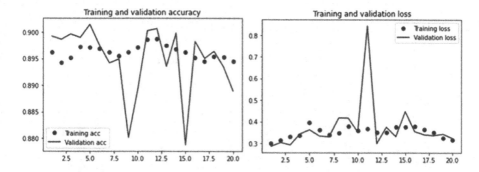

Fig. 5. (a) and (b) illustrate the training and validation accuracy plus training and validation loss with 20 numbers of epochs.

Table 1. Parameter table for CNN model

Parameters	Values
Batch size	32 for input 64 for output
Optimizer	Rmsprop
Learning rate	0.1
Stride	1
Epochs	20
Filter size	32 for input 64 for hidden and 1 for output
Loss function	Binary crossentropy

6   Results

Initially, the performances of classification algorithms were evaluated for all the feature vectors used. Four ML classifiers were chosen: k-nearest neighbors (KNN), Decision Tree (DT), Support Vector Machine (SVM) and Naïve Bayes (NB).The parameters used for the classifiers were set to the default parameters in sklearn. Overfitting did not occur due to cross-validation, removal of unrequired features and training of more percentage of data. The accuracy, specificity and sensitivity of the models are presented in Fig. 6. It is very evident that the best accuracy is 0.997 using KNN model, Decision tree (DT) acquired an accuracy of 0.984, and Support vector machine (SVM) showed 0.957 accuracy; more than 90 of classification performance is achieved for all three attributes of specificity, sensitivity and accuracy for the three ML models. On the contrary it can be seen that NB achieved the least accuracy of 0.522. The distance based algorithms such as K-means, Support vector machine (SVM) and KNN are highly affected by the scaling of features as they use the distances to compute the similarity between the data points. Whereas Naïve Bayes algorithm is information based algorithm which is least affected by the scaling hence evident from the results achieved. The performances of all the classification models are presented in receiver

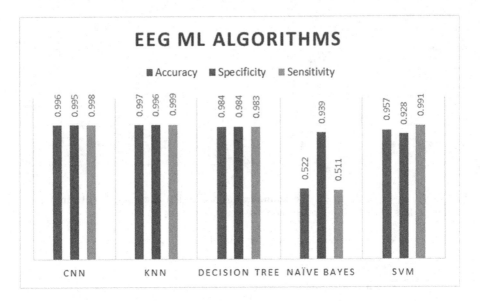

Fig. 6. Illustrates the achieved results by machine learning and deep learning models, with the accuracy, specificity and sensitivity computed by the proposed method.

operating characteristic curve (ROC) true positive rate and false positive rate are the parameters plotted and shown in Fig. 7. Later, a deep learning architecture is designed to evaluate the brain signals of normal and MDD subjects. More than 90 of classification performance is achieved for all three attributes of specificity, sensitivity and accuracy. The CNN model proposed performs exceptionally well with an accuracy of 0.996 as shown in the Fig. 6.

ROC curve

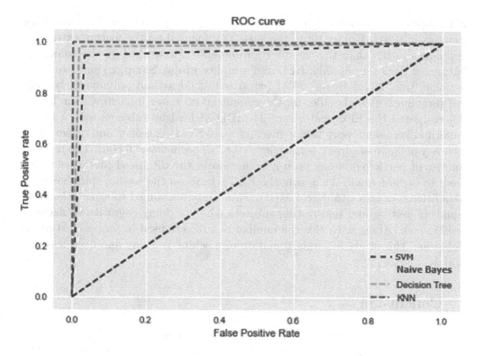

Fig. 7. Shows the ROC curve of the models proposed.

7 Discussion

Ahmadlou in 2012 [15] had worked on 12 normal and 12 depressed subjects in resting state while using an Enhanced- PNN model he preprocessed the data by Wavelets and Fourier transform (spectral bands) and worked on the non-linear features of EEG signals extracted from the beta band only. He also concluded that the MDD and normal subjects can be differentiated better in the beta band rather than alpha band which opposed the previous studies. He achieved an accuracy of 0.913 for his proposed work. EEG feature extractor named kernel eigen-filter-bank common spatial pattern (KEFB-CSP) was developed by Liao in the year 2017 [16], he used SVM classifier to differentiate 20 normal and 20 depressed subjects and EEG signals were obtained from all the 5 bands (alpha, beta, gamma, delta and theta), which achieved an accuracy of 0.812 in the same year Batchman [17] analyzed the linear and non-linear features of EEG signals of EEG signals; higuchi's fractal dimension (HFD), detrended fluctuation analysis DFA and Spectral asymmetry index (SASI) and preprocessed the data by Fourier transform. The EEG signals of 13 depressed and 13 normal controls were analyzed by applying Logistic Regression (LR) and achieved the accuracy of 0.85. In the year 2019 Xiaowei Li [18] analyzed the EEG signals of 14 MDD 14 normal subjects in resting state and used different feature generation strategies and proposed a convolutional neural network (CNN) model and acquired the accuracy of 0.847. Cukic [19] in the year 2020 focused on the feature extraction techniques rather than the classification methods. He worked on the non-linear features of EEG signals only; HFD and sample entropy (SampEn) and later used Decision Tree, Naïve Bayes, SVM (consisted of linear and polynomial kernel), and Random Forest classifier for the classification. Later in 2020, Chien-Te Wu [20] evaluated the EEG features of 24 MDD 31 healthy subjects with a model conformal kernel support vector machine (CK-SVM) classifier and achieved an accuracy of 0.836 accuracy, sensitivity = 0.875, specificity = 0.806). The reduced number of participants has been a limitation in the discussed literature which needs to be addressed. Analyzing the EEG signals on the resting state has been a traditional practice to detect MDD. This study has aimed to screen the EEG signals of resting and non-resting subjects who are doing cognitive or decision making task. Along with this the number of subjects used in proposed study is higher and this study has amalgamation of machine learning and deep learning models.

8   Conclusion

MDD can result in change of brain dynamics which is revealed by the EEG signals. Therefore a comprehensive study was done on EEG signals to detect depression using deep learning and machine learning models. The finest accuracy of 0.997 and 0.996 in classifying Major depressive disorder and healthy subjects was achieved by K-nearest neighbors and convolutional neural networks. Whereas Decision tree (DT) acquired an accuracy of 0.984, Support vector machine (SVM) showed 0.957 accuracy while Naïve Bayes (NB) had least accuracy of 0.522. The inflated values of specificities may intimate that the proposed method of work could be used for clinical applications. For avoiding the complications in the model selection of minimum number of features is encouraged as it will help in the simple interpretation; resulting in less computational burden of system which is to be commercialized. So, the proposed method to diagnose the depressed patients from healthy subjects can aid the medical care experts for early intervention and prevention of this detestable disease.

References

1. Abásolo, D., Escudero, J., Hornero, R., Gómez, C., Espino, P.: Approximate en- tropy and auto mutual information analysis of the electroencephalogram in Alzheimer's disease patients. Med. Biol. Eng. Comput. 46(10), 1019–1028 (2008)
2. Olbrich, S., Tränkner, A., Chittka, T., Hegerl, U.: Schönknecht P Functional connectivity in major depression: increased phase synchronization between frontal cortical EEG-source estimates. Psychiatry Res. Neuroimaging 222, 91–99 (2014)
3. Anand, A., et al.: Activity and connectivity of brain mood regulating circuit in depression: a functional magnetic resonance study. Psychiatry 57, 1079–1088 (2005)

4. Bae, J.N., MacFall, J.R., Krishnan, K.R.R., Payne, M.E., Steffens, D.C.: Taylor WD Dorsolateral prefrontal cortex and anterior cingulate cortex white matter alterations in late-life depression. Biol. Psychiatry **60**, 1356–1363 (2006)
5. Fingelkurts, A.A., Fingelkurts, A.A., Rytsälä, H., Suominen, K., Isometsä, E.: Kähkönen S Impaired functional connectivity at EEG alpha and theta frequency bands in major depression. Hum. Brain Mapp. **28**, 247–261 (2007)
6. Zhang, F.-F., et al.: Brain structure alterations in depression: psychoradiological evidence. CNS Neurosci. Ther. **24**(11), 994–1003 (2018)
7. Mumtaz, W., Xia, L.K., Ali, S.S.A., Yasin, M.A.M., Hussain, M., Malik, A.S.: Electroencephalogram (EEG)-based computer-aided technique to diagnose major depressive disorder (MDD). Biomed. Sign. Process. Control **31**, 108–115 (2017)
8. Qin, Y., Xu, P., Yao, D.: A comparative study of different references for EEG default mode network: the use of the infinity reference. Clin. Neurophysiol. **121**, 1981–1991 (2010)
9. Webb, S.P.: Recognition. Oxford University Press Inc, New York (1999)
10. Hansen, M., Dubayah, R., Defries, R.: Classification trees: an alternative to traditional land cover classifiers. Inte. J. Remote Sens. **17**(5), 1075–1081 (1996)
11. Acharya, U.R., Sudarshan, V.K., Adeli, H., et al.: A novel depression diagnosis index using nonlinear features in EEG signals. Europ. Neurol. **74**(1–2), 79–83 (2016)
12. Hearst, M., Dumais, S., Osman, E., Platt, J., Scholkopf, B.: Support vector machines. IEEE Intell. Syst. Appl. **13**(4), 18–28 (1998)
13. Faust, O., Ang, P.C.A., Puthankattil, S.D., Joseph, P.K.: Depression diagnosis support system based on EEG signal entropies. J. Mech. Med. Biol. **14**(3), 1450035 (2014)
14. Witten, I.H., Frank, E.: Data Mining: Practical Learning Tools and Techniques, 2nd edn. Elsevier, Amsterdam, pp. 90–97 (2005)
15. Ahmadlou, M., Adeli, H., Adeli, A.: Fractality analysis of frontal brain in major depressive disorder. Int. J. Psychophysiol. **85**, 206–211(2012)
16. Liao, S.C., Wu, C.T., Huang, H.C., Cheng, W.T.: Major depression detection from EEG signals using kernel eigen-filter-bank common spatial patterns. Sensors **17**(6), 1385 (2017)
17. Bachmann, M., et al.: Methods for classifying depression in single channel EEG using linear and nonlinear signal analysis. Comput. Meth. Prog. Biomed. **155**, 11–17 (2018)
18. Lia, X., Zhanga, X., Zhua, J., Maoa, W.: Shuting Suna. Depression recognition using machine learning methods with different feature generation strategies, China (2019)
19. Čukić, M., Stokić, M., Simić, S., Pokrajac, D.: The successful discrimination of depression from EEG could be attributed to proper feature extraction and not to a particular classification method. Cogn. Neurodyn. **14**(4), 443–455 (2020). https://doi.org/10.1007/s11571-020-09581-x
20. Wu, C.-T., Dillon, D.G., Hsu, H.-C.: Depression detection using relative EEG power induced by emotionally positive images and a support vector machine. Appl. Sci. **8**(8), 1244. Taiwan (2018)

Document Analysis and Understanding

Islamophobic Hate Speech Detection from Electronic Media Using Deep Learning

Qasim Mehmood[(✉)], Anum Kaleem, and Imran Siddiqi

Department of Computer Science, Bahria University, Islamabad 44000, Pakistan
01-249182-018@student.bahria.edu.pk,
{anumkleem.buic,imran.siddiqi}@bahria.edu.pk

Abstract. Islamophobic hate speech is the indiscriminate negative attitude and behavior towards Muslims and Islam. Speech indicating prejudice against Muslims has negatively impacted the perceptions of Islam. Online platforms like Twitter have carved out policies to stop users from promoting Islamophobic hate speech, however, such content still exists which causes problems for Muslim communities globally. Hence, it becomes pivotal to find solutions to eradicate such speech from social media platforms. This paper presents an effective methodology for Islamophobic hate speech identification in online tweets using deep learning techniques. The proposed technique relies on feature extraction using a one-dimensional Convolutional Neural Network and classification using Long Short-Term Memory network based classifier. The proposed technique is validated on a dataset comprising of 1290 pre-processed online tweets and an accuracy of more than 90% is reported.

Keywords: Hate speech · Islamophobia · Word embeddings · Convolution Neural Networks (CNN) · Bi-directional Long Short-Term Memory (LSTM)

1 Introduction

The history of hateful content on print and electronic media is spanned over many decades. Due to rapid growth of the Internet and the availability of low-cost devices, the number of social and electronic media users has increased tremendously in the recent past. A downside of this growth is the increase in conflicts, hate speech, cyber trolling and bullying. In this domain, several research studies have been carried out on recognition of hate speech including gender, racism, religion, color, disability and citizenship. Among these, the focus of our current research lies on hate speech identification and more specifically the Islamophobic hate speech. Islamophobia composed of the term 'Islam' with the postfix 'phobia', refers to the 'fear of Islam'. Multiple mediums of expression like text, audio, images or videos are commonly exploited to promote hate speech by online users.

© Springer Nature Switzerland AG 2022
C. Djeddi et al. (Eds.): MedPRAI 2021, CCIS 1543, pp. 187–200, 2022.
https://doi.org/10.1007/978-3-031-04112-9_14

Islamophobic content has resulted in biasness, discrimination, and exclusion of Muslims in societies from social, civic, and political life [1].

Hate speech in the form of tweets, posts, or articles has caused problems for inhabitants of Muslim communities living in the western countries, especially after the 9/11 attacks. According to the Runnymede trust in the United Kingdom, Islamophobia existed in premise before the September 11, 2001 incident, but after these terror attacks it has increased significantly. The Runnymede trust, also identified eight components of Islamophobia in a report published in 1997. A followup report was produced in 2004, which deduced that the aftermath of the terror attacks had made life more difficult for Muslims in the United Kingdom and other countries [2]. Moreover, the report also stated that it is almost impossible to stop the domino of Islamophobic statements from spreading over social media [3]. Hence, there is a strong need to develop tools and techniques to identify and classify derogatory hate speech against Muslims at large.

Though social media platforms like YouTube, Twitter and Facebook have established usage policies that forbid hate speech [4–6], still they fail to eradicate such content completely. It is therefore important to develop solutions that can automatically identify hate speech and suggest the required measures. Several research studies have been carried out on recognition of classical hate speech including gender [7–9] racism [10–12] and religion [13–15]. The literature is relatively limited when it comes to Islamophobic hate speech identification [16].

This paper presents an effective method for identification of Islamophobic hate speech from online tweets. The technique relies on converting the pre-processed tweets to word embeddings which are subsequently fed to one-dimensional convolutions. A bi-directional Long Short-Term Memory network (LSTM) is then employed for classification. The key highlights of this study are outlined in the following.

- An effective technique for identification of Islamophobic hate speech from online tweets is presented.
- A combination of 1D convolutions with Recurrent Neural Networks (RNN) is employed for feature learning and classification.
- A comprehensive experimental study is carried out using different variants of RNNs and the reported results validate the effectiveness of the proposed method.

The content of this paper is divided into five sections. Section 2 presents an overview of the relevant literature primarily focusing on the recent trends in this domain. Section 3 introduces the dataset, pre-processing and the details of the proposed methodology. Experimental results and the related discussion are detailed in Sect. 4 while Sect. 5 concludes this paper with a recall of our key findings.

2   Related Work

This section discusses some notable contributions to hate speech identification using pattern classification techniques. Formally, hate speech is defined as the *'negative speech against a person or members of groups identified by protected characteristics that express the speaker's emotions or feelings'* [17]. In general, the social media platforms (like Twitter) provide an open space to its users to share their views. While this freedom of speech has many positive and constructive aspects, it also propagates biasness or negativity, as a result of conflicts. Consequently, social and electronic media are being continuously used to attack people with hateful content. Due to huge volume of such content, naturally, human inspection to identify hate content is not practical and there is a need to have effective automatic analysis techniques which can identify hate speech so that corrective measures can be taken.

Studies indicate that a tweet's polarity is an important indicator of a potential hateful content [18]. Typically, the polarity is classified into three categories: clean, offensive, and hateful [19,20]. From the view point of methodology, identification of hate speech has been investigated using a variety of techniques. These include lexical, machine learning, hybrid and, deep learning-based approaches.

The lexical-based approaches rest on the idea that the most important part of classification task is to understand the lexical phrases. Such techniques were introduced in the early 1990s s for understanding semantic and grammatical patterns of a sentence [21]. Among these methods, a study by MacDonald et al. [22] presented feature extraction from text including patterns of language, grammar, manually created rules and domain base knowledge. Likewise, Ruwandika et al. [3] also employed a lexical approach for identification of hate speech. In [23], Gitari et al. presented a three step methodology for classification of hate speech. In the first step, a rule-based approach is used to detect the subject text. In the second step, a lexicon for hate speech is developed. These lexicon are used as features based on 'negative polarity words', 'hate verbs' and 'theme-based grammatical patterns'. These three types of features are used to classify text as hate speech. Though simple and intuitive, lexicon-based methods are not very robust in terms of performance.

Machine learning approaches are among the most popular techniques applied to classification of text in general and hate speech identification in particular. Among well-known studies, Davidson et al. [24] present a multi-class classifier to distinguish between hate speech, offensive language, and politically correct text. The authors employed logistic regression with L2 regularization to build a model, which produced effective results. In [16], Yasseri et al. presented a study to distinguish between Islamophobic and non-Islamophobic hate speech on tweets. The authors classify hate speech as weak or strong, for which they have created a text-only model using one-hot encoding. Secondly, they derived the non-text features which include sentiment polarity and count of swear words, speech parts, and named entities. For classification, six different methods are investigated. These include Naïve-Bayes, random forest, logistic regression, decision tree and Support Vector Machine (SVM). Among these, a multi-class SVM produced the most effective results. In another study, Sahi et al. [25] also proposed a model to automatically detect derogatory speech in online tweets. Among the investigated classifiers, authors concluded that Naïve Bayes and SVM outperform other methods.

Combination of multiple techniques (hybrid approaches) have also been employed for hate speech identification. Among such methods, Wester et al. [26] have proposed a hybrid of learning-based and lexical-based approaches for classification of hate speech. The authors used lexicon-based approach to extract complex syntactic and semantic features which are subsequently fed to a learning algorithm. Results suggest that this hybrid model produced better results as opposed to individual lexical and learning methods. In another work, Nagaraju et al. [27] employs a hybrid model for sentiment analysis on football specific tweets. The model uses a combination of Glove, CNN and LSTM for classification and reports promising results.

In the recent years, thanks to developments in different areas of neural networks and deep learning, end-to-end trainable features extractors and classifiers have been proposed [28]. In most cases, deep learning techniques [29] are fast replacing the handcrafted features with automated machine-learned features and classification. In one such study, Saksesi et al. [13], employs a dataset of 1235 tweets from Balai Bahasa of West Java province, Indonesia which were labeled for the binary classification task (hate speech or no hate speech). The technique relies on pre-processing the text and converting words in embeddings while classification was carried out using an LSTM. In the context of the current pandemic, Kumar et al. [30] implemented sentiment analysis on coronavirus public reviews. The authors employed Glove, CNN and bi-directional LSTM for classification of public views. Likewise, Vimali et al. [31] also employs LSTMs for text based sentiment analysis.

A critical review of the existing techniques on the problem of hate speech identification suggests that LSTMs have emerged as a popular choice of researchers in the recent years. While most of the existing techniques target sentiment analysis or identify hate speech in general, the specific problem of Islamophobic hate speech is relatively less explored and makes the subject of our study. The technique proposed in this regard is presented in the following section.

3   Methods

The proposed methodology to identify Islamophobic hate speech relies on a deep learning-based solution. The data is first pre-processed with key steps of case folding, tokenization, cleaning, stemming and removal of stop words. The pre-processed data is then converted to word embeddings using Word2Vec and the resulting sequence of vectors is fed to one-dimensional convolutional layers to extract meaningful features. A bi-directional Long Short-Term Memory network is subsequently employed for sequence modeling and classification. An overview of key processing steps is illustrated in Fig. 1 while the details of each of these steps along with the dataset employed in our study are presented in the following sections.

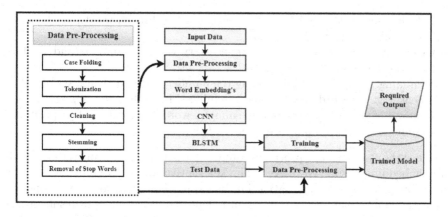

Fig. 1. An overview of key processing steps in the proposed method

3.1 Dataset

While several datasets have been developed for sentiment analysis and hate speech identification, to the best of our knowledge no public dataset is available that is specific to Islamophobic hate speech. Consequently, for the experimental study of our system, we collected multiple publicly available datasets of tweets and filtered out their subsets with purely Islamophobic hate speech content. Likewise, tweets related to Islam but without any hate content were also collected to serve as negative examples for model training. The data was labeled into positive ('1') and negative ('0') examples. We collected a total of 1290 tweets out of which 1032 were employed in the training and 258 in the test set. 10% of training data was employed for validation during the model training phase. A summary of the dataset is presented in Table 1.

Table 1. Statistics of the collected dataset

Total tweets		1290	
Negative tweets	566	Positive tweets	724
Training set	1032	Test set	258

3.2 Data Pre-processing

Data pre-processing is a typical task in text classification that includes cleaning the data and representing it in an appropriate form for further processing. In our study, data pre-processing includes case folding, tokenization, cleaning, stemming and removal of stop words (Fig. 2), as outlined in the following.

- Case Folding: is the conversion of all characters in the text to lower case letters.

- Tokenization: is the division of text stream into phrases, words, symbols etc. These units are termed as tokens.
- Cleaning: is the process to filter unnecessary words, characters and symbols from the text e.g. '@', 'RT', 'https://', '#' etc.
- Stemming: comprises of minimizing the number of different indexes of a document, e.g. the words 'useful' and 'usefulness' have the same semantic.
- Removal of stop words: the non-meaningful words comprising of prepositions, conjunctions, or pronouns are removed from text.

Once the standard pre-processing steps are carried out, we convert the words into embeddings using Word2Vec. The key motivation of an embedding representation is to exploit the relationship between different words (unlike one-hot encoding which treats each word as an independent entity). As a result of this process, each word in the pre-processed tweet is represented by a 300 dimensional vector.

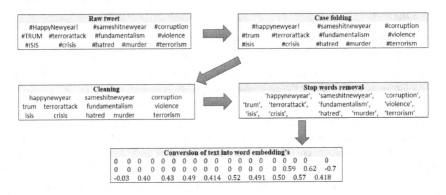

Fig. 2. An overview of pre-processing steps employed in our study

3.3 Feature Extraction and Classification

To identify tweets with Islamophobic hate speech, we propose a deep learning-based framework that combines feature extraction and classification in a single module. A combination of 1D Convolutional Neural Network with (different variants of) Recurrent Neural Network is employed for this purpose. The 1D convolutional layers extract robust hierarchical feature representations while the recurrent layers exploit the sequential information in the input tweets to categorize them into positive and negative examples.

From the view point of architectural details, the model comprises of seven convolutional layers with progressively increasing number of filters (from 32 to 512). All conv layers use the ReLU activation function while max pooling is employed to control the spatial dimension (which also prevents over-fitting). The conv layers are followed by a stack of two bi-directional LSTM layers with 64 and 128 hidden units respectively. LSTMs are preferred over simple RNNs due to their ability to model long-term dependencies in the input sequence. Likewise, the motivation of using bi-direction layers is to traverse the input sequence in both forward and backward directions hence exploiting the past as well as the future information to model the sequence. Finally, a single neuron at the output layer (with sigmoid activation function) is employed in the binary classification framework. A generalized overview of the C-BLSTM model is presented in Fig. 3 while the complete architecture of the model is summarized in Table 2. The total number of trainable parameters in the proposed model sums to 21,55,521.

4   Experimental Results and Analysis

To evaluate the effectiveness of the proposed technique, we carried out a comprehensive series of experiments. All experiments are carried out using the dataset distribution listed in Table 1 while the performance is quantified using classification accuracy.

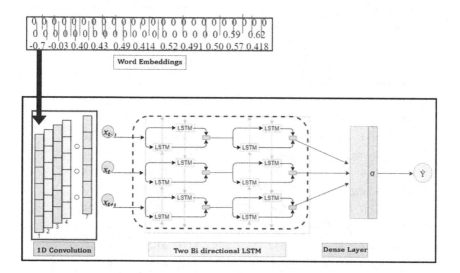

Fig. 3. General architecture of the model with 1D conv layers followed by bi-directional LSTM layers

In the first series of experiments, we directly feed the tweets (represented as embedding vectors) to different variants of RNNs without any convolutional layers to serve as the baseline results. We have employed the vanilla RNNs, GRUs and LSTMs both in single and bi-directional modes. The results of these experiments are summarized in Table 3 which allows drawing some interesting conclusions. In all cases, using bi-directional layers results in an enhanced classification accuracy as opposed the single-direction layers. This is very much natural as exploiting the future information in a sequence contributes to performance improvement. Among the different variants, LSTMs outperform GRUs and simple RNNs. Another interesting observation is that in most cases, the difference between the performance on the training and the test sets is not very high indicating that the model does not over-fit.

In the second series of experiments, we introduce convolutional layers to study the impact of feature learning from raw embeddings. The results of these experiments are presented in Table 4 where it can be seen that in all cases including the convolutional layers serves to significantly enhance the classification accuracy. The highest accuracy is reported by the combination of CNN with bi-directional LSTM reading 90.13%. A comparative overview of the results presented in Table 3 and Table 4 is also illustrated in Fig. 4 indicating the effectiveness learning robust representations through conv layers.

Table 2. Architectural details of proposed 1D CNN + BLSTM model

Layers	Filter size	No. of filters	Output shape	Parameters
Embedding	Vector Size = 300		(150, 300)	15,00,000
Conv1D 1	3	32	(150, 32)	28,832
MaxPooling1D (Pool Size = 2)			(75, 32)	0
Conv1D 2	3	64	(75, 64)	6,208
MaxPooling1D (Pool Size = 2)			(37, 64)	0
Conv1D 3	3	64	(37, 64)	12,352
MaxPooling1D (Pool Size = 2)			(18, 64)	0
Conv1D 4	3	128	(18, 128)	24,704
MaxPooling1D (Pool Size = 2)			(18, 128)	0
Conv1D 5	3	128	(18, 128)	49,280
MaxPooling1D (Pool Size = 2)			(18, 128)	0
Conv1D 6	3	256	(18, 256)	65,792
MaxPooling1D (Pool Size=2)			(18, 256)	0
Conv1D 7	3	512	(18, 512)	2,62,656
MaxPooling1D (Pool Size = 2)			(18, 512)	0
Bidirectional LSTM (Hidden Units: 64)			(18, 64)	1,39,520
Bidirectional LSTM (Hidden Units: 128)			(128)	66,048
Dense layer			(1)	129
Total parameters				21,55,521
Trainable parameters				21,55,521
Non-Trainable parameters				0

We also carried out a number of ablation studies to study the evolution of system performance as a function of number of training examples (Fig. 5), the number of layers in the convolutional (Fig. 6) and the recurrent (Fig. 7) parts of the model. The performance naturally improves with the increase in the number of training examples. Likewise, the performance varies with respect to the number of layers in the model but the variation is not very dramatic indicating the stability of the model.

Table 3. Classification performance with different variants of RNNs

Recurrent network	Training accuracy	Test accuracy
RNN	70.62	68.62
Bi-directional RNN	72.01	70.14
LSTM	74.11	71.58
Bi-directional LSTM	78.09	75.33
GRU	67.91	66.82
Bi-directional GRU	77.60	73.50

Table 4. Classification performance with convolutional and recurrent layers

Recurrent network	Training accuracy	Test accuracy
CNN + RNN	85.59	83.84
CNN + Bi-directional RNN	88.01	85.17
CNN + LSTM	89.11	86.82
CNN + Bi-directional LSTM	92.39	90.13
CNN + GRU	84.60	83.07
CNN + Bi-directional GRU	89.60	87.21

We also present a performance overview of known studies on this problem (Table 5). It is however important to mention that an objective comparison of different techniques is not possible as the reported methods have been evaluated on different datasets with different experimental protocol. The studies are listed with the motivation of providing readers with an idea on the current state-of-the-art on the problem of hate speech identification and the comparison is more of subjective rather than objective. An overall classification accuracy of more than 90% by our system is indeed quite promising.

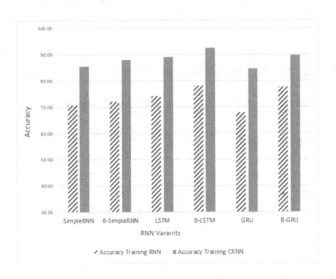

Fig. 4. Performance comparison of recurrent nets with raw embeddings and conv layers

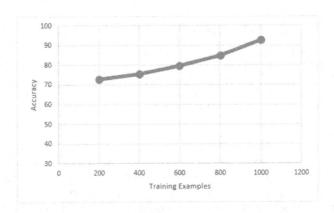

Fig. 5. Classification accuracy as a function of the number of training examples

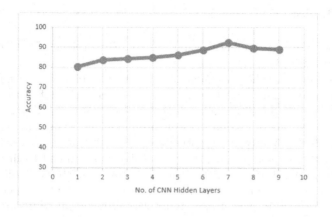

Fig. 6. Classification accuracy as a function of number of conv layers

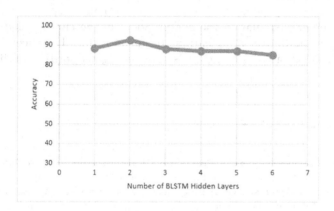

Fig. 7. Classification accuracy as a function of number of BLSTM layers

Table 5. Performance comparison with existing techniques

Reference	Classifier	Dataset	Results(%)
B. Vidgen 2019 [16]	Word Embeddings, gloVe Multi class SVM	4000 tweets	83.00
Y. Kim 2014 [32]	Word Embeddings, CNN	Online tweets	89.00
N.D.T. Ruwandika 2018 [3]	Naïve bayes Tf-idf	1080 tweets	71.90
A. Sucia Saksesi 2018 [13]	Word Embeddings, RNN	1235 tweets	88.00
Nagaraju Y. 2021 [27]	Glove, CNN, LSTM	10007 tweets	85.00
Proposed technique	Word Embeddings, CNN, Bi-directional LSTM	1290 tweets	90.13

5   Conclusion

Islamophobic hate speech identification is a complex problem due to challenges like context sensitive text and non-availability of standard datasets. In this paper, we have presented, an effective technique for classification of such hate speech from online tweets. The technique relies on learning robust feature representations from input tweets using a sequence of convolutional layers while bidirectional LSTMs are employed for sequence modeling. Experimental study on a dataset of nearly 1300 tweets reported a classification accuracy of 90.13%.

In our further exploration on the same subject, we intend to first enhance the size of the dataset and make the compiled data publicly available. Furthermore, in addition to a binary classification problem, specific hate speech classes can also be identified to pose it as a multi-class problem. In addition to tweets, the system can also be extended to identify such hate speech from articles and News. Another possible extension is to analyze the content of News and entertainment channels by generating audio transcriptions of spoken content and applying techniques similar to the one proposed in the current study. From a technical viewpoint, adversarial learning techniques which have been applied to the sentiment analysis problem, can also be investigated for the specific case of Islamophobic hate speech.

References

1. Shield for Muslims (31), 18 July 2021. https://shieldformuslims.wordpress.com/
2. Trust, R.: Islamophobia: a challenge for us all. Runnymede Trust UK **39**(11). www.runnymedetrust.org/uploads/publications/pdfs/islamophobia.pdf
3. Ruwandika, N., Weerasinghe, A.: Identification of hate speech in social media. In: 2018 18th International Conference on Advances in ICT for Emerging Regions (ICTer), pp. 273–278 (2018). IEEE
4. Inc, Y.: Youtube inc. youtube community guidelines [online]. Soc. Media Usage Policy **25**, 3389–3402 (2020)
5. Inc, T.: Twitter inc. the twitter rules [online]. Twitter Usage Policy **9**, 3389–3402 (2020)
6. Inc, F.: Facebook inc. facebook comment policy [online]. Facebook Usage Policy **6**, 3389–3402 (2020)
7. KhosraviNik, M., Esposito, E.: Online hate, digital discourse and critique: exploring digitally-mediated discursive practices of gender-based hostility. Lodz Pap. Pragmat. **14**(1), 45–68 (2018)
8. Weston-Scheuber, K.: Gender and the prohibition of hate speech. QUT Law Justice J. **12**(2), 132–50 (2012)
9. Cowan, G., Khatchadourian, D.: Empathy, ways of knowing, and interdependence as mediators of gender differences in attitudes toward hate speech and freedom of speech. Psychol. Women Q. **27**(4), 300–308 (2003)
10. Frías-Vázquez, M., Arcila, C.: Hate speech against central American immigrants in Mexico: analysis of xenophobia and racism in politicians, media and citizens, pp. 956–960 (2019)

11. Hernández, T.K.: Hate speech and the language of racism in Latin America: a lens for reconsidering global hate speech restrictions and legislation models. U. Pa. J. Int'l L. **32**, 805 (2010)
12. Matamoros-Fernández, A.: Platformed racism: The mediation and circulation of an Australian race-based controversy on twitter, facebook and youtube. Inf. Commun. Soc. **20**(6), 930–946 (2017)
13. Saksesi, A.S., Nasrun, M., Setianingsih, C.: Analysis text of hate speech detection using recurrent neural network. In: 2018 International Conference on Control, Electronics, Renewable Energy and Communications (ICCEREC), pp. 242–248. IEEE (2018)
14. Bonotti, M.: Religion, hate speech and non-domination. Ethnicities **17**(2), 259–274 (2017)
15. ElSherief, M., Kulkarni, V., Nguyen, D., Wang, W.Y., Belding, E.: Hate lingo: a target-based linguistic analysis of hate speech in social media. arXiv preprint arXiv:1804.04257 (2018)
16. Yasseri, T., Vidgen, B.: Detecting weak and strong islamophobic hate speech on social media. J. Inf. Technol. Polit. 2019 **17**(1) (2019)
17. Brown, A.: What is hate speech? part 1: the myth of hate. Law Philos. **36**(4), 419–468 (2017)
18. Calvert, C.: Hate speech and its harms: a communication theory perspective. J. Commun. **47**(1), 4–19 (1997)
19. Al-Hassan, A., Al-Dossari, H.: Detection of hate speech in social networks: a survey on multilingual corpus (2019)
20. Gaydhani, A., Doma, V., Kendre, S., Bhagwat, L.: Detecting hate speech and offensive language on twitter using machine learning: An n-gram and tfidf based approach. arXiv preprint arXiv:1809.08651 (2018)
21. Sarvabhotla, K., Pingali, P., Varma, V.: Sentiment classification: a lexical similarity based approach for extracting subjectivity in documents. Inf. Retr. **14**(3), 337–353 (2011)
22. MacDonald, M.C.: Lexical representations and sentence processing: an introduction. Lang. Cogn. Process. **12**(2–3), 121–136 (1997)
23. Gitari, N.D., Zuping, Z., Damien, H., Long, J.: A lexicon-based approach for hate speech detection. Int. J. Multimed. Ubiquitous Eng. 2015 **10**(4), 215–230 (2015)
24. Davidson, T., Warmsley, D., Macy, M., Weber, I.: Automated hate speech detection and the problem of offensive language. arXiv preprint arXiv:1703.04009 (2017)
25. Şahi, H., Kılıç, Y., Sağlam, R.B.: Automated detection of hate speech towards woman on twitter. 2018 3rd International Conference on Computer Science and Engineering (UBMK) 2018, pp. 533–536. IEEE (2018)
26. Wester, A., Øvrelid, L., Velldal, E., Hammer, H.L.: Threat detection in online discussions. In: Proceedings of the 7th Workshop on Computational Approaches to Subjectivity, Sentiment and Social Media Analysis, pp. 66–71 (2016)
27. Hegde, S.U., Zaiba, A., Nagaraju, Y., et al.: Hybrid CNN-LSTM model with glove word vector for sentiment analysis on football specific tweets, pp. 1–8. IEEE (2021)
28. Shi, B., Bai, X., Yao, C.: An end-to-end trainable neural network for image-based sequence recognition and its application to scene text recognition. IEEE Trans. Pattern Anal. Mach. Intell. **39**(11), 2298–2304 (2016)
29. Goodfellow, I., Bengio, Y., Courville, A., Bengio, Y.: Deep learning 1 (2016)
30. Mengistie, T.T., Kumar, D.: Deep learning based sentiment analysis on COVID-19 public reviews, pp. 444–449. IEEE (2021)

31. Vimali, J., Murugan, S.: A text based sentiment analysis model using bi-directional LSTM networks, pp. 1652–1658. IEEE (2021)
32. Kim, Y.: Convolutional neural networks for sentence classification. arXiv preprint arXiv:1408.5882 (2014)

A Semi-automatic Document Screening System for Computer Science Systematic Reviews

Abdelhakim Hannousse[1][(✉)] and Salima Yahiouche[2]

[1] University of 8 May 1945 Gulema, BP 401, 24000 Guelma, Algeria
hannousse.abdelhakim@univ-guelma.dz
[2] LRS Laboratory, Badji Mokhtar University, BP 12, 23000 Annaba, Algeria
salima.yahiouche@univ-annaba.dz

Abstract. The elaboration of systematic reviews has become a common practice in computer science after being exclusively related to healthcare and medical sciences. The process incorporates several steps to collect and analyze relevant papers to answer a set of well-formulated research questions. The search process starts by exploring different sources and digital libraries. This often results in a huge number of documents. After deduplication, the metadata of all the retrieved documents are checked for relevance before being approved for inclusion in the review. This task is known to be long and tiresome. In this paper, we propose a semi-automatic system that helps in reducing the efforts required for screening papers. The proposed system combines unsupervised and semi-supervised machine learning models and makes use of the domain ontology. Several features are extracted from metadata and used for classification. With the adoption of semi-supervised learning, researchers are only asked to manually label a subset of retrieved papers. Those papers are used to train a semi-supervised model which can then automatically classify the remaining papers. The proposed system is experimented with seven datasets built from pre-elaborated systematic reviews in computer science. We found that the system can save 50% of the efforts reaching up to 89% in terms of macro F1-score and up to 97% in terms of accuracy.

Keywords: Systematic reviews · Information retrieval · Document classification · Automation · Machine learning

1 Introduction

A systematic review is a scientific report synthesizing existing scientific evidences in a particular research topic [15]. It involves a broad bibliographic search, classification and analysis of all relevant scientific documents retrieved from different sources. Systematic reviews allow researchers and professionals, in a specific field, to access the latest results of valid scientific evidences through a single document. They thus help in making decisions, specifying type of interventions and

C. Djeddi et al. (Eds.): MedPRAI 2021, CCIS 1543, pp. 201–215, 2022.
https://doi.org/10.1007/978-3-031-04112-9_15

future directions [6]. The elaboration of systematic reviews has become a widely adopted research methodology in various scientific fields, including computer science. It seeks to answer clearly formulated research questions by synthesizing existing and valuable scientific data and evidences. These are identified according to a well-defined and approved research protocol. In fact, a systematic review differs from a regular survey by two main points: (1) requires an exhaustive search and selection of scientific articles published on the targeted research topic; a systematic review may also include valuable scientific evidences that has not been published through official publication channels; those resources are called gray literature; (2) adopts explicit and concise criteria approved by a network of experts for the selection and evaluation of collected publications.

Developing systematic reviews is known to be a long and tedious task [1,17]. More than one expert (at least two) should be involved throughout the process. Given the enormous amount of available scientific evidences and the variety of publication channels to be explored, different questions arise during the development of such kind of research, we quote as an example: Why choose certain publications and reject others? How to classify the found publications? Marshall et al. [16] conducted an experiment by investigating the opinion of experienced authors on useful features for proper automation of systematic reviews; the study selection is reported as one of the most useful features for such tools.

In this paper, we contribute by developing a machine learning based system for the automation of paper screening. This phase is essential in systematic reviews to identify what papers need to be included or excluded from the review. The decision is based on the relevance and provided details to the research topic. In order to reduce the efforts required for manually screening a huge number of published papers, the proposed system uses a subset of manually screened papers to train classifiers and predict the inclusion decision of the remaining papers. Due to the nature of the classification problem (i.e.; huge number of unlabeled data), the proposed system incorporates a combination of unsupervised and semi-supervised learning models. Only metadata are used for training and testing models instead of full-texts. Full texts require to be collected first and need advanced preprocessing steps specifically to deal with supplementary contents such as images and tables [5]. The metadata used in this study are extracted from Semantic Scholar[1] search engine through a provided API. The proposed system is validated through experimenting seven datasets built from recent and well-established systematic reviews in computer science.

The reminder of this paper is organized as follows. Section 2 discusses related work. Section 3 describes the architecture and details the proposed system. Section 4 presents the conducted experiments to validate the system. Section 5 presents and discusses the obtained results and Sect. 6 concludes the paper.

---

[1] Semantic Scholar home page: https://www.semanticscholar.org/.

2   Related Work

In this section, we describe the research issues and we discuss some of the recent contributions to tackle those issues in the two subsequent sections receptively.

2.1   Research Issues

The laborious nature of the systematic review elaboration process has led to the development and use of series of tools that provide automated support. A number of process steps are error prone and time consuming when done manually. Automation is needed to support researchers in building rigorous systematic reviews in less time and with minimal effort. Specifically, existing tools[2] show a lack contribution in the selection phase of the elaboration process. They only manage the manual selection of papers and identify conflicts. The problem is mainly due to [15]: (1) diverse terminology and related concepts are used in papers (2) less adoption of structured abstracts, (3) diverse criteria are adopted for selection, and (4) complexity of screening full papers. Consequently, several studies revealed the need for appropriate tools for the automation of the selection phase [1,16,17]. The recent study of Cairo et al. [4] revealed an increasing interest in using artificial intelligence and machine learning techniques to automate the study selection phase in systematic reviews.

2.2   Research Contributions

Felizardo et al. [7] proposed the use of Visual Text Mining (VTM) techniques to validate the study selection task. Content and citation maps are generated; these are used to visualize the similarity between already selected papers and correct some choices. In this work, we focus on assisting the elaboration of study selection instead of validating pre-elaborated selections as in [7].

Yu and Menzies in [28,29] provided a paper screening tool named FAST[2]. The proposed tool assists researchers in the selection of relevant papers using active learning and paper ranking following their similarities to already included papers. It also indicates when to stop screening based on a similarity threshold value with the remaining papers. The major problem of FAST[2] and active learning in general resides on the selection of seed papers. The quality of those papers greatly affects the whole process and may lead to poor prediction rates. González-Toral et al. [11] contributed to the selection of seed papers. They proposed ranking papers following a hybrid method incorporating different similarities including relevance of papers to the research questions. In the contrary to those studies, we use a combination of unsupervised and semi-supervised learning. The prediction starts when a reasonable number of papers is manually labeled.

Silva et al. [24] used a Naïve Bayes classifier trained on pre-selected papers to predict the inclusion of the remaining papers. The prediction probabilities of the classifier are used to sort those papers for manual screening. The process stops

---

[2] The systematic review toolbox: http://systematicreviewtools.com.

when no further acceptance of papers is made by the reviewers. Bag of Words extracted from titles and abstracts are used as inputs to the classifier. In our work, additional features extracted from metadata are used for classification.

Portenoy and West [20] proposed a framework that uses the citation network provided by the Web of Science (WoS) to find relevant papers. To avoid the cold start problem, they suppose that the search process starts with a set of predefined studies. Those studies are used to collect more relevant papers based on text similarities, the citation network and an unsupervised community detection algorithm (Infomap). This study treats paper selection as a recommendation problem. They focus on identifying relevant papers from a single source (WoS) without referring to false positives which is not feasible for systematic reviews.

Dinter et al. [25] developed a decision support system for automatic collection and screening of papers. The proposed system performs a federated search [8] in three search engines (Springer[3], Elsevier[4] and PubMed[5]) using their provided APIs. Therefore, input queries are automatically adapted to match the format of each search engine. Retrieved papers are split into two parts. The first part is manually screened and used to train a Convolutional Neural Network (CNN). The trained model is then used to predict the inclusion of the second part of papers (i.e.; not yet screened papers). However, it is well-known that deep learning models require a huge number of data for training; this will increase the number of papers that need to be screened manually. In the contrary, semi-supervised learning adopted in this paper may reduce the workload of researchers.

3   Proposed System

The proposed system incorporates the use of multiple machine learning models in a stacking way. Therefore, unsupervised machine learning algorithms are used first to cluster the papers following their different pairwise relationships and their outputs are used as inputs to a semi-supervised learner for final decision. The overall process of the proposed system is depicted in Fig. 1.

Input features of unsupervised models are extracted from Semantic Scholar (S2) metadata collected for each paper. Besides titles and abstracts, we make use of number of pages, list of authors, citations and references. All those metadata are extracted from S2 making use of Semantic Scholar API[6]. Each unsupervised model is charged to group the papers according to a specific type of features.

3.1   Adopted Features

In this section we describe the list of features adopted for classifying papers. Each feature is given with a brief description and the rational behind its adoption.

---

[3] Springer Nature: https://www.springer.com.
[4] Elsevier Science Direct: https://www.elsevier.com/.
[5] PubMed - National Library of Medicine: https://pubmed.ncbi.nlm.nih.gov.
[6] Semantic Scholar API: https://pypi.org/project/semanticscholar/.

Most of those features are automatically retrieved from Semantic Scholar API. Table 1 lists the returned metadata for each query by S2 API.

The features adopted in this study are classified into three main categories: *general features*, *pairwise features* and *topic modeling features*.

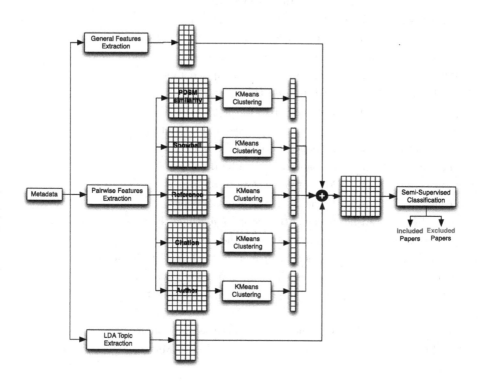

Fig. 1. Classification process

General Features: include features related to individual papers. Three features of this kind are experimented in this study: *number of pages, number of citations* and *query relevance*.

1. *Number of pages*: It is recommended, in systematic reviews, to include full papers instead of short papers of duplicate studies due to their clarity, self- and detailed contents [15]. Detailed studies are important for the data extraction phase in the systematic review process. Therefore, we consider the number of pages of each paper p. This information is extracted from the metadata of each paper as follows:

$$\text{nb\_pages}(p) = \text{endPage}(p) - \text{startPages}(p) + 1$$

2. *Number of citations*: Highly cited papers are expected to have substantial scientific impact and significant contribution to the body of knowledge [18].

Table 1. Structure of the metadata returned by Semantic Scholar (S2) API.

Attribute	Type	Description
id	string	S2 generated research paper ID
title	string	Title of the research paper
paperAbstract	string	Abstract of the research paper
entities	list	List of topics extracted from the paper
fieldsOfStudy	list	Research domains addressed by the paper
s2Url	string	URL to S2 research paper details page
s2PdfUrl	string	URL to the PDF file on S2
pdfUrls	list	External URLs to the PDF file
authors	list	Authors with a generated ID and name
inCitations	list	S2 paper IDs citing the paper
outCitations	list	S2 paper IDs cited by the paper
year	int	Year of publication of the paper
venue	string	Name of the venue of the paper
journalName	string	Name of the journal publishing the paper
journalVolume	string	Journal volume of the paper
journalPages	string	Pages of the papers of the form *"startPage-endPage"*
sources	list	Sources where the paper was retrieved
doi	string	Digital object identifier of the paper
doiUrl	string	Doi link
pmid	string	Identifier of the paper used by PubMed
magId	string	Identifier of the paper used by Microsoft Academic Graph

Therefore, they are likely to be included in systematic reviews. Number of citations is measured considering the list of citations given by Semantic Scholar.

$$\mathrm{nb\_citations}(p) = |\mathrm{inCitations}(p)|$$

3. *Query relevance:* In systematic reviews, papers are retrieved through querying a pre-defined set of well-known digital libraries. The relevance of papers to the queries depends on the algorithm adopted by each search engine. In this study, we measure the relevance of each paper to the expanded query used to retrieve them. Original queries are expanded with terms from the Computer Science Ontology (CSO) [21]. In this study, original queries are expanded with direct sub-topics and super-topics of each term in the query. The query relevance is calculated applying the following steps:

(a) transform the query Q into a conjunctive normal form with n clauses :

$$Q = (t_{11} \vee t_{12} \vee ... \vee t_{1p}) \wedge (t_{21} \vee t_{22} \vee ... \vee t_{2q}) \wedge ... \wedge (t_{n1} \vee t_{n2} \vee ... \vee t_{nl})$$

(b) for each clause c in a query Q, we get an expanded set of terms by considering the original terms themselves together with the direct subtopics and supertopics in CSO of each term. Therefore, the expanded set of terms of a clause c is calculated as follows where $terms(c)$ refers the set of terms in the clause c.

$$expand(c) = \bigcup_{i=1}^{|terms(c)|} \{t_i\} \cup \text{CSO}_{subtopics}(t_i) \cup \text{CSO}_{supertopics}(t_i)$$

(c) finally, calculate the query relevance using the following formula:

$$Query\_relevance(p, Q) = \frac{\sum_{c \in Q}(w_c \times \sum_{t \in expand(c)} occurrence(t, p))}{\sum_{c \in Q} w_c}$$

where $occurrence(t,p)$ counts the number of occurrences of the term t in the title and abstract of the paper p. In this study, we suppose that the weights w_i associated to each clause c in Q are as follows: $w_1 = 1$ and $w_{i+1} = w_i + 1$. This way, the terms of the next clause are privileged since they describe more detailed topics compared with the terms of its predecessor clause. This is inspired from the PICO (Population, Intervention, Comparison, Outcome) method that is widely adopted in defining search strings in systematic reviews [15].

Pairwise Features: features of this category identify the pairwise relatedness of retrieved papers. 4 pairwise relatedness measures are considered in this study:

1. *Common citations*: papers with common citations are likely to have common topics. Making use of S2 metadata, this feature is measured as follows:

$$cite\_relatedness(p_1, p_2) = \begin{cases} 1, & \text{if } |\text{inCitations}(p_1) \cap \text{inCitations}(p_2)| > 0; \\ 0, & \text{otherwise} \end{cases}$$

2. *Common references*: similarly, papers with common references are likely to be addressing similar topics. This feature is measured as follows:

$$ref\_relatedness(p_1, p_2) = \begin{cases} 1, & \text{if } |\text{outCitations}(p_1) \cap \text{outCitations}(p_2)| > 0; \\ 0, & \text{otherwise} \end{cases}$$

3. *Common authors*: articles published within short time period with common authors are likely to be related to the same topic.

$$auth\_relatedness = \begin{cases} 1, & \text{if } |\text{ authors}(p_1) \cap \text{authors}(p_2)| > 0 \\ 0, & \text{otherwise} \end{cases}$$

4. *Snowballing*: a paper p_1 included in the references list (backward snowballing) or in the citations list (forward snowballing) of another paper p_2 is likely to have similar topics as p_2.

$$\text{snb\_relatedness}(p_1, p_2) = \begin{cases} 1, & \text{if id}(p_1) \in \text{inCitations}(p_2) \cup \text{outCitations}(p_2) \\ 0, & \text{otherwise} \end{cases}$$

5. *Pairwise document similarity measure (PDSM)*: This measure is adopted due to its efficiency in classifying documents compared with other traditional similarity measures [19]. The PDSM similarity measure is based on the term frequency and the number of terms that appear in at least one of the two documents. Accordingly, given two papers p_1 and p_2 and a list of vocabulary terms *vocab*, the PDSM is defined as:

$$\text{pdsm}(p_1, p_2) = \frac{\sum_{i=1}^{|vocab|} \text{Min}(tf_{1i}, tf_{2i})}{\sum_{i=1}^{|vocab|} \text{Max}(tf_{1i}, tf_{2i})} \times \frac{in(p_1, p_2) + 1}{|vocab| - out(p_1, p_2) + 1}$$

where tf_{ji} represents the frequency of the *ith* vocabulary term in paper j, $in(p_1, p_2)$ describes the number of present terms of p_1 in p_2 and $out(p_1, p_2)$ represents the number of p_1 terms absent in p_2.

Topic Modeling Features: are abstract topics that can be discovered through analyzing the titles and abstracts of retrieved papers. This is a useful technique for revealing the hidden semantic structures in texts. We consider the probability of a paper to be part of each topic resulted from a probabilistic topic modeler.

3.2   Classification Process

In the proposed classification process, two unsupervised machine learning algorithms are used: KMeans [26] and LDA [3]. The former is adopted for grouping the papers based on pairwise features. Therefore, five independent KMeans models are adopted, each is used for clustering papers based on a specific pairwise feature. The LDA model is used to get topic modeling features. In order to boost the performance of used models, we make use of the grid search method [10]. KMeans models are tuned by varying the number of clusters from 2 to 100 by step of 1. The optimal number of clusters is the one providing the maximum value of the *Silhouette* score. We adopt the use of a parallelized LDA version (LDAMulticore[7]) that enables the use of all CPU cores to speed up the training phase. The hyperparameters of the LDA model are tuned as follows and the values providing the best *Coherence* score are adopted:

- we vary the *alpha* parameter value of LDA from 0.01 to 1 by step of 0.3. We also consider the two predefined values *symmetric* and *asymmetric*.
- similarly, we vary the *beta* parameter value from 0.01 to 1 by step of 0.3 in addition to the predefined value *symmetric*.

---

[7] LDAMulticore: https://radimrehurek.com/gensim_3.8.3/models/ldamulticore.html.

– the number of topics are varied from 2 to 11 by step of 1.

Finally, the models are combined in a stacking way. Therefore, the outputs of the five KMeans models and the LDA model are combined with the three general features. The resulted matrix of values is fed to a semi-supervised model for final prediction. In this study, we make use of a self-training method [30]. Using such technique, a base classifier is firstly trained on a small set of available labeled papers. The classifier is then used to label the remaining papers. New labeled papers with a high degree of confidence are added to the learning data. The classifier is re-trained on the new papers and the procedure is repeated until a stop criterion is satisfied. This self-training method enables wrapping traditional supervised learning algorithms to become semi-supervised learners. The overall classification process is given in Algorithm 1.

4   Experimentation

Due to the absence of complete datasets, we experiment the proposed system with the datasets provided in our previous work [14]. Each dataset presented in [14] incorporates the set of included studies for a specific SLR stated by the correspondent authors, extracted and saved in a readable format (.bib). In order to get a reasonable set of excluded studies, we applied the same query for each SLR into Scopus[8], we adopted the same inclusion criteria as mentioned in original SLRs: period, type and language of publications. The set of studies returned by Scopus and not included in SLRs are considered as excluded studies. The complete list of included and excluded papers for each SLR used in this study is made available for users at Github for further experiments[9]. The metadata of all the studies are completed by querying Semantic Scholar using the DOI of papers. The resulting datasets and their configurations are given in Table 2.

Different supervised classifiers are used as base models for the semi-supervised learner. For performance evaluation, we use k-fold cross-validation and the following two metrics:

1. *Accuracy*: is defined as the ratio of correct predicted papers regarding the total number of papers. It is calculated using the following formula:

$$\text{Accuracy} = \frac{\text{TP} + \text{TN}}{\text{TP} + \text{TN} + \text{FP} + \text{FN}}$$

   In the context of this study, True Positive (TP) designates the number of correct predictions of included papers where True Negative (TN) designates the number of correct predictions of excluded papers. Similarly, False Positive (FP) designates the number of incorrect predictions of included papers where False Negative (FN) designates the number of incorrect predictions of excluded papers.

---

[8] Scopus abstract and citation database: https://www.scopus.com.

[9] Datasets for automatic screening of papers: https://github.com/hannousse/Semantic-Scholar-Evaluation.

Input : P: metadata of retrieved papers, tr: training rate, m: base model
Output: $P_{included}$, $P_{excluded}$
$F_{pdsm} = [\ ]; F_{snowball} = [\ ]; F_{reference} = [\ ]; F_{citation} = [\ ]; F_{authorship} = [\ ]$
/* Tune KMeans models one for each pairwise feature   */
for $ft \in \{pdsm, snowball, reference, citation, authorship\}$ do
   $S \leftarrow 0$
   for $i \leftarrow 2$ to 100 do
      $model \leftarrow KMeans(k{=}i)$
      $labels \leftarrow model.fit\_predict(get(ft,P))$
      $silhouette \leftarrow silhouette\_score(get(ft,P), labels)$
      if $silhouette > S$ then
         $S \leftarrow silhouette$
         $F_{ft} = make\_numeric(labels)$
      end
   end
end
/* Tune an LDA model for titles and abstracts of papers   */
$alpha \leftarrow [\ 0.01, 0.31, 0.61, 0.91, symmetric, asymmetric]$
$beta \quad \leftarrow [\ 0.01, 0.31, 0.61, 0.91, symmetric]$
$coherence \quad \leftarrow 0$
for $a \in alpha$ do
   for $b \in beta$ do
      for $nb\_topic \leftarrow 2$ to 11 do
         model $\leftarrow LDAMulticore(get(text,P), a, b, nb\_topic)$
         c $\leftarrow CoherenceModel(model)$
         if $c > coherence$ then
            $coherence \leftarrow c$
            $F_{topics} = make\_numeric(model.topics)$
         end
      end
   end
end
/* Concatenate all the features to form the final feature vector   */
$F \leftarrow concat(F_{pdsm}, F_{snowball}, F_{reference}, F_{citation}, F_{authorship}, F_{topics},$
$generalFeatures(P))$
/* Build a semi-supervised model with a specified traininig rate   */
$model \leftarrow self\_training(m)$
/* Make predictions   */
$P_{included}, P_{excluded} = model.predict(F, rate{=}tr)$
return $P_{included}$, $P_{excluded}$

Algorithm 1: Classification process for the automatic screening of papers

2. *Macro F1-score:* is defined as the mean of class-wise F1-scores. Therefore, the Macro F1-score is obtained by averaging F1-scores computed for each class and calculated as follows:

$$\text{Macro F1-score} = \frac{1}{2}(\text{F1-score}_{included} + \text{F1-score}_{excluded})$$

Table 2. Experimented datasets.

ID	Ref.	#Included	#Excluded	Total
D1	[2]	21	35	56
D2	[9]	24	82	106
D3	[12]	22	305	327
D4	[13]	128	432	560
D5	[22]	64	417	481
D6	[23]	69	173	242
D7	[27]	54	217	271

The F1-score for each class indicates the best trade-off between precision and recall of that class. The F1-score of a class i is obtained by applying the following formula:

$$\text{F1-score}_i = 2 * \frac{\text{Precision}_i * \text{Recall}_i}{\text{Precision}_i + \text{Recall}_i}$$

where Recall and Precision are measured as follows:

$$\text{Recall} = \frac{TP}{TP + FN} \qquad \text{Precision} = \frac{TP}{TP + FP}$$

5   Results and Analysis

By applying the proposed system described in Sect. 3 to the set of built datasets described in Table 2, we obtained the best results using the RF classifier as a base model for the self-training algorithm. The results are shown in Table 3.

Table 3. Performance of the system with RF as base classifier

Dataset	Recall (%)	Precision (%)	Macro F1 (%)	Accuracy (%)
D1	80.48	85.00	81.84	83.93
D2	83.59	88.43	85.66	90.57
D3	86.90	90.02	88.39	97.21
D4	93.74	79.56	84.33	91.40
D5	87.09	74.57	78.54	87.94
D6	92.05	87.41	89.09	90.50
D7	88.49	80.17	83.13	88.24

The results shown in Table 3 are obtained using 50% of labeled papers for training. By 50%, half of the included papers and the same number of excluded papers are used to initiate the semi-supervised learner. As can be seen from Table 3, the system provides the higher Macro-F1-score (89.09%) with D6 and the lower score (78.54%) with D5. Higher recall (93.74%) is obtained with D4 where higher precision (90.02%) is obtained with D3. This is due to the difference of natures of the datasets and their incorporated metadata. Besides RF, 5 other classifiers are tested: Decision Tree (DT), Naïve Bayes (NB), Support Vector Machine (SVM), Logistic Regression (LR) and Stochastic Gradient Descent (SGD). Due to space limitation, only the results on D3 for all the experimented classifiers are shown in Table 4. The second best classifier was DT that provided 80.58% in terms of Macro F1-score.

Table 4. Performance comparison using different base classifiers for the semi-supervised learner - case of D3

Classifier	Recall (%)	Precision (%)	Macro F1 (%)	Accuracy (%)
DT	92.49	74.69	80.58	93.87
NB	81.66	58.44	56.67	73.54
SVM	82.70	64.08	68.00	87.47
LR	79.79	65.93	69.97	89.97
SGD	58.88	52.17	45.63	62.67
RF	86.90	90.02	88.39	97.21

Figure 2 shows the performance of the system by varying the ratio of the training subset from 10 to 50 by step of 10. The results show that the performance of the system drastically decreases for D1, D3 and D7 but gradually decreases in the case of D2, D4 and D6. A closer look at the values of features, we found that the included papers of D2, D4 and D6 are strongly connected to each others either by having common authors, references or citations which is not the case for D1, D3 and D7. This affects the predictions of models trained on pairwise features. Moreover, the queries used for retrieving papers of D1, D3 and D7 incorporate general terms such as *"goal"* and *"crystal"*. This produces inaccurate expansion of queries with terms from the CSO ontology which in turn affects the importance of the query-relatedness feature.

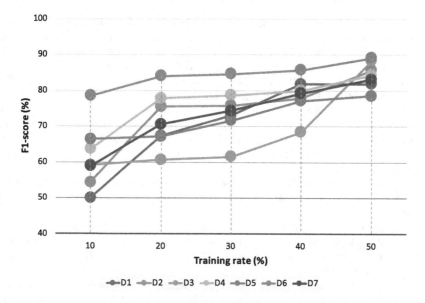

Fig. 2. Effect of varying the training ratio

6 Conclusion

The automation of the systematic review process is becoming a necessity to reduce the time and efforts needed to perform such valuable research studies. In this paper, we contributed by developing and experimenting a system for the automatic selection of relevant papers through analyzing merely their metadata obtained from Semantic Scholar search engine. The proposed system makes use of unsupervised and semi-supervised machine learning to predict the inclusion or the exclusion of papers into/from a specific systematic review. The results show that by labeling 50% of included papers, the system automatically labels the remaining papers with a macro-F1-score up to 89.09%. As a perspective, we plan to enhance the performance of the proposed system by: (1) introducing new features, (2) experimenting more classification techniques such as incremental learning and (3) building larger datasets by querying more search engines.

References

1. Al-Zubidy, A., Carver, J.C., Hale, D.P., Hassler, E.E.: Vision for SLR tooling infrastructure: prioritizing value-added requirements. Inf. Softw. Technol. **91**, 72–81 (2017). https://doi.org/10.1016/j.infsof.2017.06.007
2. Alhammad, M.M., Moreno, A.M.: Gamification in software engineering education: a systematic mapping. J. Syst. Softw. **141**, 131–150 (2018). https://doi.org/10.1016/j.jss.2018.03.065
3. Blei, D.M., Ng, A.Y., Jordan, M.I.: Latent Dirichlet allocation. J. Mach. Learn. Res. **3**, 993–1022 (2003). https://doi.org/10.5555/944919.944937

4. Cairo, L.S., de Figueiredo Carneiro, G., da Silva, B.C.: Adoption of machine learning techniques to perform secondary studies: a systematic mapping study for the computer science field. In: Filipe, J., Smialek, M., Brodsky, A., Hammoudi, S. (eds.) Proceedings of the 21st International Conference on Enterprise Information Systems, ICEIS 2019, Heraklion, Crete, Greece, 3–5 May 2019, pp. 351–356. SciTePress (2019). https://doi.org/10.5220/0007780603510356
5. Dieste, O., Padua, A.G.: Developing search strategies for detecting relevant experiments for systematic reviews. In: 2013 ACM/IEEE International Symposium on Empirical Software Engineering and Measurement, Madrid, Spain, 20–21 September 2007, pp. 215–224. IEEE Computer Society (2007). https://doi.org/10.1109/ESEM.2007.19
6. Dybå, T., Kitchenham, B.A., Jørgensen, M.: Evidence-based software engineering for practitioners. IEEE Softw. **22**(1), 58–65 (2005). https://doi.org/10.1109/MS.2005.6
7. Felizardo, K.R., Andery, G.F., Paulovich, F.V., Minghim, R., Maldonado, J.C.: A visual analysis approach to validate the selection review of primary studies in systematic reviews. Inf. Softw. Technol. **54**(10), 1079–1091 (2012). https://doi.org/10.1016/j.infsof.2012.04.003
8. Ghafari, M., Saleh, M., Ebrahimi, T.: A federated search approach to facilitate systematic literature review in software engineering. Int. J. Softw. Eng. Appl. **3**(2), 13–24 (2012). https://doi.org/10.5121/ijsea.2012.3202
9. Ghasemi, M., Amyot, D.: From event logs to goals: a systematic literature review of goal-oriented process mining. Requirements Eng. **25**(1), 67–93 (2019). https://doi.org/10.1007/s00766-018-00308-3
10. Ghawi, R., Pfeffer, J.: Efficient hyperparameter tuning with grid search for text categorization using KNN approach with BM25 similarity. Open Comput. Sci. **9**(1), 160–180 (2019). https://doi.org/10.1515/comp-2019-0011
11. González-Toral, S., Freire, R., Gualán, R., Saquicela, V.: A ranking-based approach for supporting the initial selection of primary studies in a systematic literature review. In: XLV Latin American Computing Conference, CLEI 2019, Panama, Panama, 30 September–4 October 2019, pp. 1–10. IEEE Computer Society (2019). https://doi.org/10.1109/CLEI47609.2019.235079
12. Goulão, M., Amaral, V., Mernik, M.: Quality in model-driven engineering: a tertiary study. Softw. Qual. J. **24**(3), 601–633 (2016). https://doi.org/10.1007/s11219-016-9324-8
13. Guinea, A.S., Nain, G., Traon, Y.L.: A systematic review on the engineering of software for ubiquitous systems. J. Syst. Softw. **118**, 251–276 (2016). https://doi.org/10.1016/j.jss.2016.05.024
14. Hannousse, A.: Searching relevant papers for software engineering secondary studies: semantic scholar coverage and identification role. IET Softw. **15**(1), 126–146 (2021). https://doi.org/10.1049/sfw2.12011
15. Kitchenham, B.A., Budgen, D., Brereton, P.: Evidence-Based Software Engineering and Systematic Reviews. Chapman & Hall/CRC, Boca Raton (2015)
16. Marshall, C., Kitchenham, B.A., Brereton, P.: Tool features to support systematic reviews in software engineering - a cross domain study. e-Informatica Softw. Eng. J. **12**(1), 79–115 (2018). https://doi.org/10.5277/e-Inf180104
17. Michelson, M., Reuter, K.: The significant cost of systematic reviews and meta-analyses: a call for greater involvement of machine learning to assess the promise of clinical trials. Contemp. Clin. Trials Commun. **16**, 100443 (2019). https://doi.org/10.1016/j.conctc.2019.100443

18. Molléri, J.S., Petersen, K., Mendes, E.: Towards understanding the relation between citations and research quality in software engineering studies. Scientometrics **117**(3), 1453–1478 (2018). https://doi.org/10.1007/s11192-018-2907-3
19. Oghbaie, M., Mohammadi Zanjireh, M.: Pairwise document similarity measure based on present term set. J. Big Data **5**(1), 1–23 (2018). https://doi.org/10.1186/s40537-018-0163-2
20. Portenoy, J., West, J.D.: Constructing and evaluating automated literature review systems. Scientometrics **125**(3), 3233–3251 (2020). https://doi.org/10.1007/s11192-020-03490-w
21. Salatino, A.A., Thanapalasingam, T., Mannocci, A., Osborne, F., Motta, E.: The computer science ontology: a large-scale taxonomy of research areas. In: Vrandečić, D., et al. (eds.) ISWC 2018. LNCS, vol. 11137, pp. 187–205. Springer, Cham (2018). https://doi.org/10.1007/978-3-030-00668-6_12
22. Santos, J.A.M., Rocha-Junior, J.B., Prates, L.C.L., do Nascimento, R.S., Freitas, M.F., de Mendonça, M.G.: A systematic review on the code smell effect. J. Syst. Softw. **144**, 450–477 (2018). https://doi.org/10.1016/j.jss.2018.07.035
23. Shahin, M., Babar, M.A., Zhu, L.: Continuous integration, delivery and deployment: a systematic review on approaches, tools, challenges and practices. IEEE Access **5**, 3909–3943 (2017). https://doi.org/10.1109/ACCESS.2017.2685629
24. Silva, G., Neto, P.S., Moura, R.S., Araujo, A.C., da Costa Castro, O.C., Ibiapina, I.: An approach to support the selection of relevant studies in systematic review and systematic mappings. In: 8th Brazilian Conference on Intelligent Systems BRACIS 2019, Salvador, Brazil, 15–18 October 2019, pp. 824–829. IEEE Computer Society (2019). https://doi.org/10.1109/BRACIS.2019.00147
25. Van Dinter, R., Catal, C., Tekinerdogan, B.: A decision support system for automating document retrieval and citation screening. Expert Syst. Appl. **182**, 115261 (2021). https://doi.org/10.1016/j.eswa.2021.115261
26. Vassilvitskii, S., Arthur, D.: k-means++: the advantages of careful seeding. In: Proceedings of the Eighteenth Annual ACM-SIAM Symposium on Discrete Algorithms, New Orleans Louisiana, USA, 7–9 January 2006, pp. 1027–1035. ACM (2006). https://dl.acm.org/doi/10.5555/1283383.1283494
27. Yang, C., Liang, P., Avgeriou, P.: A systematic mapping study on the combination of software architecture and agile development. J. Syst. Softw. **111**, 157–184 (2016). https://doi.org/10.1016/j.jss.2015.09.028
28. Yu, Z., Kraft, N.A., Menzies, T.: Finding better active learners for faster literature reviews. Empir. Softw. Eng. **23**(6), 3161–3186 (2018). https://doi.org/10.1007/s10664-017-9587-0
29. Yu, Z., Menzies, T.: Fast2: an intelligent assistant for finding relevant papers. Expert Syst. Appl. **120**, 57–71 (2019). https://doi.org/10.1016/j.eswa.2018.11.021
30. Zhu, X.: Semi-supervised learning literature survey. Technical report TR 1530, University of Wisconsin, July 2008

Handwriting Based Personality Traits Identification Using Adaptive Boosting and Textural Features

Abdellatif Gahmousse[1]([✉]) [iD], Rabeb Yousfi[1] [iD], and Chawki Djeddi[1,2] [iD]

[1] Department of Mathematics and Computer Science, Larbi Tebessi University, Tebessa, Algeria
{abdellatif.gahmousse,c.djeddi}@univ-tebessa.dz
[2] LITIS Lab, University of Rouen, Rouen, France

Abstract. Computer analysis of personality traits through handwriting product is becoming increasingly an important thing, mainly because of the deep integration of AI techniques in many fields, such as recruitment services, pedagogy, and mental health diagnostics. Various research studies have shown that there are numerous dimensions of information which can be extracted from a writer's handwriting product. This information had helped reveal writer's gender, identity, age, and also several personality features. Hence, our work aimed at identifying the personality traits of a writer according to Five Factor Model (FFM), by exploiting the textural features of his handwriting product. Thus, the Edge Hinge technique was introduced to extract the textural information found in handwriting images. The exploited dataset for the evaluation of this work consists of a new corpus, dedicated to the experience of the personality traits problem on a group of 285 subjects by instrumentalizing FFM approach. We used several classifiers such as, the Random Forest, Support Vector Machine, and Adaboost in order to choose the best one. The experimental work resulted in higher identification rates than those in the literature, through introducing a combination of classifier technique based on Adaboost to improve performance.

Keywords: Personality Traits identification · Handwritten Documents · Adaboost and Textural Features

1 Introduction

The identification of individual's personality traits from their handwriting product has been the subject of numerous researches by psychologists. However, their computer science counterparts have not yet given this problem the importance it deserves. After a deep dive in the literature of the field of computerized identification of personality traits, several research trends have been identified. The first trend is mainly based on the concept of automating graphology skills by integrating techniques for capturing and detecting features such as letters/words sizes, letters/word slants, baseline, spaces, and pen pressure. On the other hand, a second trend of research lets the Deep Learning classifiers do the work of discovering and extracting implicit features in text images.

© Springer Nature Switzerland AG 2022
C. Djeddi et al. (Eds.): MedPRAI 2021, CCIS 1543, pp. 216–227, 2022.
https://doi.org/10.1007/978-3-031-04112-9_16

Furthermore, another one is based mainly on the fact that a text image is just a texture. Therefore, we look for global features such as Edge Hinge, Histograms of oriented Gradient, Oriented Basic Image Features Column, Contourlets, and Gray Level Co-occurrence Matrices in order to use them as reference data for training models and classes' prediction.

In 2015, Joshi [1] proposed a method for predicting personality traits from graphological features extracted from an individual's handwriting such as baseline, margin, slant of words, and height of T-bar. The exploited dataset was generated from 100 text samples that were examined by graphological experts. The system was based on the K-NN classifier; no clear results have been published.

The following year, Fallah et al., in his paper [2] worked on a personality feature detection system using a Persian handwriting. The dataset collected handwritten records from 70 people, using the MMPI model for psychological assessment. Accordingly, the proposed system goes through a pre-processing phase which aims at minimizing noise and applying contour smoothing, followed by a segmentation phase. To reduce the data to be processed, two families of features were used. The first is Text Independent Features (TIFs) which are margin value, word expansion, character sizes, line spaces, word spaces, word tilts and others (graphological features). The second is Text Dependent Features (TDFs) represented in Higher-order local auto-correlation (HLAC). Hence, the system based on ANN classifier achieved a recognition level of 61%, demonstrating the superiority of text-dependent features over TIPs.

A different work published in [3] addressed the topic of identifying personality traits by considering 23 graphological features such as maximum, minimum, average size of letters, ratio, spaces between letters, etc. Also, Relevant Features were selected to feed four machine learning classifiers: ANN, AdaBoost, KNN, and SVM. In addition, Hyperparameter tuning was applied to get optimal parameters for each classifier with an accuracy of 62.5–83.9%. Furthermore, Experimental work observed that on-line features were more sensitive for personality traits compared to off-line feature.

Based on the FFM model for personality trait evaluation, Gavrilescu [4] proposed a 3-layer architecture integrating artificial neural networks. The first layer performed the role of text image normalization and local features extraction. The second layer did the feature mapping, while the last one played the role of the classifier. The proposed approach was carried out on a dataset of 128 subjects. In the end, the resulted model had a rate of 84.4% in intra-subject and 80.5% in inter-subject predictions.

On the other hand, Lemos et al. [5] worked on other types of personality traits such as optimistic, pessimistic, balanced, independent, pragmatic, etc. This was done by proposing an approach starting with a pre-processing phase, followed by a conversion of the samples into black and white images. At the end, a Convolutional Neural Network was used to extract implicit features from handwritings and also predict the subject's traits.

The multimedia information processing for personality and social networks analysis contest (MIPPSNA) was a very important benchmark for the topic of identifying personality traits from handwriting product [6]. In a competitive context several approaches were proposed to be tested on the so-called HWxPI dataset [7] based on FFM. Indeed, an approach based on (HoG) as a textural feature has been implemented by integrating SVM as a classification tool. A second method was also set up integrating the CNNs from the 418 colored training set sample; 216 patches were also obtained from each sample after converting them into black and white images. In addition, the implemented CNN was composed of 5 convolutional layers for feature extraction and three fully connected layers for classification.

Separately from the MIPPSNA contest, another work based on the HWxPI dataset was published [8]. An approach based on textural features was proposed considering the text image as a texture. The authors preferred to follow the simplest way, by directly applying feature extraction (OBIFC technique) on the original samples especially since OBIFC is known to be effective with noisy images, besides this was the case for the HWxPI samples that were stafflined. As the classification problem was of the Multi-label Classification type, it led us to use the Rank-SVM technique with a Radial Basis Function kernel, followed by a grid search to optimize the parameters. Finally, the personality trait identification results of the proposed method were superior to those presented in the MIPPSNA competition.

Recently, Umair presented a suitable approach [9] for predicting personality traits through handwriting product. However, to implement the proposed approach the author created a new database (due to the unavailability of the handwritten dataset, which links FFM traits to handwriting samples). In the first step, the samples were converted to grey scale along with extracting implicit features from scanned images using CNN. In the end, a neural network was trained by back-propagation to learn the patterns from the extracted features and determine the FFM personality traits. The result of the test on randomly written samples obtained an overall prediction accuracy of 59.73%. A similar work [10] treating theHWxPI dataset and using CNNs obtained an accuracy of 50.23%.

In short, this paper will begin by presenting the data corpus, the proposed method, and its main components. Additionally, a section is dedicated to explain the experimental process and the classification technique. To conclude, results and discussion will be presented followed by a conclusion and future perspectives.

2 Data Corpus

In a recent work [9] and because of the lack of Datasets in the field, the author found it necessary to create his own dataset in order to be able to answer the problems of identifying personality traits from the HW product. His dataset consists of 285 subjects, each of whom participated with one dependent and one independent text. The FFM-based IPIP questionnaire was used to assess each subject. Consequently, the obtained results (integer values between 0 and 100) were assigned as labels to the text images under the FFM classes: Extraversion, Neuroticism, Agreeableness, Conscientiousness, and Openness to experience (ENACO). A categorization on three levels (low, medium and high) was also used to transform the integer values into qualitative values (Fig. 1).

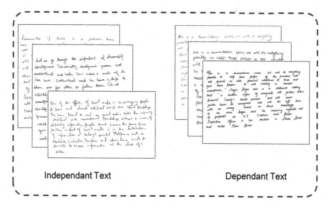

Fig. 1. Dataset samples

To demonstrate, all the values that are less than 33 are labeled as low (L), while the ones that sit between 34 and 66 are labeled as Medium (M), and, lastly, the values that are greater than or equal to 67 are labeled as High (H). The table below provides some statistical highlights of the dataset.

Table 1. Samples Distribution on the five personality traits and their values [9].

Personality trait	Samples by class values		
	Low (L)	Medium (M)	High (H)
Extroversion	152	310	108
Neuroticism	174	306	90
Consciousness	214	274	82
Agreeableness	218	278	74
Openness	402	134	34
Total	**1160**	**1302**	**389**

3 Proposed Method

The proposed method takes the presented dataset corpus as a training/testing base as presented in the table below. The segmentation protocol established on this dataset randomly puts 70% of the samples in the training dataset and 30% of the samples in the test dataset. Our approach does not differentiate between the two dataset corpora (dependent texts and independent texts), but it considers as a single one.

Also, our method considers the handwriting product as a texture and for that reason Edge Hinge technique is applied to extract the features to be analyzed. These features will be processed as digital vectors of one dimension (Fig. 2).

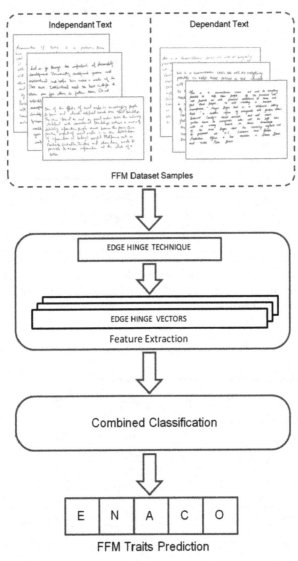

Fig. 2. Proposed method

A comparative study was established searching the correlation of the different FFM classes with the different EH technique configurations. Thus, several vectors of different EH configurations were used to represent the same sample. This analysis revealed that some FFM classes of the same sample are better represented by one EH configuration than another. Therefore, the best EH configurations were chosen for each class. In the next phase, the resulted EH vectors will be handled separately from the others. Whereas, in order to choose the best classifier, several ones were tested, which lead to Ada-boost to be the chosen one for this experimental study.

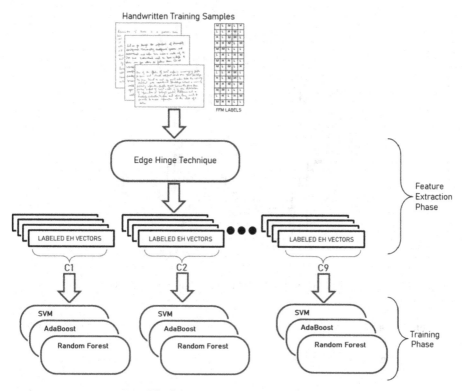

Fig. 3. Experimental training phase

3.1 Feature Extraction

The proposed personality trait identification system is based on a set of attributes such as orientation, curvature and texture that are estimated by computing Edge-HINGE distributions [11]. In order to capture the curvature of the contour, as well as its orientation, the hinge distributions are used.

The main idea is to consider in the neighborhood not one, but two edge fragments emerging from the central pixel and then calculate the joint probability distribution of the orientations of the two fragments. In all the experiments that will be presented in the following sections, we have considered detailed fragments ranging from 4 pixels to 9 pixels. Figure 3 shows a graphical description of the characteristics of the edge hinges (Table 2).

3.2 Combined Classification and Experimentation

In order to properly tune our classification process, we had to go through the following steps. First, we had to go through all the possible EH Configurations from C1 to C6 for each of the classifiers dedicated to this experimental study. Thus, we could search and analyze the prediction results for each of the configurations. Adaboost showed a high sensitivity and better results compared to SVM and Random Forest. (See Table 3.)

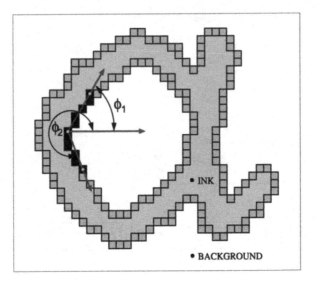

Fig. 4. Graphical overview for edge-hinge method [10]

Table 2. An overview of the implemented EH configurations and their dimensionality

Edge hinge fragment	Description	Feature vector dimension
C1: 4 pixels	Edge hinges distribution with a 4 pixel fragment	576
C2: 5 pixels	Edge hinges distribution with a 5 pixel fragment	1024
C3: 6 pixels	Edge hinges distribution with a 6 pixel fragment	1600
C4: 7 pixels	edge hinges distribution with a 7 pixel fragment	2304
C5: 8 pixels	Edge hinges distribution with a 8 pixel fragment	3136
C6: 9 pixels	Edge hinges distribution with a 9 pixel fragment	4096

Second, results shown in Table 3 led us to choose Adaboost to become the classifier of the proposed system. Also, it should be noted that, with the Adaboost results for the different FMM classes presented in Table 4, we could observe that the first EH configuration C1 showed a high prediction of 90.64% with the Extraversion class and 82.45% for the Conscientiousness class, compared to the other EH configurations. The second EH configuration had the highest average rate compared to the other EH configurations, especially for the Openness to Experience class. Again, the fourth configuration had the

Table 3. Overall identification rates recorded using Random Forests (RF), Support Vector Machines (SVM) and the Adaptive BOOSTING algorithm (ADABOOST)

Edge hinge configurations	Global Identification rate		
	Random forest	SVM	AdaBoost
C1	53.68%	48.88%	82.57%
C2	49.94%	54.50%	**82.92%**
C3	50.76%	54.50%	79.29%
C4	49.59%	54.50%	82.10%
C5	49.00%	54.50%	77.66%
C6	49.82%	54.50%	81.40%

Table 4. Results for the five personality traits prediction using Adaboost algorithm.

Edge Hinge Configurations	E	N	A	C	O	Average
C1	**90.64 %**	83.04 %	83.04 %	**82.45 %**	73.68 %	**82.57 %**
C2	85.96 %	84.79 %	84.79 %	**82.45 %**	**76.60 %**	**82.92 %**
C3	88.88 %	78.94 %	78.94 %	82.45 %	67.25 %	79.29 %
C4	89.47 %	81.28 %	81.28 %	**82.45 %**	76.02 %	**82.10 %**
C5	84.79 %	78.94 %	78.94 %	77.77 %	67.83 %	77.65 %
C6	83.04 %	**85.38 %**	**85.38 %**	80.11 %	73.09 %	81.40 %

third highest average recognition rate reaching 89.47% for the Extraversion class and a rate of 76.02% for Openness to Experience.

This time, and to take better advantage of the EH configurations with high rates (C2, C1 and C4), we used three instances of the Adaboost classifier, each one them trained one of selected feature vectors. Therefore, the test phase was carried out by combining the Adaboost trained models results through a Majority Voting technique, as explained in the Fig. 4. It should be noted that there was an improvement in the prediction rate compared to the prediction based on unique EH vector, and this can be seen in summary in the next section (Fig. 5).

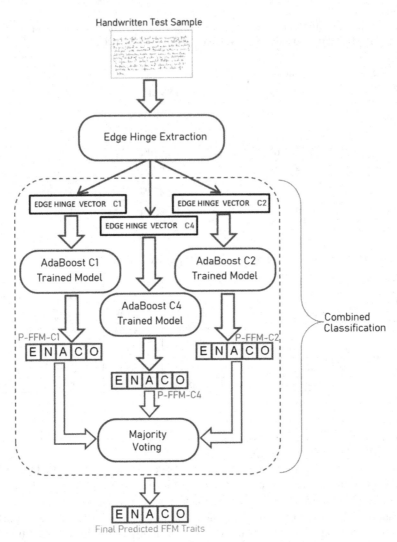

Fig. 5. Combined classification overview in the test step

4   Results and Discussion

Experimental trials with SVM classifier as well as for RF could not exceed 54.5% and 53.68% respectively with EH Features. Although, the EH distributions with configurations (C2, C1 and C4) achieved better overall prediction rates with the AdaBoost algorithm, see Table 3. Openness to experience is the best characterized feature by all the considered features using SVM and Random Forest classifiers, while extraversion trait is the best characterized feature by the AdaBoost algorithm (90.64%) using the same features, see Table 4.

The main observation is that the technique of combining classifiers has contributed in the enhancement of the prediction performance, as can be seen in the table below (Table 5).

Table 5. Comparison of the previous results with those of the Adaboost classifier combination

Edge Hinge Configurations	E	N	A	C	O	Average
C2,C1,C4	88.49 %	83.43 %	83.43 %	82.45 %	**77.30 %**	**83.02 %**
C2	85.96 %	84.79 %	84.79 %	82.45 %	76.60 %	82.92 %
C1	90.64 %	83.04 %	83.04 %	82.45 %	73.68 %	82.57 %
C4	89.47 %	81.28 %	81.28 %	82.45 %	76.02 %	82.10 %

On the data corpus side, it should be mentioned that the used dataset is still small and needs further expansion to become more representative. Looking at Table 1, it can be seen that the dataset is unbalanced with respect to the distribution of samples over the 5 FFM classes. Moreover, it is clear that the number of samples to learn with a 'High' value on the 5 classes is small compared to 'Low' and 'Medium' values. For example, the number of samples with a 'Low' value on 'Openness to experience' class is 402, whilst the number of samples with a 'High' value on the same class is 34 samples. This can have a negative impact on the performance of classifiers as was the case for SVM and Random Forest.

Finally, the obtained results clearly demonstrate the potential of the instrumented features as well as the AdaBoost algorithm and the classifier combination technique for the identification of personality traits. Then, we also report a comparison of our system with state-of-the-art systems of the last four years reported in the literature. The comparisons are summarized in Table 6.

Table 6. Comparison of the performance of handwriting-based personality trait prediction systems.

Paper	Features	Classification	Dataset	Inventory model	Results
Fallah et al.(2016) [2]	TIFs & HLAC	HMM & ANN	70 Subjects	MMPI	70%
Gavrilescu et al. (2018) [4]	Graphological Features	ANN	128 Subjects	FFM	80.5%
UmairShahid (2020) [9]	/	CNN	285 Subjects	FFM	59.73%

(continued)

Table 6. (*continued*)

Paper	Features	Classification	Dataset	Inventory model	Results
Gahmousse et al. (2020) [8]	OBIFC	Rank-SVM	418 Subjects	FFM	58.6%
Proposed Method (2021)	Edge Hinge	Combined Classification based AdaBoost	285 Subjects	FFM	**83.02%**

5 Conclusions and Future Works

In this paper, we presented a method for the prediction of personality traits from handwriting product. The method instrumented the Edge Hinge as a feature extraction technique and exploited the EH configurations range. Experimental work on several classifiers led to choose Adaboost algorithm as the best classifier characterizing the EH features. As a result, Experimental results with Adaboost on several EH configurations revealed that some configurations characterize one class better than another, and this led us to adopt the combination of Trained AdaBoost Models to end up with a Majority Voting technique for each class. The results were promising and are shown in the comparison of the proposed method with other works that used the same dataset or used the FFM model.

As future perspectives, we plan to continue working on this dataset, trying to inset other textural features, combining them in order to find better solutions. Also, we plan to conduct experimental tests with the cross-validation technique, especially since the dataset is unbalanced. Furthermore, we plan to search for possible correlations between the personality traits and the two data corpus provided in the used dataset.

References

1. Joshi, P., Agarwal, A., Dhavale, A., Suryavanshi, R., Kodolikar, S.: Handwriting analysis for detection of personality traits using machine learning approach. Int. J. Comput. Appl. **130**, 40–45 (2015)
2. Fallah, B., Khotanlou, H.: Identify human personality parameters based on handwriting using neural network. In: Artificial Intelligence and Robotics (IRANOPEN), pp. 120–126. IEEE. (2016)
3. Chen, Z., Lin, T.: Automatic personality identification using writing behaviors: an exploratory study. Behav. Inf. Technol. **36**(8), 839–845 (2017)
4. Gavrilescu, M., Vizireanu, N.: Predicting the big five personality traits from handwriting. EURASIP J. Image Video Process. **2018**(1), 57 (2018)
5. Lemos,N., Shah, K., Rade, R., Shah, D.: Personality prediction based on handwriting using machine learning. In: 2018 International Conference on Computational Techniques, Electronics and Mechanical Systems (CTEMS), pp 110–113. IEEE (2018)
6. Ramirez, G., et al.: Overview of the multimedia information processing for personality & social networks analysis contest. In: International Conference on Pattern Recognition Workshop Proceedings (2018)

7. Ramirez, G., Villatoro, E., Jiménez-Salazar, H.: TxPI-u: a resource for personality identification of undergraduates. J. Intell. Fuzzy Syst. **34**(5), 2991–3001 (2018)
8. Gahmousse, A., Gattal, A., Djeddi, C., Siddiqi, I.: Handwriting based personality identification using textural features. In: 2020 International Conference on Data Analytics for Business and Industry: Way Towards a Sustainable Economy (ICDABI). IEEE (2020)
9. Umair, S.: Identification of personality traits using computerized analysis of handwriting, Master thesis of Computer Science, Department of Computer Science, Bahria University,(2020)
10. Valdez-Rodríguez, J.E., Calvo, H., Felipe-Riverón, E.M.: Handwritten Texts for personality identification using convolutional neural networks. In: Zhang, Z., Suter, D., Tian, Y., Branzan Albu, A., Sidère, N., Jair Escalante, H. (eds.) ICPR 2018. LNCS, vol. 11188, pp. 140–145. Springer, Cham (2019). https://doi.org/10.1007/978-3-030-05792-3_13
11. Bulacu, M., Schomaker, L.R.B.: Text-independent writer identification and verification using textural and allographic features. IEEE Trans. on Pattern Analysis and Machine Intelligence (PAMI), Special Issue - Biometrics: Progress and Directions, **29**(4), 701–717 (2007)

An Automated Approach for Analysing Students Feedback Using Sentiment Analysis Techniques

Shpetim Sadriu[1], Krenare Pireva Nuci[1(✉)], Ali Shariq Imran[2], Imran Uddin[3], and Muhammad Sajjad[2,3]

[1] Faculty of Computer Science and Engineering,
University for Business and Technology, Pristina, Kosovo
krenare@gmail.com
[2] Faculty of Information Technology and Electrical Engineering,
Norwegian University of Science and Technology (NTNU), Gjøvik 2815, Norway
[3] Department of Computer Science, Islamia College University Peshawar,
Peshawar 25000, Pakistan

Abstract. Conducting and evaluating continuous student feedback is essential for any quality enhancement cell (QEC) within an education institution. Students' feedback based on their personal opinions can play a vital role in ensuring quality education. However, students' subjective opinions are often ignored due to time constraints or a lack of adequate analysis strategies. Therefore, to automate the quality assurance process, two classification models (i.e., based on Monkey learn API and SentiWord using TextBlob) are proposed to analyze students' feedback data. The results shows that the model employing MonkeyLearn performs nearly 22% points better than the Textblob on the Albanian language dataset obtained from 114 students' responses, achieving 72.12% accuracy.

Keywords: Sentiment analysis · MonkeyLearn · TexBlob · Machine learning · Artificial intelligence · Opinion mining · Emotion classification

1 Introduction

The pandemic of COVID-19 transpose the daily routine and lifestyle of people all over the world. It has also affected the education system and make them shift from in-campus classes into online classes. This switching in the education system induces many unseen consequences including student aptitude, response, learning ability. Therefore, mechanisms should be devised to evaluate the quality of education in online teaching. The traditional approach was to conduct post-class procedures by the quality assurance office. This is usually concretized by collecting feedback from the students about teachers and the courses on prescribed proforma having some predefined questions. This feedback only consists of quantitative data which is not sufficient because qualitative aspects are ignored, such

© Springer Nature Switzerland AG 2022
C. Djeddi et al. (Eds.): MedPRAI 2021, CCIS 1543, pp. 228–239, 2022.
https://doi.org/10.1007/978-3-031-04112-9_17

as student's sentiments at the time of feedback. This poses a challenge to combine quantitative data with qualitative data to elucidate the outcome of the current education scenario through more detailed analysis of students' feedback. The quantitative analysis of student feedback (based on prescribed questions about a course, teacher or assessment) is usually carried out through statistical analysis, whereas the qualitative analysis needs to take into account the students opinion about a particular subject or teacher in their styles, reflecting their state of mind. These opinions can be negative, positive or neutral. To dig out the real essence of their opinion, Sentiment Analysis of opinions is carried out. It is a sub branch of natural language processing (NLP) that aims to extract the sentiments from the text [3,4]. Sentiment Analysis is used to classify the intent of text, whether it is positive, neutral or negative sentiment, and is considered as text classification problem [5,10,21]. Millions of people express their sentiments and opinions in blogs, wikis, social networks and forums [18,20]. These sentiments and opinions are analyzed to monitor public opinion for decision-making [18,21], for example, election results have been predicted in studies by analyzing Twitter posts [16] and social trends related to COVID-19 [8].

In opinion mining, opinions are categorized into positive, negative and neutral while in sentiment analysis different emotions such as love, joy, surprise, anger, sadness, and fear are extracted from the text to evaluate the intended sentiments of the writer. Literature study reveals that there are numerous state-of-the-art machine learning and deep learning based techniques conducting opinion mining and sentiment analysis [3]. The feedback expressed by the students through text-note in the evaluation proforma can be used to evaluate the sentiments of the students. The sentiment analysis plays a vital role to evaluate the overall attitude, feedback and behaviors of the students versus teachers, courses and institutions in the educational system [6]. From the sentiment analysis, it can be easily identified what is the overall status of the students against any course, teacher or institution. Consequently, based on these findings, a different aspect of teaching and learning can be fine-tuned and overall educational policy can be reformed.

This study aims to facilitate the quality enhancement cell (QEC) for analyzing students qualitative feedback by proposing an automated approach for analyzing the sentiments from the captured data. This study follows the previous study conducted by [2] as part of the project supported by the Ministry of Education, Science, Technology and Innovation for the innovation of quality assurance offices within the Higher Education Institutions amidst COVID-19 pandemic crises. The project aimed to document the transformation of in-campus classes to online classes at Kosovo Universities and identified the technological infrastructure for the online classes during COVID-19 lockdown. The key contribution of this study is the collection of 114 students' feedback in Albanian language and applying two state-of-the-art polarity assessment models.

The rest of this paper is organized as follows: Sect. 2 discusses the related work concerning sentiment analysis in the education domain, while Sect. 3 discusses the methodology approach, including the methods and instruments used in this research paper. In Sect. 4 the results are presented, while Sect. 5 concludes the research study and emphasizes the achieved results.

2   Related Work

Researchers have used the sentiment analysis technique in multiple domains for analysing the users' feedback, particularly, students feedback in the education domain. For instance, [13] presented a comprehensive review of aspect-based sentiment analysis approaches in education domain. The paper focuses on the student's opinions towards teachers, courses and institutions. Moreover, according to a study [1], text classification models based on deep learning techniques gained massive popularity in recent years. Deep neural models can achieve incredible results in sentiment analysis tasks. The authors in [26] emphasized the effectiveness of 3W-CNN for sentiment classification on four benchmark data-sets. The study showed 3W-CNN has achieved higher performance compared to convolution Neural Network(CNN) and Naive Bayes - Support Vector Machine (NB-SVM) with 85.8% accuracy. The accuracy of both CNN and NB-SVM on MR data-set was almost equal, but the convergence of CNN was faster.

Sindhu et al. in [22] applied the Long short-term memory (LSTM) model. In it, they initially performed aspect extraction (six aspects extracted: teaching pedagogy, behaviour, knowledge, assessment, experience and general) attaining accuracy up to 91%, following with the sentiment polarity detection by achieving 93% accuracy. The data-set included the opinions of 40 students. Further, Lee et al. proposed a methodology for identifying keywords by discriminating positive and negative sentences [14]. They classified the word based on weakly supervised learning using CNN. Furthermore, [15, 24] proposed models to classify polarity to identify words with high polarity scores using English and Korean language. The models include CNN-Rand, CNN-Static, CNN-Non-Static, CNN-2 channel and CNN-4 channel. Whereas, the work conducted in [15], used deep neural network similar to [7,11]. Moreover, there are certain classification models with pseudo-document generation and self-training modules that use unlabeled data for model refinement. This is a flexible method for handling weak supervision types that can integrate existing deep neural model for text classification. According to Kastrati et al. [11], 80.64% (F1 score) was achieved using weakly supervised framework for aspect-based sentiment analysis whereas for broader course-related aspects the F1 score was 65.64%.

Estradaa et al. in [7] tried to indicate polarity for positive and negative labels (senti-TEXT) as well as polarity with positive, negative learning centered emotions (eduSERE: engaged, excited, bored and frustrated). Moreover, evolutionary algorithm EvoMSA was used to investigate the effectiveness of different architectures (CNN, one LSTM, hybrid between CNN and LSTM and BERT) based on accuracy classification and polarity with learning-centred emotions. The research achieved 95% of accuracy for sentiTEXT and 84% of accuracy for eduSERE. Wang in his work [23] showed that using recurrent Neural network (RNN) the system can achieve significant performance in text categorization. In his study, the author presented disconnected recurrent neural network (DRNN) with positive invariance in combination with RNN. For reaching higher accuracy in text categorization, the author proposed the use of DRNN model, to improve RNN and CNN model.

According to Yang et al. [25], there are two main challenges when classifying sentiment in text:

- Sentiment classification is highly domain-dependent and the efficiency of the trained model is not guaranteed in every domain.
- The quantity of labeled data plays important role in the quality of the classifier, it becomes difficult to evaluate the classifier when there is limited labeled data in a domain.

Therefore, the researchers focused on learning high-level features that can generate sentiment classifications in other domains toward global classifiers. The proposed model is based on aggregation between labeled and un-labeled data from multiple domains by learning new feature representations. The experiment used multi-domain sentiment classification by comparing methods within in-domain classifier and multi-domain classifier.

According to [1,7], aspect-based sentiment analysis (ABSA) plays a key role in predicting polarity of text through NLP. To get precise sentiment expression from ABSA, they propose a model named Attention-based Sentiment Reasoner (AS-Reasoner). The study used English and Chinese language datasets for capturing sentiment similarity between two words in a single sentence and computed weights for global attention from a global perspective. Finally, Kastrati et al. in [12] used sentiment rich representation as an impact of deep learning document classification which increased the performance score by five percentage resulting in 78.10% (F1 score).

This research study differs from the previous discussed research by using existing text analysis APIs such as MonkeyLearn and TextBolob in a dataset constructed from data collected using the primary data collection method in Education domain. The students feedback is initially collected in the Albanian Language. The analysis of the captured feedback is performed at the sentence level. Furthermore, the effectiveness of this technique is realized by comparing the accuracy of the classified sentiments using each of the aforementioned APIs.

3   Methodology

For this research paper, a prototype in Python language is developed. The prototype is fed with 624 paragraphs of opinions expressed by 114 student in Albanian language from the Faculty of Computer Science at the University for Business and Technology, Kosovo.

The experiment followed three phases. As shown in Fig. 1 the first phase dealt mainly with the construction of dataset. The dataset includes three sentiment and seven emotion classes. The maximum length of the sentences in the dataset is 108 words, the minimum is 1 word, whereas the average length of the sentences is 28 words.

The students opinion [19] is processed in sentence level, which then is manually labeled into three sentiment classes (see Fig. 1, sentiment column): positive (1), neutral (2), and negative (3). The distribution in both sentiment classes is

Emotions	Sentiment	Data (ALB)	Data (ENG)
4	3	Per shkak të gjendjes së krijuar si pasojë e pandemisë edhe ne sikur shumica e institucioneve në Kosovë kemi qenë të detyruar që të vijojmë ligjëratat online	Due to the situation created as a result of the pandemic, we, like most institutions in Kosovo, have been forced to attend online lectures
5	1	Gjatë ligjëratave nuk kanë munguar as projektet e ndryshme prej të cilëve kemi përfituar shumë dhe këto projekte edhe pse nga distanca mendoj se kanë qenë mjaft të dobishme	During the lectures there were also various projects from which we benefited a lot and these projects, although from a distance I think they were quite useful
2	1	Në përgjithësi mund të them se gjatë kësaj periudhe të vështirë kemi arritur të përfundojmë me sukses procesin mësimor online	In general I can say that during this difficult period we have managed to successfully complete the online learning process

Fig. 1. A snapshot of the labelled dataset depicting emotion and sentiment category along with the actual feedback data.

imbalanced, 75% are with positive polarity, 0.11% neutral, and 13% negative. With respect to emotional labeling, the authors followed the Parrot model [17]. The Parrot model encapsulates the emotional classifications based on primary aspects such as: love (6), joy (5), surprise (4), anger (3), sadness (2), fear (1), and neutral (0) (Fig. 2).

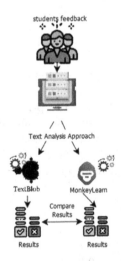

Fig. 2. High-level overview of the proposed methodology.

The second phase follows the creation of the models using two different text analysis approaches i.e., TextBlob API (see Fig. 3) and Monkey Learn API (see Fig. 4) for extracting the sentiment and emotion of the sentences. In both models the Python Flask is used as stack technology for pre-processing dataset and converting data automatically from CSV into JSON format. A Google translation API is also employed to transltate Albanian langauge into English for further processing with MonkeyLearn. An incentive for using two types of APIs is to observe the difference in the classification accuracy using state-of-the-art technology.

To evaluate the proposed model in the third phase, the authors used Precision, Recall, Accuracy and F1 score as evaluation metrics.

TextBlob is an NLP library for Python and it is used for part-of-speech tagging, noun phrase extraction and sentiment analysis. It aims to provide access to a common text processing operation through its interface. In our case, we used the model for performing the sentiment classification of the collected data following the steps depicted in Fig. 3.

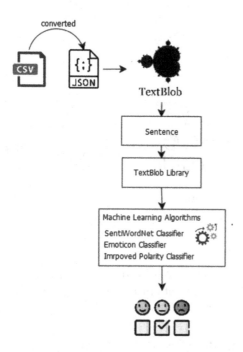

Fig. 3. Sentiment analysis using TextBlog

As shown in Fig. 3, the dataset is initially converted from CSV format into JSON. This is followed by SentiWord Classifier (SWNC), which implements NaiveBayesAnalyzer. NaiveBayesAnalyzer uses Natural Language ToolKit (NLTK) with Emoticon Classifier (EEC) and Improved Polarity Classifier (IPC).

In the second model using MonkeyLearn API (see Fig. 4) on the other hand, the authors integrated Google translate API for language translation, as the MonekyLearn API can not process Albanian language. Additionally, combining MonkeyLearn API and Google-Translate API [9] for Albanian to English translation in real-time shows higher precision (see Table 4). MonkeyLearn API is text-analysis API that allows developers to process textual data for classification. It implements machine learning models for sentiment analysis, keyword extraction and topic detection.

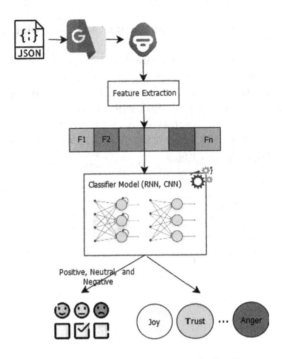

Fig. 4. Sentiment analysis using MonkeyLearn

4   Results

This section presents the results obtained with TextBlob and MonkeyLearn API for sentiment polarity assessment. In the following subsection, we also present the metrics used to evaluate the models.

4.1   Evaluation Metrics

To evaluate the models' performance for predicting sentiment polarity results, we employed precision, accuracy, recall, and F1 score. These are derived from the confusion matrix which is composed of true positives (TP), true negatives (TN), false positives (FP), and false negatives (FN), as described below:

Accuracy - It is the percentage of correctly predicted instances from total instances.

$$Accuracy = \frac{(TP + TN)}{TP + FP + TN + FN} \tag{1}$$

Precision - Precision is the percentage of correctly classified samples for the particular class out of all predicted labels for that class.

$$Precision = \frac{TP}{(TP + FP)} \tag{2}$$

Recall - The recall is the percentage of all predicted samples for the particular class relation with actual labels for that class.

$$Recall = \frac{TP}{(TP + FN)} \tag{3}$$

F1-score - F1 score is a combination of both precision and recall, it can be interpreted as the harmonic mean of precision and recall.

$$F1 - score = \frac{2 \times (\text{Precision} \times \text{Recall})}{(\text{Precision} + \text{Recall})} \tag{4}$$

4.2   Polarity Prediction Using Textblob and MonkeyLearn

The TextBlob API uses a range from -1 to 1 for sentiment classification. The negative responses are assigned -1, 0 for neutral, and $+1$ for positive sentiment. Table 1 shows that the TextBlob model predicted 165 sentences as negative out of 624 in total (i.e. 26.44%), 147 responses with neutral polarity (23.56%), and the rest of 312 sentences as positive (50%). Whereas, the MonkeyLearn API predicted 98 negative sentences (15.71%), 85 responses with neutral polarity (13.62%), and the rest of 441 sentences with positive polarity (70.67%).

Table 1. MonkeyLearn versus TextBlob API prediction

Sentiment classification	MonkeyLearn (%)	TextBlob (%)
Positive	70.67	50
Neutral	13.62	23.56
Negative	15.71	26.44

The validation of the results for the model using MonkeyLearn for predicting the sentiment polarity (positive, neutral and negative) is performed using the confusion matrix, and Table 2 shows the classification report. It can be seen that the model based on MonkeyLearn was 72% accurate.

The same approach for validating the results for the model using TextBlob for predicting the three classes of sentiment polarity is performed, and Table 3 shows the classification report. TextBlob achieved an accuracy of 50%.

Table 2. Classification report for MonkeyLearn model

	Precision	Recall	F1-Score	Support
−1	0.44	0.51	0.47	84
0	0.28	0.33	0.31	72
1	0.87	0.82	0.84	468
Accuracy			0.72	624
Macro avg	0.53	0.55	0.54	624
Weighted avg	0.74	0.72	0.73	624

Table 3. Classification report for TextBlob model

	Precision	Recall	F1-Score	Support
−1	0.19	0.38	0.26	84
0	0.11	0.22	0.15	72
1	0.86	0.57	0.68	468
Accuracy			0.50	624
Macro avg	0.39	0.39	0.36	624
Weighted avg	0.68	0.50	0.56	624

Table 4, presents the comparison results of the prediction for both models with respect to accuracy, precision (avg.), recall (avg.) and F1-Score (avg.). The model using MonkeyLearn resulted with higher accuracy (72%) compared to TextBlob (50%).

Table 4. Accuracy (%), Precision (Avg%), Recall (Avg%) and F1-Score results for MonkeyLearn and TexBlob API

Model	Accuracy	Precision	Recall	F1-Score
MonkeyLearn API	0.72	55	53	54
TextBlob API	0.50	39	39	36

4.3 Emotion Identification Using MonkeyLearn

In addition to sentiment classification, we further analyszed the emotions expressed in the feedback by students employing MonkeyLearn emotion classifier API. We classified the emotions into distinct categories defined by the Parrot model i.e. love, joy, surprise, anger, sadness, and fear [17]. We further had few instances in our dataset that didn't depict any significant emotions, which we classified as neutral.

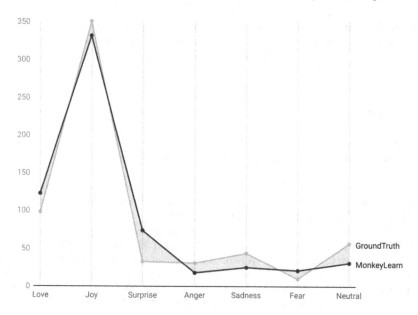

Fig. 5. Emotion classification using MonkeyLearn model

The results in Fig. 5 shows that Joy emotion dominated with 351 sentences (56%), followed by Love emotion with 98 responses (16%). The model predicted 32 (5%) responses as Surprise and Anger, While Sadness was recorded in 44 responses (7%) and the last emotion class Fear, appeared in 10 response sentences (2%). Finally, we have included Neutral emotion category for the dataset instances that are not satisfied with Parrot emotions, containing 57 sentences (9%).

5   Conclusion

This research paper studied two automated models for sentiment analysis of student's feedback to predict the sentiment polarity and identify emotions. To predict the sentiment polarity, the first model uses TextBlob API, whereas the second model uses MonkeyLearn API. The latter model is further utilized to identify seven emotional categories from the students' feedback, following the Parrot Model classification. Results from both TextBlob and MonkeyLearn models are validated using a ground truth dataset, which is constructed from 114 students' feedback (624 sentences with average length of 28 words) as part of the quality enhancement cell procedure for the Faculty of Computer Science and Engineering at The University for Business and Technology in Kosovo. The results shows that the model using MonkeyLearn achieved a sentiment polarity classification accuracy of 72.12% compared to the model using Texblob, with 50.48%.

Acknowledgment. The authors would like to thank the Ministry of Education, Science, Technology and Innovation in Kosovo for supporting this research, as part of the project: The impact of COVID-19 pandemic in teaching and learning in Higher Education Institutions in Kosovo.

References

1. Apuk, V., Nuci, K.P.: Classification of pedagogical content using conventional machine and deep learning model. WiPiEC J. Works Progr. Embed. Comput. **7**(1) (2021)
2. Baftiu, E., Nuci, K.P.: The transformation process from in-campus classes into online classes due to the Covid-19 situation-the case of higher education institutions in Kosovo. arXiv preprint arXiv:2104.03896 (2021)
3. Birjali, M., Kasri, M., Beni-Hssane, A.: A comprehensive survey on sentiment analysis: approaches, challenges and trends. Knowl. Based Syst. 107134 (2021)
4. Chaturvedi, I., Cambria, E., Welsch, R.E., Herrera, F.: Distinguishing between facts and opinions for sentiment analysis: survey and challenges. Inf. Fusion **44**, 65–77 (2018). https://doi.org/10.1016/j.inffus.2017.12.006, https://www.sciencedirect.com/science/article/pii/S1566253517303901
5. Choi, Y., Lee, H.: Data properties and the performance of sentiment classification for electronic commerce applications. Inf. Syst. Front. **19**(5), 993–1012 (2017). https://doi.org/10.1007/s10796-017-9741-7
6. Edalati, M., Imran, A.S., Kastrati, Z., Daudpota, S.M.: The potential of machine learning algorithms for sentiment classification of students' feedback on MOOC. In: Arai, K. (ed.) IntelliSys 2021. LNNS, vol. 296, pp. 11–22. Springer, Cham (2022). https://doi.org/10.1007/978-3-030-82199-9_2
7. Estradaa, M.L.B., Cabada, R.Z., Bustillos, R.O., Graff, M.: Opinion mining and emotion recognition applied to learning, ELSEVIER. Expert Syst. Appl. **150**, 12 (2020)
8. Imran, A.S., Daudpota, S.M., Kastrati, Z., Batra, R.: Cross-cultural polarity and emotion detection using sentiment analysis and deep learning on Covid-19 related tweets. IEEE Access **8**, 181074–181090 (2020)
9. Google Cloud Translate, INC.: Translation. https://cloud.google.com/translate. Accessed 28 2006
10. Ju, S., Li, S.: Active learning on sentiment classification by selecting both words and documents. In: Ji, D., Xiao, G. (eds.) CLSW 2012. LNCS (LNAI), vol. 7717, pp. 49–57. Springer, Heidelberg (2013). https://doi.org/10.1007/978-3-642-36337-5_6
11. Kastrati, Z., Imran, A.S., Kurti, A.: Weakly supervised framework for aspect-based sentiment analysis on students reviews of MOOCs. IEEE Access **4**, 2016(4(10.)) (2017)
12. Kastrati, Z., Imran, A.S., Yayilgan, S.Y.: The impact of deep learning on document classification using semantically rich representations, research gate, no. 10, 25 (2019)
13. Kastrati, Z., Dalipi, F., Imran, A.S., Pireva Nuci, K., Wani, M.A.: Sentiment analysis of students' feedback with NLP and deep learning: a systematic mapping study. Appl. Sci. **11**(9), 3986 (2021)
14. Lee, G., Jeong, J., Seo, S., Kim, C., Kang, P.: Sentiment classification with word attention based on, knowledge-based systems. Knowl. Based Syst. **152**(10) (2018)

15. Meng, Y., Shen, J., Zhang, C., Han, J.: Weakly-supervised neural text classification, department of computer science, university of at Illinois Urbana-champaign, IL, USA, no. 10, pp. 983–992 (2018)
16. O'Connor, B., Balasubramanyan, R., Routledge, B.R., Smith, N.A.: From tweets to polls: linking text sentiment to public opinion time series. In: Fourth International AAAI Conference on Weblogs and Social Media (2010)
17. Parrott, W.: Emotions in Social Psychology. Psychology Press, Philadelphia (2001). 978-0863776830
18. Ramírez-Tinoco, F.J., Alor-Hernández, G., Sánchez-Cervantes, J.L., Olivares-Zepahua, B.A., Rodríguez-Mazahua, L.: A brief review on the use of sentiment analysis approaches in social networks. In: CIMPS 2017. AISC, vol. 688, pp. 263–273. Springer, Cham (2018). https://doi.org/10.1007/978-3-319-69341-5_24
19. Rrustemi, V., Nuci, K.P.: Aspect based sentiment analysis using deep learning techniques. Thesis, Work in Progress (2021)
20. Saleh, M.R., Martín-Valdivia, M.T., Montejo-Ráez, A., Ureña-López, L.: Experiments with SVM to classify opinions in different domains. Expert Syst. Appl. 38(12), 14799–14804 (2011)
21. Schuller, B., Mousa, A.E.D., Vryniotis, V.: Sentiment analysis and opinion mining: on optimal parameters and performances. Wiley Interdisc. Rev. Data Min. Knowl. Discov. 5(5), 255–263 (2015)
22. Sindhu, I., Daudpota, S.M., Badar, K., Bakhtyar, M., Baber, J., Nurunnab, D.M.: Aspect based opinion mining on student s feedback for faculty teaching performance evaluation. IEEE Access 7(10), 108729–108741 (2019)
23. Wang, B.: Disconnected recurrent neural networks for text categorization. Joint Laboratory of HIT and iFLYTEK, iFLYTEK Research, Beijing, China (20118)
24. Wojcik, K., Tuchowski, J.: Feature based sentiment analysis. In: 3rd International Scientific Conference on Contemporary Issues in Economics, Business and Management EBM 2014, no. 269093520 (2014)
25. Yang, F., Mukherjee, A., Zhang, Y.: Leveraging multiple domains for sentiment classification. In: Proceedings of COLING 2016, the 26th International Conference on Computational Linguistics: Technical Papers, pp. 2978–2988 (2016)
26. Zhang, Y., Zhang, Z., Miao, D., Wang, J.: Three-way enhanced convolutional neural networks for sentence-level sentiment classification. ELSEVIER (10), 55–64 (2018)

Keyword Spotting in Modern Handwritten Documents Using oBIFs

Douaa Yousfi[1]([✉]), Abdeljalil Gattal[2], Chawki Djeddi[2,3], Imran Siddiqi[4], and Ameur Bensefia[5]

[1] Laboratory of Mathematics, Informatics and Systems (LAMIS), University of Larbi Tebessi, Tebessa, Algeria
douaa.yousfi@univ-tebessa.dz
[2] Department of Mathematics and Computer Science, Larbi Tebessi University, Tebessa, Algeria
{abdeljalil.gattal,c.djeddi}@univ-tebessa.dz
[3] LITIS Laboratory, University of Rouen, Rouen, France
[4] Bahria University, Islamabad, Pakistan
imran.siddiqi@bahria.edu.pk
[5] Higher Colleges of Technology, CIS Division, Abu Dhabi, UAE
abensefia@hct.ac.ae

Abstract. Spotting keywords in modern handwritten documents is an interesting problem that allows to search, index, and classify document images. This paper investigates the word spotting problem in a segmentation-based framework where features extracted from word images are employed to match a query keyword with those in a reference base. More specifically, we employ oriented basic image features (oBIFs) to characterize the word images while matching is carried out by computing the distance (similarity) between word images in the feature space. Experimental study of the system is carried out using the dataset of the ICFHR 2014 word spotting competition and promising results are reported in terms of P@K precision and mean average precision (mAP).

Keywords: Word spotting · Modern Handwritten documents · Oriented Basic Image Features (oBIFs)

1 Introduction

In the recent years, word spotting has emerged as a highly effective technique for information retrieval and large-scale indexing of datasets of handwritten documents. Word spotting was proposed as an alternative to full transcription to retrieve keywords from document images. A typical word spotting system includes a set of documents (reference base), and, when provided with a query item, the system outputs a collection of documents that are relevant to the query. In this perspective, word spotting systems are similar to the traditional information retrieval systems. Formally, word spotting (WS) is the task of retrieving all instances of a given query word from collections of document images (typically handwritten) using image matching techniques without the involvement of an OCR.

© Springer Nature Switzerland AG 2022
C. Djeddi et al. (Eds.): MedPRAI 2021, CCIS 1543, pp. 240–250, 2022.
https://doi.org/10.1007/978-3-031-04112-9_18

As a function of the input query type, word spotting methods are divided into two broad categories, Query-by-Example (QbE) and Query-by-String (QbS). In the QbE approach, the user provides an image of the word as query whereas the QbS approach allows the user to provide the query in the form of text. In many cases, the provided query string is converted to an image which is subsequently employed in the QbE framework. On the other hand, from a methodological viewpoint, word spotting techniques are distinguished into segmentation-based and segmentation-free approaches. In segmentation-based approaches, the queried words can be directly compared with the segmented word images [1] while segmentation-free techniques rely on comparing parts of documents to match the query [2] without any segmentation into semantically meaningful entities (words for example).

A typical word spotting system includes the key components of preprocessing, segmentation, feature extraction, and matching; feature extraction and matching steps being the focus of the current study. Feature extraction is the most critical part of any pattern matching system. Effective feature representations can lead to high performance even with simple matching techniques. This study investigates the effectiveness of oriented-basic image features (oBIFs) for spotting of handwritten keywords. Features extracted from segmented handwritten words are compared with those of the query images using a number of distance metrics. As a function of degree of similarity, documents containing the queries keyword are returned to the user. Details of the proposed technique are presented in Sect. 3 of the paper. Prior to these details, we present an overview of notable studies on the problem of word spotting in Sect. 2. Section 4 introduces the experimental study along with the reported results and discussion. At the end, we conclude the paper in Sect. 6 with a summary of our findings and a discussion on avenues of further research on this subject.

2 Related Work

Keyword spotting has remained an attractive area of research for the pattern classification community, both for handwritten and printed documents. Among one of the notable works on this subject, Llados et al. [3] carried out a comparative study to assess the performance of different descriptors for spotting keywords in historical documents using a query-by-example framework. Dynamic Time Warping (DTW) based matching is employed as the baseline while other features include bag of visual words, a pseudo-structural model, and a structural approach that represents words as graphs. Experimental study on the George Washington dataset and a collection of marriage records revealed that the bag of words (statistical) features outperforms the other representations.

In another study, Kovalchuk et al. [4] exploit histogram of oriented gradients (HOG) and local binary patterns (LBP) with nearest neighbor matching to present an efficient word spotting method. Experimental study on the dataset of the ICFHR 2014 Handwritten Keyword Spotting Competition [5] reported promising retrieval performance. A statistical method based on the Harris corner detector is presented by Rothfeder et al. [6] to compare segmented word images. The correspondence between angular points is employed to classify word images by similarity. Matches between these points are established by comparing local windows and using the sum of the squares of differences

(SSD). Experiments were carried out on two datasets of historical documents with 2372 (good quality) and 3262 (poor quality) images and reported average precision of 62.5% and 15.5% respectively.

Among other known methods, Aldavert et al. [7] propose a query-by-string framework where images of words in the learning set are represented by both textual and visual representations. The textual representation is based on n-grams of characters while the visual representation relies on the bag of visual words scheme. The two representations are fused and projected into a sub-vector space using the latent semantic analysis method. This transformation allowed, from a textual query, to retrieve instances of words that were represented only by the visual modality.

In addition to various research studies, efforts have also been made to objectively evaluate the advancements on the problem through organization of international competitions. The most notable of these is the Handwritten Keyword Spotting Competition [5] in conjunction with the International Conference on Frontiers in Handwriting Recognition (ICFHR). The competition included two task, segmentation-based and segmentation-free spotting. Among the participating systems the highest mean average precisions for the two tasks read 33.80 and 52.40 respectively on the Modern and Bentham dataset.

A summary of notable word spotting based techniques reported in the literature is presented in Table 1. It can be seen that though the performance of different studies varies as a function of the technique as well as the dataset employed, in general, the reported mean average precision (mAP) values are low and offer substantial potential to the research community to come up with robust solutions for this challenging problem.

Table 1. Performance comparison of well-known keyword spotting systems reported in the literature

Study			Database	mAP
Methods	Features	Metric		
Llados et al. (2012) [3]	BoVW	Cosine distance	George Washington	42.20
			Barcelona Cathedral	30.00
Kovalchuk et al. (2014) [4]	HOG and LBP	L2 distance	George Washington	50.10
			Lord Byron	90.70
Rothfeder et al. (2003) [6]	Corner Feature	L2 distance	Reasonable quality images of GW	62.57
Aldavert et al. (2013) [7]	Textual descriptor and BoVW	Cosine distance	All words as queries (GW)	56.54
			In vocabulary queries (GW)	76.20
Best system in [5]	HOG and LBP	L2 distance	Modern Dataset	33.80
	HOG and LBP	L2 distance	Bentham dataset	52.40

3   Proposed Methods

The proposed method in the current study relies on a segmentation-based approach where the location of words in the document images is provided in the ground truth. The technique is based on two key steps, extraction of features from the word images and word matching. A graphical overview of the method is presented in Fig. 1 while the details of feature extraction and matching are presented in the following sections.

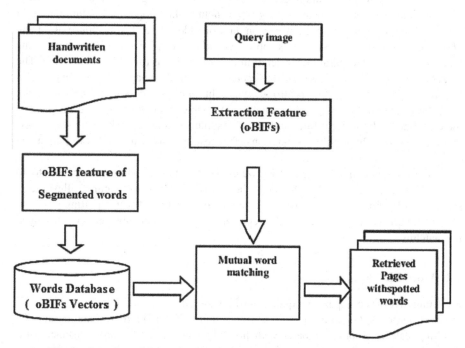

Fig. 1. Overview of the proposed segmentation-based wordspotting technique

3.1   Feature Extraction

Choosing a robust feature representation is the most critical step in any pattern matching problem. The key objective of feature extraction is to represent the (word) images in such that objects (words) with similar morphological properties tend to cluster together in the feature space while those with different visual appearance are apart. In other words, the idea is to seek features which minimize the intra-class and maximize inter-class similarities. For the problem under study, words represent the objects of interest and are employed for feature extraction. A wide variety of statistical and structural features, extracted from handwritten words, have been investigated in the literature for problems like handwriting recognition, writer identification and classification of writing styles, in addition to word spotting. Among these, we have chosen to employ the oriented basic image features (oBIFs) [8, 9]. The oBIFs have been successfully applied to a number of pattern classification problems like texture classification [8], digit recognition [10], writer identification [9, 11, 12], gender classification [13] and handwriting-based personality identification [14].

The oBIF descriptor is an extension to the basic image features (BIFs) [8, 9] where the computation involves labeling each location in the image into one of the seven local symmetry classes. The symmetry types include flat, slope, dark rotational, light rotational, dark line on light, light line on dark or saddle-like. The response of a bank of six derivative-of-Gaussian filters (up to second order) of size is determined by the scale parameter σ. The parameter ε determines if a location is to be classified as flat. The local orientation that can be assigned to each location in the image depends on the local symmetry type. If the location is attributed to light rotational, dark rotational, or the flat class, no orientation is assigned. A total of n possible orientations can be assigned to the dark line on light, light line on dark and saddle-like classes, while the slope class includes a total of 2n possible orientations. This results in a feature vector of dimension $5n + 3$.

In our implementation of the oBIFs, we fix the orientation quantization parameter to $n = 5$. This results in a total of 28 entries in the oBIFs dictionary. Figure 2 illustrates a sample word encoded using the oBIFs. From the perspective of word spotting problem, we encode all words using the oBIFs representation which is subsequently employed for matching.

3.2 Word Matching

Matching involves comparing a query word image with those in the reference base for retrieval purposes. Given a query word, we compute its oBIFs representation and the resulting feature vector is compared with those of all the reference words. Distance (similarity) between two feature vectors is computed using the city-block distance [15] while a number of other metrics are also investigated. These include the Euclidean distance, cosine similarity, hamming distance, correlation coefficient, Spearman's correlation and Chebychev distance. The sensitivity of matching performance to the type of metric is presented later in the paper.

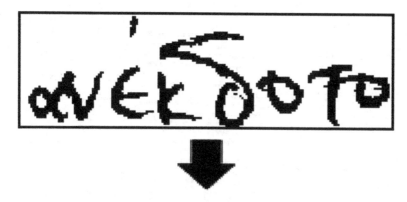

Fig. 2. Example of oBIFs computation for a handwritten word image for $\sigma = 2$ and $\sigma = 4$ while $\varepsilon = 0.001$.

4   Experimental Results

The experimental study of the proposed method is carried out on the contemporary dataset from the ICFHR 2014 Competition on Handwritten Keyword Spotting (H-KWS 2014) [5] for the segmentation-based track where the locations of the word images within the document are provided. The dataset consists of handwritten documents from the ICDAR 2009 handwritten segmentation contest [16], written in four languages (English, French, German, and Greek). The reference base has a total of 100 document images (25 for each of the four languages) and 300 query word images. Samples of document images from the dataset are illustrated in Fig. 3.

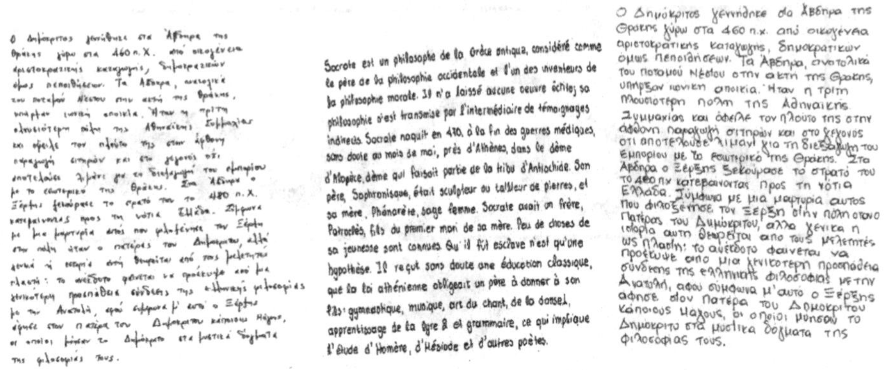
Socrate est un philosophe de la Grèce antique, considéré comme
le père de la philosophie occidentale et l'un des inventeurs de
la philosophie morale. Il n'a laissé aucune oeuvre écrite; sa
philosophie s'est transmise par l'intermédiaire de témoignages
indirects. Socrate naquit en 470, à la fin des guerres médiques,
sans doute au mois de mai, près d'Athènes, dans le dème
d'Alopèce, dème qui faisait partie de la tribu d'Antiochide. Son
père, Sophronisque, était sculpteur ou tailleur de pierres, et
sa mère, Phénarète, sage femme. Socrate avait un frère,
Patroclès, fils du premier mari de sa mère. Peu de choses de
sa jeunesse sont connues. Qu'il fût esclave n'est qu'une
hypothèse. Il reçut sans doute une éducation classique,
que la loi athénienne obligeait un père à donner à son
fils: gymnastique, musique, art du chant, de la danse,
apprentissage de la lyre et grammaire, ce qui implique
l'étude d'Homère, d'Hésiode et d'autres poètes.

Fig. 3. Samples of handwritten document images from the ICFHR competition dataset

To quantify the system performance in different experiment, we employ the standard metrics include the Top retrieved words (P@k) and the mean Average Precision (mAP). For completeness, these metrics are elaborated in the following:

- P@k, the precision at ***k*** is obtained by computing the precision at a given cut-off rank, considering only the ***k*** top-most results returned by the system [17]. In out experiments, we report the results for three values of ***k*** (1, 5 and 10). Formally, P@k measure is defined as:

$$P@k = \frac{|\{relevant\ words\} \cap \{k\ retrieved\ words\}|}{|\{k\ retrieved\ \ words\}|} \tag{1}$$

- The mean Average Precision (mAP) for a given set of query images, is the mean of the average precision scores for each query. The Average Precision for a query is defined as:

$$AP = \frac{\sum_{k=1}^{n}(p(k) * rel(k))}{|\{retrieved\ words\}|} \tag{2}$$

where rel(k) takes the value 1 if a word at rank k is relevant and the value 0 otherwise.

We carried out a series of experiments to evaluate the effectiveness of the oBIF features for spotting words in document images. The 100 document images in the ICFHR 2014 competition dataset are employed as the reference base while six-word images (illustrated in Fig. 4) are employed as query samples.

In the first series of experiments, we study the impact of the scale parameter σ (σ ∈ {1,2,4,8,16}) in computing the oBIF features. City-block distance is employed as distance metric for matching purposes in these experiments while the parameter ε is fixed to a small value of 0.001. The performance in terms of Top1, Top5, Top10 and mAP is summarized in Fig. 5 while the performance for few of the combinations of scale parameter is presented in Table 2.

It can be seen from Table 1 that the matching performance varies as a function of the scale parameter in computing the oBIFs. The oBIF features generated and combined

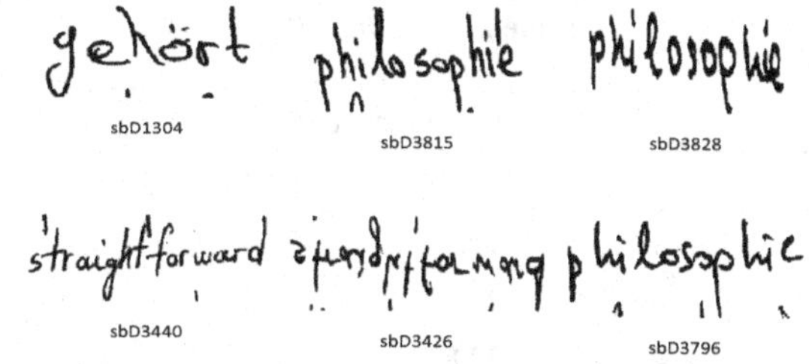

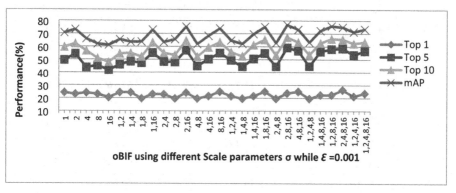

Fig. 4. Samples of the selected query words from the modern dataset

using the values of the scale parameter $\sigma = 2,8,16$ outperform the other configurations reporting a mAP of 76.86%. The performance on other metrics reads a Top-1 precision of 23.77%, Top-5 of 59.23%, and Top-10 of 67.16%. The best performance rates of these experiments are summarized in Table 2.

Fig. 5. The performance of the proposed method using oBIFs

Table 2. Performance with different parameters in computing obifs

oBIFs Parameter		Size	Performance (%)			
ε	σ		Top 1	Top 5	Top 10	mAP
0.001	1	23	24.15	49.42	59.50	70.59
	2	23	22.97	54.17	62.19	73.11
	4	23	24.04	43.74	56.58	65.88
	8	23	23.00	45.24	50.76	61.96
	16	23	20.41	41.60	47.83	61.04
	1,2	46	24,25	45,97	54,42	65,33
	1,4	46	24,25	48,39	54,88	63,48

(*continued*)

Table 2. (*continued*)

oBIFs Parameter		Size	Performance (%)			
ε	σ		Top 1	Top 5	Top 10	mAP
	1,8	46	19,6	47,17	52,03	63,63
	1,16	46	22,97	55,07	63,18	72,87
	2,4	46	22,86	48,17	54,84	63,32
	2,8	46	19,6	47,92	53,5	65,53
	2,16	46	24,15	57,17	64,55	75,31
	4,8	46	19,6	44,84	52,18	61,91
	4,16	46	21,58	50,3	59,37	68,26
	8.16	46	24,95	54,96	63,32	74,02
	1,2,4	69	21,47	49,45	55,61	64,64
	1,4,8	69	19,6	44,42	52,55	62,11
	1,4,16	69	21,58	50,57	61,2	69,6
	1,8,16	69	25,05	54,82	65,28	75,26
	2,4,8	69	19,6	44,51	53,36	62,72
	2,8,16	69	23.77	**59.23**	**67.16**	**76.86**
	4,8,16	69	25,05	56,68	63,47	73,2
	1,2,4,8	92	19,6	44,72	53,64	63,32
	1,4,8,16	92	22,49	56,11	62,85	72,28
	1,2,8,16	92	22,49	58,1	66,04	75,91
	2,4,8,16	92	**26.34**	58.65	65.64	75.02
	1,2,4,16	92	21,47	53,55	62,47	71,4
	1,2,4,8,16	92	23,77	56,64	63,55	73,52

In addition to the city-block distance, we also evaluated the best configuration of oBIFs using different metrics and the corresponding results are presented in Table 3. It can be observed from the reported results that with few exceptions, the performance of different metrics is more or less similar. The highest mAP is reported using the correlation measure and reads 78.89%. These results are quite promising and validate the effectiveness of oBIFs for characterizing word images. It should also be noted that we do not carry out any pre-processing in the word images and the features are directly extracted from the raw images.

Table 3. Performance of the proposed method as a function of different distance metrics

oBIFs Parameter	Distance Type	*Top 1*	*Top 5*	*Top 10*	*mAP*
$\varepsilon = 0.001$ and $\sigma = 2,8,16$	City-block	23.77	**59.23**	67.16	76.86
	Euclidean	**27.83**	56.37	65.51	76.26
	Cosine	26.44	59.07	68.44	78.28
	Hamming	10.47	26.40	30.71	40.41
	Correlation	26.44	59.06	**68.81**	**78.89**
	Spearman	23.08	49.62	59.18	69.65
	Chebychev	24.14	52.76	61.75	72.90

5 Conclusions and Future Works

This study targeted the problem of word spotting in handwritten documents and investigated the effectiveness of oriented basic image features (oBIFs) in characterizing handwritten words. Features were extracted (and combined) using different configurations of oBIFs parameters and a number of distance metrics were employed to compare a query word image with those in the reference base. The system was evaluated on the modern dataset from the ICFHR 2014 Competition on Handwritten Keyword Spotting (H-KWS 2014) and the preliminary results obtained in our experiments are quite encouraging.

Our further study on this subject will include an investigation of other statistical as well as structure features. Furthermore, in addition to the conventional features, data driven feature learning is also planned to be investigated. Furthermore, the matching which presently relies on instance-based classification can be further enriched by model-based classification.

References

1. Greibus, M., Telksnys, L.: Speech keyword spotting with rule based segmentation. Inf. Softw. Technol. **403**, 186–197 (2013)
2. Rusinol, M., Aldavert, D., Toledo, R., Llads, J.: Efficient segmentation-free keyword spotting in historical document collections. Pattern Recogn. **48**(2), 545–555 (2015)
3. Llados, J., Rusinol, M., Fornes, A., Fernandez, D., Dutta, A.: On the influence of word representations for handwritten word spotting in historical documents. IJPRAI **26**(5), 1263002 (2012)
4. Kovalchuk, A., Wolf, L., Dershowitz, N.: A simple and fast word spotting method. In: 14th International Conference on Frontiers in Handwriting Recognition (ICFHR), pp. 3–8 (2014)
5. Pratikakis, I., Zagoris, K., Gatos, B., Louloudis, G., Stamatopoulos, N.: Icfhr 2014 competition on handwritten keyword spotting (H-KWS 2014). In: 14th International Conference on Frontiers in Handwriting Recognition (ICFHR), pp. 814–819 (2014)
6. Rothfeder J., Feng S., Rath T. Using corner feature correspondences to rank word images by similarity. In: Conference on Computer Vision and Pattern Recognition Workshop, Madison, USA, pp. 30–35 (2003)

7. Aldavert, D., Rusiñol, M., Toledo, R., Lladós, J.: Integrating visual and textual cues for query-by-string word spotting. In: Proceedings of the International Conference on Document Analysis and Recognition, pp. 511–515 (2013)
8. Newell, A.J., Griffin, L.D., Morgan, R.M., Bull, P.A.: Texture-based estimation of physical characteristics of sand grains. In: 2010 International Conference on Digital Image Computing: Techniques and Applications, pp. 504–509 (2010)
9. Newell, A.J., Griffin, L.D.: Writer identification using oriented basic image features and the delta encoding. Pattern Recogn. **47**(6), 2255–2265 (2013)
10. Gattal, A., Djeddi, C., Chibani, Y., Siddiqi, I.: Isolated handwritten digit recognition using oBIFs and background features. In: Proceedings - 12th IAPR International Workshop on Document Analysis Systems, DAS 2016 (2016). https://doi.org/10.1109/DAS.2016.10
11. Gattal, A., Djeddi, C., Siddiqi, I., Al-Maadeed, S. Writer identification on historical documents using oriented basic image features. In: Proceedings of International Conference on Frontiers in Handwriting Recognition, ICFHR 2018-August, 369–373 (Institute of Electrical and Electronics Engineers Inc., 2018)
12. Abbas, F., Gattal, A., Djeddi, C., Siddiqi, I., Bensefia, A., Saoudi, K.: Texture feature column scheme for single and multi-script writer identification. IET Biometrics **10**(2), 179–193 (2021). https://doi.org/10.1049/bme2.12010
13. Gattal, A., Djeddi, C., Siddiqi, I., Chibani, Y.: Gender classification from offline multi-script handwriting images using oriented Basic Image Features (oBIFs). Expert Syst. Appl. **99**, 155–167 (2018)
14. Gahmousse, A., Gattal, A., Djeddi, C., Siddiqi, I.: Handwriting based personality identification using textural features. In: 2020 International Conference on Data Analytics for Business and Industry: Way Towards a Sustainable Economy (ICDABI), Sakheer, Bahrain, pp. 1–6 (2020). https://doi.org/10.1109/ICDABI51230.2020.9325664
15. Mitra, D., Sarkar, P., Roy, P.: Face recognition by city-block distance classifier in supervised machine learning. IJRAR **6**, 21653 (2019)
16. Gatos, B., Stamatopoulos, N., Louloudis, G.: ICDAR2009 handwriting segmentation contest. Int. J. Doc. Anal. Recogn. **14**(1), 25–33 (2011)
17. Wang, P., Eglin, V., Garcia, C., Largeron, C., Llados, J., Fornes, A.: A novel learning-free word spotting approach based on graph representation. In: 11th IAPR International Workshop on Document Analysis Systems (DAS), pp. 207–211 (2014)

Artificial Intelligence and Intelligent Systems

Real-Time Detection of Traffic Anomalies Near Roundabouts

Anima Pramanik[1(✉)], Sobhan Sarkar[2], Chawki Djeddi[3,4], and J. Maiti[1,5]

[1] Department of Industrial and Systems Engineering, IIT Kharagpur, Kharagpur 721302, India
apramanik17@gmail.com, jhareswar.maiti@hotmil.com
[2] Information Systems and Business Analytics, IIM Ranchi, Ranchi 834008, Jharkhand, India
sobhan.sarkar@iimranchi.ac.in
[3] Department of Mathematics and Computer Science, Larbi Tebessi University,
Tebessa, Algeria
c.djeddi@univ-tebessa.dz
[4] LITIS Lab, University of Rouen, Rouen, France
[5] Centre of Excellence on Safety Engineering and Analytics, IIT Kharagpur, Kharagpur
721302, India

Abstract. Visual analytics can bridge the gap between computational and human approaches for detecting traffic anomalies near the round-about, making the data analysis process more transparent. The main problem with anomaly detection is the unavailability of anomalous data as they do not occur frequently. Moreover, there is a variety in the characteristics of the same real-time scenario. A solution is proposed to handle these issues using unsupervised learning which mainly encloses the detection of vehicles, road, roundabout violations, and traffic jams near the round-about. Initially, vehicles, roads, and round-about are detected based on Histogram of Gradient (HoG) feature descriptor and color information. Then, optical flow is applied to the detected vehicles for obtaining their trajectory information. Finally, the round-about violation is detected based on the position and angle between the centre of the round-about and the vehicle trajectory. Additionally, the number of vehicles near the round-about is computed for detecting the traffic jam. The effectiveness of the proposed algorithm is demonstrated over 30 real-time traffic videos. Some additional comparative studies are done over the benchmark data YouTube8M. Through an extensive study, it can be concluded that our proposed algorithm is superior to some state-of-the-arts.

Keywords: Round-about violation · Traffic jam · Video analytics · Road safety

1 Introduction

For the past few decades, real-time traffic anomaly detection, especially using video analysis, has become a very important subject. It has been an integral subject of traffic management and Intelligent Transportation Systems (ITS), helping in anomaly detection and thereby reduction of occurrences of escalation of accidents, especially on road, and enhancing road safety. Traffic anomaly refers to the unusual/unnatural behavior

C. Djeddi et al. (Eds.): MedPRAI 2021, CCIS 1543, pp. 253–264, 2022.
https://doi.org/10.1007/978-3-031-04112-9_19

corresponding to either vehicle or pedestrian. Such examples are speed violation, jamming, overtaking, illegal parking, oncoming traffic, and illegal turn. These are acted as the reasons for traffic accidents. As per the road crash studies, it has been observed that traffic accidents predominantly happen in the vicinity of the roundabout (i.e., road intersection) due to either jamming or illegal turn [4, 10, 11]. Therefore, we intend to analyze these traffic behavior near the roundabout.

Road congestion or traffic jam seriously affect human's everyday's life. Initially, a traffic jam is detected by a person standing at a heavy traffic area. Later, with the advancement of image processing and deep learning, the development of an automated system for the detection of traffic jams is attracting more and more interest [9]. Image processing-based conventional studies for the detection of traffic jams has gained much attention [9]. While, deep learning has remained the more popular choice due to its proficiency in object detection, it has limitations in anomaly detection [19]. Deep learning is restricted to the training classes. Moreover, there is a variety in the characteristics of same real-time scenario [21]. Therefore, unsupervised learning (i.e., image processing) is adopted in this study for traffic anomaly detection. Image processing-based conventional studies for the detection of traffic jam mainly consist of background monitoring, foreground object detection, feature extraction, training, and traffic jam estimation [13]. In these processes, training background is time-consuming. Moreover, some factors, including light illumination, camera shaking, and certain change in the scenario can affect these processes. To address these issues, an optical flow-based Spatio-temporal feature for each detected foreground object is used for the estimation of traffic jams. As the results of optical flow techniques are not consistent over the sequence of frames, optical flow based measurement is done for each frame wherever it is applicable. Then, based on the criteria, frames containing anomaly are detected and stored. The gaps between these detected frames are computed. If the gap between two frames is less than four (experimentally found suitable), then all the frames present in between these two frames are considered as resultant frames for the corresponding anomaly (i.e., traffic jam).

Several accidents happen near the roundabout due to the pre-event, namely 'illegal U turn'. In [2], low-level features are used for event modeling. Here, initially, a co-occurrence matrix is obtained between Spatio-temporal features. Then, this matrix is used by the Markov model for estimating the anomaly 'illegal U turn' from the future data. The statistical method with a heuristic approach is proposed in [15]. Another technique is proposed in [12], which is based on Latent Dirichlet Allocation (LDA) with Gaussian Mixture Model (GMM). Inter distances among nearer objects are not considered in these methods for motion estimation. Moreover, 'illegal U turn' near the roundabout is still an open problem. To address these issues, color and inter-distance features are used for the detection of illegal U-turns near the roundabout.

In this study, a vision-based system is developed for the detection of traffic jams and illegal U-turns near the roundabout. Initially, background estimation is done by extracting the foreground objects from the video/image frame. Then, the Histogram of Oriented Gradient feature descriptor is used over the background for the roundabout modelling. For the classification task, the Support Vector Machine (SVM) algorithm is used. On the other hand, Farneback Optical Flow is used over the detected foregrounds for obtaining the adaptive traffic motion flow. Density-based motion flow is used to define the traffic jam. Additionally, the direction of motion flow and inter-distance between the detected roundabout and motion flow is used for classifying the illegal U-turn. This method is applied to a set of collected traffic videos containing both normal and abnormal scenarios. Moreover, a comparative study is done to prove the effectiveness of the proposed method over some state-of-the-arts. This method avoids the necessity of a large database, making use of common traffic jams and illegal U-turn videos as benchmarks.

The rest of the article proceeds as follows: the literature review is presented in Sect. 2. Section 3 explains the proposed methodology. Results are reported in Sect. 4. Finally, we conclude the study in Sect. 5 with limitations and scopes for the future works.

2   Literature Review

Traffic jam and illegal U-turn detection near the roundabout consist of two phases: moving object detection, and feature analysis and classification. Foreground detection can be done by deducting the background from the frame. For background subtraction, MOG [17,28], GMM [5], and MOG2 [34] are used. Background Detection is usually a computationally expensive task, with the intensity of the moving object pixels determined as a mathematical function of the neighborhood pixels. Deep learning approaches [14,16,30] are very good in object detection tasks, but these are restricted to the training samples. Moreover, GPU is required for processing, which may not be affordable always. Therefore, we use an unsupervised technique for moving object detection and background subtraction.

For the detection of a roundabout violation, the detection of the round-about (i.e., Region of Interest (RoI)) was done with the help of template matching or basic color based thresholding considering the neighbouring environment to have similar pixel values in all frames. Roundabout detection is a relatively unexplored field, with only a few previously designed algorithms. A threshold matching approach using features like shape, size and color was implemented to decipher the roundabout from the video with multiple stationary elements. As very few state-of-the-arts are present for traffic anomaly detection near the roundabout, it is an open field for research. The floor detection algorithm was used to detect motor able parts of the road for jamming detection to separate instances from mass parking. The technique combines three visual cues for evaluating the likelihood of horizontal intensity edge line segments belonging to the boundary of a roadway and other objects. For the detection of illegal U-turns, the direction of motion flow is used in [1]. These are restricted to occlusion and lighting illumination. To address all these issues, we have developed a method based on the density and direction and inter-distance of optical motion flow for the detection of both traffic jams and illegal U-turns near the roundabout. This is enumerated in the following section.

3 Proposed Methodology

The video-based traffic anomaly detection method near the roundabout is displayed in Fig. 1. The methodology mainly consists of four steps: i) foreground object detection, ii) roundabout detection, iii) feature extraction, and iv) feature analysis for traffic anomaly classification. Proposed Foreground object detection is done using background subtraction, as depicted in Sect. 3.1. Roundabout is detected based on the HoG feature descriptor, as explained in Sect. 3.2. For each detected foreground object, optical flow-based features are extracted, as shown in Sect. 3.3. Finally, rules are generated based on the optical features for the classification of traffic jams and illegal U-turns near the roundabout.

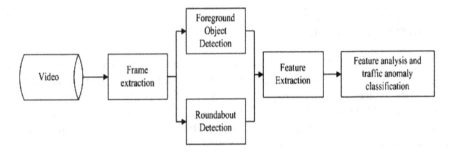

Fig. 1. Flowchart of the proposed methodology.

3.1 Foreground Object Detection

Foreground object detection refers to the scanning and searching for an object in a frame or video. Here, each frame in a video is subtracted from its previous frame to get the values of only those pixel values which change and the change is caused by motion. Then, for each pixel location in the frame, we check the number of changes less than a threshold, say Th_1. The pixel location where maximum no change in pixel intensity obtained is considered as background. The regions corresponding to foreground objects are extracted by subtracting the background regions from the video frame. Then, clusters/granules are formed over these regions for separating the foreground objects. Cluster formation is done based on spatial similarity. Let F_i^t be the i-th cluster formed in the t-th frame. Then, this cluster must follow Eq. (1), as follows:

$$\left| F_i^t(x,y) - F_i^t(x+j, y+k) \right|_{j,k=-1,0,1} \leq Th_2 \tag{1}$$

where (x, y) represents the position of a pixel in x and y co-ordinates.

3.2 Roundabout Detection

The motivation behind the detection of the roundabout is to detect common traffic anomalies, such as traffic jams and riders violating the 'keep left instruction. We aim to detect such anomalies by detecting the roundabout and observing directional flows and density around it. Traffic jam is detected based on density. Whereas, illegal U-turn can be estimated if the direction of the velocity vector is not along the left of the roundabout.

In order to detect the stationary round about, first, background is detected. As said in the previous section, based on the two thresholds Th_1 and Th_2, background is detected. Once all the stationary objects were identified, the next task was to isolate the circular red-colored roundabouts from the other backgrounds. This was done as a basic color based thresholding approach as most of our sample space consisted of red colored. To preserve this information, RGB image is converted to HSV [20]. Histogram of Oriented Gradients (HoG) feature descriptor is used over the stationary objects for feature extraction. In this process, initially, a window of having size (11×11) slides over the original HSV-converted image. HoG is obtained for the background region present within this window. We are looking for contour feature, which is mainly focused on orientation and magnitude of local features using the traditional HoGs method [3]. As the size of this filter is much less compared to the original input feature space, SVM can work effectively for both training and testing. Moreover, the effects of background clutter and perspective distortion are also be re-solved due to extracting the features from the aforesaid small sized window. HOG descriptor keeps in account the shape of a roundabout and hence is more robust. After the detection of foreground objects and roundabout, traffic anomalies near the roundabout are detected as depicted in the next section.

3.3 Traffic Anomalies Near the Roundabout

Two types of traffic anomalies, such as traffic jams and illegal U-turns are detected near the roundabout. Initially, roundabout and road are detected, and then these traffic anomalies are identified. Road detection, traffic jams, and illegal U-turns are explained in the following sub-sections:

Road Detection: The initial challenge was to identify the presence of roads in the videos. Colour-based thresholding was done to identify the roads. To take into consideration, the different 'appearance' of the roads during different times of the day, the image frames were considered in their HSV format. This ensured that we successfully avoided using brightness as a direct parameter, instead only including the chromatic notion of brightness, intensity. Various points of the images were then marked with a binary notation, grey or not grey. To make sure that we have detected the entire segments of roads, we used all the 'grey' marked points to construct a graph. The external points of the cluster were then interpolated to approximately determine what part of the ground we define as motorable.

Traffic Jam Detection: To detect occurrences of jamming, it was necessary to detect the collection of vehicles occurring in an unusually small area. The size of the area is determined from the detected background which gives us a clear estimate of the area of motorable roads. It was also essential to keep in mind that jamming would be a traffic anomaly only if this occurred in the driving space. The parking spaces were first identified by running image processing techniques on frames, where a parking space was defined by a roadside area, demarcated with white stripes. Occurrences of jamming in the parking area on either side of the road could be ignored since jamming in these spaces would have no potential risk.

After the detection of roundabout and road over frames, these are used for further processing. Then, the parking space is segregated from the driving space. Based on locality, a certain area of width d, measured from the boundary of the road was allotted for parking on both sides of the road. Thus, we were successfully able to identify the road area and also segregate the parking area from the driving area. After the detection of the parking space area, we have measured the density (number of vehicles present in an area). If density values exceed a threshold Th_3, then, it is termed a traffic jam.

All moving objects were further evaluated to determine whether the center of the clustered bounding boxes (formed over the detected moving objects) lay within the driving area. Thus, all these moving objects with centers that occurred in the parking space were removed. The directional velocity of bounding boxes was first calculated. If a certain number of bounding boxes were having the same directional velocity, the distance between the boundaries of the two bounding boxes was calculated. In case the bounding boxes were overlapping or the distance was less than a certain threshold, the instance was classified as a jamming situation.

Detection of Illegal U-Turn: After the detection of moving objects, optical flow is applied over each to find their motion flow. Then, the angle between the motion flow and center of the roundabout is measured. If the angle is greater than 90°C, then it is considered an illegal U-turn.

4   Results and Discussions

In this section, the experimental setup, dataset used, and experimental results are explained in the following sub-sections.

4.1   Experimental Setup

The algorithms for the detection of traffic jams and illegal U-turns are coded in Python 3.6 (Anaconda) in Windows using an Intel processor clocked at 2.50 GHz with 8 GB of memory. The libraries used are 'cv2', 'NumPy', and 'imutils'. The original input used in this study is having size of (256×256) Then, a filter having size of (11×11) is sliding over this input feature space for extracting the background pixels which are further used for extracting the HoG feature. A number of 9 bins and 20 °C angle are used for HoG formation. In this experiment, thresholds $Th_1 = 2, Th_2 = 5$, and $Th_3 = 10$ are found experimentally suitable.

4.2   Datasets Used

The effectiveness of the proposed methodology is demonstrated over the 20 real-time traffic videos acquired from YouTube8M [29] and an integrated steel plant in India. These videos consist of three situations, including traffic jams, illegal U-turns, and normal scenarios. Each video is recorded with the duration of 1 to 4 min. Low illumination and occlusion effects are present in these videos. In most cases, road crashes near the roundabout occur due to these two traffic anomalies (i.e., traffic and illegal U-turn), which are considered in this study. As real-time video data is used in this study, by characteristic, this data is unbalanced.

4.3   Experimental Results

In this study, initially, the foreground object and its motion flow are detected. Then, roundabout detection is done. Thereafter, traffic jams and illegal U-turns are detected. Finally, a comparative study is presented.

Detection Results for Foreground and Its Motion Flow: Here, first, the background is detected based on the Gaussian noise removal and size-based contour thresholding, as shown in Fig. 2a. No other pre-processing step is used for noise removal task. Then, the background is subtracted from the input frame to define foreground objects, as shown in Fig. 2b. After the detection of the foreground object, optical flow is applied over it to find the motion flow, as shown in the same figure. As an example, optical flow applied to heavy traffic is shown in Fig. 2c. From these figures, it is evident that the method applied for foreground and its motion flow detection is effective, even in case of heavy traffic.

Detection Results for Roundabout: As our research is on anomaly detection near roundabout, so the detection of roundabout is the prior task. The detection result for the roundabout is shown in Fig. 2d. From this figure, it is seen that roundabout is detected correctly based on the HoG based feature descriptor over HSV values. This proves the effectiveness of our proposed method for roundabout detection.

Detection Results for Traffic Jam and Illegal U-turn: The detection result for traffic jams is shown in Fig. 2e. From this figure, it is seen that several moving objects in a given space which has been detected not to be a parking space. The road has been separated and the detection has been performed only on the areas classified as road. As we can observe that more than a certain number of objects having the same optical flow and cluttered at a given spot for a certain time is detected as a jamming incident.

Detection Results for Illegal U-turn: Detection results for illegal U-turns are illustrated in Fig. 2f. From this figure, it is evident that the angle between moving vehicles and roundabouts is greater than ninety degrees. Therefore, it is considered an illegal U-turn. Output image as shown in Fig. 2f proves the effectiveness of the proposed method.

Fig. 2. (a) Output with Gaussian Noise removal and Size-based contour thresholding; (b) Optical flow over the Background Subtracted Output; (c) Optical flow output for traffic; (d) HSV-color-shape based Roundabout Detection; (e) Traffic Jam Detection at a non-parking location; and (f) Illegal U-turns detection.

Comparative Study: To prove the effectiveness of our algorithms, we have conducted a comparative study between developed algorithms and some state-of-the-art algorithms for the detection of two traffic anomalies (i.e., traffic jam and illegal U turn near the roundabout) in traffic videos acquired from the plant. Three performance metrics, including mean average accuracy (%), mean average precision (%), and speed (frame per second (fps)) are used in this comparative study. 5-fold cross validation is done in this study, to see the robustness of the proposed method. As one video may contains more than one violation for any kind of traffic anomaly. As an example, one or more than one traffic jam or illegal U turn can be happened in one video. Therefore, for each video, average accuracy and average precision are obtained under each-fold validation. After, 5-fold cross validation, five average accuracies and five average precision are obtained. From these values, mean average accuracy is obtained by calculating the mean of all five average accuracies. In the same way, mean average precision is also computed. In the case of jamming detection, TJDUIP [13] and RCDITA [32] are used for comparative study. Whereas, VIUT [31] and TVHCC [1] are used as a comparative study for illegal U-turn detection. Comparative results for traffic jams and illegal U-turns are shown in Table 1 and Table 2, respectively. From Table 1, it is evident that our proposed algorithm is superior to TJDUIP and RCDITA for traffic jam detection. On the other hand, our proposed algorithm is superior to VIUT and TVHCC for the detection of illegal U-turns in terms of mean average accuracy, mean average precision, and speed.

Table 1. Comparative study for traffic jam detection.

Algorithms	Mean average accuracy (%)	Mean average precision (%)	Speed (fps)
TJDUIP	78.1	91.3	2
RCDITA	81.7	94.2	6
Proposed	93.5	98.3	14

Table 2. Comparative study for illegal U-turn detection.

Algorithms	Mean average accuracy (%)	Mean average precision (%)	Speed (fps)
VIUT	83.6	92.7	3
TVHCC	87.2	96.1	5
Proposed	91.6	98.6	14

5   Conclusions

Traffic accidents near the roundabout mainly happen due to two traffic anomalies, namely traffic jam and illegal U turn. Thus, a system is required to automatically detect these anomalies and consequently, a signal can be sent to the control room to manage the traffic. In this way, a probability of a mishap can be reduced. As a consequence, the road safety is enhanced. Therefore, in the present study, we have developed a method for detecting the aforesaid two traffic anomalies. The method consists of four stages: (i) moving object and motion flow detection, (ii) roundabout detection, (iii) feature extraction, and (iv) feature analysis and classification. Here, foreground objects, road, and round-about are detected based on the Histogram of Gradient (HoG) [18] feature descriptor and spatio-color information. Optical flow is applied on the detected vehicles for obtaining their trajectory information. Round-about violation is detected based on the position and angle between the center of the round-about and the vehicle trajectory. The effectiveness of the proposed method has been demonstrated over 20 traffic videos acquired from the YouTube8M and an integrated steel plant in India. In addition, a comparative study is conducted to prove its superiority over some state-of-the-arts. However, our method is restricted to the day light and monocular vision. More number of features can be considered in the future studies to make the method more robust. Another potential future works could be the use of efficient clustering techniques [22,26,27] on features to club into feature-clusters, which may increase the performance of anomaly detection algorithm. Another interesting domain is the generation of rules [7,8], which may help in anomaly detection more accurately. Moreover, fuzziness or inconsistency handling using fuzzy logic [6,33] or rough set theory [23,24] could also be considered as a potential research avenue in this domain. In addition, the developed method can be embedded in a decision support system [25] to take a prompt and efficient decision on traffic anomalies on road.

Acknowledgement. The work is done under UAY project, Government of India (GOI), funded by Ministry of Education & Ministry of Steel (GOI), and Tata Steel Limited. We acknowledge the Centre of Excellence in Safety Engineering and Analytics (CoE-SEA) (www.iitkgp. ac.in/department/SE), IIT Kharagpur and Safety Analytics & Virtual Reality (SAVR) Laboratory (www.savr.iitkgp.ac.in) of Department of Industrial & Systems Engineering, IIT Kharagpur for experimental/computational and research facilities for this work.

References

1. Athanesious, J., Srinivasan, V., Vijayakumar, V., Christobel, S., Sethuraman, S.C.: Detecting abnormal events in traffic video surveillance using superorientation optical flow feature. IET Image Proc. 14(9), 1881–1891 (2020)
2. Cui, L., Li, K., Chen, J., Li, Z.: Abnormal event detection in traffic video surveillance based on local features. In: 2011 4th International Congress on Image and Signal Processing, vol. 1, pp. 362–366. IEEE (2011)
3. Dalal, N., Triggs, B.: Histograms of oriented gradients for human detection. In: 2005 IEEE Computer Society Conference on Computer Vision and Pattern Recognition (CVPR 2005), vol. 1, pp. 886–893. IEEE (2005)
4. Daniels, S., Brijs, T., Nuyts, E., Wets, G.: Explaining variation in safety performance of roundabouts. Accident Anal. Prevention 42(2), 393–402 (2010)
5. Friedman, N., Russell, S.: Image segmentation in video sequences: A probabilistic approach. arXiv preprint arXiv:1302.1539 (2013)
6. Hamamoto, A.H., Carvalho, L.F., Sampaio, L.D.H., Abrão, T., Proença, M.L., Jr.: Network anomaly detection system using genetic algorithm and fuzzy logic. Expert Syst. Appl. 92, 390–402 (2018)
7. Heinrich, M., Gölz, A., Arul, T., Katzenbeisser, S.: Rule-based anomaly detection for railway signalling networks. arXiv preprint arXiv:2008.05241 (2020)
8. Hela, S., Amel, B., Badran, R.: Early anomaly detection in smart home: a causal association rule-based approach. Artif. Intell. Med. 91, 57–71 (2018)
9. Huang, L.l., Tang, Y.p., Meng, Y.: Research on road congestion state detection based on machine vision. J. Chin. Comput. Syst. 35(1), 148–153 (2014)
10. Hydén, C., Várhelyi, A.: The effects on safety, time consumption and environment of large scale use of roundabouts in an urban area: a case study. Accid. Anal. Prev. 32(1), 11–23 (2000)
11. Imprialou, M.I.M., Quddus, M., Pitfield, D.E.: High accuracy crash mapping using fuzzy logic. Transp. Res. Part C: Emerg. Technol. 42, 107–120 (2014)
12. Jeong, H., Yoo, Y., Yi, K.M., Choi, J.Y.: Two-stage online inference model for traffic pattern analysis and anomaly detection. Mach. Vis. Appl. 25(6), 1501–1517 (2014). https://doi.org/10.1007/s00138-014-0629-y
13. Nagaraj, U., Rathod, J., Patil, P., Thakur, S., Sharma, U.: Traffic jam detection using image processing. Int. J. Eng. Res. Appl. 3(2), 1087–1091 (2013)
14. Pathak, A.R., Pandey, M., Rautaray, S.: Application of deep learning for object detection. Procedia Comput. Sci. 132, 1706–1717 (2018)
15. Patino, L., Ferryman, J.: Multiresolution semantic activity characterisation and abnormality discovery in videos. Appl. Soft Comput. 25, 485–495 (2014)
16. Pérez-Hernández, F., Tabik, S., Lamas, A., Olmos, R., Fujita, H., Herrera, F.: Object detection binary classifiers methodology based on deep learning to identify small objects handled similarly: Application in video surveillance. Knowl.-Based Syst. 194, 105590 (2020)

17. Piccardi, M.: Background subtraction techniques: a review. In: 2004 IEEE International Conference on Systems, Man and Cybernetics (IEEE Cat. No. 04CH37583), vol. 4, pp. 3099–3104. IEEE (2004)
18. Pramanik, A., Djeddi, C., Sarkar, S., Maiti, J., et al.: Region proposal and object detection using hog-based CNN feature map. In: 2020 International Conference on Data Analytics for Business and Industry: Way Towards a Sustainable Economy (ICDABI), pp. 1–5. IEEE (2020)
19. Pramanik, A., Pal, S.K., Maiti, J., Mitra, P.: Granulated RCNN and multi-class deep sort for multi-object detection and tracking. IEEE Trans. Emerg. Topics Comput. Intell. **6**(1), 171–181 (2021)
20. Pramanik, A., Sarkar, S., Maiti, J.: Oil spill detection using image processing technique: an occupational safety perspective of a steel plant. In: Abraham, A., Dutta, P., Mandal, J., Bhattacharya, A., Dutta, S. (eds.) Emerging Technologies in Data Mining and Information Security. AISC, vol. 814, pp. 247–257. Springer, Singapore (2019). https://doi.org/10.1007/978-981-13-1501-5_21
21. Pramanik, A., Sarkar, S., Maiti, J.: A real-time video surveillance system for traffic pre-events detection. Accid. Anal. Prev. **154**, 106019 (2021)
22. Pramanik, A., Sarkar, S., Maiti, J., Mitra, P.: Rt-gsom: rough tolerance growing self-organizing map. Inf. Sci. **566**, 19–37, 106019 (2021)
23. Rawat, S.S., Polavarapu, V.A., Kumar, V., Aruna, E., Sumathi, V.: Anomaly detection in smart grid using rough set theory and k cross validation. In: 2014 International Conference on Circuits, Power and Computing Technologies [ICCPCT-2014], pp. 479–483. IEEE (2014)
24. Sarkar, S., Baidya, S., Maiti, J.: Application of rough set theory in accident analysis at work: a case study. In: 2017 Third International Conference on Research in Computational Intelligence and Communication Networks (ICRCICN), pp. 245–250. IEEE (2017)
25. Sarkar, S., Chain, M., Nayak, S., Maiti, J.: Decision support system for prediction of occupational accident: a case study from a steel plant. In: Abraham, A., Dutta, P., Mandal, J., Bhattacharya, A., Dutta, S. (eds.) Emerging Technologies in Data Mining and Information Security. AISC, vol. 813, pp. 787–796. Springer, Singapore (2019). https://doi.org/10.1007/978-981-13-1498-8_69
26. Sarkar, S., Ejaz, N., Maiti, J.: Application of hybrid clustering technique for pattern extraction of accident at work: a case study of a steel industry. In: 2018 4th International Conference on Recent Advances in Information Technology (RAIT), pp. 1–6. IEEE (2018)
27. Sarkar, S., Lodhi, V., Maiti, J.: Text-clustering based deep neural network for prediction of occupational accident risk: a case study. In: 2018 International Joint Symposium on Artificial Intelligence and Natural Language Processing (iSAI-NLP), pp. 1–6. IEEE (2018)
28. Sen-Ching, S.C., Kamath, C.: Robust techniques for background subtraction in urban traffic video. In: Visual Communications and Image Processing 2004, vol. 5308, pp. 881–892. International Society for Optics and Photonics (2004)
29. Thomas, S.S., Gupta, S., Subramanian, V.K.: Event detection on roads using perceptual video summarization. IEEE Trans. Intell. Transp. Syst. **19**(9), 2944–2954 (2017)
30. Tong, K., Wu, Y., Zhou, F.: Recent advances in small object detection based on deep learning: a review. Image Vis. Comput. **97**, 103910 (2020)
31. Wang, W., Zhou, Y., Cai, Q., Zhou, Y.: A research on detection algorithm of vehicle illegal U-Turn. In: Liang, Q., Liu, X., Na, Z., Wang, W., Mu, J., Zhang, B. (eds.) CSPS 2018. LNEE, vol. 517, pp. 1089–1099. Springer, Singapore (2020). https://doi.org/10.1007/978-981-13-6508-9_132
32. Wei, L., Hong-ying, D.: Real-time road congestion detection based on image texture analysis. Procedia Eng. **137**, 196–201, 103910 (2016)

264   A. Pramanik et al.

33. Wijayasekara, D., Linda, O., Manic, M., Rieger, C.: Mining building energy management system data using fuzzy anomaly detection and linguistic descriptions. IEEE Trans. Industr. Inf. **10**(3), 1829–1840 (2014)
34. Zivkovic, Z.: Improved adaptive gaussian mixture model for background subtraction. In: Proceedings of the 17th International Conference on Pattern Recognition, 2004. ICPR 2004, vol. 2, pp. 28–31. IEEE (2004)

A Two-Stage Framework for Diverse Traffic Light Recognition Based on Individual Signal Detection

Ssu-Yun Lin and Huei-Yung Lin$^{(\boxtimes)}$

Department of Electrical Engineering, National Chung Cheng University,
Chiayi 621, Taiwan
lin@ee.ccu.edu.tw

Abstract. The detection of traffic lights is an indispensable part of advanced driver assistance systems. This paper presents a new two-stage detection framework which is able to recognize various types of traffic signals. Different from the techniques based on the direct detection of traffic lights, we consider the individual signal bulbs as targets for detection and recognition. In our two-stage approach, the first detection stage aims to achieve a very low miss rate on the traffic signal bulbs with possibly high false positives. It is then followed by the second recognition stage to single out the correct traffic signals using a classification network. The proposed method overcomes the diverse traffic light detection problem due to various arrangements of signal bulbs in different countries. It is also capable of simultaneously detecting individual traffic signals including the arrow lights. Thus, the categories of traffic light states for classification and training can be reduced. The experiments carried out using our road scene images and public datasets have demonstrated the feasibility of the proposed technique.

Keywords: Traffic light detection · Arrow light identification · Autonomous vehicle

1 Introduction

To reduce traffic accidents and avoid traffic congestion, intelligent vehicles have to deal with various road conditions, and response quickly according to available information. Among the driving data related to the traffic infrastructure, the observation of traffic lights is the most important since it provides the indication of stop or go during driving. If the traffic light detection result is incorrect, or there is no enough response time for the driver to make a decision, serious car accidents or severe consequences could occur. Thus, the traffic light detection techniques need to meet the accuracy and real-time requirements for advanced driver assistance system (ADAS) and self-driving vehicles.

In the existing traffic light detection literature, most approaches start from identifying the whole traffic light, rather than the signal bulb itself. It is then

© Springer Nature Switzerland AG 2022
C. Djeddi et al. (Eds.): MedPRAI 2021, CCIS 1543, pp. 265–278, 2022.
https://doi.org/10.1007/978-3-031-04112-9_20

followed by the recognition of traffic signal status in a smaller restricted area. This type of two-stage detection strategy seems straightforward. However, the detection of traffic light 'box' is generally not a simple task due to its variety in different countries and regions. Figure 1 shows some traffic lights adopted in a few different locations. The signal bulbs can be arranged vertically, horizontally, or attached on the side without any specific rules. Thus, there might be potential safety issues if the entire box is used as a target for traffic light recognition. Some situations such as multiple or flashing signals further complicate the training of the detection networks.

In addition to the problems in the first stage detection, the identification of arrow lights is another important issue not properly addressed in the current traffic light detection techniques. Although the conventional algorithms can deal with basic circular signal lights fairly well, the capability of arrow light detection is still very limited. Some popular public traffic datasets (such as KITTI, LISA, etc.) do not provide sufficient arrow lights for network training and testing. This is a serious issue since the arrow lights frequently appear in many traffic scenes for direction instructions. Thus, a comprehensive traffic light detection system should also be able to recognize the green lights presented by straight, right and left arrows.

In this work, we present a technique for traffic light detection with the emphasis on the recognition of various types of traffic signals. A two-stage detection flow different from the previous approaches is proposed. In our method, the first stage aims to identify as many 'lights' as possible, followed by the second stage to recognize the true 'traffic signals'. The idea of this approach is to achieve the zero miss rate for traffic light search, even with a large number of false positives, in the first stage. The true positives are then singled out from the candidates by a sophisticated traffic signal classification network. In the experiments, the proposed technique is tested on a variety of real traffic scene images containing arrow lights. The evaluation results have demonstrated the effectiveness of our two-stage traffic light detection and recognition method for real-world applications.

2   Related Works

Due the advances of recent hardware development with the improvement on the computing power, the use of deep neural networks for learning based tasks is becoming feasible. The current convolutional neural networks applied to the road scene object detection can be divided into one-stage or two-stage approaches. In the first approach, the object detection is formulated as a regression problem. The bounding box positions and the class probabilities of targets are derived directly. The representative techniques are the YOLO series [4,14,15], which are generally faster but with lower accuracy compared with the two-stage approach. In the second approach, the object detection is regarded as a classification problem. A number of region proposals are found first, followed by target

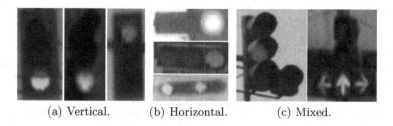

(a) Vertical.   (b) Horizontal.   (c) Mixed.

Fig. 1. Several traffic light styles adopted in different countries. There are signal bulbs arranged vertically, horizontally, or attached on the side without any specific rules. (a) is commonly seen in the US, Europe and Japan, (b) is commonly seen in Taiwan and Korea, (c) occasionally appears in Taiwan road scenes and a few regions. Some traffic light settings such as multiple or flashing signals further complicate the training process of detection networks. (Color figure online)

identification using the image features such as color, shape and texture. One representative two-stage method is the R-CNN series [9,10,16], which is generally slower but provides more accurate results.

In the traffic light detection task, the targets are relatively small in the image compared to most object detection applications. To deal with the problem on easy feature lost due to multiple convolutions, many techniques have been proposed to modify the network architectures while using other information for assistance. In [3], Behrendt *et al.* did not use the full image as input, but divided it into three equal parts for traffic light detection. They modified YOLOv3 to improve the accuracy of small target detection by increasing the number of prediction grids from 7 × 7 to 11 × 11. Weber *et al.* modified Faster R-CNN by replacing VGG-16 with Inception-v2 for feature extraction [18]. The residual network was used to retain the features of small objects after the multi-layer operations. In the previous work, Yeh *et al.* proposed a map assisted traffic light detection approach, and used YOLOv3 as the main network structure [20]. The accuracy is further improved by incorporating the lidar data to restrict the traffic light detection region.

It is worth discussing that there are very few deep learning based methods dealing with arrow signals. Most current techniques for traffic light detection only consider the basic circular lights. In [12], Vijay *et al.* used a convolutional network to find the locations of traffic signals, followed by the color identification. If the result is green, another process is carried out to verify if it is an arrow signal. Similarly, Bach *et al.* and Weber *et al.* classified the colors after finding the bounding box positions [1,17]. The shape of the color regions was then recognized for arrow signal identification. In [19], Yeh and Lin presented a two-stage traffic light detection approach for Taiwan road scenes. The first stage detection consists of four categories: red, yellow, green and arrow lights, followed by the arrow signal recognition in the second stage.

3   Method

As illustrated in Fig. 1, the identification of traffic light regions is not a trivial task. In addition to a variety of styles and arrangements, the possibility of multiple signals appeared at the same time also makes the traffic light detection more complicated. If all combinations of individual signals are treated as different classes of traffic light states, the required training data will become very large with some cases difficult to collect. This usually includes the arrow signals, which are frequently ignored in the public traffic light datasets and the traffic light detection techniques. Unlike the previous approaches starting with the detection of traffic light boxes, we present a new detection architecture entirely based on the traffic signal bulb. The flowchart of the proposed technique is shown in Fig. 2. Given an input image, the first stage uses a convolutional neural network to detect the lights, i.e., the potential traffic signals, as many as possible. In the second stage, another network is employed specifically for traffic signal classification.

Fig. 2. The flowchart of the proposed two-stage approach. The first stage is to detect the position of the traffic signal bulb, and the second stage is to eliminate the incorrect prediction and recognize the signal states. The input is a color image, and the output is the positions and states of the traffic lights.

3.1   Light Candidate Detection

The proposed technique starts with the detection of candidate traffic lights using less strict criteria. A lower threshold is adopted for the detection network to identify the possible traffic signal bulbs in the image. The objective is to avoid missing any objects of interest, so the classification of traffic signal states is not the main consideration in this stage. With a low threshold, the number of false positives can increase significantly and the precision will be relatively low. For example, some similar objects such as vehicle brake lights, color signboards and pedestrian signals will be extracted as well, and expected to be eliminated in the following stage.

To detect the traffic lights, several network structures including Faster R-CNN and YOLOv3 have been tested. Considering the traffic signal bulb is a small target in the road scene images, Faster R-CNN is adopted as the main detection framework. We first follow the basic structure of Fast R-CNN, and then develop a special method for the generation of candidate areas. The region proposal network replaces the selective search in the network model to improve the detection speed and accuracy. There are several key modules being modified: the feature extraction network, RoI generation, RoIPooling, and the classification and regression.

To achieve a higher detection accuracy, the residual network ResNet-50 is used to replace the original VGG16 in the feature extraction stage. The difference between the feature extraction network is shown in Table 1. Moreover, instead of using a single feature map, multi-scale feature maps created by feature pyramid network is adopted in the encoder [13]. Finally, in order to increase the candidate predictions to minimize the missing rate of signal bulbs, the number of outputs for each layer is increased from 1000 to 2000. The original three scales (128, 256 and 512) in the region proposal network are increased to five (32, 64, 128, 256 and 512), and a total of 15 anchors are used for the anchor box section.

Table 1. The comparison of feature extraction networks (VGG16 and ResNet-50) adopted in the proposed technique.

Output size	VGG16		ResNet-50	
112×112	3×3 conv, 64	$\times 2$	–	
56×56	maxpool		1×1 conv, 64	$\times 3$
	3×3 conv, 128	$\times 2$	3×3 conv, 64	
			1×1 conv, 128	
28×28	maxpool		1×1 conv, 128	$\times 4$
	3×3 conv, 256	$\times 3$	3×3 conv, 128	
			1×1 conv, 512	
14×14	maxpool		1×1 conv, 256	$\times 3$
	3×3 conv, 512	$\times 3$	3×3 conv, 256	
			1×1 conv, 1024	
7×7	maxpool		1×1 conv, 512	$\times 3$
			3×3 conv, 512	
			1×1 conv, 2048	
1×1	fc4096, fc4096, fc1000		average pool, fc1000	

3.2   Traffic Light Classification

With the prediction of traffic signal candidates, the objective of the second stage is to remove the false positives as well as classify the traffic light states. This is carried out by filtering the detection results with the position and object size, followed by the traffic signal recognition using a classification network. Table 2 tabulates the relationship between the size of a signal light and its distance from the vehicle. The target size in the image is used to reject some false traffic light detection results based on the physical distance. According to the traffic regulation, the safe driving distance is the vehicle speed (km/hr) multiplied by 0.5. That is, a vehicle driving at the speed of 70 km/hr should maintain a safe distance of 35 m. Thus, two situations with different traffic light detection distances are discussed in this work.

- The size of signal lights is larger than 5 × 5 in the image, which corresponds to less than 90 m.
- The size of signal lights is larger than 10 × 10 in the image, which corresponds to less than 35 m.

Alternatively, the suitable target sizes can also be determined if the distance between the vehicle and traffic light location is available from GPS and the information on the map.

Table 2. The relationship between the size of a signal light and its distance from the vehicle. The value in the table indicates the number of signal lights observed with the size (in pixel, the first column) and distance (in meter, the first row). There are no traffic lights in the range of 0–15 m due to the field-of-view of the camera.

	0–15	15–30	30–45	45–60	60–75	75–90	90–105
1 × 1–4 × 4	–	1	5	5	3	5	5
5 × 5–9 × 9	–	–	1	3	13	18	134
10 × 10–14 × 14	–	9	10	16	109	738	545
15 × 15–19 × 19	–	2	52	176	1043	201	31
20 × 20–24 × 24	–	21	262	481	125	4	–
25 × 25–29 × 29	–	189	858	327	11	1	–
30 × 30–34 × 34	–	6	5	1201	40	–	–
35 × 35–39 × 39	–	65	5	377	26	–	–
40 × 40 and up	–	302	5	149	1	–	–

In addition to the filtering according to the size, the traffic light location in the image is also verified. Since the traffic lights must be above the ground, the first stage detection results appeared in the road area will be considered as false positives. For the road surface detection, the semantic segmentation technique ICNet is adopted [21]. Due to the high labor cost of the semantic segmentation labeling, we do not generate the segmentation ground-truth on our own dataset. The network is trained using the public dataset CityScape [7], so some conditions in the Taiwan road scenes, such as fences and viaducts, cannot be segmented accurately. Nevertheless, this road surface extraction module is not part of the main system architecture yet provides additional restriction for removing the false traffic light detection.

To further take the advantage of road scene image properties, the vanishing point is used to provide a fixed forbidden zone for traffic light filtering. It is also used to improve the road surface segmentation. In this work, the vanishing point is derived using the method proposed by Chaudhury et al. [5]. The vanishing point location in the image will remain static and fixed if the camera's orientation is not changed. Figure 3 shows the road surface area obtained by semantic segmentation and the vanishing point. The first-stage detection results in the color regions (road surfaces) will be removed from the participation in traffic signal classification.

(a) Road surface extraction.   (b) Constrained with vanishing point.

Fig. 3. The road surface extraction results obtained by semantic segmentation (ICNet) and the vanishing point.

After the road surface segmentation, several neural networks are used to identify the false positives and recognize the traffic signals. To select the best architecture for this task, five network structures, AlexNet, VGG16, ResNet-50, ResNet-101 and ResNetXt50, are used for the evaluation with different optimizers. We adopt stochastic gradient decent (SGD) and adaptive moment estimation (Adam) as the optimizers for comparison. In our evaluation on the public traffic light datasets, VGG16 is able to identify the incorrect traffic lights more accurately and require less training time. It also comes with a smaller network architecture, and therefore is adopted as the main network structure in our implementation.

3.3 Dataset

Table 3 shows several public datasets currently available and commonly used for the evaluation of traffic light detection. Our objective is to detect and recognize the individual light signals, but most of them cannot be directly adopted for training. Only the Korea dataset[1] has the traffic light boxes arranged horizontally, the rest are arranged vertically. There are no arrow light signals in LISA, Bosch and DriveU datasets [2,8], but LISA provides the single light annotation [11]. Among them, the WPI dataset is the only traffic light dataset with arrow signal annotation [6].

---

[1] https://www.acelab.org/traffic-light-dataset.

272   S.-Y. Lin and H.-Y. Lin

Table 3. The public datasets currently available and commonly used for traffic light detection. Not all datasets contain arrow lights and the necessary annotation. There are also different arrangements (horizontal or vertical) for the traffic signals. The traffic lights in LISA and Bosch datasets are small and unclear, and relatively more difficult to identify. (* indicates the number of classes for testing only.)

	LISA	Bosch	DriveU	WPI	Korea
Resolution	1280×960	1280×720	2048×1024	1920×1028	2048×1068
No. of Images	43,007	13,427	–	–	25,882
No. of Classes	7	15, 4*	344	12	3
Arrangement	Vertical	Vertical	Vertical	Vertical	Horizontal
Single Light Annotation	Yes	No	No	Yes	Yes
Arrow Light	Rare	Rare	Rare	Yes	Yes
Arrow Light Annotation	Rare	Rare	Rare	Yes	No

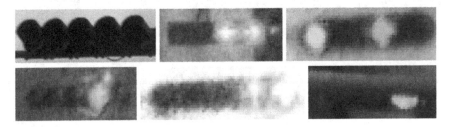

Fig. 4. The traffic lights which are unrecognizable or largely occluded are excluded in the network training. (Color figure online)

The annotation of our own dataset is carried out with two types. In the first stage detection, the whole images are used to label the individual signal lights, including their positions and types (red, yellow, green, arrow left, arrow straight and arrow right, totally 6 classes). To avoid extracting obscure features for training, the traffic lights which are unrecognizable or occluded (as shown in Fig. 4) are excluded from the network training. The numbers of training images for 'red', 'yellow', 'green', 'arrow left', 'arrow straight' and 'arrow right' are 6275, 1350, 5175, 498, 1964 and 2067, respectively.

The objective of the second stage is to distinguish different traffic signals and remove the false positives caused by color, shape and other factors in the first stage detection. To obtain the true positive training samples, the six categories of traffic signals are extracted from the training images. The derivation of false positive training data is more difficult since they need to be collected from the false positives labeled in the first stage detection. A few samples of these cases are shown in Fig. 5. Since the incorrect detection results are not extracted or assigned manually, this will require a fairly large amount of first stage detection outputs. The number of training samples in the experiments for 'red', 'yellow', 'green', 'arrow left', 'arrow straight', 'arrow right' signals and false positives are 4637, 801, 4270, 267, 825, 817 and 602, respectively.

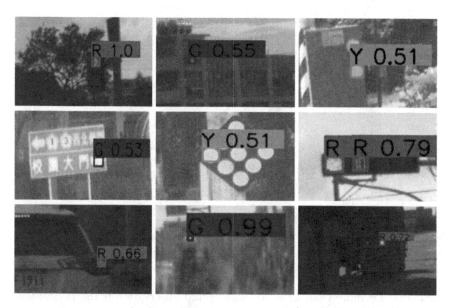

Fig. 5. The false positives frequently obtained in the first stage detection results, including pedestrian lights, brake lights, traffic signs, etc.

4   Experiments

We collect the road scene images with traffic lights using two Basler aca2040 35gc cameras for network training and testing. The focal lengths of the cameras are set as 3.5 mm and 12 mm to acquire the images with different fields-of-view (FOVs). Figure 6 shows the numbers of traffic signals in different categories. The numbers of red and yellow signals are much larger than others as expected, since the images without traffic lights are not included. The statistics of the traffic signals in terms of their image region sizes are illustrated in Fig. 7. It shows the distribution with the majority ranges from 5×5 to 20×20, and no arrow signals for the sizes larger than 40×40. To deal with this data imbalance problem, we first add 400 images with 830 'arrow left' signals from the Korea dataset. Additional 130 arrow signals (left, straight and right) are extracted from the open street images provided by Mapillary[2]. Finally, the data augmentation is carried out with blur, illumination change, rotation and translation to provide another 1315 arrow signals.

The performance evaluation is carried out with two application scenarios: the traffic signals in the images are larger than 5×5 and 10×10 pixels for the long range and close range detection, respectively. Table 4 shows the comparison of the results using the first stage detection only and the proposed two-stage approach. The table indicates that our two-stage detection technique has significant improvement on the mAPs. The accuracy on the important arrow left signals

---

[2] https://www.mapillary.com/.

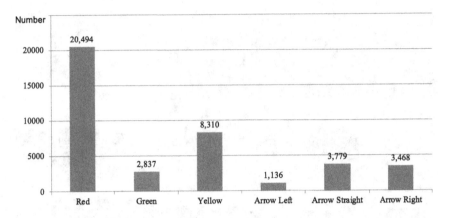

Fig. 6. The numbers of traffic signals in different categories. There are much more red and yellow traffic signals than others in general road scene image captures.

is increased for more than 40%. An unexpected observation is the performance drop on the yellow lights. This is due to the yellowish objects appeared in the street scenes, which make the second-stage signal light classification more difficult. Moreover, the current networks are not sensitive enough to distinguish the red and yellow lights very well, which needs to be optimized in the future investigation. This is also the reason that the yellow signals for the targets greater than 5 × 5 perform better compared to those greater than 10 × 10 (Fig. 8).

Table 4. The comparison of the results obtained from the first stage detection only and our two-stage approach for the target size larger than 5 × 5 and 10 × 10.

	5 × 5		10 × 10	
Method	First stage	Our method	First stage	Our method
Red	82.1%	83.6%	84.1%	87.6%
Yellow	89.1%	81.5%	85.2%	82.4%
Green	75.5%	77.6%	91.3%	93.4%
Arrow Left	36.7%	79.4%	36.4%	80.9%
Arrow Straight	80.3%	86.6%	83.4%	91.2%
Arrow Right	76.9%	83.0%	74.3%	83.0%
Average	73.4%	81.9%	75.8%	86.4%

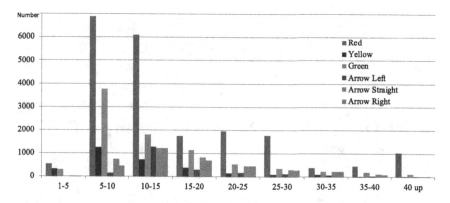

Fig. 7. The numbers of traffic signals versus their sizes in the images. The majority of the traffic signals have the sizes range from 5 × 5 to 20 × 20.

The proposed algorithms are tested on a PC with an Intel Core i7 CPU and an Nvidia GeForce GTX 1070 Ti 8G GPU. It takes about 26 s to load the weights of the architecture with three networks. The processing time for a single image is approximately 680 ms. It takes several milliseconds in the first stage detection and 460 ms to reject the false positives using the constraints based on the road surface segmentation and vanishing point. The second stage classification takes about 4.2 ms in average. Since the pre-filtering step spends about 60% of the total processing time, the overall computation can be further reduced with more efficient road surface extraction algorithms.

We also use our own image data for training, and carry out the evaluation on several public datasets. The mAPs for LISA, Bosch and WPI are 14.6%, 6.6% and 81.2%, respectively. In LISA and Bosch datasets, the sizes of most traffic signals are in the range between 5 × 5 and 10 × 10, which belong to the difficult cases for small object detection. The colors and shapes of the traffic lights in WPI are similar to ours, and therefore the comparable results are achieved. Since the images captured by different cameras have the color aberration, it will affect the detection result significantly for the features highly depending on the colors. Figure 9 illustrates the distributions of hue values for LISA, Bosch, WPI and our datasets. It shows that the color distribution of Bosch dataset is very different from others. The arrow signals in the WPI dataset fairly overlap with ours, while the LISA dataset has the values shifted to the right. Consequently, our traffic light detection approach is effective but sensitive to the signal colors in these public datasets.

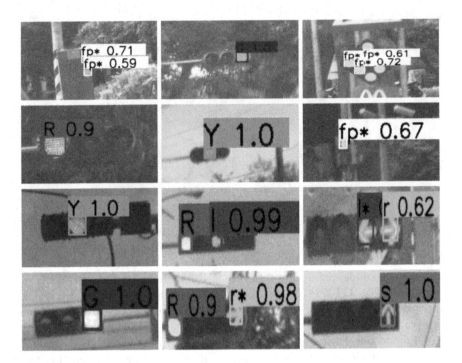

Fig. 8. The traffic light detection results using the proposed two-stage framework. R, Y, G, l, s, r, fp denote red, yellow, green, arrow left, arrow straight, arrow right, false positive, respectively. The symbol * indicates that the result of the second classification stage is different from the first detection stage. (Color figure online)

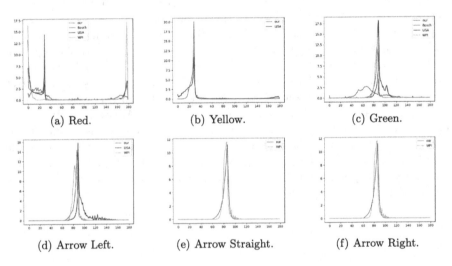

Fig. 9. The distributions of hue values in the HSI color space for LISA, Bosch, WPI and our datasets. (Color figure online)

5 Conclusion

In this paper we propose a new two-stage framework for traffic light detection and recognition. Different from the existing methods which rely on the characteristics of the traffic light region detection, we consider the individual signal lights as targets to avoid the problem caused by the different traffic light arrangement in different countries. The proposed technique is able to deal with multiple lights involving arrow signals, and the number of categories for training and testing is greatly reduced. In the experiments, the performance evaluation is carried out using our road scene images as well as the public datasets. The results have demonstrated the feasibility of the proposed method for diverse traffic light detection with arrow signals.

Acknowledgment. The support of this work in part by the Ministry of Science and Technology of Taiwan under Grant MOST 106-2221-E-194-004 and the Advanced Institute of Manufacturing with High-tech Innovations (AIM-HI) from The Featured Areas Research Center Program within the framework of the Higher Education Sprout Project by the Ministry of Education (MOE) in Taiwan is gratefully acknowledged.

References

1. Bach, M., Stumper, D., Dietmayer, K.: Deep convolutional traffic light recognition for automated driving. In: 2018 21st International Conference on Intelligent Transportation Systems (ITSC), pp. 851–858. IEEE (2018)
2. Behrendt, K., Novak, L., Botros, R.: A deep learning approach to traffic lights: detection, tracking, and classification. In: 2017 IEEE International Conference on Robotics and Automation (ICRA), pp. 1370–1377 (2017). https://doi.org/10.1109/ICRA.2017.7989163
3. Behrendt, K., Novak, L., Botros, R.: A deep learning approach to traffic lights: detection, tracking, and classification. In: 2017 IEEE International Conference on Robotics and Automation (ICRA), pp. 1370–1377. IEEE (2017)
4. Bochkovskiy, A., Wang, C.Y., Liao, H.Y.M.: Yolov4: Optimal speed and accuracy of object detection. arXiv preprint arXiv:2004.10934 (2020)
5. Chaudhury, K., DiVerdi, S., Ioffe, S.: Auto-rectification of user photos. In: 2014 IEEE International Conference on Image Processing (ICIP), pp. 3479–3483 (2014). https://doi.org/10.1109/ICIP.2014.7025706
6. Chen, Z., Huang, X.: Accurate and reliable detection of traffic lights using multiclass learning and multiobject tracking. IEEE Intell. Transp. Syst. Mag. **8**(4), 28–42 (2016). https://doi.org/10.1109/MITS.2016.2605381
7. Cordts, M., et al.: The cityscapes dataset for semantic urban scene understanding. In: Proceedings of the IEEE Conference on Computer Vision and Pattern Recognition (CVPR) (2016)
8. Fregin, A., Muller, J., Krebel, U., Dietmayer, K.: The driveu traffic light dataset: introduction and comparison with existing datasets. In: 2018 IEEE International Conference on Robotics and Automation (ICRA), pp. 3376–3383 (2018). https://doi.org/10.1109/ICRA.2018.8460737
9. Girshick, R.: Fast r-cnn. In: Proceedings of the IEEE International Conference on Computer Vision, pp. 1440–1448 (2015)

10. Girshick, R., Donahue, J., Darrell, T., Malik, J.: Rich feature hierarchies for accurate object detection and semantic segmentation. In: Proceedings of the IEEE Conference on Computer Vision and Pattern Recognition, pp. 580–587 (2014)
11. Jensen, M.B., Philipsen, M.P., Møgelmose, A., Moeslund, T.B., Trivedi, M.M.: Vision for looking at traffic lights: issues, survey, and perspectives. IEEE Trans. Intell. Transp. Syst. **17**(7), 1800–1815 (2016). https://doi.org/10.1109/TITS.2015.2509509
12. John, V., Zheming, L., Mita, S.: Robust traffic light and arrow detection using optimal camera parameters and gps-based priors. In: 2016 Asia-Pacific Conference on Intelligent Robot Systems (ACIRS), pp. 204–208. IEEE (2016)
13. Lin, T., Dollár, P., Girshick, R., He, K., Hariharan, B., Belongie, S.: Feature pyramid networks for object detection. In: 2017 IEEE Conference on Computer Vision and Pattern Recognition (CVPR), pp. 936–944 (2017). https://doi.org/10.1109/CVPR.2017.106
14. Redmon, J., Divvala, S., Girshick, R., Farhadi, A.: You only look once: unified, real-time object detection. In: Proceedings of the IEEE Conference on Computer Vision and Pattern Recognition, pp. 779–788 (2016)
15. Redmon, J., Farhadi, A.: Yolo9000: better, faster, stronger. In: Proceedings of the IEEE Conference on Computer Vision and Pattern Recognition, pp. 7263–7271 (2017)
16. Ren, S., He, K., Girshick, R., Sun, J.: Faster R-CNN: towards real-time object detection with region proposal networks. In: Advances in Neural Information Processing Systems, pp. 91–99 (2015)
17. Weber, M., Huber, M., Zöllner, J.M.: Hdtlr: a CNN based hierarchical detector for traffic lights. In: 2018 21st International Conference on Intelligent Transportation Systems (ITSC), pp. 255–260. IEEE (2018)
18. Weber, M., Wolf, P., Zöllner, J.M.: Deeptlr: a single deep convolutional network for detection and classification of traffic lights. In: 2016 IEEE Intelligent Vehicles Symposium (IV), pp. 342–348. IEEE (2016)
19. Yeh, T.W., Lin, H.Y.: Detection and recognition of arrow traffic signals using a two-stage neural network structure. In: The 6th International Conference on Vehicle Technology and Intelligent Transport Systems (VEHITS) (2020)
20. Yeh, T.W., Lin, S.Y., Lin, H.Y., Chan, S.W., Lin, C.T., Lin, Y.Y.: Traffic light detection using convolutional neural networks and lidar data. In: 2019 International Symposium on Intelligent Signal Processing and Communication Systems (ISPACS), pp. 1–2. IEEE (2019)
21. Zhao, H., Qi, X., Shen, X., Shi, J., Jia, J.: ICNet for real-time semantic segmentation on high-resolution images. In: Ferrari, V., Hebert, M., Sminchisescu, C., Weiss, Y. (eds.) ECCV 2018. LNCS, vol. 11207, pp. 418–434. Springer, Cham (2018). https://doi.org/10.1007/978-3-030-01219-9_25

Enhancing Vehicle Networks Performance by Cache-Aided Non-Orthogonal Multiple Access (CA-NOMA)

Abdullah Saad Zeki$^{(\boxtimes)}$ and Muhammad Ilyas$^{(\boxtimes)}$

Altinbas University, Istanbul, Turkey
203720140@ogr.altinbas.edu.tr, muhammad.ilyas@altinbas.edu.tr

Abstract. The emergence of heterogeneous wireless devices and the increasing demand for advanced applications such as autonomous driving and vehicle internet represent a real challenge to the Quality of Services (QoS) in-vehicle networks. These challenges are related to high spectrum efficiency, high reliability, and low latency. In this paper, the Cache-Aided Non-Orthogonal Multiple Access (CA-NOMA) technique was used as one of the possible solutions to overcome these challenges. Also, (NOMA) was shown as a major contributor to the increase in the volume of data compared to (OMA). This technology contributes to improving the performance of the system by using the information in the cache, where this process is done without the need for consent of the subscriber who owns the cache, as well as ensuring that there is no interference in the privacy of subscribers or access to their personal files, as each vehicle stores common files and provides them using the principle of (NOMA). We tried to reduce the load on traffic by increasing the probability of successful decoding; this contributes to improving spectrum efficiency. Through the simulation results, it was concluded that the (CA-NOMA) technique increases the system efficiency by 23.6% compared without caching in the Vehicle networks.

Keywords: Cache · CA-NOMA · NOMA · QoS · Vehicle network first section

1 Introduction

With the rapid development of communication networks, the increasing demand for new complex and resource-intensive applications, the diversity in subscriber traffic [1], the different environments, and the random demands of subscribers, it has become necessary to think of new practical solutions to deal with these changes [2]. It is envisaged that the vehicles will have a qualitative leap in the field of the amount of information exchange and the speed of traffic. The size of the files is large due to the downloading of common files by many subscribers [3]; also, downloading these files from (BS) leads to additional consume of connection resources, which causes an increase in the cost of the network [4, 5]. One of the new technologies in (5G) that help in overcoming these obstacles by overcoming the high data volume is the cache technology, where the common files are stored in the vehicle in advance without the need to fetch data from the network,

© Springer Nature Switzerland AG 2022
C. Djeddi et al. (Eds.): MedPRAI 2021, CCIS 1543, pp. 279–287, 2022.
https://doi.org/10.1007/978-3-031-04112-9_21

which leads to increased spectrum efficiency and reduced latency [6], for example, when the user in a particular car needs information about the road, he takes it from memory installed in the nearby car without returning to the base station (BS) as shown in Fig. 1, so installing the cache modules at the end of the user greatly contributes to increasing the efficiency of the network and reducing the load on the(BS) [7].

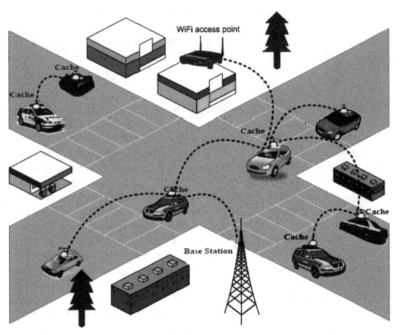

Fig. 1. Illustrate information exchange in-vehicle networks.

With the development of technology and the increase in the volume of new applications, it has become necessary to employ new technologies that deal with these applications [8], (NOMA) has been shown as a technology with important benefits; it has greatly contributed to the increase in data transfer rate by allowing services to be delivered to manyusers, that is at the same time and at the same frequency depending on the energy field or coding field, using Successive Interference Cancellation (SIC) cancels out other users' signals and treat them as noise. [9], and thus, the use of the two techniques are employed together (CA-NOMA) greatly contributes to increasing the efficiency of the network, as the vehicle can take advantage of the contents of the cache in the nearby vehicles directly without having to go back to the base station, this reduces the load on traffic between cars and the base station, thus taking advantage of the bandwidth savings this makes it easy to deal with new applications, such as self-driving and internet connection [10].

2   Related Works

2.1   Caching

This technology helps reduce traffic loads on BS by storing common information in vehicles, which leads to increased spectrum efficiency and enhanced data transmission rate [11]. Where the cache contains two vertical phases when communicating between vehicles: 1-cache phase: in this phase, the base station provides the vehicles with the information most used by users, as the data is transmitted during times of non-congestion and stored in the vehicle's cache, 2-request phase: in this phase the cache supplies the nearby vehicles with the information they need and have available to them [12].

2.2   Non-Orthogonal Multiple Access (NOMA)

(NOMA) is a technology developed in wireless systems to improve network performance compared to (OMA), in which OMA system sends data based on either time division or frequency division, as shown in Fig. 2. The NOMA system works on the principle of non-orthogonality, allowing several subscribers to subscribe to a specific frequency band. The purpose of this technology is to increase capacity and thus work to save energy, which has a significant impact on the economy and the environment. NOMA work is based on either (power domain) or (code domain), where more than one user is served on the same frequency [13].

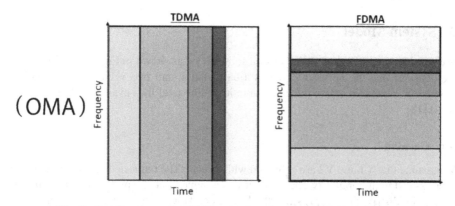

Fig. 2. Sending data using OMA technology based on TDMA or FDMA.

In power technology, the base station employs Superposition Coding (SC) to transmit users' data by sharing frequency and time with allocating a certain part of the power to each user as shown in Fig. 3, while at the receiver, thedesired signal is distinguished through (SIC) where it works to cancel Interfering and selecting the desired signal [14].

2.3   Cache-Aided NOMA

Due to the flexibility of (NOMA), it has made it easy to integrate with other technologies such as cache. When (CA-NOMA) technique is added to the vehicle network; some

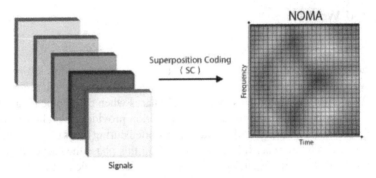

Fig. 3. Sending data using NOMA technology.

achieved results can be recorded. In addition to the huge number of users provided by (NOMA) [15], the network capacity is also enhanced through cache technology, as temporary storage in vehicles allows quick access to the required files without overloading the connection links between the vehicles and the base station, which reduces the need for additional spectrum resources [16]. It can also be seen that caching the requested data content in vehicles results in reduced computational delay and improved (QoS) for users. The need to provide a high level of data has become very necessary to deal with advanced applications, such as team games for subscribers in different regions, telehealth, and autonomous driving [17].

3   System Model

We consider a system that serves several subscribers, as shown in Fig. 1. For simplicity, we consider that the network contains a base station and two vehicles. Each vehicle contains a cache that stores information in it, andthe total files available at the BS is T = 10 [18].

3.1   Caching

We assume that V1 and V2 are equipped with a cache.The requested data content by the user has different popularity.Therefore, it was assumed that the popularity of the files is formed by distributing (Zipf) since the law of (Zipf) works to sort words according to the repeatedly incidence of their existence [19]. The repeated incidence of each word is inversely commensurate with its order number.

$$F(r) = \frac{A}{r^\epsilon} \qquad (1)$$

where r represents the order of repeatedwords, F(r) is repeatedly incidence of r, (A) is a constant, (ϵ) is the popularity coefficient. If we consider that the total number of files required is (F_{total}) therefore, the popularity of the files is calculated as follows in Eq. (2)

$$G(f) = \frac{\frac{1}{f^\epsilon}}{\sum_{i=1}^{F_{total}} \frac{1}{i^\epsilon}} \qquad (2)$$

With the popularity profile mentioned above, the optimal caching strategy will be to cache from the most popular file to the least popular file [20].

3.2 Optimal Power Allocation

We assume that both V1 and V2 have the files in their cache, and the file is successfully decrypted if the received SINR is greater than a given threshold, which might be different for different files. For simplicity, we allow these thresholds and noise variance (σ) to be unity. Therefore, the probabilities of successful decoding at V1 and V2 are given in Eq. (3) and Eq. (4)

$$P_{v1} = P\{\frac{\propto Pg_1^2}{\sigma_1^2}\} \tag{3}$$

$$P_{v2} = P\{\frac{(1-\propto)Pg_2^2}{\sigma_2^2}\} \tag{4}$$

where ($\propto$) presents Power Allocation Factor (PAF), (g_1) and (g_2) is thechannel gains at V1 and V2, respectively [21].

4 Simulation Result

In this section, simulation results will be presented that shows the contribution of the cache with NOMA to improve the performance of the fifth-generation system. All the simulations are performed using *MATLAB©*. It is necessary to strive for an optimal

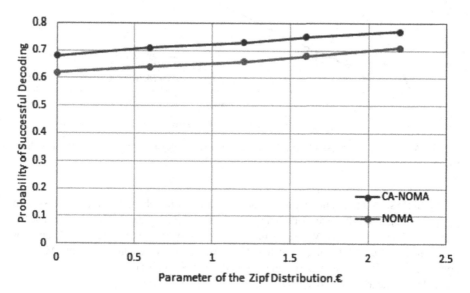

Fig. 4. Performance comparison of CA-NOMA and NOMA systems for different values of (ϵ).

distribution of power and strive for high levels of probability of successful decoding to ensure delivery to all subscribers.Since the files stored in memory are arranged based on a Zipf distribution, priority will be given to the most common files over others. Figure 4 shows the comparison in the performance of the system with or without cache for different values of (ϵ).

It shows that the cache in vehicles improves the performance of (CA-NOMA) since files that are requested by anotherperson may be cached, and the composite increases with the size of the cache. We also present that the higher the parameter value (ϵ), the more likely the decoding will succeed, which leads to a decrease in the response time and thus an increase in the efficiency of the car network. Figure 5 shows the probability of successful decryption with the increase in transmission power. It is noticeable that with the presence of the cache, the probability increases dramatically, and this shows that with the use of the cache, the requests of subscribers can be met without referring to the base station, where if the information of a particular user is stored in the cache of a nearby user shared with him in the same sub-channel, the information can be used to remove interference.

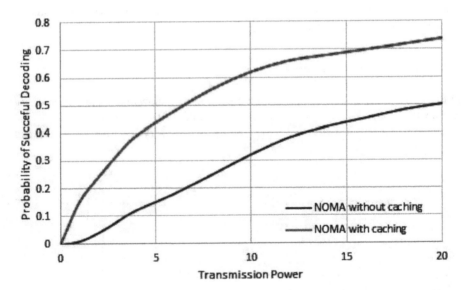

Fig. 5. Possibility of successful decryption with increased transmission power with or without cache.

Figure 6 shows the contribution of cache placement in vehicles to improving system performance; when the size of the cache at each vehicle increases, the chance that the requested files of V1 and V2 being increases, thereby increasing the performance of cache-aided NOMA, we also note that the performance of cache added NOMA and conventional NOMA are exactly equal when the cache size is zero, in other words when no cache is placed in the vehicles.

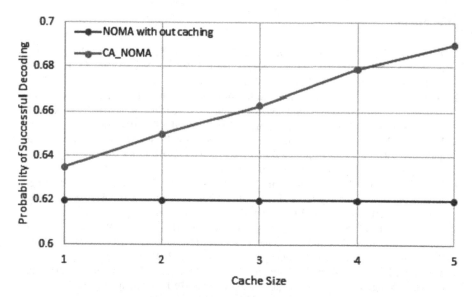

Fig. 6. The effect of caching placement in composites to improve system performance compared to traditional NOMA in terms of variation of the probability of successful decoding.

5   Conclusion and Future Work

This paper presented (CA-NOMA), which is one of the important techniques in improving the performance of the vehicle networks in 5G, especially when there are many users. The results of the analyzes showed the contribution of this new technology to reducing interference between signals, as the subscriber obtains requests from the cache at the nearby subscriber, even without the user permission, as it effectively contributes to the ease of data transmission. The primary goal is to increase the quality of services by increasing the likelihood of subscribers receiving the desired signals successfully. The advantages offered by (NOMA) compared to (OMA) were also clarified, and how it contributed enormously to the increase in the volume of data transfer. in addition, the use of cache content distribution based on popularity contributes effectively to increasing spectrum efficiency, Moreover, it was shown how the cache placement in vehicles improved the performance of the system compared to when vehicles were free of it. The benefit of this technology can be increased by working to increase the flexibility in accessing the required files, where it is possible to work on split cache's files into sections. Furthermore, work on the development of priority selection for the distribution of files in vehicles.

References

1. Xiang, L., Ng, D.W.K., Ge, X., Ding, Z., Wong, V.W.S., Schober, R.: Cache-aided non-orthogonal multiple access: the two-user case. IEEE J. Sel. Top. Sig. Process. 13(3), 436–451 (2019). https://doi.org/10.1109/JSTSP.2019.2907864
2. Gurugopinath, S., Al-Hammadi, Y., Sofotasios, P.C., Muhaidat, S., Dobre, O.A.: Non-orthogonal multiple access with wireless caching for 5G-enabled vehicular networks. IEEE Netw. 34(5), 127–133 (2020). https://doi.org/10.1109/MNET.011.1900564
3. Moghimi, M., Zakeri, A., Javan, M.R., Mokari, N., Ng, D.W.K.: Joint radio resource allocation and cooperative caching in PD-NOMA-based HetNets. IEEE Trans. Mob. Comput. 1–18 (2020). https://doi.org/10.1109/TMC.2020.3034618
4. Yang, Z., Liu, Y., Chen, Y., Al-Dhahir, N.: Cache-aided NOMA mobile edge computing: a reinforcement learning approach. IEEE Trans. Wirel. Commun. 19(10), 6899–6915 (2020). https://doi.org/10.1109/TWC.2020.3006922
5. Huynh, L.N.T., Pham, Q.V., Nguyen, T.D.T., Hossain, M.D., Shin, Y.R., Huh, E.N.: Joint computational offloading and data-content caching in NOMA-MEC networks. IEEE Access 9, 12943–12954 (2021). https://doi.org/10.1109/ACCESS.2021.3051278
6. Wang, X., Chen, M., Taleb, T., Ksentini, A., Leung, V.C.M.: Cache in the air: exploiting content caching and delivery techniques for 5G systems. IEEE Commun. Mag. 52(2), 131–139 (2014). https://doi.org/10.1109/MCOM.2014.6736753
7. Ding, Z., et al.: Application of non-orthogonal multiple access in LTE and 5G networks. pp. 1–16 (2015). http://arxiv.org/abs/1511.08610
8. Zhang, J., Zhang, X., Wang, W.: Cache-enabled software-defined heterogeneous networks for green and flexible 5G networks. IEEE Access 4, 3591–3604 (2016). https://doi.org/10.1109/ACCESS.2016.2588883
9. Dai, L., Wang, B., Yuan, Y., Han, S., Chih-Lin, I., Wang, Z.: Non-orthogonal multiple access for 5G: Solutions, challenges, opportunities, and future research trends. IEEE Commun. Mag. 53(9), 74–81 (2015). https://doi.org/10.1109/MCOM.2015.7263349
10. Di, B., Song, L., Li, Y., Han, Z.: V2X.pdf. no. December, pp. 14–21 (2017)
11. Yacoub, M.: Multiple access. Wirel. Technol. 63–118 (2001). https://doi.org/10.1201/9781420041156-c3
12. Oviedo, J.A., Sadjadpour, H.R.: Leveraging edge caching in NOMA systems with QoS requirements. In: CCNC 2018 - 2018 15th IEEE Annual Consumer Communications and Networking Conference, vol. 2018-January, pp. 1–5 (2018). https://doi.org/10.1109/CCNC.2018.8319188
13. Gurugopinath, S., Sofotasios, P.C., Al-Hammadi, Y., Muhaidat, S.: Cache-aided non-orthogonal multiple access for 5G-enabled vehicular networks. IEEE Trans. Veh. Technol. 68(9), 8359–8371 (2019). https://doi.org/10.1109/TVT.2019.2929741
14. Ding, Z., Lei, X., Karagiannidis, G.K., Schober, R., Yuan, J., Bhargava, V.K.: A survey on non-orthogonal multiple access for 5G networks: research challenges and future trends. IEEE J. Sel. Areas Commun. 35(10), 2181–2195 (2017). https://doi.org/10.1109/JSAC.2017.2725519
15. Kaneko, M., Randrianantenaina, I., Dahrouj, H., Elsawy, H., Alouini, M.-S.: On the opportunities and challenges of NOMA-based fog radio access networks: an overview. IEEE Access 8, 205467–205476 (2020). https://doi.org/10.1109/access.2020.3037183
16. Tang, Z., He, J.: NOMA enhanced 5G distributed vehicle to vehicle communication for connected autonomous vehicles. In: MobiArch 2020 – Proceedings of 2020 ACM MobiArch 2020 15th Workshop on Mobility in the Evolving Internet Architecture. Part Mobicom 2020, pp. 42–47 (2020). https://doi.org/10.1145/3411043.3412505

17. Rezvani, S., Mokari, N., Javan, M.R., Jorswieck, E.A.: Resource allocation in virtualized CoMP-NOMA HetNets: multi-connectivity for joint transmission. IEEE Trans. Commun. 1–54 (2021. https://doi.org/10.1109/TCOMM.2021.3067700
18. Liu, J.: Vehicular Networks, pp. 1–17. Wiley 5G Ref (2019). https://doi.org/10.1002/978111 9471509.w5gref091
19. Yin, Y., Liu, M., Gui, G., Gacanin, H., Sari, H., Adachi, F.: QoS-oriented dynamic power allocation in NOMA-based wireless caching networks. IEEE Wirel. Commun. Lett. **10**(1), 82–86 (2021). https://doi.org/10.1109/LWC.2020.3021204
20. Alabbas, R., Hassnawi, L.A., Ilyas, M., Pervaiz, H., Abbasi, Q.H., Bayat, O.: Performance enhancement of safety message communication via designing dynamic power control mechanisms in vehicular ad hoc networks. Comput. Intell. (April), 1–23 (2020)
21. Liu, Y., Zhao, J., Li, M., Wu, Q.: Intelligent reflecting surface aided MISO uplink communication network: feasibility and power minimization for perfect and imperfect CSI. IEEE Trans. Commun. **69**(3), 1975–1989 (2021)

Performance Analysis of Hard Decision and Soft Decision Algorithms Over *In Vivo* Radio Channel

Mohanad Mezher[1]([⊠]) and Amjed Razzaq AlAbbas[2]

[1] The University of Mashreq, Baghdad, Iraq
mohanad.ahmed@uom.edu.iq
[2] Alsalam University College, Baghdad, Iraq

Abstract. BER performance of soft and hard decisions over *in-vivo* radio channel using ultra-wideband (UWB) frequencies (3.10–10.60 GHz) is presented in this paper. BER performance is calculated by comparing the message decoded by soft and hard decision algorithms with the transmitted message. This article compares the BER performance of soft and hard decisions over in vivo radio channels with Eb/No = (0–14 dB). We used MATLAB for this experiment. BER performance is better with a soft decision decoding algorithm in the log domain than with a hard decision algorithm, regardless of the Eb/No Levels.

Keywords: BER · Implantable devices · In vivo communication · Wireless body area networks · Ultra wideband

1 Introduction

1.1 An Overview for *In-Vivo* Radio Channel

The quality of life for many people has improved dramatically as a result of biomedical engineering technological advances. With the goal of meeting the demand for breakthrough biomedical technology and better healthcare quality, research into wireless body area networks (WBANs) has gotten a lot of attention in recent years [1]. Some of this cutting-edge technology includes wireless in vivo sensors and actuators like pacemakers, nerve stimulators, wireless capsule endoscopes (WCEs), and others. These new in-vivo wireless medical devices, along with associated technologies, offer a cost-effective and scaleable solution, as shown in [2]. They can also be used in conjunction with wearable devices. Depending on the signal path, the in vivo channel is considered a very noisy channel with a lot of fading (Bones, Flesh, Blood, Muscles and Skins). It's possible to provide continuous health monitoring with less surgical invasiveness by using in vivo-WBAN devices (Fig. 1) [7]. The longer the data is collected, the more reliable the analysis will be for clinicians, allowing them to use big data instead of data obtained during brief hospital visits [4]. In order to fully exploit and expand the potential of WBANs for practical applications, it is necessary to accurately assess the propagation of

© Springer Nature Switzerland AG 2022
C. Djeddi et al. (Eds.): MedPRAI 2021, CCIS 1543, pp. 288–300, 2022.
https://doi.org/10.1007/978-3-031-04112-9_22

electromagnetic (EM) waveforms in an in vivo communication environment (implant-to-implant and implant-to-external device) and obtain accurate channel models. Creating and using such a model is necessary for a variety of reasons, including achieving high data rates, meeting link budgets, locating appropriate operating frequencies, and developing efficient antennas and transceivers, including digital baseband transmitter/receiver algorithms [5]. In order to improve the efficacy of in vivo-WBAN devices, research into the in vivo wireless communication channel is essential [6]. It's still early days for the in vivo wireless communication research, but compared to the on-body wireless communication channel, there have been very few studies done so far. The in vivo channel differs from the more familiar wireless cellular and Wi-Fi settings in that the EM wave propagates through a relatively lossy environment inside the body and the primary scatterers are located close to the antenna (Fig. 2) [6].

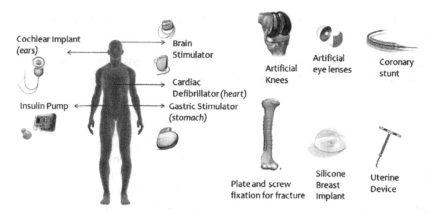

Fig. 1. Different implantable medical devices.

Various communication protocols, operational frequencies, and antenna designs are taken into consideration when presenting the current state of in vivo channel characterization in this work [8]. This work also highlights important research issues. There is also numerical and experimental characterization of the in vivo wireless communication channel. These findings are intended both to increase public awareness of this important communication medium and to stimulate further investigation into it.

In vivo-WBANs and their additional technologies will have a significant impact on healthcare in the future, given their enormous potential and critical importance [9]. For dependable, efficient, and high-performance communication systems, accurate channel models are essential if they are to be fully utilized for practical applications. By carefully evaluating link budgets, these models are needed to protect the safety of biological tissues as well as improve service quality metrics like high data rates, low bit-error rates, and low latency. For all their attention paid to studying on-body wireless communication channels (linkages between implants and external devices), researchers have only looked at a small subset of in vivo wireless communication channels. Antenna near-field characteristics are different from those of the more common wireless cellular or Wi-Fi settings because

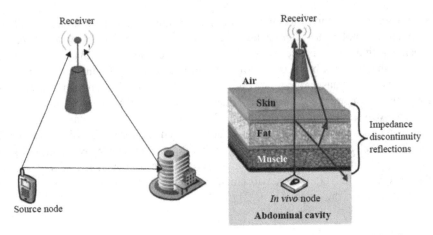

Fig. 2. The classical communication channel compared with the *in vivo* channel.

electromagnetic (EM) waves propagate through a very lossy environment inside the body and dominant scatterers are present.

1.2 *In Vivo* Communication System

A communication system's performance can be described by a matrix. While BER is an important measure, it is not the only one to consider. Because of the way bits are conveyed from transmitter to receiver in a communication system, they can be represented as a digital stream of binary integers with ones and zeros. Researchers are working to make implanted devices including cardiac pacemakers, medication delivery devices, and defibrillators ready for general public usage. The size of implanted devices is a serious issue since they cannot be put in the human body. Researchers want to make implants as tiny as possible without compromising functioning [12]. New antenna designs are being studied to help the gadget communicate with other devices using Wi-Fi, 3G, 4G, and 5G technologies. Using these antennas in a better wireless communication system will help researchers shrink implantable devices. [13] Illustrates this. It is tough to charge or change the implant's battery everyday once it is in place (see [14] for more information). The introduction of fifth-generation (5G) technology might hypothetically enhance the battery life of these devices by up to ten years. Because of the body's dense structure, a signal has trouble transmitting properly, resulting in inter-symbol interference (ISI) as detailed in [15]. See [10] for a full look at several types of antennas available for future implants that can aid in reliable connection between implantable devices and external conventional communication equipment. [5] Presents in vivo communication channel physiognomies. An ex-vivo device's antenna placement highlights the location-dependent elements of in-vivo communication and the shift in signal propagation that impacts communications. [16] "A mathematical channel model for in-vivo communication is created at ultra-wideband frequencies utilizing measurement data acquired from tests performed with a human corpse," says [17]. The necessity for medical support and ethical authorization makes testing time-consuming and costly. The mathematical modeling of ultra-wideband in vivo radio channels [18] allows researchers to simulate with minimal experimental equipment. The experimental analysis in [19] shows that in vivo communication is site independent. In vivo communication models fail badly, encouraging researchers to dig deeper and find new models [20]. To quickly adopt and commercialize the technology for the benefit of the end user, a full examination will be required in the near future [21].

1.3 Viterbi Algorithm

A large number of industries and users rely on storage media devices. As information technology advances, so does the demand for data storage media [22]. Directly attached storage, network attached storage, and storage area networks [23] are three forms of storage medium. For data loss prevention, storage media reliability is crucial. The data storage industry faces difficulties such device lifetime, reliability, and failure. Despite this, most data storage industries do not explore more dependable and fault-tolerant solutions [24]. Rather, they work on improving backup and recovery solutions. Between 3 and 5 years, hard disk drives appear to be the most reliable storage medium. In serious business, hard disk drives are coupled in RAID systems, with enhanced backup frequency, signaling low user trust in the equipment and other possible environmental catastrophes. According to a 2010 Microsoft study report, most faulty hard disks are replaced. Microsoft data centers report replacing hard drives at a rate of about 78% [25].

Here are the findings of an investigation. Hard disk failures account for 70% of server failures, RAID controllers for 6%, RAM for 5%, and miscellaneous factors for 18% [26]. Thus, hard disks are the most commonly replaced component and the most common cause of server failure [27]. Improved storage medium error correction or recovery procedures can increase data reliability. Its usage in data encoding and decoding with NTCs in Forward Error Correction (FEC) has encouraged research into its use in storage media to improve data reliability [28]. New technique reduces calculation complexity while maintaining performance. The computational complexity of convolutional coding was one of their drawbacks [29]. Storage media failures continue to be reported in high numbers despite Reed Solomon being nearly the only algorithm used in error correction. As a result, the authors propose an error correcting technique (locked Convolutional encoder with Enhanced Viterbi Algorithm decoder) to improve storage medium reliability.

2 Soft and Hard Decisions

The decoding of code words received through noisy channels is a difficult task in error correction [30]. The sender adds redundant bits or parity bits to the message before sending it, generating code words. After that, the code words are sent across computer networks [31]. To recover the original data, the receiver checks the arriving code words and conducts decoding or error correction. If there are no errors, that is, the code words match exactly, it is simple to decode the data by removing the parity bits. If no match is found, however, more advanced decoding algorithms are used. The two types of decoding procedures are depicted in the diagram (Fig. 3).

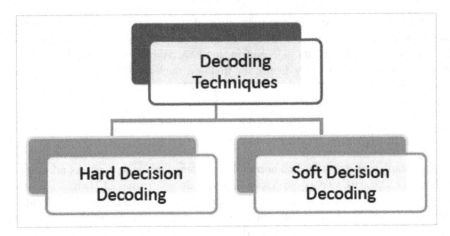

Fig. 3. The techniques of decoding.

It's called hard decision decoding because it considers each bit as either 1 or 0, depending on whether it came from the threshold stage of the receiver. Upon receiving a pulse, it takes a voltage sample and compares it to a preset threshold voltage. Voltages over the threshold are decoded as 1, while voltages below it are decoded as 0. Regardless of how near the voltage is to the threshold, the decoding is performed. As a class of algorithms, Soft decision decoding decodes a stream or block of bits by taking into account a variety of possible values. It takes into account the accuracy of each received pulse when estimating the amount of incoming data. Viterbi decoders, which decode convolutional codes, frequently employ soft-decision decoders.

2.1 Hard Decision Decoding

A parity encoder and communication channel (which attenuates data randomly) make up our communication model. The message bits "01" are applied to the parity encoder, and the output code word "011" is obtained as a result [32].

The channel transmits the codeword "011" as the result of the operation. A value of "0" is represented by "0 Volt," while a value of "1 Volt" is transmitted. The channel reduces the strength of the signal, resulting in a distorted waveform being seen by the receiver. Using the threshold voltage as a guide, the hard decision decoder decides what action to take. The threshold voltage in this scenario is set at 0.5 volts (in the middle of the "0" and "1" Volt range). The hard decision detector in the receiver identifies the bit state as "0" if the voltage level is below the threshold and as "1" if the voltage level is above the threshold at each sampling instant (as indicated in the picture above). As a result, "001" is returned as the outcome of the hard decision block. According to this "001" output, it's probable that the message bits cannot be retrieved effectively because "001" isn't a legitimate code word (compare this to all the potential code words listed above). The decoder computes the shortest Hamming distance for each case by comparing the output of the hard decision block with all potential code words (as illustrated in the table below).

Table 1. The output of hard decision block.

All possible code words	Hard decision output	Hamming distance
000	001	1
011	001	1
101	001	1
110	001	3

A valid code word has a minimum Hamming distance, and the decoder's responsibility is to select one that has that minimal Hamming distance. The minimal Hamming distance in our situation is "1," and there are three code phrases that are valid at this separation. With three options to pick from, there is a 1/3 chance of decoding the proper code word ("001" – that's what we sent). As a result, the chance of recovering our data is only 1/3 when using hard decision decoding.

2.2 Soft Viterbi Decoding

If the code word is received by a soft decision decoder, it is tested against all potential codes and only the one with the least Euclidean distance is picked [33]. In summary: Soft decision decoding improves decision making by adding more reliability information (such as Euclidean distance or log-likelihood ratio).

The Viterbi decoder can do hard or soft decision decoding. To make a hard decision, the received symbol is quantized to either "0" or "1". With a threshold of 1, the received bit is a one. Soft decision quantizers are multi-layer quantizers. Instead than defining thresholds, it uses information about the received symbol's dependability to improve error correction (Fig. 5). By comparing received code words to all possible code words, the shortest Euclidean distance is chosen. Voltage samples match to parity bits given when reading data [35]. Before decoding, the decoder receives voltage samples from the stream and digitizes them. To summarize, soft decoding helps decision making by delivering more reliable data. We don't use a threshold because it's subjective, but the read sequence is real. Compile two metric pathways, then sum, compare, and choose the survivor path's little distances. There are various soft decision volt-age levels for each sample moment (Fig. 5). On determines the Euclidean distance using the received signal and all available code words. Use the smallest or longest distance in Euclidean space. The soft choice uses all voltage levels to make a decision in this case. Soft decision decoding improves receiver performance by roughly 2 dB over hard decision decoding. Read signal 0.7V, 0.4 V, 0.22 V is a convolutional error code. The soft Viterbi algorithm seeks for the output sequence that is closest to r in terms of Euclidean distance. The encoder input sequence that follows the best path determines the most likely message sequence. The output code words are expressed as "OVolts" for zero and "1Volts" for one. The signal degrades after storage and must be re-read as distorted data. Distance between read signal and all possible code words can be computed using soft choice. The decoder then chooses the shortest Euclidean distance between the decoded words and their matches. The soft decision uses all the information from the various voltage levels to create a choice (Fig.4).

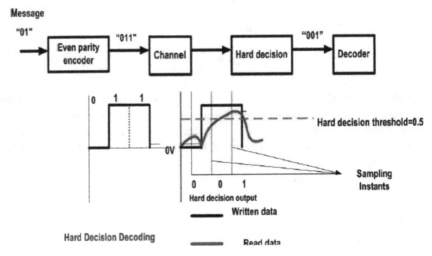

Fig. 4. Hard decision decoding.

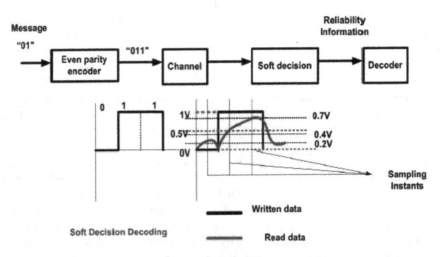

Fig. 5. Soft decision decoding.

This method compares the code words that have been read against all other possible code words to determine which one is closest to the one that has been read. Because the output bit is represented by a multilayer soft value, the decoding only works with quantized real values.

A $^1/_2$ Viterbi decoder with four states (S0, S1, S2, and S3) is shown in Fig. 6. Originally, the code words were (1, 1), (−1), (−1) and (1, −1) were written to the stor-age media devices, and the read codes were (0.7, 0.8), (0.9, 0.7), (0.7, 0.6) and The Euclidean distance at time T is equal to the sum of all of its individual pathways. Comparing the accumulated distances, the path with the shortest cumulative Euclidian distance is found. For example, at time T=0, the cumulative distance between S0 and S0 is 6.13 while the cumulative distance between S0 and S1 is 0.13. Because it has the smallest cumulative Euclidian distance, our route will be S0 to S1. The cumulative distances from S0 to S0 are 5.28 at time T = 4, 6.88 at time T = 3, 10.48 at time T = 4, 3.23 at time T = 4, 8.88 at time T = 4, 8.08 at time T = 4, and 9.68 at time T = 4 respective ly. As of now, our survivor path is determined by the minimal cumulative Euclidian distance of 3.23.

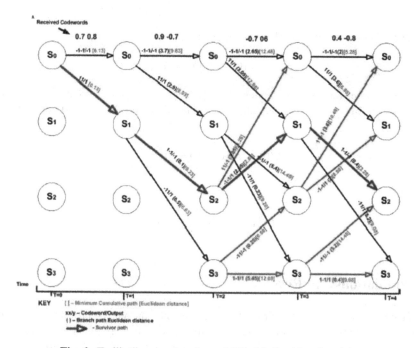

Fig. 6. Trellis diagram showing soft Viterbi algorithm decoder.

The concept of belief propagation underpins soft-decision decoding. The sum-product algorithm is a message transmission algorithm with a soft decision-making process. They are given as log-likelihood ratios in sum product decoding. The matrix of a binary variable is represented by a single value using log likelihood ratios (LLR). The sum-product algorithm resembles the bit-flipping method in that it is a soft decision message-passing algorithm. As opposed to bit flipping algorithms, SPA uses probabilities of information bits to express each choice.

Important terms in the algorithm are in equations below:

The check nodes calculate their response message;

$$r_{jt}(0) = \frac{1}{2} + \frac{1}{2}_{\left(\frac{tsvj}{t}\right)} G\left(1 - 2q_{tj}(1)\right) \tag{1}$$

$$r_{jt}(1) = 1 - r_{jt}(0) \tag{2}$$

Now the message nodes update their response message to check nodes

$$q_{jt}(0) = k_{tj}(1 - p_t) \underset{jF_{sc_i/j}}{G} \left(r_j F_t(0)\right) \tag{3}$$

$$q_{jt}(1) = k_{tj}(p_t) \underset{jF_{s_i/j}}{G} \left(r_j F_t(1)\right) \tag{4}$$

Constant *Kij* are chosen in such a way to ensure that

$$q_{tj}(0) + q_{tj}(1) = 1 \tag{5}$$

At this point the message nodes also update their current estimation C_i' of their message C_i. This is done by calculating the probabilities for 0 and 1 and voting for the bigger one.

$$Q_i(0) = k_i(1 - p_i) \underset{j \text{ sci}}{G} \left(r_{ji}(0)\right) \tag{6}$$

And

$$Q_i(1) = k_i(p_i) \underset{jsc_i}{G} \left(r_{ji}(1)\right) \tag{7}$$

3 Simulations and Results

MATLAB was used to run the simulations and conduct the analysis for this article. The quantity of code words, iterations, and decoding algorithms employed in this study are all taken into consideration when doing the analysis. The number of iterations specifies how many times the received code word is reviewed before a final decision is made.

This study employed two alternative decoding algorithms. They are algorithms for soft decision decoding and methods for hard decision decoding. Decoding algorithms that use both soft and hard decisions are used to code the 100000 code words. Both of these methods utilize an iterative decoding strategy. This simulation goes through 50 iterations. Table 2 summarizes the results of a performance comparison between decoding based on hard and soft decisions. As Eb/No increased, the number of errors dropped (Table 1).

Table 2. Performance analysis of hard decision and soft decision decoder.

$E_b/N_o dB$ Values	No. of errors for hard decision	No. of errors for sft decision
0	0.4912	0.4912
1	0.4905	0.4905
2	0.4908	0.4283
3	0.4782	0.355
4	0.4682	0.2788
5	0.3983	0.1287
6	0.313	0.02967
7	0.1919	0.005
8	0.09924	0.0003876
9	0.03803	0.00004243
10	0.01006	0.00000013
11	0.001965	0
12	0.0002961	0
13	0.00003699	0
14	0.00000011	0

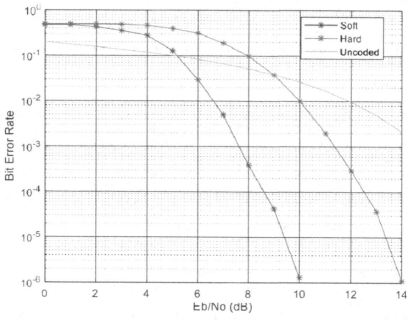

Fig. 7. BER performance comparison between soft decision and hard decision over *in vivo* radio channel.

Table 2 shows that the number of soft decision errors is zero for Eb/No dB 11, 12, 13, and 14. However, practically all Eb/No values contain an error when subjected to a hard decision decoding process. Consider the Eb/No = 10 for the comparative study. The number of errors in hard decision decoding for Eb/No = 10 is 0.01006. However, the soft decision decoding error rate for the identical Eb/No is 0.00000013. As a result, soft choice decoding offers remarkable decoding performance. Both probability and the log domain can be used for soft decision decoding. Comparing the log domain to the probability domain, log decoding has a lower level of decoding complexity. Soft decision decoding was simulated in this work log domain. Figure 6 compares the results of BER-based hard decision decoding with those of BER-based soft decisions (Fig. 7).

We can deduct from the graph that for a 10 dB Eb/No, BER 10^{-6} is attained when using soft decision decoding. However, the same BER of 14 dB Eb/No is produced when using hard decision decoding. When compared to hard decision decoding, soft decision decoding offers a 2–3 dB code boost. We may conclude from the simulation findings that soft decision decoding outperforms hard choice decoding in terms of performance.

4   Conclusion

To ensure mistake-free communication, make sure your forward error correction technique is up to date. One of the most effective error-correction codes is the FEC code, which uses soft and hard decision algorithms. However, the BER's performance is solely determined by the decoding algorithm's design and selection. There was a comparison of the BER performance of a soft decision decoding method with a hard decision decoding algorithm in the log domain Different Eb/No levels were used in the comparison. No matter what Eb/No level you use, the log domain's soft decision decoding method outperforms the hard decision decoding algorithm in terms of BER performance. Both decoding algorithms provide good BER performance over an in vivo channel at a half-code rate.

References

1. Mezher, M., Ilyas, M., Bayat, O., Abbasi, Q.H.: Bit error rate performance of in-vivo radio channel using maximum likelihood sequence estimation. In: 2020 International Conference on Electrical, Communication, and Computer Engineering (ICECCE), pp. 1–4 (2020). https://doi.org/10.1109/ICECCE49384.2020.9179248
2. Ilyas, M., et al.: Evaluation of ultra-wideband in vivo radio channel and its effects on system performance. Trans. Emerging Telecommun. Technol. 30(1), e3530 (2019)
3. Demir, A.F., et al.: In vivo wireless channel modeling. arXiv preprint arXiv:1902.08199 (2019)
4. Obaid, S.M., Elwi, T.A., Ilyas, M.: Fractal minkowski-shaped resonator for noninvasive biomedical measurements: blood glucose test. Progress Electromagnetics Res. C 107, 143–156 (2021)
5. Ilyas, M., Bayat, O., Abbasi, Q.H.: Experimental analysis of ultra wideband in vivo radio channel. In 2018 26th Signal Processing and Communications Applications Conference (SIU), pp. 1–4. IEEE, May 2018
6. Abbasi, Q.H., Member, S., Nasir, A.A., Member, K.Y.: Cooperative In-Vivo Nano-Network Communication at Terahertz Frequencies Nano-Micro Interface Relay Nodes Data-Analysis Nano-Routers, vol. 3536, no. c, pp. 1–5 (2017)

7. Rathore, H., Mohamed, A., Guizani, M.: Deep learning-based security schemes for implantable medical devices. In: Energy Efficiency of Medical Devices and Healthcare Applications, pp. 109–130. Academic Press (2020)
8. Ilyas, M., Ucan, O.N., Bayat, O., Yang, X., Abbasi, Q.H.: Mathematical modeling of ultra wideband in vivo radio channel. IEEE Access **6**, 20848–20854 (2018)
9. Demir, A.F., Z. E. Ankaralı, Q. H. Abbasi, E. Serpedin, and H. Arslan, "T 32 Ill,", June 2016
10. Ilyas, M., Bayat, O., Ucan, O.N., Imran, M.A., Abbasi, Q.H.: Location dependent channel characteristics for implantable devices. In: 2019 International Conference on Advances in the Emerging Computing Technologies (AECT), pp. 1–4. IEEE, February 2020
11. Anatomical, H., Demir, A.F., Member, S., Ankarali, Z.E., Member, S., Abbasi, Q.H.: Anatomical Region-Specific In Vivo Wireless Communication Channel Characterization, June 2017
12. Szivek, J.A., Roberto, R.F., Margolis, D.S.: In Vivo Strain Measurements from Hardware and Lamina during Spine Fusion, pp. 243– 250 (2005)
13. Alomainy, A., Hao, Y., Yuan, Y., Liu, Y.: Modelling and characterisation of radio propagation from wireless implants at different frequencies. In 2006 European Conference on Wireless Technology, pp. 119–122. IEEE, September 2006
14. Shubair, R.M., Elayan, H.: A survey of in vivo WBAN communications and networking: research issues and challenges. In 2015 11th International Conference on Innovations in Information Technology (IIT), pp. 11–16. IEEE. November 2015
15. Yang, K., Hussain, Q., Chopra, N., Munoz, M.: Nano Communication Networks Effects of non-flat interfaces in human skin tissues on the in-vivo Tera-Hertz communication channel. Nano Commun. Netw., pp. 1–9 (2015)
16. Hussein, E.D., Qasem, N., Jameel, M.S., Ilyas, M., Bayat, O.: Performance optimization of microstrip patch antenna using frequency selective surfaces for 60 GHz. In 2020 28th Signal Processing and Communications Applications Conference (SIU), pp. 1–4. IEEE, October 2020
17. Elias, J., Mehaoua, A.: Energy-aware topology design for wireless body area networks. In: 2012 IEEE International Conference on Communications (ICC) (pp. 3409–3410). IEEE, June 2012
18. Özdogan, Ö., Member, S., Björnson, E., Member, S.: Massive MIMO with spatially correlated rician fading channels, vol. 67, no. 5, pp. 1–17 (2019)
19. Khan, J.Y., Yuce, M.R., Bulger, G., Harding, B.: Wireless body area network (WBAN) design techniques and performance evaluation. J. Med. Syst. **36**(3), 1441–1457 (2012)
20. Science, C., Mary, Q.: Characterisation of the In-vivo Terahertz Communication Channel within the Human Body Tissues for Future Nano-Communication Networks, no, September 2015
21. Chopra, N., Upton, J., Philpott, M., Alomainy, A.: Characterization of Volumetric Change in Collagen using THz Time Domain Spectroscopy for In-Body Nanonetworks, vol. 1, pp. 1–2
22. Singh, M., Wassell, I.J.: Comparison between soft and hard decision decoding using quaternary convolutional encoders and the decomposed CPM model. In: IEEE VTS 53rd Vehicular Technology Conference, Spring 2001. Proceedings (Cat. No. 01CH37202), vol. 2, pp. 1347–1351. IEEE, May 2001
23. Zheng, S., Zhou, X., Chen, S., Qi, P., Yang, X.: DemodNet : Learning Soft Demodulation from Hard Information Using Convolutional Neural Network, pp. 1–5
24. Hassan, K., Michael, K., Mrutu, S.I.: Design of s oft viterbi algorithm decoder enhanced with non t ransmittable c odewords for storage media, vol. 7, no. 1, pp. 1–11 (2017)
25. Alhasan, A., Audah, L., Alabbas, A.: Energy overhead evaluation of security trust models for IoT applications. J. Theor. Appl. Inf. Technol. **98**, 69–77 (2020)
26. Khan, I., Zafar, M.H., Ashraf, M., Kim, S.: Computationally Efficient Channel Estimation in 5G, pp. 1–12 (2018)

27. Hussein, Y.M., Mutlag, A.H., Al-nedawe, B.M.: Comparisons of Soft Decision Decoding Algorithms Based LDPC Wireless Communication System Comparisons of Soft Decision Decoding Algorithms Based LDPC Wireless Communication System (2021)
28. Jose, R., Pe, A.: Analysis of hard decision and soft decision decoding algorithms of LDPC codes in AWGN. In: 2015 IEEE International Advance Computing Conference (IACC), pp. 430–435. IEEE, June 2015
29. Alabbas, A.R., et al.: Performance enhancement of safety message communication via designing dynamic power control mechanisms in vehicular ad hoc networks. Comput. Intell. 37(3), 1286–1308 (2021). https://doi.org/10.1111/coin.12367
30. Alvarado, A., Member, S., Agrell, E., Member, S.: Replacing the Soft- decision FEC Limit Paradigm in the Design of Optical Communication Systems (2015)
31. Jeon, T., Yoon, S., Kim, K.: Performance of Iterative Soft Decision Feedback Equalizers for Single-Carrier Transmission, vol. 12, no. 3, pp. 1280–1285 (2017)
32. Hewavithana, T.C., Brookes, M.: Soft decisions for dqpsk demodulation for the viterbi decoding of the convolutional codes, pp. 17–20 (2003)
33. Phamdo, N., Alajaji, F.: Soft-decision demodulation design for COVQ over white, colored, and ISI Gaussian channels. IEEE Trans. Commun. 48(9), 1499–1506 (2000)
34. Theses, M., Liu, S.: Digital Commons @ Michigan Tech Soft-decision equalization techniques for frequency selective MIMO channels Soft- Decision Equalization Techniques for Frequency Selective MIMO Channels
35. Abbasi, Q.H., Alomainy, A., Hao, Y.: Antenna diversity techniques for enhanced networks in healthcare (2014)

The Thermal Modeling for Underground Cable Based on ANN Prediction

Abdullah Ahmed Al-Dulaimi[1]([✉]) [iD], Muhammet Tahir Guneser[1] [iD],
and Alaa Ali Hameed[2] [iD]

[1] Karabuk University, Karabuk 78100, Turkey
2038171016@ogrenci.karabuk.edu.tr
[2] Department of Computer Engineering, Istinye University, Istanbul, Turkey
alaa.hameed@istinye.edu.tr

Abstract. Many factors affect the ampacity of the underground cable (UC) to carry current, such as the backfill material (classical, thermal, or a combination thereof) and the depth at which it is buried. Moreover, the thermal of the UC is an effective element in the performance and effectiveness of the UC. However, it is difficult to find thermal modeling and prediction in the UC under the influence of many parameters such as soil resistivity (ρ_{soil}), insulator resistivity ($\rho_{insulator}$), and ambient temperature. In this paper, the calculation of the UC steady-state rating current is the most important part of the cable installation design. This paper also applied an artificial neural network (ANN) to develop and predict for 33 kV UC rating models. The proposed system was built by using the MATLAB package. The ANN-based UC rating is achieves the best performance and prediction for the UC rating current. The performance of the proposed model is superior to other models. The experiment was conducted with 200 epochs. The proposed model achieved high performance with low MSE (0.137) and the regression curve gives an excellent performance (0.99).

Keywords: Underground cables performance · Cable ampacity · Thermal modeling · Thermal backfill · Heat transfer · Artificial neural network (ANN)

1 Introduction

The electric power distribution industry has grown over the past two decades, which has resulted in an increased demand for electricity. The methods of distribution, on the other hand, have remained largely unchanged. Overhead and underground power lines are the two primary means of distributing electricity, and both methods have their benefits and drawbacks.

The transmission line of an underground power cable can carry as much electricity as necessary. It is possible to transmit maximum electric current without exceeding cable temperature limits thanks to the cable's ampacity. The maximum current that a cable can carry is meant by the term "cable ampacity." The temperature has a direct impact on the amount of current flowing through the transmission cable. The temperature of a conductor rises when it's subjected to high current. Power cable insulation

© Springer Nature Switzerland AG 2022
C. Djeddi et al. (Eds.): MedPRAI 2021, CCIS 1543, pp. 301–314, 2022.
https://doi.org/10.1007/978-3-031-04112-9_23

will fail if exposed to too high temperatures (higher than the steady-state temperature). Transmission line failure is thus caused. XLPE-insulated power cables lead to excessive conductor temperatures of over 90 C, causing in unsafe transmission line operation.

In literature reviews, several studies have shown that adding a small amount of thermal backfill material around a power cable significantly increases the cable's ampacity based on thermal analysis [1, 2]. The current ratings of buried cables are determined using various of approaches that all use a constant value for the soil thermal conductivity [3, 4]. An important factor affecting the current carrying ampacity of the cable is the formation of dry zones in the soil around the cable, as these dry zones cause moisture migration within the soil. Where the factor of reducing the dry areas around the cables has been proposed [5]. Liquid water, vapor, and heat flow in an UC based thermal system were compared using the new numerical model developed by the authors. Experimental verification of transient calculations of the finite element method showed a strong correlation between cable temperature and soil water content [6]. The thermal conductivity of soil rises with increasing porosity and water saturation of the pores [7, 8].

The numerical thermal analysis of high voltage UC in sinusoidal currents with multilayer soil was presented in a study. Analysis of the results of determining the thermal properties of a multilayered soil has been completed [9]. An analytical model using the finite element method was presented [10]. By using the Finite Element Method (FEM), cable ampacity and thermal behavior were calculated with single or multi-core cables buried or in ducts and in flat or trefoil formation, and the effect of soil resistivity variance was observed [11, 12]. A study was presented for the thermal resistivity of underground power cables using a one-dimensional thermal-electrical model [13].

Artificial intelligence has been used in many electrical applications, including state estimation of the power system, predicting the life of lithium batteries in electric vehicles, and determining faults in the electrical transmission system for UCs. An ANN can predict the failure risk of medium voltage UC linked to overhead distribution lines can be predicted using an ANN [14]. A number of modern algorithms were used to predict the sheath current before buried the cable underground, and the most influential factors on the current sheath were identified [15]. Artificial intelligence was used to predict the thermal conductivity and the process of heat flow through the soil was revealed as it was a thermomechanical process [16]. Utilizing ANN, a standard model for soil thermal conductivity was developed. The results of bivariate correlations and ANN-based soil thermal conductivity prediction variables were also examined and discussed. Next, the model's performance was assessed and compared to that of four other soil thermal conductivity models that had previously been developed [17]. The cables ampacity ensures that the maximum electric current can be transferred without exceeding the cable's maximum allowable temperature. The term cable ampacity describes the amount of current the cable can carry [18, 19]. The temperature has a direct effect on the amount of current flowing through the transmission cable. The temperature of the conductor rises due to the high current. During extremely high temperatures (above the steady-state temperature), the insulation of a power cable breaks down.

The main objective of this paper studies for UC performance systems using ANN. A thermal-electrical is use to transform complex heat transfer problems into simple electric circuit problems. The intelligent systems-based UC rating study of underground lines involves steady-state rating calculation and conductor temperature calculation based on peak loadings with computational the MATLAB package. Finally, the proposed system using simulated data has been developed to estimate and predict the UC steady-state rating current.

In the next section, a geometric model for UC is discussed. In Sect. 3, describes the modeling of internal and external thermal resistance for UC. A detailed description of the mathematical model of ground cables and boundary condiconditions is given in Sect. 4. Section 5 shows the proposed ANN-based UC rating, and the proceeding of the ANN Learning model. Section 6, presenting the simulation results. Finally, the proposed study concluded in the Sect. 7.

2   A Geometric Model for Underground Cable Used

The UC used in this experiment has a cross-sectional area of 300 mm^2 and medium voltage (33 kV). Figure 1a depicts the number of cable layers and their respective diameters. The outer diameter is 83.95 mm, while the conductor diameter is 39.8 mm. In addition,

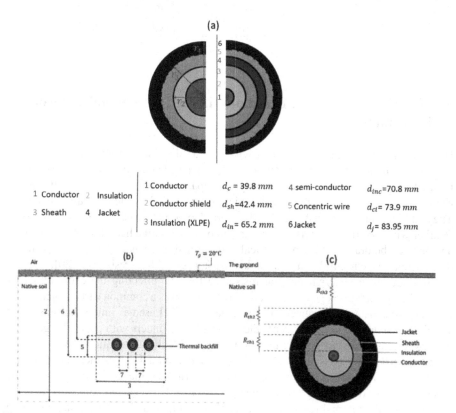

Fig. 1. The model architecture of the underground cable a) layers and the layers radius for 33 kV underground power cable, b) Arrangement of UC in terms of geometry, c) The cable's thermal resistance, both internally and externally.

Fig. 1b depicts the soil surface temperature in contact with the cable and the materials used to backfill the cable. The cable backfill size is critical because it has the greatest impact on the cable ampacity to carry the current. Table 1 displays the UC geometry dimensions. In this paper the resistivity of aluminum conductor is $\rho = 0.0042$ km/w, XLPE type insulator is $\rho = 3.5$ km/w, mother soil (slurry) is $\rho = 0.8$ km/w and soil thermal backfill is $\rho = 0.65$ km/w.

Table 1. Geometry dimensions of the used UC.

Variable	Value	Unit
1	4	m
2	2.34	m
3	2	m
4	0.8	m
5	0.5	m
6	1	m
7	20	cm

3 Modeling of Thermal Resistance in the Internal and External Environments

Heat transfer coefficients and soil resistivity, play a role in determining cable rating values, on which the thermal circuit depends. This means that as accuracy increases in the thermal circuit parameters, the cable carrying ampacity increases. The conductive material in the power cable generates heat, which is then stifled by the insulating materials. The materials ability to resist heat flow is referred to as its thermal resistance. Engineers familiar with electrical circuits can use an analogy to describe heat flow. As a result, an analogy can be drawn between electrical and thermal resistance. the ratio of potential difference to the current flowing through a resistor is called its resistance [20].

Soil acts as an external thermal resistance for UC, affecting the cable ampacity ratings. The calculation of external thermal resistance was a common early project focus for many scientists and engineers. Early researchers [21] used a similar thermoelectric circuit to design ground cables as parallel conductive cylinders with equal charges. The external thermal resistance was calculated using Goldenbergs equations derived based on the superposition's assumption. A single insulated buried cables thermal resistance can be easily determined by starting with the external thermal resistance of a bundle before applying overlay [22]. The internal resistance between the conductor and the insulator and the internal resistance between the insulator and the jacket are shown in Fig. 1c. The external resistance between the jacket and the soil is also shown in Fig. 1c. Also, we can see the radii of the cable layers in Fig. 1a.

4   A Mathematical Model for Underground Cables

The mathematical model has been used to calculate the current rating for UC [23], through this situation, the cable ampacity to carry current can be calculated. Heat is transferred from the conductor to the surrounding soil and environment via conduction in UC [24]. With the ampacity of the cable, can transfer as much electric current as possible while still keeping the cable within safe operating temperatures [25]. The conductor's temperature has a significant impact on the cable's ability to carry current. From the conductor to the surrounding soil, heat dissipation and diffusion significantly impact UC system performance evaluations, which affects the cable's ampacity to carry current.

The boundary condition must be specified when computing the model. Heat conduction occurs in two dimensions in a UC system, and only the cable core and insulation are subjected to the heat source condition.

For the steady-state condition [14], The two-dimensional heat conduction equation

$$\frac{\partial}{\partial x}\left(k\frac{\partial T}{\partial x}\right) + \frac{\partial}{\partial y}\left(k\frac{\partial T}{dy}\right) + q_\omega = 0 \tag{1}$$

where q_ω is the amount of heat that can be generated per unit volume.

Equations (2–5) show the constant surface temperature, constant surface heat flux, perfectly insulated, and convection on the surface, respectively.

$$T_{(x_x=0,t)} = T_{\text{surface}} \tag{2}$$

$$-k\frac{\partial T}{\partial x}\bigg]_{x=0} = q_s \tag{3}$$

$$\frac{\partial T}{\partial x}\bigg]_{x=0} = 0 \tag{4}$$

$$-k\frac{\partial T}{\partial x}\bigg]_{x=0} = H[T_\infty - T_{x=0}] \tag{5}$$

5   Proposed of ANN-Based Underground Cable Rating

ANN is used to solve AC/DC motor control problems, estimation power electronic systems, power system stability, and transmission line faults due to its rapid implementation. This paper used an ANN system to design the modeling and prediction for 33 kV UC performances. Moreover, the proposed algorithm applied on the specification for UC. Figure 2 shows the structure of the ANN-based UC ratings for 33 kV UC. two inputs for ANN are soil resistivity and insulator resistivity to predict the UC ratings. Where these parameters affect the ampacity of the cable to carry current. Among many types of ANN, in this paper has used the backpropagation (BP) training method. Figure 2 shows three layers, which are input, hidden and output layers. Proposed of the ANN-based UC rating program is designed by MATLAB software.

The BP network training algorithm includes three phases: data feed model, associated error return, and weight adjustment. ANN trained by batch mode and training data is used to train the ANN taken from the UC classification. The training data consider of inputs, soil resistivity, insulator resistivity and target output.

The forward feed phase begins by receiving all input signals (X_i) and sending them to each of the hidden nodes ($Z_1, \ldots Z_j$). Hidden node calculates the net and activation function using:

$$net_j = b_{0j} + \sum_{j=1}^{P} w_{ij} X_i \tag{6}$$

$$Z_j = f(net_j) \tag{7}$$

where, X_i, $i = 1, 2$ is the inputs, Z_j, $j = 1, 2, \ldots, P$ is the outputs hidden layer, w_{ij} Is the weights between the hidden and input layer and b_{0j} is the bias weights between the input and hidden layer. In this study 40 nodes are used in the hidden layer and the sigmoid activation function is expressed in the following equation:

$$f(net_j) = \frac{2}{1 + e^{-net_j}} - 1 \tag{8}$$

Then, the output of the hidden nodes (Zj) is sent to each output node. The output node calculates the activation function and net activation function using:

$$net_k = b_{0k} + \sum_{k=1}^{n} w_{jk} Z_j \tag{9}$$

$$UGC = f(net_k) \tag{10}$$

where, UC rating (UCR) is the output of the final layer, w_{jk} is the weight between the output and hidden layers and b_{0k} is the bias weight between the output and hidden layers.

In this study, the linear activation function as shown in this equation:

$$f(net_k) = net_k \tag{11}$$

BP training algorithm begins to produce small value networks. The error is calculated for each ANN output unit by subtracting the UN ANCR output from the UCR target data the error is based on an account (δ_k). Error$_k$ distributes the error in the UCR output unit and updates all data for the previous layers in the equation:

$$\delta_k = error_k f'(net_k) \tag{12}$$

Where the weights Change (Δw_{jk}) between the output layer and hidden layer is computed by δ_k and the bias weight change (Δb_{0k}) is calculated as:

$$\Delta w_{jk} = l_r \delta_k Z_j \tag{13}$$

$$\Delta b_{0k} = l_r \delta_k \tag{14}$$

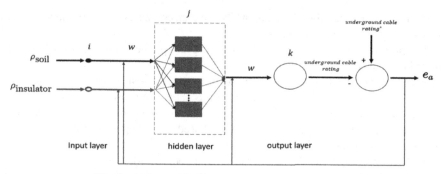

Fig. 2. ANN-based underground cable rating network

The factor δ_j In the hidden layer is calculated where l_r is learning rate. It is dependent on δ_k and derivative of its activation function in the equation:

$$\delta_j = f'\left(net_j\right) \sum_{k=1}^{n} w_{jk}\delta_k \tag{15}$$

weights Change (Δw_{ij}) between hidden and input layer is computed by δ_j and the bias weights change (Δb_{0j}) is calculated by equations:

$$\Delta w_{ij} = l_r \delta_j X_i \tag{16}$$

$$\Delta b_{0j} = l_r \delta_j \tag{17}$$

The last step is updating (weights) by applying the equations:

$$w_{ij}(new) = w_{ij}(old) + \Delta w_{ij}$$

$$b_{0j}(new) = b_{0j}(old) + \Delta b_{0j}$$

$$w_{jk}(new) = w_{jk}(old) + \Delta w_{jk}$$

$$b_{0k}(new) = b_{0k}(old) + \Delta b_{0k} \tag{18}$$

6   Results and Discussion

The steady-state rating current values are calculated using mathematical calculations (mathematical model) and then these values are entered into the (FEM) to show the temperature distribution around the cables. Those previously obtained values using mathematical calculations (mathematical model) are entered into the ANN to calculate the prediction values, as we see in Fig. 3. Consequently, using (FEM) shows the temperature distribution around the cables based on ANN and then compares the results and indicates the percentage of accuracy and error.

The proposed ANN is designed the modeling and prediction for 33 kV UC ratings model in this paper. UC data obtained through built the program of mathematical model of for UC rating. This training data consists of two inputs: soil resistivity and insulator resistivity and one output data is UC rating. In this paper, ANN uses three layers, namely input, hidden, and output layers. The activation function in the hidden and output layers are sigmoid and linear, respectively. An ANN-based UC rating approach is also developed and it has a good performance approach. In this work, the learning rate applied in the ANN system is 0.1 and the number of hidden nodes is 20.

Table 2 shows the actual values of soil resistivity, insulator resistivity and the input values to be prediction using the ANN to predict the steady-state rating current.

Figure 4 shows the input data values bigger than the predicted data values for the steady-state rating current, which gives a highly accurate prediction rate. The current values to be predicted were calculated in advance using mathematical model calculations and then compared to the predicted values.

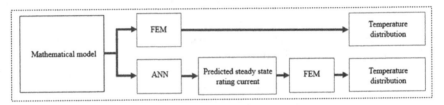

Fig. 3. Steps of the proposed model

Table 2. Test values.

Actual value (mathematical model)			Input value to prediction	
ρ_{soil}	$\rho_{insulator}$	ρ_{soil}	$\rho_{insulator}$	
0.8	1–4	0.5	1–4	
1	1–4	0.55	1–4	
1.2	1–4	0.6	1–4	
1.4	1–4	0.65	1–4	
1.6	1–4	0.7	1–4	
1.8	1–4	0.75	1–4	
2	1–4	0.8	1–4	

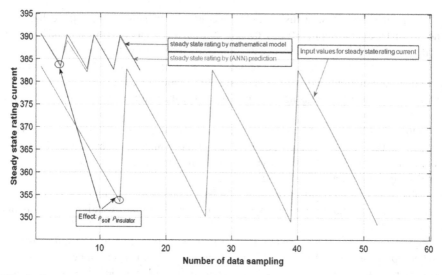

Fig. 4. Steady-state rating current: Input, actual and prediction current for underground cable.

Figure 5a shows the mathematical model calculation results between the resistivity of soil and UC rating with change in insulator resistivity. Insulator resistivity is changed between (1 to 4) in this test. Figure 5a shows the relationship between soil resistivity with UC is inverse when the insulation Resistivity is inconstant.

Figure 5b shows the mathematical model calculation results between the resistivity of the insulator and UC rating with change in soil resistivity. In this experiment, soil resistivity is changed between (0.8 to 2). Figure 5b shows the relationship between resistivity of insulator with UC is a direct relationship, but when the effect of soil resistivity value changes (inconstant) the relationship becomes inverse.

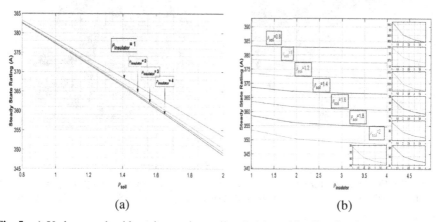

(a)   (b)

Fig. 5. a) Underground cable rating against soil resistivity with effect insulator resistivity, **b)** Underground cable rating against insulator resistivity with effect soil resistivity

Figure 6a shows Heat diffusion and temperature distribution around the cable, considering that the cable depth is 0.8 m, the soil thermal resistivity 0.8 (km/w), and insulator thermal resistivity 1 (km/w). Power cable ampacity increased with decreases in the insulators resistivity, which cooled and regulated the heat transfer around the power cables. A condensed temperature distribution outside the conductor can be seen decreasing the conductors temperature. This heat dissipation makes the cable more able to carry a large amount of current.

Figure 6b shows Heat diffusion and temperature distribution around the cable. When considering the 3.5 (km/w) thermal resistivity of the insulator, the same variables were used. Increasing the thermal resistivity of the insulator causes a decrease in the power cable's ampacity to transmit electric current.

Cable system temperatures of interest, selected ampacity, or other relevant thermal circuit parameters can be used as objective functions (thermal resistivity or boundary conditions [26].

Figure 7a shows a steady-state rating current prediction. (0.5 to 0.8) soil resistivity has been proposed as values to predict the current state for each value increment of insulator resistivity between (1 to 4) as we see in Table 2 it is clear that the predicted current value is close to the actual current value (mathematical model calculation).

Figure 7b shows a steady-state rating prediction. (1 to 4) insulator resistivity has been proposed as values to predict the current state for each value increment of soil resistivity between (0.5 to 0.8) as we see in Table 2 it is clear that the predicted current value is very close to the actual current value. Figure 7b also shows that a slight change in the actual value of the current leads to a relatively bigger change in the value to be predicted. However, the accuracy rate is very high with a small error rate.

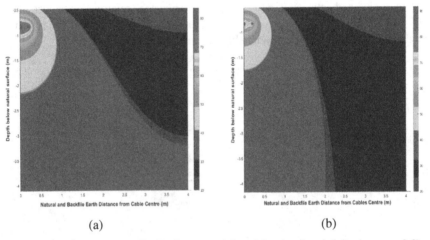

(a)   (b)

Fig. 6. The FEM temperature distribution around the cable, **a)** soil resistivity ($\rho_{soil} = 0.8$) and insulator resistivity ($\rho_{insulator} = 1$), **b)** soil resistivity ($\rho_{soil} = 0.8$) and insulator resistivity ($\rho_{insulator} = 3.5$)

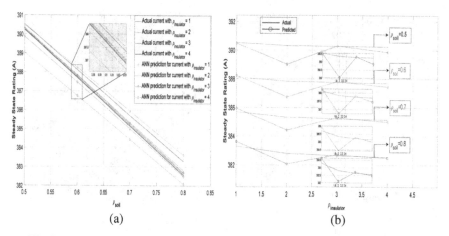

Fig. 7. ANN steady-state rating prediction **a)** Insulator resistivity, **b)** Soil resistivity

In Fig. 8a one sample of the predicted values using an artificial neural network was used, which are (0.8) soil resistivity and (1) insulator resistivity. It was taken into account that the value of the steady-state rating current slightly increased during the prediction process as shown in Fig. 7b. The results show that the temperature distribution in Fig. 8a, depending on the artificial neural network, is very close to the real temperature distribution.

In Fig. 8b Another sample of predicted values based on the ANN was used: (0.8) soil resistivity and (3.5) insulator resistivity. The figure shows the temperature distribution results around the power cables depending on the change in the steady-state rating current value when it is predicted. Whereas, the slight change of the rating current led to a convergence between the actual temperatures distribution and the temperatures distribution based on the artificial neural network.

Figure 9(a, b) shows the mean square error (*mse*) decreases for each epoch until it reaches very close to zero at 200 epochs. The regression curve is achieved an excellent performance to reach 0.99. The proposed ANN-based UC rating is validated with two effects on the UC rating: soil resistivity and insulator resistivity. Also, the figure shows indicate the best validation performance of the neural network and show the gradient, mu and training curves of the process. The minimum gradient was decided as 10^{-2} for the goal in the training process. The training has reached the goal at the 200 epochs. The gradient and mu (the neural network's weight changes) change over time and the number of validation checks is shown in Fig. 9. These outputs of the training process indicate a successful state of the neural network.

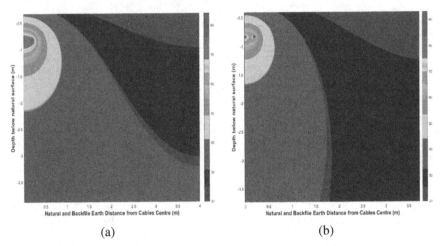

(a)   (b)

Fig. 8. The FEM temperature distribution around the cable (based on ANN), **a)** soil resistivity (ρ_{soil} = 0.8) and insulator resistivity ($\rho_{insulator}$ = 1), **b)** soil resistivity (ρ_{soil} = 0.8) and insulator resistivity ($\rho_{insulator}$ = 3.5)

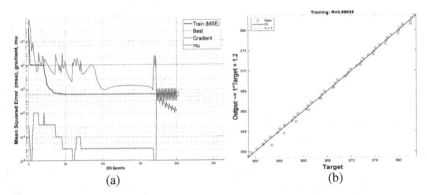

(a)   (b)

Fig. 9. a) Performance of ANN, **b)** Regression

7 Conclusion

Designers and project engineers need additional variables provided during the cable testing process, this paper plays a crucial role in providing them. Approximate assumptions lead to a large margin of error, so before entering the power distribution, you must ensure that all factors affecting the power distribution and cable reliability are in good condition. The use of the artificial intelligence prediction method in UCs is considered very effective from a practical and economical point of view, as it gives excellent results that are close to reality and saves the prices of the tools used to calculate these variables. The paper presented two important factors that affect the temperature distribution around the cable: the soil resistivity and the insulator resistivity. The results show the convergence between the actual values calculated using the mathematical model and the predicted values based on the artificial neural network. In the future, it is possible to study the influence of other factors that have a high impact on the cables ampacity to carry the current and the temperature distribution around the power cables.

References

1. Anders, G.J.: Rating of electric power cables: ampacity computations for transmission, Distribution, and Industrial Applications. IEEE (1997)
2. De Leon, F., Anders, G.J.: Effects of backfilling on cable ampacity analyzed with the finite element method. IEEE Trans. Power Delivery 23(2), 537–543 (2008)
3. Hegyi, J., Klestoff, A.Y.: Current-carrying capability for industrial underground cable installations. IEEE Trans. Ind. Appl. 24(1), 99–105 (1988)
4. Anders, G.J., Napieralski, A., Kulesza, Z.: Calculation of the internal thermal resistance and ampacity of 3-core screened cables with fillers. IEEE Trans. Power Delivery 14(3), 729–734 (1999)
5. Gouda, O.E., El Dein, A.Z., Amer, G.M.: Effect of the formation of the dry zone around underground power cables on their ratings. IEEE Trans. Power Delivery 26(2), 972–978 (2010)
6. Kroener, E., Vallati, A., Bittelli, M.: Numerical simulation of coupled heat, liquid water and water vapor in soils for heat dissipation of underground electrical power cables. Appl. Therm. Eng. 70(1), 510–523 (2014)
7. Peters-Lidard, C.D., Blackburn, E., Liang, X., Wood, E.F.: The effect of soil thermal conductivity parameterization on surface energy fluxes and temperatures. J. Atmos. Sci. 55(7), 1209–1224 (1998)
8. Rees, S.W., Adjali, M.H., Zhou, Z., Davies, M., Thomas, H.R.: Ground heat transfer effects on the thermal performance of earth-contact structures. Renew. Sustain. Energy Rev. 4(3), 213–265 (2000)
9. Ocłoń, P., Cisek, P., Pilarczyk, M., Taler.: Numerical simulation of heat dissipation processes in underground power cable system situated in thermal backfill and buried in a multilayered soil. Energy Conversion Manage. 95, 352–370 (2015)
10. Ocłoń, P., et al.: The performance analysis of a new thermal backfill material for underground power cable system. Appl. Thermal Eng. 108, 233–250 (2016)
11. Sahar, A.M., Wissink, J., Mahmoud, M.M., Karayiannis, T.G., Ishak, M.S.A.: Effect of hydraulic diameter and aspect ratio on single phase flow and heat transfer in a rectangular microchannel. Appl. Therm. Eng. 115, 793–814 (2017)
12. Diaz-Aguiló, M., De León, F., Jazebi, S., Terracciano, M.: Ladder-type soil model for dynamic thermal rating of underground power cables. IEEE Power Energy Technol. Syst. J. 1, 21–30 (2014)
13. Papagiannopoulos, I., Chatziathanasiou, V., Exizidis, L., Andreou, G.T., De Mey, G., Więcek, B.: Behaviour of the thermal impedance of buried power cables. Int. J. Electr. Power Energy Syst. 44(1), 383–387 (2013)
14. Orille-Fernández, Á.L., Khalil, N., Rodríguez, S.B.: Failure risk prediction using artificial neural networks for lightning surge protection of underground MV cables. IEEE Trans. Power Delivery 21(3), 1278–1282 (2006)
15. Akbal, B.: Applications of artificial intelligence and hybrid neural network methods with new bonding method to prevent electroshock risk and insulation faults in high-voltage underground cable lines. Neural Comput. Appl. 29(8), 97–105 (2017). https://doi.org/10.1007/s00521-017-2860-8
16. Zhang, T., Wang, C.J., Liu, S.Y., Zhang, N., Zhang, T.W.: Assessment of soil thermal conduction using artificial neural network models. Cold Regions Sci. Technol. 169, 102907 (2020)

17. Zhang, N., Zou, H., Zhang, L., Puppala, A.J., Liu, S., Cai, G.: A unified soil thermal conductivity model based on artificial neural network. Int. J. Thermal Sci. **155**, 106414 (2020)
18. Ocłoń, P.: The effect of soil thermal conductivity and cable ampacity on the thermal performance and material costs of underground transmission line. Energy **231**, 120803 (2021)
19. Fu, C.Z., Si, W.R., Quan, L., Yang, J.: Numerical study of heat transfer in trefoil buried cable with fluidized thermal backfill and laying parameter optimization. Mathematical Problems in Engineering (2019)
20. Pilgrim, J., Lewin, P., Gorwadia, A., Waite, F., Payne, D.: Quantifying possible transmission network benefits from higher cable conductor temperatures. IET Gener. Transm. Distrib. **7**(6), 636–644 (2013)
21. Kelly, D.K., Jancauskas, J.R.: Cable sizing-avoid shortcuts and do it right. In: IECEC 96. Proceedings of the 31st Intersociety Energy Conversion Engineering Conference, vol. 4. IEEE (1996)
22. Hanna, M.A., Chikhani, A.Y., Baxter, M., Salama, M.M.A.: Thermal Modelling of cables in conduits:(Air gap consideration). In: Proceedings 1995 Canadian Conference on Electrical and Computer Engineering, vol. 1. IEEE (1995)
23. Al-dulaimi, A.A., Güneser, M.T., Hameed, A.A.: Investigation of thermal modeling for underground cable ampacity under different conditions of distances and depths. In: International Symposium on Multidisciplinary Studies and Innovative Technologies, pp. 1–5 (2021)
24. Kroener, E., Vallati, A., Bittelli, M.: Numerical simulation of coupled heat, liquid water and water vapor in soils for heat dissipation of underground electrical power cables. Appl. Thermal Eng. **70**(1), 510–523 (2014)
25. de Lieto Vollaro, R., Fontana, L., Vallati, A.: Experimental study of thermal field deriving from an underground electrical power cable buried in non-homogeneous soils. Appl. Thermal Eng. **62**(2), 390–397 (2014)
26. Al-Saud, M.S., El-Kady, M.A., Findlay, R.D.: A novel finite-element optimization algorithm with applications to power cable thermal circuit design. In: 2007 IEEE Power Engineering Society General Meeting. IEEE (2007)

Layer-Wise Relevance Propagation for Smart-Grid Stability Prediction

Türkücan Erdem and Süleyman Eken[(✉)]

Information Systems Engineering Department, Kocaeli University, 41001 Izmit, Turkey
suleyman.eken@kocaeli.edu.tr

Abstract. Smart grids find energy prices by comparing consumer demand with supply data. Since this is a time-sensitive process they need to predict smart grid stability dynamically. Power grid frequency rises in times of overproduction and decreases in times of underproduction. Using this feature of the grid, Decentral Smart Grid Control (DSGC) ties the grid frequency to energy price and gives us a mathematical model stability prediction. However, this solution comes with "fixed input" and "stability" issues. For solving this in a previous work we suggested using deep learning (DL) models. We compared multiple DL models, found one with 99.62% and showed DL models can give new insights to simulated grid stability prediction. However, since DL models are black boxes, the model lacked any information about why and how the system works. In general, this opaqueness of DL models stands in between them and wide-spread use in engineering. In this paper we used Layer-Wise Relevance Propagation (LRP) to find relevance scores of each input and to make our system human understandable. We show that the most important input in the DSGC system is reaction times of participants, followed by price elasticity coefficient and power consumption or generation have little to none effect on stability.

Keywords: Smart grids · Decentral Smart Grid Control · Layer-Wise Relevance Propagation · Deep learning · Smart grid stability prediction

1 Introduction

The European Union Commission Task Force for Smart Grid defines smart grid as "A Smart Grid is an electricity network that can cost efficiently integrate the behavior and actions of all users connected to it – generators, consumers and those that do both – in order to ensure economically efficient, sustainable power system with low losses and important levels of quality and security of supply and safety…" [1]. It allows two-way connections between its users. It works by collecting consumer demand data, comparing supply information, and producing a price value for electricity. This price information is sent to consumers so they can decide their energy usage. Since this is time sensitive, predicting grid stability dynamically is necessary for success.

Since frequency of the grid increases in the time of excessive production and decreases in time of underproduction, all information needed for finding energy prices

C. Djeddi et al. (Eds.): MedPRAI 2021, CCIS 1543, pp. 315–328, 2022.
https://doi.org/10.1007/978-3-031-04112-9_24

can be gotten from measuring frequency [2]. DSGC described in [2] and assessed in [3] gives us a mathematical model for grid stability prediction; however, execution of these models relies on significant simplifications. One way of manipulating this model is running simulations with fixed values for one subset of variables and fixed value distributions for the rest of data. As described in [4] this leads to two issues referred to as "fixed inputs" and "equality" issues. For overcoming this in a previous work [5] we suggested using DL models for predicting smart grid stability. We found a model with 99.62% accuracy and showed that deep learning models gave new insights into the system.

However, DL models also come with their issues. Although deep learning methods have become popular in the literature with their high success rates in the last few decades, they have disadvantages compared to the methods they replace, such as decision trees. Deep learning methods are referred to as 'black-box'es in the literature [6]. Unlike models whose decisions can be explained and interpreted by humans, such as decision trees, the decision mechanisms of black box models are hidden behind the curtain. This prevents widespread use in places where it is important to know the inner working mechanisms. For this, the subject of explainable artificial intelligence (XAI) has been given importance in the literature for a while.

XAI aims to produce more explainable models while at the same time keeping the high-performance rate that makes AI popular in the first place; thus, avoiding shortcomings of methods such as Gradient Boosted Machines (GBM) that turn weak learners into strong learners but lose some of the intelligibility at this stage. By making the deep learning model explainable:

- Causal relationships between variables can be found.
- Predictions about the operation of the system can be given.
- Reliable descriptions of models can provide confidence to users of the model.
- Impartiality can be achieved by identifying prejudices.
- It allows the developer and people from other disciplines to be more involved during model creation.
- It provides security [7].

For all these reasons, in this paper we propose using Layer-Wise Relevance Propagation (LRP) to find the relevance of each input so we can explain and interpret the model. By achieving this we hope we can increase the adaptation of DL models for smart grid stability prediction.

2 Related Works

2.1 Big Data Analytics in Smart Grids and Smart Grid Stability

For smart grids big data is generated from diverse sources such as users, PMU's, smart energy meters, smart readers and more. For communication purposes they use WiFi, Zigbee, Z-wave and alike. Hashem et al. [8] show the hardships of managing and processing the big data from smart grids and other applications of smart cities. They propose a business model with the purpose of managing big data. They also show that despite hardships big data and big data analytics can play a big part in smart cities. This big data produced by smart grid can be divided into two categories: utility and supplementary data sources. Utility category can include data taken from the likes of PMU, SCADA and IED. Supplementary data includes data taken from additional sources, like GPS and GIS data. Shady S. Refaat et al. [9] show how all this big data continuously produced by the smart grid can impact stability and reliability.

Seref Sagiroğlu et al. [10] in their paper reviews literature for big data in smart grid. They find that renewable energy systems require big data analytics. However technological developments in big data and smart grids are pushing the limits of our IT infrastructure. On top of that they argue that in literature there are not enough articles to apply smart grid analytics. Ghorbanian et al. [11] survey issues in smart grids related to big data. They show that since big data comes from multiple and distributed sources, and storing bulky and big data is difficult, it is difficult to plan analytics for big data. However even if we can store this data since this data consists of private and sensitive information there needs to be systems for security and privacy. Most importantly they argue that AI analysis of systems lacks representation, and it is essential to provide proper representation for interpretation of systems.

To overcome the simplifications inherent to the DSGC model Venayagamoorthy introduce situational awareness (SA). SA means the perception of elements in each space and time. One part of the desired intelligent systems is sense-making agents and intelligent sense making agents are needed. Article finds NN, Fuzzy Logic Swarm Intelligence and adaptive critic designs are promising for this purpose. Also, Wide Area Monitoring (WAM) is necessary [12]. Arzamasov et al. [4] propose a way to overcome simplifications of NSCG. They investigated the system for unique design points and applied DT to results. Delays over 8s found to destabilize the system. However, for a consumer reacting in over 8 s the system may be stable if another consumer is reacting fast enough, and the average reaction time is moderate. Power consumed and generated found to have no effect on stability.

2.2 XAI and Interpretability

For their superior ability to represent non-linear relationships, ease of use and robustness to noise ANN models are long popular in literature. However, they suffer from being 'black-box' models. Their opaqueness stands in between them and widespread use in fields like engineering, medicine, and law [13]. Attempts at extracting rules from ANN come with issues like limiting their capabilities or requiring specific learning models. However, Gregor et al. in 1999 proposed a pedagogical method for extracting rules from ANN's without these issues called ANN-DT. Proposed algorithm creates a univariate decision tree from the trained network. For each node, the algorithm decides which variable to split the data set with. For attribute and parity selection in nodes, two variations were created, ANN-DT(e) using weighted variance minimization and ANN-DT(s) using attribute importance analysis. Both algorithms use greedy pruning. Proposed algorithm is compared to CART on three fronts, namely: cosine and sine curves, abalone, and sap flow data sets. Positive results are achieved, and one advantage of the presented algorithm is that its cost only grows linearly with neural network size [14].

Zilke et al. [15] mention that studies like the one above conducted in the 1990s only work on single-layer NNs. The DeepRED algorithm is presented for extracting rules from DNNs. This algorithm, which is decompositional, extracts rules for each class, processes the layer for each class in descending order, and finds the behavior of each layer in terms of the previous layer. Finally, it combines the rules it has found in each layer. Because of this it can reveal hidden features. The basis of DeepRED is the CRED algorithm, which cannot be applied to DNNs. For the pre-processing, the pruning technique is borrowed from RxREN. Algorithm is controlled by the class dominance and minimum class database parameters. In result, DeepRED finds rules successfully, the rules found for complex problems are understandable to humans, RxREN pruning helps to create more understandable rules, and it can create quality rules independent of training dataset size.

Kovalerchuk and Neunhaus [16] argue that explainability is not just another dimension of machine learning but a main dimension on which all other dimensions depend. They propose an algorithm called Dominance Classifier and Predictor (DCP) that opens new avenues for visual information discovery and analytical computation. The proposed algorithm serves to provide visual explanation as well as mathematical or written explanations. The Wisconsin Breast Cancer dataset (WBCD) is used as the dataset. The proposed algorithm consists of 5 stages: creating class dominance intervals, combining voting methods and intervals, learning the parameters, visualizing the dominance structure, and explaining the prediction. In the chosen voting method, the number of votes is determined by the ratio of those who are in the class to those who are not, the number of votes is limited, and the minimum range is limited. In the visualization part, each dimension is shown as a separate column. In each column the majority positive and negative ranges are shown along with missing ranges in the training set. Although the algorithm does not achieve as high a performance as SVM and ANN, it offers a higher performance rate than other explainable models.

Bach et al. [17] present Layer-Wise Relevance Propagation (LRP), which shows the contribution of each pixel to the classification. The model assumes that classifiers can be decomposed into multiple layers. These layers can be feature extraction or algorithm parts that work on computed features. This assumption is shown to be correct on BoW, non-linear SVM and NN. LRP assumes a relevance score R for each dimension and in FNN finds the R score in the next layer which is closer to the input layer. LRP is not a certain method but a set of rules. These are: R is kept the same for each layer and the sum of R coming into a node equals the sum of R coming out from the same node. Because of this, for NNs different propagation rules can be used for calculating relevance. As a result, a heatmap is created. This heatmap shows that class relevant properties can be many things such as edges, structural parts such as corners, areas with a certain color, and local features.

Amarasinghe et al. [18] show that model-based methods for anomaly detection require a priori knowledge and mathematical knowledge. That is why data-based systems stand out in this field, and DNNs come to the fore among these systems. However, it is vital to know whether the high-performance rates of DNNs are due to the right reasons or due to some artifacts in the dataset. The article provides an interface for DNNs to achieve this. In addition to anomaly detection this interface gives a confidence rate for detection, presents a written explanation, and shows the important variables behind this decision. By using this interface offline, the authorized person is expected to check the system before the system is installed. To achieve this, the proposed algorithm separates the combined function of DNN using LRP and shows the average relationship of each input.

Intrusion Detection (IDs) is key for malicious attack detection on physical systems. However, due to the mentioned black box restriction, it is necessary to know the reason for misclassifications to prevent future attacks. Marino et al. [19] provide an AI interface for this. It uses adverse machine learning to annotate detections. It finds out which entries cause the most misclassification from the difference between the modified and original sample. By visualizing these differences, inferences can be made as 'Normal samples are classified as DOS because'. While the same decomposition rule was applied to all layers in early implementations of LRP, it has become more popular lately to assign different decomposition rules based on positions and layers in NN. It is claimed that the rules established with this composite strategy protect against gradient destruction and provide object discrimination. Kohlbrenner et al. [20] set out to quantify these claims on ImageNet and PascalVOC datasets. They create computational maps for both the composite and orthodox models. The article shows that the LRP model with composite implementation not only provides better representative feature maps, but also solves the gradient destruction problem of the old solutions and improves object localization and gradient destruction. Also, the composite method can assign a negative relevance score to class-contradictory features with just only a single modified backpropagation.

Lauritsen and et al. uses LRP and Temporal Convolutional Network (TCN) for their explainable AI warning score system (xAI-EWS). The system predicts acute critical illness from patients' electronic health records and enables the possibility for explaining the predictions [21]. Song and et al. uses gradient boosting with decision trees implemented in a discrete-time survival network (DS-GBT) for acute kidney injury (AKI) prediction. Using Shapely Additive exPlanations (SHAP), they explain the prediction system and validate the model externally [22]. El-Sappagh et al. proposes a model for explainable Alzheimer's Disease (AD) prediction. They use datasets taken from Alzheimer's Disease Neuroimaging Initiative (ADNI) for employing a comprehensive list of modalities. Using Random Forest (RF), they create a two-layer model and with SHAP they calculate feature contributions and rank them by influence [23]. Maloca et al. utilizes Traceable Relevance Explainablity (T-REX) with Convolutional Neural Network for correctly predicting and explaining the automatic optical coherence tomography (OCT) image segmentation [24]. Jiménez-Luna et al. investigates multiple algorithmic concepts of XAI in the context of drug discovery. They argue that for ensuring XAI methods serve their purpose, at least for now, solutions require cooperation between experts from multiple disciplines. They also argue that due to the lack of a method that caters all the needs of XAI, a jury approach for combining multiple XAI methods will play a key role in the short and middle term [25]. Yang et al. uses Bayesian teaching to propose modelling the human explaniee and formalizing the role of it. This method improves the predictive capacity for how well the user can predict the model's judgement, which is also called fidelity [26].

3   XAI for Smart-Grid Stability Prediction

3.1   Optimized Deep Models

In a previous work [5] we used an optimized deep learning model for smart grid stability prediction to overcome fixed inputs and equality issues of the DSGC system. We've used the same dataset used in this article. For preparation scaling was performed on the dataset. We compared multiple deep learning models for both original and augmented dataset. We used 'ReLU' activation function in hidden layers and 'sigmoid' activation in the output layer for all models. We also wanted to test the effect of different optimizers. For this purpose, we used Adam [27], SGD [28] and Nadam [29] optimizers. On top of this we also tested for different epoch and K values of the KFold cross-validation engine.

Tables for all tests are given in the article. What we found can be summed up as:

- For both data sets the model with the best performance was "288–288-24–12-1".
- For "288–288-24–12-1" and other models Nadam optimizer gave the best results. Compared to Adam optimizer its run times were a little slower but such minor differences in run times can be ignored.
- Doubling the fold number to 20 but halving the epoch number to 25 gave comparable results for the original dataset but for the augmented dataset the results were worse.

We compared our best DL model with 99.62% with other state-of the art models and showed that stability prediction has promising results in terms of local stability analysis. However, one of the downsides of the proposed model and all 'black box' systems is that it lacks any explanation about the system. For this reason, in this paper we propose using Layer-Wise Relevance Propagation (LRP) introduced in [15] for finding the relevance score of inputs.

3.2   Layer-Wise Relevance Propagation

LRP helps to identify key features by back propagating the prediction made by the network back on the network. It assumes relevance score R to each input and uses special local propagation rules. As stated LRP is not a fixed model but a set of rules. These rules work while backpropagation is implemented: R is kept the same for each layer and the sum of R coming into a node equals the sum of R coming out from the same node. R score passed to neurons of lower layer is achieved by this general rule:

$$R_J = \sum_k \frac{z_{jk}}{\sum_j z_{jk}} R_k \tag{1}$$

LRP can be used with CNNs, FNNs and LSTMs as long as it uses ReLU activation function. Its inputs can be videos, images, text and other things. Since LRP is a set of rules instead of a fixed method, different propagation rules that adhere to the principles can be used. So, over the years, different LRP rules have emerged as well as different LRP uses as discussed in [20]. Some of these rules are:

- LRP-Z (LRP-0): Distributes the relevance score to neuron activation by the contribution rate of each input according to the following rule [30]:

$$R_J = \sum_k \frac{a_j w_{jk}}{\sum_{0,j} a_j w_{jk}} R_k \qquad (2)$$

- LRP-Epsilon: It is the first development on the LRP-0 rule. It adds a small positive epsilon variable to the denominator. The role of epsilon is to absorb some relevance when the contributions to the activation of the target neuron are weak or conflicting. As epsilon increases, only the most noticeable results surpass this absorption. This ensures that the resulting features are fewer in number and have less noise. Its formula is as follows:

$$R_J = \sum_k \frac{a_j w_{jk}}{e + \sum_{0,j} a_j w_{jk}} R_k \qquad (3)$$

- LRP-Alpha Beta: Its formula is as follows:

$$R_i = \sum_j (\alpha \frac{(x_i w_{ij})^+}{\sum_i (x_i w_{ij})^+} - \beta \frac{(x_i w_{ij})^+}{\sum_i (x_i w_{ij})^+}) R_J \qquad (4)$$

For this rule, α and β values are selected such that $\alpha - \beta = 1$, thus providing the relevance preservation rule. If α and β is selected as $\alpha = 1$ $\beta = 0$, the following rule, also called the Z + rule, is obtained [31]:

$$R_i = \sum_j \frac{(x_i w_{ij})^+}{\sum_i (x_i w_{ij})^+} R_J \qquad (5)$$

- Deep Taylor w^2: If the input space is unconstrained, the nearest root point is searched along the gradient and following rule is obtained [32]:

$$[x_j]_i = \frac{w_{ij}^2}{\sum_{i'} w_{i'j}^2} x_j. \qquad (6)$$

4 Experimental Analysis

4.1 Building Dataset

We use a dataset from stability simulations done on a 4-node star topology network as described in [33]. It is synthetic in nature. It consists of 10.000 samples but since the grid is symmetric, we augment the original data set 3! times so augmented dataset consists of 60.000 samples. It has 3 measurements for 4 nodes, so it has 12 inputs, and it has 2 dependent variables. Input name followed by 1 means supplier node, otherwise means consumer node.

Inputs are:

- 'tau1' to 'tau4': The reaction time of each participant. Takes a real value between 0.5 and 1.0
- 'p1' to 'p4': Nominal power consumed(negative) or produced(positive) by each participant. Takes a real value between -2.0 and -0.5 for consumer nodes. Since total power consumed equals, power generated $p1 = -(p2 + p3 + p4)$
- 'g1' to 'g4': price elasticity coefficient. Take a real value between 0.05 and 1.00

Dependent variables are:

- 'stab': the maximum real part of the characteristic differential equation root (if positive, the system is linearly unstable; if negative, linearly stable).
- 'stabf': a categorical (binary) label ('stable' or'unstable'). If 'stab' is higher than 0 then 0 else 1.

'stab' and 'stabf' are related so we choose to drop 'stab'. Since the dataset values are from simulation; all features have fixed ranges, do not have any missing values and distributions are mostly uniform across to board with 'p1' being the exception, which follows a normal distribution with the skew value of -0.013.

4.2 Experimental Setup and Experiment

For LRP purposes, we have a few libraries that work on Python or other programming languages. Among these choices, we prefer to use the "iNNvestigate" proposed by M.Alber et al. from TU-Berlin in [34]. The reason for this is that it allows tensorflow-based models directly, unlike libraries that only work on the Caffe-like libraries introduced in [35]. Since iNNvestigate runs on Python 3.6, TensorfFlow 1.12 and Cuda 9.x, we create a virtualenv with these libraries. In addition to the specified libraries, we load the libraries required for visual mathematical operations such as numpy, matplotlib, seaborn, pandas.

In the previous sub-section, we discuss different LRP rules. "iNNvestigate" offers us these rules and 'Ignore Bias' versions for LRP-Z and LRP-Epsilon, where biases are ignored. These are compared in Fig. 1.

If we examine Fig. 1, we see that all relevance values for LRP Alpha-Beta are extremely high compared to relevance values of rules like LRP-Epsilon, LRP-Z. Also, when biases are ignored for LRP-Z and LRP-Epsilon, we see that slight differences become large. The reason there are so many differences between all the rules is that, as mentioned in [20], these rules were meant to be used with each other and in certain parts of the network. This composite method, which is shown in Fig. 2, is one of the preferred ways to use LRP, but since these studies are done with inputs such as pictures and videos and have much more hidden layers than our network, we prefer to use a single LRP rule for all layers. We think that the use of a single rule will not make a significant difference in the result, but it will cost less in terms of time and computation. The most accepted rules in the literature for stand-alone use in the network are LRP-Z and LRP-Epsilon. We preferred to use LRP-Epsilon since it is an improvement on top LRP-Z.

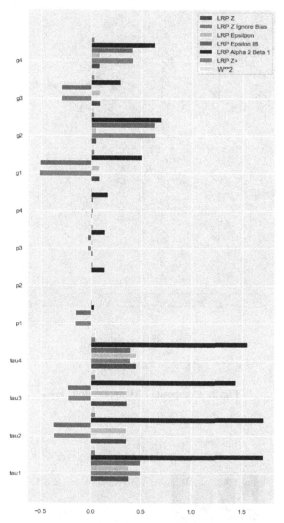

Fig. 1. Comparison of different LRP rules

In Fig. 3, the relevance scores found with the use of LRP-Epsilon in all layers are given.

When we examine Fig. 3, we see that 'tau', that is, the reaction time of the participants in the network has the highest relevance scores ('tau1' = 0.3809; 'tau2' = 0.3731; 'tau3' = 0.3614; 'tau4' = 0.3857). We observe that the next highest score, the variable 'g', that is, the price elasticity coefficient, is around 5.5 times less ('g1' = 0.0705; 'g2' = 0.0845; 'g3' = 0.0858; 'g4' = 0.0621) When we examine 'p', that is, e energy use/consumption, we see that the relevance score is around 0 which is negligible.('p1' = -0.0044; 'p2' = -0.00156; 'p3' = −0.0035; 'p4' = 0.0025) When examining the researches on smart grids in the literature, we could see the importance of the reaction times of the network participants for the smart grid; The fact that relevance scores affect more than all other

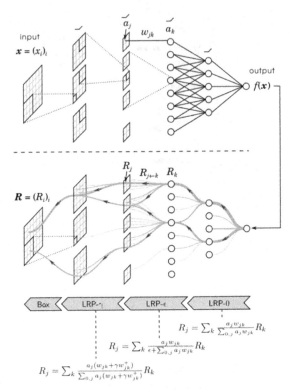

Fig. 2. Composite LRP application [36]

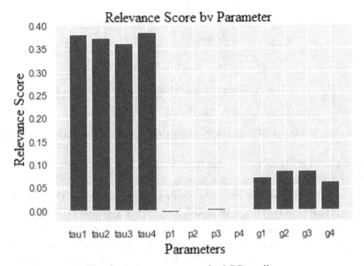

Fig. 3. Relevance scores for LRP-epsilon

inputs in our dataset supports this finding. Gorzałczany et al. [37] make rule inference on the same data set as ours, is examined, it turns out that it found comparable results with ours. When listing which inputs are most important for the rules, reaction time comes first, after that comes price elasticity. For energy consumption/generation they find significance values below 0.001 for p1, p2, p3 and p4. Since consumption in the system will always be equal to production, consumption and production values do not affect the stability of the system in our case.

5 Conclusion and Future Works

Smart grids allow two-way communication between its users. It works by comparing supply and demand data and offering an energy price for consumers. Since this process is time sensitive it is necessary to find a way to dynamically find smart grid stability. For this purpose, DSGC uses the fact that frequency rises and decreases in times of overproduction and underproduction and gives us a mathematical model for smart grid stability prediction. However, to implement this model some simplifications are made and because of this it has some problems.

To overcome these problems in a previous work, we compared different DL models and parameters and found models with accuracy up to 99.62% However the suggested DL model, along with all other DL models, comes with its problems. The deep learning model, which is a black box, does not give us any information about the prediction mechanism of the system. XAI, which has been popular in the literature for a while, aims to make these models explainable and interpretable and thus, it aims to predict the functioning of the system, to give confidence to users and to provide security [7]. For this purpose, we use LRP technology to interpret and understand the model we proposed.

LRP works by backpropagating the prediction made by the network over the network and determining a relevance score for each input. Instead of being an LRP specific model, A definition consisting of the constraints that layer-by-layer relevance scores are preserved and that the relevance score arriving at each neuron is equal to the outgoing relevance score. Therefore, there is more than one rule in literature and more than one use of these rules. We compare multiple rules on a single rule network, and we choose the LRP-Epsilon rule because it is the most accepted method for use in single rule networks with a literature search.

With the LRP-Epsilon rule, we use LRP on our deep learning model and obtain relevance scores for our inputs. We discover that the most important variable for grid stability is the response time of users on the network to changes in the network. We see that the price elasticity coefficient's relevance score is around 15–20% of response time' relevance score. At the same time, we see that the nominal power consumed or produced by the nodes has no appreciable effect on the stability of the network. We decide that this is because the amount of energy consumed and produced in the network is always equal.

We offer a solution with XAI to the black box problem, which is one of the biggest problems of deep learning, and we aim to increase the usability of the model we previously proposed.

References

1. i-SCOOP. https://www.i-scoop.eu/industry-4-0/smart-grids-electrical-grid
2. Schäfer, B., Grabow, C., Auer, S., Kurths, J., Witthaut, D., Timme, M.: Taming instabilities in power grid networks by decentralized control. Eur. Phys. J. Spl. Topics **225**(3), 569–582 (2016). https://doi.org/10.1140/epjst/e2015-50136-y
3. Sinopoli, B., Schenato, L., Franceschetti, M., Poolla, K., Sastry, S.: Optimal linear LQG control over lossy networks without packet acknowledgment. In: 45th IEEE Conference on Decision and Control, San Diego. IEEE (2006). https://doi.org/10.1109/CDC.2006.377017
4. Arzamasov, V., Böhm, K., Jochem, P.: Towards concise models of grid stability. In: 2018 IEEE International Conference on Communications, Control, and Computing Technologies for Smart Grids (SmartGridComm), Aalborg. IEEE (2008). https://doi.org/10.1109/SmartG ridComm.2018.8587498
5. Breviglieri, P., Erdem, T., Eken, S.: Predicting smart grid stability with optimized deep models. SN Comput. Sci. **2**(2), 1–12 (2021). https://doi.org/10.1007/s42979-021-00463-5
6. Stepin, I., Alonso, J.M., Catala, A., Pereira-Fariña, M.: A survey of contrastive and counter-factual explanation generation methods for explainable artificial intelligence **9**, 11974–12001 (2021). https://doi.org/10.1109/ACCESS.2021.3051315
7. Arrieta, A.B., et al.: Explainable artificial intelligence (XAI): concepts, taxonomies, opportunities and challenges toward responsible AI **58**, 82–115 (2020). https://doi.org/10.1016/j. inffus.2019.12.012
8. Hashem, I.A.T., et al.: The role of big data in smart city. **36**(5), 748–758 (2017). https://doi. org/10.1016/j.ijinfomgt.2016.05.002
9. Refaat, S.S., Mohamed, A., Abu-Rub, H.: Big data impact on stability and reliability improvement of smart grid. In: 2017 IEEE International Conference on Big Data (Big Data), Boston, pp. 1975–1982. IEEE (2017). https://doi.org/10.1109/BigData.2017.8258143
10. Sagiroglu, S., Terzi, R., Canbay, Y., Colak, I.: Big data issues in smart grid systems. In: 2016 IEEE International Conference on Renewable Energy Research and Applications (ICRERA), Birmingham, pp. 1007–1012. IEEE (2016). https://doi.org/10.1109/ICRERA.2016.7884486
11. Ghorbanian, M., Dolatabadi, S.H., Siano, P.: Big data issues in smart grids: a survey **13**(4), 4158–4168 (2019). https://doi.org/10.1109/JSYST.2019.2931879
12. Venayagamoorthy, G.K.: Intelligent sense-making for smart grid stability. In: 2011 IEEE Power and Energy Society General Meeting, Detroit, pp. 1–3, IEEE (2011). https://doi.org/ 10.1109/PES.2011.6039876
13. Zednik, C.: Solving the black box problem: a normative framework for explainable artificial intelligence. Philosophy Technol. **34**(2), 265–288 (2019). https://doi.org/10.1007/s13347-019-00382-7
14. Schmitz, G.P.J., Aldrich, C., Gouws, F.S.: ANN-DT: an algorithm for extraction of decision trees from artificial neural networks **10**(6), 1392–1401 (1999). https://doi.org/10.1109/72. 809084
15. Zilke, J.R., LozaMencía, E., Janssen, F.: DeepRED – rule extraction from deep neural Networks. In: Calders, T., Ceci, M., Malerba, D. (eds.) DS 2016. LNCS (LNAI), vol. 9956, pp. 457–473. Springer, Cham (2016). https://doi.org/10.1007/978-3-319-46307-0_29
16. Kovalerchuk, B., Neuhaus, N.: Toward efficient automation of interpretable machine learning. In: 2018 IEEE International Conference on Big Data (Big Data), Seattle, pp. 4940–4947. IEEE (2018). https://doi.org/10.1109/BigData.2018.8622433
17. Bach, S., Binder, A., Montavon, G., Klauschen, F., Müller, K.R., Samek, W.: On pixel-wise explanations for non-linear classifier decisions by layer-wise relevance propagation **10**(7) (2015). https://doi.org/10.1371/journal.pone.0130140

18. Amarasinghe, K., Kenney, K., Manic, M.: Toward explainable deep neural network based anomaly detection. In: 11th IEEE International Conference Human System Interaction, Gdansk. IEEE (2018). https://doi.org/10.1109/HSI.2018.8430788
19. Marino, D.L., Wickramasinghe, C.S., Milos, M.: An adversarial approach for explainable AI in intrusion detection systems. In: IECON 2018 - 44th Annual Conference of the IEEE Industrial Electronics Society. IEEE, Washington (2018). https://doi.org/10.1109/IECON.2018.8591457
20. Kohlbrenner, M., Bauer, A., Nakajima, S., Binder, A., Samek, W., Lapuschkin, S.: Towards best practice in explaining neural network decisions with LRP. In: 2020 International Joint Conference on Neural Networks (IJCNN), pp. 1–7, Glasgow. IEEE (2020). https://doi.org/10.1109/IJCNN48605.2020.9206975
21. Lauritsen, S.M., et al.: A explainable artificial intelligence model to predict acute critical illness from electronic health records 11(3852) (2020). https://doi.org/10.1038/s41467-020-17431-x
22. Song, X., et al.: Cross-site transportability of an explainable artificial intelligence model for acute kidney injury prediction 11(5668) (2020). https://doi.org/10.1038/s41467-020-195 51-w
23. El-Sappagh, S., Alonso, J.M., Islam, S.M.I., Sultan, A.M., Kwak, K.S.: A multilayer multimodal detection and prediction model based on explainable artificial intelligence for Alzheimer's disease 11(2660) (2021). https://doi.org/10.1038/s41598-021-82098-3
24. Maloca, P.M., et al.: Unraveling the deep learning gearbox in optical coherence tomography image segmentation towards explainable artificial intelligence 4(170) (2021). https://doi.org/10.1038/s42003-021-01697-y
25. Jiménez-Luna, J., Grisoni, F., Schneider, G.: Drug discovery with explainable artificial intelligence 2, 573–584 (2020). https://doi.org/10.1038/s42256-020-00236-4
26. Yang, S.C.H., Vong, W.K., Sojitra, R.B., Folke, T., Shafto, P.: Mitigating belief projection in explainable artificial intelligence via Bayesian teaching 11(9863) (2021). https://doi.org/10.1038/s41598-021-89267-4
27. Zhang, Z.: Improved Adam optimizer for deep neural networks. In: 2018 IEEE/ACM 26th International Symposium on Quality of Service (IWQoS)., pp. 1–2 IEEE, Banff (2018). https://doi.org/10.1109/IWQoS.2018.8624183
28. Cutkosky. A., Orabona F.: ImMomentum-based variance reduction in non-convex SGD. In: Advances in Neural Information Processing Systems, vol. 32 (2020)
29. Jakovetić, D., Xavier, J., Moura, J.M.F.: Fast distributed gradient methods 59(5), 1131–1146 (2014). https://doi.org/10.1109/TAC.2014.2298712
30. Montavon, G., Binder, A., Lapuschkin, S., Samek, W., Müller, K.-R.: Layer-wise relevance propagation: an overview. In: Samek, W., Montavon, G., Vedaldi, A., Hansen, L.K., Müller, K.-R. (eds.) Explainable AI: Interpreting, Explaining and Visualizing Deep Learning. LNCS (LNAI), vol. 11700, pp. 193–209. Springer, Cham (2019). https://doi.org/10.1007/978-3-030-28954-6_10
31. Samek, W., Montavon, G., Binder, A., Lapuschkin, S., Müller, K.R: Improved Adam optimizer for deep neural networks. In: NIPS 2016 Workshop on Interpretable ML for Complex Systems (2016)
32. Montavon, G., Lapuschkin, S., Binder, A., Samek, W., Müller, K.B.: Explaining nonlinear classification decisions with deep Taylor decomposition 65, 211–222 (2017). https://doi.org/10.1016/j.patcog.2016.11.008
33. Schäfer, B., Matthiae, M., Timme, M., Witthaut D.: Decentral smart grid control 17 (2015). https://doi.org/10.1088/1367-2630/17/1/015002
34. Alber, M., et al.: iNNvestigate Neural Networks! 20(93), 1–8 (2019)

35. Lapuschkin, S., Binder, A., Montavon, G.,Müller, K.R., Samek, W.: The LRP toolbox for artificial neural networks **17**(114), 1–5 (2016)
36. Heatmmaping. http://www.heatmapping.org/
37. Gorzałczany, M.B., Piekoszewski, J, Rudziński, F.: A modern data-mining approach based on genetically optimized fuzzy systems for interpretable and accurate smart-grid stability prediction **13**(10), 1–5 (2019). https://doi.org/10.3390/en13102559

Abalone Age Prediction Using Machine Learning

Seda Guney[1], Irem Kilinc[1], Alaa Ali Hameed[3], and Akhtar Jamil[2(✉)]

[1] Istanbul Sabahattin Zaim University, 34303 Istanbul, Turkey
{seda.guney,irem.kilinc}@std.izu.edu.tr
[2] National University of Computer and Emerging Sciences, Islamabad, Pakistan
akhtar.jamil@nu.edu.pk
[3] Department of Computer Engineering, Istinye University, Istanbul, Turkey
alaa.hameed@istinye.edu.tr

Abstract. Abalone is a marine snail found in the cold coastal regions. Age is a vital characteristic that is used to determine its worth. Currently, the only viable solution to determine the age of abalone is through very detailed steps in a laboratory. This paper exploits various machine learning models for determining its age. A comprehensive analysis of various machine learning algorithms for abalone age prediction is performed which include, backpropagation feed-forward neural network (BPFFNN), K-Nearest Neighbors (KNN), Naive Bayes, Decision Tree, Random Forest, Gauss Naive Bayes, and Support Vector Machine (SVM). In addition, five different optimizers were also tested with BPFFNN to evaluate their effect on its performance. Comprehensive experiments were performed using our data set.

Keywords: Machine learning · Neural networks · Abalone · Back propagation neural networks

1 Introduction

Abalones are types of single-shelled marine snails found in the cold coastal waters worldwide, majorly found along the coastal regions of some countries such as Australia, Western North America, South Africa, New Zealand, and Japan [1]. The age of the abalone is highly correlated to its prices as it is the sole factor used to determine its worth [2]. However, determining the age of abalone is a highly involved process that is usually carried out in a laboratory.

Technically, rings are formed in the inner shell of the abalone as it grows gradually at a rate of one ring per year. To get access to the inner rings of an abalone, the shell's outer rings need to be cut. After polishing and staining, a lab technician examines a shell sample under a microscope and counts the rings. Because some rings are hard to make out using this method, 1.5 is traditionally added to the ring count as a reasonable approximation of the age of the abalone [1]. Knowing the correct price of the abalone is important to both the farmers and consumers. In addition, knowing the correct age is also crucial to environmentalists who seek to protect this endangered species.

© Springer Nature Switzerland AG 2022
C. Djeddi et al. (Eds.): MedPRAI 2021, CCIS 1543, pp. 329–338, 2022.
https://doi.org/10.1007/978-3-031-04112-9_25

Due to the inherent inaccuracy in the manual method of counting the rings and thus calculating the age, researchers have tried to employ physical characteristics of the abalone such as sex, weight, height, and length to determine its age. Thus, by applying machine learning on a dataset containing a large number of training samples of physical measurements of abalone, its age can be predicted quickly and more accurately.

Machine learning algorithms are data-driven approaches that can effectively recognize certain patterns. Over the last decade, machine learning techniques have been successfully applied across various domains such as for Unicode symbols identification [3], classification of large data sets [4], ordinal classification [5], etc. Among machine learning approaches, the most successful and widely used techniques include Artificial neural networks (ANN), KNN, random forest, Gauss Naïve Bayes and SVM. These techniques have been widely used to solve many pattern recognition problems, which include both classification and regression.

The literature review indicates that the artificial intelligence approaches for abalone age prediction are not sufficient. A detailed search for literature for abalone on popular databases such as Google Scholar, Web of Science, and Scopus showed that only a few papers were found. In [6] authors proposed a feed-forward multi-layer perceptron model to predict the age of abalone. The model was trained with the Lavenberg-Marquardt backpropagation algorithm. Experimental demonstrated that the error rate gradually decreased as the number of hidden layers increased. Obtained results showed the robustness and effectiveness of this model as it achieved high classification accuracy.

Similarly, in [7], the authors proposed a regression-based artificial neural network to determine abalone age. They employed a relatively shallower network with three hidden layers for prediction. The physical measurements of the abalone were used as features, and the results were highly accurate.

Similarly, in [8], the authors applied a convolutional neural network (CNN) model. The authors experimented with various network architectures and different types of convolutions. Also, the deep learning-based approach was compared with conventional machine learning methods. The deep learning-based method achieved 79.09% classification accuracy, which was much better than conventional approaches.

In this study, we exploit the power of seven different machine learning algorithms for abalone age prediction. The algorithms included BPFFNN, K-nearest neighbor, Naive Bayes, decision tree, random forest, Gauss naive Bayes, and support vector machine. In addition, five different optimizers were also tested with BPFFNN to evaluate their effect on its performance.

The rest of the paper is organized as follows: Section 2 describes the related works. Section 3 presents the proposed method and the dataset used. In Sect. 4, obtained experimental results are presented. Finally, we complete the paper with concluding remarks in Sect. 5.

2 Materials and Methodology

2.1 Dataset

The abalone dataset was obtained from UCI Machine Learning Repository [3]. The dataset consists of 4176 samples with eight numerical features along with labels. These features represent the physical characteristics of abalone, such as gender, length, height, diameter, whole weight, shucked weight, viscera weight, shell weight, and rings. The distances were measured millimetres, while the weight values were measured in grams. Gender, a categorical feature, has been converted into numerical features, and all values were transformed to numerical.

We categorized the abalone into three age groups: G1: below 7, G2: between 7 and 16, G3: above 16. These ages groups were represented as G1 = 1, G2 = 2 and G3 = 3. For some algorithms, such as ANN the input labels were proceeded to represent them as one hot-vector representation.

2.2 Classification

This section briefly summarizes the classification and optimization algorithms used in this study.

Artificial Neural Networks (ANNs). ANNs consist of neurons arranged in layers. The first layer is called the input, while the last layer is referred to as the output layer. Hidden layers are placed between input and output layers to map the input to the output. The perceptron equation is as follows:

$$y = \varphi \left(\sum_{i=1}^{n} W_i * x_i \right) \tag{1}$$

where φ is the activation function, X is the input, and W is the weight vector.

$$p_c = \frac{e W^{r+b}}{\sum_{i=1}^{L} e W_{i}^{r+b_i}} \tag{2}$$

We exploited both categorical hinge (3) as well as mean squared error (4) as loss functions in our experiments. In order to find an optimal accuracy and evaluate the effectiveness of optimization algorithms, proposed neural network model were trained separately with Stochastic Gradient Descent, Adagrad, RMSprop, Adam, Nadam optimization algorithm respectively.

$$\text{MSE} = \sum_{i=1}^{n} \left(y_i - \hat{y}_i \right)^2 \tag{3}$$

In this study, five layers were used; one input, three hidden, and one output layer. The number of neurons on input and output were selected according to input feature size and output classes. The number of neurons at the hidden layers were empirically calculated and was set to 70. ReLu activation function was used in all layers except the output layer, which used softmax. The learning rate was set to 0.01.

K-Nearest Neighbor. KNN is one of the oldest, simple and efficient supervised machine learning algorithms. It has been applied in various applications, including problems of classification or regression. It is a non-parametric classification method that means it does not require any prior information about the data distribution.

KNN employs distance measures to learn and classify the samples. We applied three distance measurements Euclidian, Minkowski, and Manhattan. We found that Euclidian distance was better for our data set [9]. For KNN algorithm, the selection of K, which is the number of neighbours, plays a crucial role. For any point p, the closest K neighbours are selected, and the decision is based on the majority vote of these k-neighbours.

Naive Bayes. Naïve Bayes is a classical classification algorithm that is based on Baye's Theorem. It assumes that the predictors are independent. The main objective is to maximize the posterior probabilities for each class. Theoretically, it results in a minimum error rate and has resulted in worked well for various real-world applications.

Consider the input data X with hypothesis H, prior P(H|X); the posterior probability can be estimated as follows

$$P(H|X) = P(X|H)P(H)/P(X) \tag{4}$$

Decision Tree. A decision tree is a simple supervised learning algorithm that can be employed for both classification and regression tasks. It continuously split the data into smaller subset based on some criteria. Then a voting mechanism is followed to make the final decision [10, 11]. There are two main types of decision trees: classification trees and regression trees. The classification trees are the ones where the output variable is discrete, while in the case of regression trees, the output variable is continuous.

To construct the decision tree, entropy and information gain are generally employed [12, 13]. The process iteratively continues splitting the data at each node until the leaves are pure. To avoid the overfitting problem, a limit on the depth of the decision tree is also introduced.

The information gain for each attribute is calculated using the following equations:

$$Gini\ index = 1 - \sum_{i=1}^{c} p_i^2 \tag{5}$$

$$Gain\ ratio = \frac{Information\ gain}{Split\ information} \tag{6}$$

Random Forest. Random forests are ensemble techniques that are widely used for both classification and regression. They employed multiple decision trees for training and testing. This makes them more robust compared to a single decision tree. The random forest algorithm generates an independent random vector θ_k from the previous random vectors which is then distributed to all trees. The trees are grown during training stage using the random vector θ_k, that will result in a tree-structured classifiers $\{h(x, \theta_k), k = 1, ...\}$. The generalization error is calculated by [15]:

$$PE* = PX, Y(mg(X, Y) < 0) \tag{7}$$

where X and Y are random vectors and mg is the margin function.

Gauss Naive Bayes. The Gaussian Naïve Bayes classifier is a special case of Naïve Bayes in continuous case.

$$f(x) = \frac{1}{\sigma\sqrt{2\pi}} e^{\frac{-(x-\mu)^2}{2\sigma^2}} \tag{8}$$

In practice, we assume that each of the probability function has a Gaussian distribution, only need to calculate mean μ and variance σ^2 to obtain the density in Eq. (10).

$$(x_i|\omega_i) = f(x_k) \tag{9}$$

This classifier is called Gaussian Naïve Bayes. In which we need to compute the mean μ_i and variance σ^2 of each training samples of classes ω_i.

Support Vector Machines. Support Vector Machine (SVM) is a non-paramatric classifier. Basically, SVM is basically a linear binary classifier that assigns a class label to test data for classification. It tries to maximize the margin between the two classes. However, it can also be adopted to non-linear data by applying kernel techniques. An SVM constructs a hyperplane in an infinite-dimensional space which is used for classification or regression. This hyperplane is obtained by finding the maximum separation between two classes with the nearest training data points. These data points are termed as support vectors. SVM is a highly powerful model that can produce optimal accuracy even in the presence of lower training samples.

3 Experimental Results

A number of experiments were performed to obtain the optimal parameters for each model. All the experiments were performed on the standard Intel (R) Core (TM) İ5-7200U CPU @ 2.50GHz computer in an Anaconda environment with Python as the programming language. The training dataset consists of 4176 samples. These samples were divided into training consisting of 2923 samples (70%) and testing 1253 samples (30%) subsets.

The Training accuracy with different optimizers is shown Fig. 1. BPFFNN model obtained high accuracy for both training and testing. Moreover, Adadelta optimizer scored better compared to other optimizers with BPFFNN (89% training and 88% testing). The figure shows that all optimizers produced similar results except Sgd optimizer.

In Fig. 2 the convergence of five different optimization algorithms is illustrated in terms of training loss over the epochs. BPFFNN model had a lower training loss with Adagrad optimizer. Sgd starts with a rapid descent, but after 150 epoch stops improving. Rmsprop, Adadelta and Adam optimizers seem to perform almost the same (Fig. 3).

Table 1 shows the confusion matrix for a multiclass classification problem with three classes (1, 2 and 3). As seen in the table, TP_1 is the number of true positive samples in the class 1, that is, the number of samples that are correctly classified from class 1. E_{12}

is misclassified samples, i.e., the samples from class 1 that were incorrectly classified as class 2. Accordingly, the false negative in the 1 class (FN_1) is the sum of all class 1 samples that were incorrectly classified as class 2 or 3, i.e., is the sum of E_{12} and E_{13}.

Briefly, FN of any class is equal to the sum of a row except value TP. The false positive (FP) of any class is equal to the sum of a column except the value TP. The true negative (TN) of any class is equal to the sum of values except row of true class and the column of predicted class.

$$FN_1 = E_{21} + E_{31} \qquad (10)$$

$$FP_1 = E_{12} + E_{13} \qquad (11)$$

$$TN_1 = TP_2 + E_{32} + E_{23} + TP_3 \qquad (12)$$

Table 2 summarizes the accuracy of all the classifiers. Generally, all classifiers performed equally well, except the Gauss Naive Bayes, which obtained relatively lesser accuracy (60.88%). Moreover, the Random Forest classifier produced the highest performance on our dataset (87%) followed by SVM, which achieved an accuracy of 86.76%. Furthermore, KNN and Decision tree classifiers reach almost equal accuracy 86.28%, 86.44%, respectively. Compared with the other classifiers, the performance of the proposed model was relatively better. From the obtained results, we can conclude that the BPFFNN reached the best accuracy in the abalone age prediction task.

Table 1. The confusion matrix for a multiclass classification problem with three classes.

True	Pred		
	G1	G2	G3
G1	TP1	E21	E31
G2	E12	TP2	E32
G3	E13	E23	TP3

G1: age < 7, G2: 7 ≤ age ≤, and G3: age > 16.

The confusion matrix of the Random Forest algorithm is presented in Table 3. Obtained results demonstrate that it performs the best results for Group-2 class of the dataset. There only 8 data in Group-2 that are misclassified. One thousand forty-one data in Group 2 are classified correctly. Only 3 data classified correctly in Group-3, which shows it does not perform well.

Confusion matrix of SVM algorithm is presented in Table 4. Obtained results demonstrates that, the SVM algorithm gave the worst results after the Gauss Naïve Bayes algorithm for class 2 (between 7 and 16 age of abalone). 59 data in class 2 are misclassified, that is, FN_2.

Confusion matrix of KNN algorithm is presented in Table 5. Obtained results demonstrates that, 1006 data in class 2 are classified correctly, i.e. TP_2. Only 35 data classified

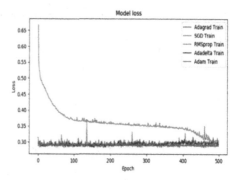

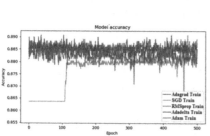

Fig. 1. Training accuracy with different optimizers

Fig. 2. Training loss for each optimizer.

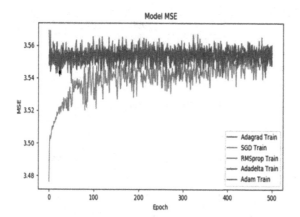

Fig. 3. Mean Square Error for different optimizers

Table 2. Comparison of applied algorithms.

No	Method	Accuracy %
1	KNN	86.28
2	Gaus Naive Bayes	60.84
3	Decision Tree	86.44
4	Random Forest	87.00
5	Support Vector Machine	86.76
6	**Proposed (BPFFNN)**	**88.25**

Table 3. Confusion matrix for random forest.

True	Pred		
	G1	G2	G3
G1	35	31	0
G2	7	1041	1
G3	0	136	3

G1: age < 7, G2: 7 ≤ age ≤, and G3: age > 16.

Table 4. Confusion matrix for SVM.

True	Pred		
	G1	G2	G3
G1	44	22	0
G2	11	990	48
G3	0	85	54

G1: age < 7, G2: 7 ≤ age ≤, and G3: age > 16.

Table 5. Confusion matrix for KNN.

True	Pred		
	G1	G2	G3
G1	41	25	0
G2	11	1006	32
G3	0	104	35

G1: age < 7, G2: 7 ≤ age ≤, and G3: age > 16.

correctly in the 3(above 16 age of abalone) class, that is, TP_3. The KNN and decision tree algorithms gave the worst results for class 1.

Confusion matrix of Gauss Naive Bayes algorithm is presented in Table 6. Obtained results demonstrates that, relevant algorithm preform the best results for 1(below 7 age of abalone) and 3 (above 16 age of abalone) class of the dataset. There only 4 data in class 1 (below 7 age of abalone) that are misclassified, that is, FN_1. The Gauss Naive Bayes algorithm gave the worst results for class 2. Only 629 data classified correctly in the 2((between 7 and 16 age of abalone)) class, i.e. TP_2. 420 data in class 2 are misclassified, that is, FN_2.

The confusion matrix of the decision tree algorithm is presented in Table 7. Obtained results demonstrate that 1018 data in class 2 are classified correctly, i.e. TP_2. Only 31 data in class 2(between 7 and 16 age of abalone) are misclassified, that is, FN_2. The decision tree algorithm gave the best results after the random forest algorithm for class

Table 6. Classification result for Gauss Naive Bayes

True	Pred		
	G1	G2	G3
G1	62	4	0
G2	108	629	312
G3	0	67	72

G1: age < 7, G2: 7 ≤ age ≤, and G3: age > 16.

2. Only 24 data classified correctly in the Group 3. The decision tree algorithm gave the worst results after the random forest algorithm for class 3. While for 3 class, it does not perform well.

Table 7. Classification result for decision tree.

True	Pred		
	G1	G2	G3
G1	41	25	0
G2	10	1018	21
G3	0	115	24

G1: age < 7, G2: 7 ≤ age ≤, and G3: age > 16.

The overall results obtained for abalone classification using the six conventional classifiers were satisfactory except Gauss Naive Bayes classifier. The proposed BPFFNN outperformed all other classifiers in terms of classification accuracy. In addition, we compared our approach with CNN based method proposed by authors in [8], which reported 79.09% accuracy. We believe that for simple datasets such as the one we used in this study, the conventional machine learning approaches are more effective than deep learning-based approaches. Even though deep learning-based approaches have shown high classification accuracy for many problems, yet they are data intensive. We prefer conventional machine learning approaches over deep learning methods for both ease of implementation and classification accuracy in scenarios like this where the dataset is small.

4   Conclusion

This paper focused on abalone age prediction using machine learning techniques. Six state-of-the-art models were employed, which are commonly used for classification tasks. We further quantified the performance of BPFFNN using five different optimizers to select the one that performs best. For our dataset, BPNN yielded the highest accuracy (88%), followed by the random forest classifier (87%). In the future, we would like to extend our method by employing an automatic feature extraction step from images of the abalone for its age prediction.

References

1. Abalone. https://en.wikipedia.org/wiki/Abalone
2. Hossain, M., Chowdhury, N.: Econometric Ways to Estimate the Age and Price of Abalone. Department of Economics, University of Nevada (2019)
3. UCI Machine Learning Repository, Abalone dataset. https://archive.ics.uci.edu/ml/datasets/ Abalone
4. Babu, A.B.: Design and development of artificial neural network based Tamil Unicode symbols identification system. IJCSI Int. J. Comput. Sci. **9**(1), 388 (2012). No 2
5. Alsabti, K., Ranka, S., Singh, V.: CLOUDS: a decision tree classifier for large datasets (1999)
6. Jabeen, K., Ahamed, K.: Abalone age prediction using artificial neural network. IOSR J. Comput. Eng. **18**(05), 34–38 (2016)
7. Misman, M.F., et al.: Prediction of abalone age using regression-based neural network. In: 2019 1st International Conference on Artificial Intelligence and Data Sciences (AiDAS), pp. 23–28. IEEE, September 2019
8. Sahin, E., Saul, C.J., Ozsarfati, E., Yilmaz, A.: Abalone life phase classification with deep learning. In: 2018 5th International Conference on Soft Computing & Machine Intelligence (ISCMI), pp. 163–167 (2018)
9. Bhatia, N.: Survey of nearest neighbor techniques. arXiv preprint arXiv:1007.0085 (2010)
10. ChiMerge, K.R.: discretization of numeric attributes. In: Proceedings of the Tenth National Conference on Artificial Intelligence (1992)
11. Han, J., Kamber, M.: Data Mining: Concepts and Techniques, 550 (2000)
12. Bramer, M.: Principles of Data Mining, vol. 180. Springer, London (2007). https://doi.org/ 10.1007/978-1-84628-766-4
13. Leung, K.S., et al.: Data mining on DNA sequences of hepatitis b virus. IEEE/ACM Transactions on Computational Biology and Bioinformatics, pp. 428–440 (2009)
14. Palaniappan, S., Awang, R.: Intelligent heart disease prediction system using data mining techniques. In: 2008 IEEE/ACS International Conference on Computer Systems and Applications. IEEE (2008)
15. Breiman, L.: Random forests. Mach. Learn. **45**, 45–49 (2001)

A Novel Optimized Method for Feature Selection Using Non-linear Kernel-Free Twin Quadratic Surface Support Vector Machine

Saptashwa Maity[1]([✉]), Arjav Rastogi[2], Chawki Djeddi[3,4], Sobhan Sarkar[5], and J. Maiti[6,7]

[1] Agricultural and Food Engineering, IIT Kharagpur, Kharagpur 721302, India
saptashwa.basilisk10@gmail.com
[2] Chemical Engineering, IIT Kharagpur, Kharagpur 721302, India
[3] Department of Mathematics and Computer Science, Larbi Tebessi University, Tebessa, Algeria
c.djeddi@univ-tebessa.dz
[4] LITIS Lab, University of Rouen, Rouen, France
[5] Information Systems and Business Analytics, IIM Ranchi, Ranchi 834008, Jharkhand, India
sobhan.sarkar@iimranchi.ac.in
[6] Department of Industrial and Systems Engineering, IIT Kharagpur, Kharagpur 721302, India
[7] Centre of Excellence on Safety Engineering and Analytics, IIT Kharagpur, Kharagpur 721302, India

Abstract. Feature Selection (FS) is an important topic in the domain of machine learning. Support Vector Machine (SVM) is one of the most popular ML models for classification tasks. Efficient feature selection may ensure enhanced classification accuracy. Although there are several feature selection algorithms in practice, they are either separately used, combinedly used with linear SVM or, used with kernel-based SVM. Additionally, there exists another problem in classification methods, which is the selection of correct kernel function. There seems to be as such no general rule for selecting a kernel that maximizes the model's performance. To handle the issues together, we propose a model called *non-linear kernel-free twin quadratic surface SVM with optimized feature selection (LTQSSVM-OFS)* which can eventually tackle both feature selection and classification tasks efficiently. We are doing feature selection in a kernel-free way by applying optimization method on a Laplacian Twin Quadratic Surface SVM classifier. We have validated our proposed model using (i) min-max approach-based SVM without FS, (ii) linear SVM, and (iii) radial basis function-based SVM models applied on four datasets, namely 'Star3642balanced', 'Diabetes', 'Health care: Heart attack possibility', and 'Blood Transfusion'. Experimental results reveal that the proposed model outperforms the other models. Additional worth noting benefit of our model is that it yields better results in case of working with fewer features.

© Springer Nature Switzerland AG 2022
C. Djeddi et al. (Eds.): MedPRAI 2021, CCIS 1543, pp. 339–353, 2022.
https://doi.org/10.1007/978-3-031-04112-9_26

Keywords: Kernel-free SVM · Twin quadratic surfaces · Laplacian matrix · Feature selection · Classification · Optimization

1 Introduction

Support Vector Machine (SVM) is a powerful and well-known classification algorithm developed by Vladimir Vapnik with his other colleagues in 1995 [26]. It has been used in diverse application domains, such as accident prediction [23–25,27], disease prediction [3], stock market trend prediction [6], time series prediction [5], so forth. SVM typically works based on a kernel function. The kernel function transforms lower-dimensional inputs into higher dimensional outputs or feature space, which makes data separable. Therefore, the classification of data points by the SVM algorithm becomes easier. Hence, the selection of a proper kernel function is very important, which is, however, a difficult task. A lot of hits and trials are required to get the appropriate SVM kernel function. It eventually consumes a large amount of time. Additionally, during classification, if the dataset is large or the number of features is high, there is a possibility that SVM may not work satisfactorily due to data size. Large size of data often leads to data redundancy, which acts as the main cause for the poor performance of SVM. Under such circumstances, noise and unimportant features can be reduced using a feature selection technique. It must be properly done to ensure that the remaining features are of high importance and necessary for the best performance of SVM. Another solution to remove the redundancy from the dataset is to reduce its dimensionality by forming hybrid features which is a combination of two or more features and then, utilize the resulting dataset for classification. This method is called dimensionality reduction. Many techniques are in existence for dimensional reduction; however, most of them are stand-alone. Instead of doing the stand-alone dimensionality reduction, if the feature selection algorithm is applied on an embedded SVM, both feature selection and classification task can be simultaneously completed; thus, reducing total computational time.

In our study, we have chosen LTQSSVM [28], on which we have applied our optimization technique to select relevant features. Initially, we used SVM-RFE on LTQSSVM for feature selection which we named LTQSSVM-FS (i.e., Laplacian Twin Quadratic Surface SVM for Feature Selection). SVM Recursive Feature Elimination (SVM-RFE) is an algorithm that aims to find a ranking of m features using the reverse sequential selection methodology. ($m \ll n$). SVM-RFE begins including all features and eliminates one at once until just m features are spared. The feature that minimizes the fluctuation of the 'weight vector norm' is the one that has to be deleted [2]. SVM-RFE generates a ranking list for the whole set of features. A subset of all these features is preserved in the lack of a termination criterion, demonstrating the best performance on a validation dataset. Laplacian Twin Quadratic Surface Support Vector Machine (LTQSSVM) is a form of non-linear support vector machine which uses twin quadratic surfaces calculated using the Laplacian matrix to classify the target variable into $\{+1, -1\}$. The LTQSSVM does not use any kernel for classification, so the time spent in choosing the appropriate kernel for classification is non-existent. It's worth noting that, instead of a non-convex problem, this approach relates to two convex quadratic layouts problems. Moreover, the two surface equations are often solved directly in their basic construction, instead of their two problems as shown in [8,16]. Manifold learning techniques [1] have recently gotten a lot of attention because they preserve the underlying geometrical configuration while preventing overfitting to the training instances. [1,7,8] have employed this technique in semi-supervised categorization. The process, however, differs from typical TSVM because quadratic surfaces are used for classification.

In summary, there are major two issues identified by our study. *First*, the selection of the suitable kernel function in SVM during classification is difficult. Since the parameters of the associated kernel have significant impact on classification performance, it is essential to select the proper kernel which eventually demands a large amount of time and effort. The *second* issue is the high dimensionality of datasets. Datasets may contain much information along with irrelevant information inside. There could be a possibility of the existence of a redundant and irrelevant set of features. Therefore, feature selection can be used under such circumstances. However, almost all the feature selection techniques used so far are stand-alone or used with linear SVM. To solve the first issue, we have used kernel-free SVM which avoids the dependencies on the selection of kernels. To address the second issue, a novel feature selection process has been incorporated in the kernel-free SVM model, which can offer an automatic feature sub-set selection and classification/prediction and thereby, consuming less time. Therefore, the objective of the study is to develop a feature selection approach that can be used upon a non-linear kernel-free SVM model. To fulfill the objective, we have developed an optimization technique to select features in a non-linear kernel-free twin quadratic SVM model and named it as non-linear kernel-free twin quadratic surface SVM with optimized feature selection (LTQSSVM-OFS). We have validated our proposed model by comparing with: (i) min-max approach-based SVM without FS, (ii) linear SVM, and (iii) radial basis function-based SVM models applied on four datasets, namely 'Star3642balanced', 'Diabetes', 'Health care: Heart attack possibility', and 'Blood Transfusion'. Finally, the comparative study reveals promising results for the validation of the proposed model.

The rest of the paper proceeds as follows: In Sect. 2, we describe some prerequisites for understanding the proposed model which is explained in Sect. 3. Section 4 reports the details of datasets used, experiments conducted and their results for the validation of our proposed model. Finally, in Sect. 5, we conclude our study by stating its limitations and the scopes for future works.

2   Prerequisites

For a better understanding of our proposed model, we have discussed below two basic algorithms as prerequisites, namely Laplacian Twin Quadratic Surface SVM (LTQSSVM) and Laplacian Twin Quadratic Surface SVM for Feature Selection (LTQSSVM-FS).

2.1   LTQSSVM

In this model, we define a set of l labeled points $\{x^i, y_i\}_{i=1}^l$ and $m-l$ unlabeled points $\{x^i\}_{i=l+1}^m$, where $x^i = \{x_1^i, x_2^i, ...x_n^i\}\epsilon R^n$ for $i = 1,2,3,...m$ and $y = \{+1,-1\}$ for $i = 1,2,3,...l$. $|I^+|$ of the labeled points are in the positive category. The rest $|I^-|$ are identified in the negative category. From (1) and (2), two quadratic surfaces can be found:

$$G_1(x) : \frac{1}{2}x^T W^+ x + (b^+)^T x + c^+ = 0 \tag{1}$$

$$G_2(x) : \frac{1}{2}x^T W^- x + (b^-)^T x + c^- = 0 \tag{2}$$

for the above mentioned two classes, in which $W^+ = (\omega_{ij}^+)\epsilon R^{nXn}$, $W^- = (\omega_{ij}^-)\epsilon R^{nXn}$, $(b^+, b^- \ \epsilon \ R^n)$ and $(c^+, c^- \ \epsilon \ R)$. In [1], a data adjacency network W_{ij}^{sim}, as mentioned in Eq. (3), depicts the familiarity of each pair of input data for manifold regularization [1].

$$W_{ij}^{sim} = \begin{cases} e^{\frac{(-||x^i - x^j||)^2}{2\sigma^2}} & , x^i \text{ and } x^j \text{ are neighbors} \\ 0 & , \text{otherwise.} \end{cases} \tag{3}$$

Here, $(-||x^i - x^j||)^2$ signifies the euclidean norm squared and σ is the parameter with the value 10 (we have considered in our study). $D\epsilon R^{mXm}$ is a diagonal matrix which also satisfies $D_{ii} = \sum_{j=1}^n W_{ij}^{sim}$. Let L be the Laplacian matrix, which can be computed as follows:

$$L = 2(D - W_{ij}^{sim}) \tag{4}$$

$$g_1(x) : \frac{1}{2}(x^i)^T W^+ x^i + (b^+)^T x^i + c^+ \ \epsilon \ R^n \tag{5}$$

$$g_2(x) : \frac{1}{2}(x^i)^T W^- x^i + (b^-)^T x^i + c^- \ \epsilon \ R^n \tag{6}$$

For calculating the classifying surfaces, we use the following two equations along with the constraints mentioned in [28].

$$\min_{W^+,b^+,c^+,\xi^+} \sum_{i\epsilon I^+}(\frac{1}{2}(x^i)^T W^+ x^i + (b^+)^T x^i + c^+)^2 + C_1^+ \sum_{i\epsilon I^-} \xi^+$$

$$+ C_2^+(||W^+||_F^2 + ||b^+||_2^2 + (c^+)^2) + C_3^+ g_1^T L g_1 \tag{7}$$

$$\text{s.t.} : \frac{1}{2}(x^i)^T W^+ x^i + (b^+)^T x^i + c^+ \geq \xi_i^+, i \ \epsilon \ I^-$$

$$\xi^+ = (\xi_1^+, \xi_2^+, ..., \xi_{I^-}^+) \geq 0$$

$$\min_{W^-,b^-,c^-,\xi^-} \sum_{i\in I^-}(\frac{1}{2}(x^i)^T W^- x^i + (b^-)^T x^i + c^-)^2 + C_1^- \sum_{i\in I^+}\xi^-$$
$$+C_2^-(||W^-||_F^2 + ||b^-||_2^2 + (c^-)^2) + C_3^- g_2^T L g_2 \qquad (8)$$
$$\text{s.t.}: \frac{1}{2}(x^i)^T W^- x^i + (b^-)^T x^i + c^- \geq \xi_i^-, i \in I^+$$
$$\xi^- = (\xi_1^-, \xi_2^-, ..., \xi_{I^+}^-) \geq 0$$

In the above Eqs. (7) and (8), L represents the Laplacian Matrix calculated in Eq. (4). g_1 and g_2 are two different arrays, each containing m elements (where m = the number of rows in the dataset) in which elements are calculated from Eqs. (5) and (6), respectively. After solving these two equations, we proceed to test our model. A new data point $x \epsilon R^n$ is allocated to either the positive or negative group, based on which of the two surfaces it is nearest to. Then, we compare our obtained results to the target variable of the test dataset and calculate the performance of the model.

2.2   LTQSSVM-FS

Laplacian Twin Quadratic Surface Support Vector Machine - Feature Selection (LTQSSVM-FS) incorporates the application of SVM-RFE on LTQSSVM. In this algorithm, we continuously eliminate the least important feature until the number of features becomes 1. The steps of the algorithm are as follows:

Step 1: Initially, train the model using all the features using (7) and (8) and select the surface having the best classification accuracy.

Step 2: Calculate the squared Euclidean norm for the surface parameters as $||W^-||_F^2$, $||b^-||_2^2$, $||W^+||_F^2$, $||b^+||_2^2$.

Step 3: Temporarily, remove the features one at a time and calculate $||W^{-(-q)}||_F^2$, $||b^{-(-q)}||_2^2$, $||W^{+(-q)}||_F^2$, $||b^{+(-q)}||_2^2$, where $||A^{(-q)}||_F^2$ denotes the squared Euclidean norm of a parameter A with feature q removed. This is obtained by removing the q th column and q th row from the existing parameter matrix.

Step 4: For each feature q, calculate $\{(||W^-||_F^2 + ||b^-||_2^2 + ||W^+||_F^2 + ||b^+||_2^2) - (||W^{-(-q)}||_F^2 + ||b^{-(-q)}||_2^2 + ||W^{+(-q)}||_F^2 + ||b^{+(-q)}||_2^2)\}$ and remove the feature with the lowest value of K.

Step 5: Repeat the steps from 2 to 5, until N (number of features) is equal to one.

The results of this approach were unsatisfactory for a lower value of N. As the number of features decreased, the classification precision became worse, and finding the value of a trade-off between the number of features and accuracy score became difficult.

3   Proposed LTQSSVM-OFS Model

In this study, we have proposed an algorithm called Laplacian Twin Quadratic Surface Support Vector Machine - Optimized Feature Selection (LTQSSVM-OFS). It is based upon the fact that the hyper-parameters, which define the best surface for classification using N features, may not be the same as the hyper-parameters defining the best surface for classification using $(N-1)$ features. Using this concept, we have defined our algorithm. The steps of the algorithm are as follows:

Step 1: Train the model using Eqs. (7) and (8).

Step 2: Test the model using the 'newSVM' function which utilizes N features. Store the accuracy score and the surface having the best classification accuracy.

Step 3: The function returns a solution array: $array_{sol} = [\ accuracy_{max}, W^+, W^-, b^+, b^-, c^+, c^-, C1^+_{maxacc}, C2^+_{maxacc}, C3^+_{maxacc}, C1^-_{maxacc}, C2^-_{maxacc}, C3^-_{maxacc}, accuracy_{array}, X_{train}, y_{train}, X_{test}, y_{test}\ ]$.
Here, $accuracy_{max}$ refers to the maximum accuracy achieved after testing the model on the test data. $W^+, W^-, b^+, b^-, c^+, c^-$ are the surface parameters, $C1^+_{maxacc}, C2^+_{maxacc}, C3^+_{maxacc}, C1^-_{maxacc}, C2^-_{maxacc}, C3^-_{maxacc}$ are the hyper-parameters used to achieve maximum accuracy, $accuracy_{array}$ is the list of all the accuracy scores achieved while testing the trained model and $X_{train}, y_{train}, X_{test}, y_{test}$ represents the training data and the test data split in that iteration.

Step 4: We start by defining a new function to select the features which take the solution array obtained in the last step as the input and gives output an array of best models for different N. We recursively train the model after removing the feature q and finally select the model with the best performance along with its accuracy score and the number of features used to train that model. After adding that model to the array, the function removes the feature which was not included in the subset of features used to define the model, and the whole process is repeated until $N = 1$. Then, the loop is broken and the function returns an array of the best performing models having the length is equal to the number of features in the dataset. The pseudo-code of the proposed LTQSSVM-OFS model is provided in Algorithm 1.

Algorithm 1: Pseudo-code for feature selection using LTQSSVM-OFS.

Input: $array_{sol}$, N= Total number of features.
Output: $model_{best}$ = Array of the best models.
Initialize $W^+_{rfe} = W^+, W^-_{rfe} = W^-, b^+_{rfe} = b^+, b^-_{rfe} = b^-, length = len(b^+), X^f_{test} = X_{test}, X^f_{train} = X_{train},, l_{col} = list(X_{test}.columns), model_{maxlist} = [], acc_{maxlist} = []$
for f_{num} in range N **do**
   $acc_{list} = [], model_list = []$
   if $len(list(X_{train^f}.columns)) \geq 1$ **then**
      for q in range $(N - f_{num})$ **do**
         $model = newSVM(X^{f-q}_{train}, y_{train}, X^{f-q}_{test}, ytest)$
         insert $accuracy_{max}$ from model into acc_{list}
         add model to $model_{list}$
      end
      Re-define X^f_{train} and X^f_{test}
      $l_{col}.remove(l_{col}[argmax(acc_{list})])$
   end
   add $model_{list}[argmax(acc_{list})]$ to $model_{maxlist}$
   $model_{best} = model_{maxlist}[argmax(acc_{maxlist})]$
end
return $model_{best}$

---

4 Data, Experiments, and Results

After the model building, the proposed model has been tested using four datasets. The performance of the model has been compared with the three state-of-the-art algorithms. In this section, the datasets used, experimental setup, and results from analyses are discussed in detail.

4.1 Datasets

We have worked predominantly on 4 datasets, named, 'Star3642balanced'[1], 'Diabetes'[2], 'Health care:Heart attack possibility'[3] and 'Blood Transfusion'[4]. These datasets are downloaded from Kaggle. They are balanced in nature which means that the number of instances of the negative class is comparable to that of the positive class. The 'Star3642balanced' dataset contains 500 rows and 7 columns, out of which one is the 'target class', one is the column with string type object and the other 5 columns contain the numerical type objects. The 'target class' and the column with string type object are removed to form X and y is formed using the 'target class' column. The 'Diabetes' dataset contains 768 rows and 9

---

[1] https://www.kaggle.com/vinesmsuic/star-categorization-giants-and-dwarfs.
[2] https://www.kaggle.com/ahmettezcantekin/beginner-datasets.
[3] https://www.kaggle.com/nareshbhat/health-care-data-set-on-heart-attack-possibility.
[4] https://www.kaggle.com/shabbir94/blood-transfusion.

columns, out of which one is the 'outcome' and the other eight columns contain numerical values. The eight columns focus on the parameters, such as 'number of pregnancies', 'age', 'blood pressure', 'skin thickness', 'glucose', 'insulin', 'bmi', and 'dpf' which affect that whether a person is diabetic or not. The *Health care: Heart attack possibility'* dataset contains 304 rows and 14 columns, out of which one is the 'target' and the other thirteen contain numerical values. Some columns, including 'sex', 'cp', and 'fbs' are categorical; whereas, others are continuous. The *'Blood Transfusion'* dataset consists of 748 rows and 5 columns, out of which the target column is 'Whether the person has donated blood in March 2007' and the other four contain numerical values.

4.2   Description of Experiments

The experiments are carried out on a PC with RAM of 16 GB. The models are developed in both Python [9,10,15] and R [22], and the convex issues are handled by IBM ILOG CPLEX 12.6.3.. The regularization parameters $C_1^+, C_2^+, C_3^+ C_1^-, C_2^-$ and C_3^- take values from the set: $\{2^{-4}, 2^{-3}, ..., 1, 2^1, ..., 2^4, 32\}$. We have used the accuracy score as the evaluation metrics because of the balanced nature of the datasets. We mainly focused on the LTQSSVM-OFS approach for feature selection and we compared it with other state-of-the-art models, which are discussed below.

(i) 'Min-Max-based SVM without Feature Selection (min-max_SVM_NO-FS or NO-FS)' refers to the approach we achieve after classifying using the [4] Algorithm 1.

(ii) 'SVM-LIN' refers to the scikit-learn version of SVM using linear kernel.

(iii) 'SVM-RBF' refers to the scikit-learn version of SVM using Gaussian kernel.

(iv) 'LTQSSVM-FS' refers to the primary approach that we mentioned for feature selection in the pre-requisite section.

Figure 1a depicts the results as obtained for 'Star3642balanced' dataset. The results are also formulated in Table 1. Here, it can be seen that the maximum accuracy score is reached using LTQSSVM. It's also worth noting that the categorization performance of LTQSSVM when we use only 2 features (selected using LTQSSVM-OFS) is better than all the other competitors compared even when they have more information. Figure 2a depicts the results as obtained for 'Diabetes' dataset. The results are also formulated in Table 2. Here, it can be seen that the maximum accuracy score is reached using SVM-RBF, when it used all 8 features for classification. However, it should also be noted that as the number of features decreased, the drop in performance in our model is way less than that of its competitors. When only 2 features were used for classification, our model performed best with an accuracy score of 0.78 whereas all other competitors got an accuracy score below 0.70. Figure 3a shows the results as obtained for 'Health care: Heart attack possibility' dataset. The results are also formulated in Table 3. In this case, the best results are obtained by SVM-RBF dataset which predicted the correct outcome with 92% accuracy when the number of features involved was nine. LTQSSVM-OFS outperforms every other method when the number of features involved is five. Figure 4a shows the results as obtained for 'Blood Transfusion' dataset. In Fig. 4, it can be seen that the LTQSSVM-OFS performs better than all the approaches. In Table 4, it can be seen that, no matter how many features are considered for classification, LTQSSVM-OFS outperforms all its competitors. The best accuracy, i.e., 77.54% is achieved when 3 features are used for classification. We built correlation heatmaps representing the correlation between different features using Pearson's R for the continuous-continuous type of feature vectors, correlation ratio for categorical-continuous type of feature vectors, and Cramer's V for the categorical-categorical type of feature vectors. Although the feature ranking that we did by using our algorithms was not the same as this correlation matrix, this correlation gave an approximate understanding of the importance of different features used in the classification. In all the tables reported, F_n means that 'n' no. of features are used for classification. For example, F_3 means 3 features are used for classification.

Table 1. Outcomes of our LTQSSVM-OFS method and all competing approaches in terms of accuracy on 'Star3642balanced' dataset

Approach used	F5	F4	F3	F2	F1
LTQSSVM-OFS	88.88%	88.88%	88.80%	88.88%	85.60%
SVM-RBF	78.41%	81.65%	83.27%	84.12%	84.80%
SVM-LIN	87.23%	87.26%	87.29%	82.47%	82.42%
NO-FS	85.00%	–	–	–	–
LTQSSVM-FS	88.88%	54.44%	52.87%	52.87%	52.87%

Table 2. Outcomes of our LTQSSVM-OFS method and all competing approaches in terms of accuracy on 'Diabetes' dataset

Approach used	F8	F7	F6	F5	F4	F3	F2	F1
LTQSSVM-OFS	80.00%	79.68%	79.68%	79.68%	79.68%	79.68%	78.12%	74.48%
SVM-RBF	82.80%	82.80%	81.77%	83.80%	83.30%	73.00%	68.75%	68.50%
SVM-LIN	80.70%	80.70%	81.25%	81.77%	82.80%	73.90%	68.20%	67.70%
NO-FS	74.50%	–	–	–	–	–	–	–
LTQSSVM-FS	80.00%	70.70%	58.80%	58.80%	58.80%	58.80%	58.80%	58.80%

In Table 1, it can be observed that the accuracy of all the approaches decreases when the no. of features decrease except in the case of SVM-RBF. Similarly, in Table 2, the accuracy of SVM-LIN and SVM-RBF increases as the no. of features decreases from six to four. In Table 3, we can observe that initially when all the features are used, SVM-RBF performs the worst but as the number of features decreases, it outperforms all other algorithms, including LTQSSVM-OFS for $n = \{8, 9\}$. LTQSSVM-OFS performs better than other algorithms for $n = \{11, 10, 5, 4\}$. In Table 4, it can be noticed that LTQSSVM-OFS dominates for all the features. Overall, the accuracy achieved after classifying this dataset is comparatively less than other datasets; however, the maximum accuracy is achieved by LTQSSVM.

Table 3. Outcomes of our LTQSSVM-OFS method and all competing approaches in terms of accuracy on 'Health care: Heart attack possibility' dataset

Approach used	F13	F12	F11	F10	F9	F8	F7	F6	F5	F4	F3	F2	F1
LTQSSVM-OFS	89.47%	89.47%	90.78%	90.78%	90.78%	89.47%	88.15%	88.15%	88.15%	85.52%	80.26%	78.94%	75.00%
SVM-RBF	68.42%	73.68%	73.68%	73.68%	92.10%	92.10%	90.78%	88.15%	82.89%	84.21%	76.31%	81.57%	81.57%
SVM-LIN	89.47%	86.84%	86.84%	86.84%	89.47%	90.78%	90.78%	85.52%	81.57%	78.94%	80.26%	81.57%	81.57%
NO-FS	82.89%	–	–	–	–	–	–	–	–	–	–	–	–
LTQSSVM-FS	89.47%	89.47%	89.47%	80.26%	82.89%	82.89%	81.57%	81.57%	80.26%	77.63%	71.05%	46.05%	46.05%

Table 4. Outcomes of our LTQSSVM-OFS method and all competing approaches in terms of accuracy on 'Blood Transfusion' dataset

Approach used	F4	F3	F2	F1
LTQSSVM-OFS	77.00%	77.54%	77.00%	76.47%
SVM-RBF	75.40%	75.40%	74.86%	74.86%
SVM-LIN	76.47%	74.86%	74.86%	74.86%
NO-FS	75.93%	–	–	–
LTQSSVM-FS	70.00%	67.91%	75.93%	75.93%

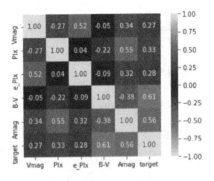

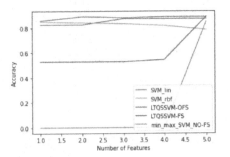

(a) Correlation Heatmap of feature vectors   (b) Plot of Accuracy vs. Number of Features

Fig. 1. Plots and matrices of 'Star3642balanced' dataset.

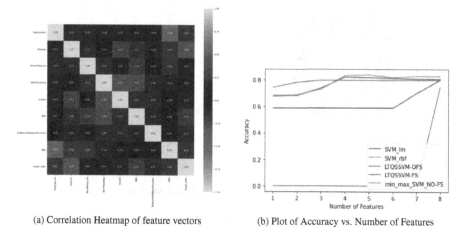

(a) Correlation Heatmap of feature vectors   (b) Plot of Accuracy vs. Number of Features

Fig. 2. Plots and matrices of 'Diabetes' dataset.

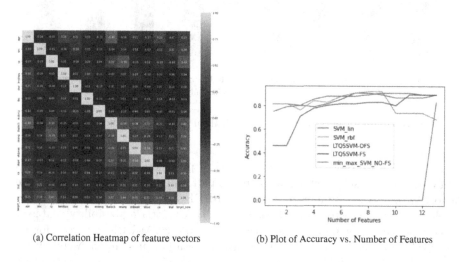

(a) Correlation Heatmap of feature vectors   (b) Plot of Accuracy vs. Number of Features

Fig. 3. Plots and matrices of 'Health care: Heart attack possibility' dataset.

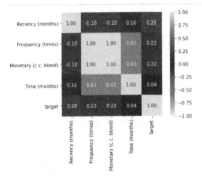
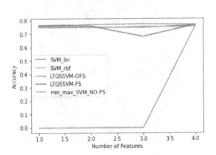

(a) Correlation Heatmap of feature vectors

(b) Plot of Accuracy vs. Number of Features

Fig. 4. Plots and matrices of 'Blood Transfusion' dataset.

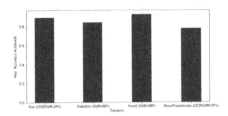
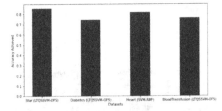

(a) Plot of Maximum Accuracy for different datasets

(b) Plot of Maximum Accuracy for different datasets when only one feature is considered

Fig. 5. Comparison of maximum classification accuracy in different datasets.

In Fig. 5a, we plotted the highest level of precision attainable for different datasets to understand which algorithm is performing the best among all other algorithms. It was found that both SVM-RBF and LTQSSVM-OFS perform well. For the 'Diabetes' and 'Health care: Heart attack possibility' datasets, maximum accuracy was achieved while applying SVM-RBF, whereas for the 'Star3642balanced' and 'Blood Transfusion' datasets, maximum accuracy was achieved by LTQSSVM-OFS. In Fig. 5b, we have plotted the maximum classification accuracy achieved when only one feature is used. LTQSSVM-OFS performs the best in this case achieving maximum accuracy in three out of four datasets. In the 'Health care: Heart attack possibility' dataset, both SVM-RBF and SVM-LIN perform equally and better than LTQSSVM-OFS when only one feature is used.

5   Conclusions

In the present study, we have proposed a new SVM model which is called non-linear kernel-free twin quadratic surface SVM with optimized Feature Selection (LTQSSVM-OFS) for optimal feature selection and classification in the machine learning paradigm. There are two major issues, from which, the concept of the model emerges. First, the unavailability of any standard method for selecting a proper kernel function of SVM, and the second one is the high-dimensionality of data. The proposed model helps in selecting important features optimally for providing the best results. Additionally, it works in a kernel-free way, thus reducing the dependency on any kernel function. Both feature selection and classification have been done using our proposed LTQSSVM-OFS model. The model has been tested using min-max approach-based SVM without FS, linear SVM, and radial basis function-based SVM models applied on four datasets, namely 'Star3642balanced', 'Diabetes', 'Health care: Heart attack possibility', and 'Blood Transfusion'. Results reveal that the proposed model outperforms the other state-of-the-arts.

The present study, however, suffers from few limitations. One of such limitations is the higher time complexity. It is recommended to use parallel computing in such conditions [23]. As future scopes, reducing the training time can be done by utilizing LTQSSVM-FS approach for feature ranking and LTQSSVM-OFS approach for surface selection. One may also plan to implement our technique on unbalanced datasets [19]. Also, this model can be used to classify images; this prospect of this model needs further investigation. The scopes for future work may be directed to multi-class classification and optimizations using meta-heuristics approaches to minimize the computation time. Furthermore, the proposed model can also be deployed on the functional data [11], or image data for segmentation [12], or can be used in decision support system [13,14,18]. Moreover, the proposed method can also be made powerful to handle uncertainty or fuzziness [17,20,21] in decision making process.

References

1. Belkin, M., Niyogi, P., Sindhwani, V.: Manifold regularization: a geometric framework for learning from labeled and unlabeled examples. J. Mach. Learn. Res. **7**(11) (2006)
2. Hamed, T., Dara, R., Kremer, S.C.: Network intrusion detection system based on recursive feature addition and bigram technique. Comput. Secur. **73**, 137–155 (2018)
3. Huang, M.W., Chen, C.W., Lin, W.C., Ke, S.W., Tsai, C.F.: DSVM and SVM ensembles in breast cancer prediction. PLoS ONE **12**(1), e0161501 (2017)
4. Jiménez-Cordero, A., Morales, J.M., Pineda, S.: A novel embedded min-max approach for feature selection in nonlinear support vector machine classification. Eur. J. Oper. Res. **293**(1), 24–35 (2021)
5. Kim, K.J.: Financial time series forecasting using support vector machines. Neurocomputing **55**(1–2), 307–319 (2003)
6. Lin, Y., Guo, H., Hu, J.: An SVM-based approach for stock market trend prediction. In: The 2013 International Joint Conference on Neural Networks (IJCNN), pp. 1–7. IEEE (2013)
7. Melacci, S., Belkin, M.: Laplacian support vector machines trained in the primal. J. Mach. Learn. Res. **12**(3), 1149–1184 (2011)

8. Morris, A.P., et al.: Large-scale association analysis provides insights into the genetic architecture and pathophysiology of type 2 diabetes. Nat. Genet. **44**(9), 981 (2012)
9. Pramanik, A., Djeddi, C., Sarkar, S., Maiti, J., et al.: Region proposal and object detection using hog-based CNN feature map. In: 2020 International Conference on Data Analytics for Business and Industry: Way Towards a Sustainable Economy (ICDABI), pp. 1–5. IEEE (2020)
10. Pramanik, A., Gorai, A., Sarkar, S., Gupta, P.: A novel feature extraction-based human identification approach using 2D ear biometric. In: 2018 IEEE Applied Signal Processing Conference (ASPCON), pp. 168–172. IEEE (2018)
11. Pramanik, A., Nande, V., Pradhan, A.S., Sarkar, S., Maiti, J.: Dynamic functional bandwidth kernel-based SVM: an efficient approach for functional data analysis. In: Hassanien, A.E., Bhattacharyya, S., Chakrabati, S., Bhattacharya, A., Dutta, S. (eds.) Emerging Technologies in Data Mining and Information Security. AISC, vol. 1286, pp. 673–681. Springer, Singapore (2021). https://doi.org/10.1007/978-981-15-9927-9_65
12. Pramanik, A., Sarkar, S., Maiti, J.: Oil spill detection using image processing technique: an occupational safety perspective of a steel plant. In: Abraham, A., Dutta, P., Mandal, J., Bhattacharya, A., Dutta, S. (eds.) Emerging Technologies in Data Mining and Information Security. AISC, pp. 247–257. Springer, Singapore (2019). https://doi.org/10.1007/978-981-13-1501-5_21
13. Pramanik, A., Sarkar, S., Maiti, J.: A real-time video surveillance system for traffic pre-events detection. Accid. Anal. Prev. **154**, 106019 (2021)
14. Pramanik, A., Sarkar, S., Maiti, J., Mitra, P.: Rt-gsom: rough tolerance growing self-organizing map. Inf. Sci. **566**, 19–37 (2021)
15. Pramanik, A., Sarkar, S., Sai Siddharth, V., Maiti, J., Mitra, P.: Semi-automated ontology creation and upgradation for rail-road incidents: a case of a steel plant in India. In: Tavares, J.M.R.S., Chakrabarti, S., Bhattacharya, A., Ghatak, S. (eds.) Emerging Technologies in Data Mining and Information Security. LNNS, vol. 164, pp. 285–294. Springer, Singapore (2021). https://doi.org/10.1007/978-981-15-9774-9_28
16. Rastogi (nee Khemchandani), R., Bharti, A.: Least squares twin extreme learning machine for pattern classification. In: Deb, D., Balas, V.E., Dey, R. (eds.) Innovations in Infrastructure. AISC, vol. 757, pp. 561–571. Springer, Singapore (2019). https://doi.org/10.1007/978-981-13-1966-2_50
17. Sarkar, S., Baidya, S., Maiti, J.: Application of rough set theory in accident analysis at work: a case study. In: 2017 Third International Conference on Research in Computational Intelligence and Communication Networks (ICRCICN), pp. 245–250. IEEE (2017)
18. Sarkar, S., Chain, M., Nayak, S., Maiti, J.: Decision support system for prediction of occupational accident: a case study from a steel plant. In: Abraham, A., Dutta, P., Mandal, J., Bhattacharya, A., Dutta, S. (eds.) Emerging Technologies in Data Mining and Information Security. AISC, pp. 787–796. Springer, Singapore (2019). https://doi.org/10.1007/978-981-13-1498-8_69
19. Sarkar, S., Khatedi, N., Pramanik, A., Maiti, J.: An ensemble learning-based undersampling technique for handling class-imbalance problem. In: Proceedings of ICETIT 2019, pp. 586–595. Springer (2020)
20. Sarkar, S., Kumar, A., Mohanpuria, S.K., Maiti, J.: Application of bayesian network model in explaining occupational accidents in a steel industry. In: 2017 Third International Conference on Research in Computational Intelligence and Communication Networks (ICRCICN), pp. 337–392. IEEE (2017)

21. Sarkar, S., Lakha, V., Ansari, I., Maiti, J.: Supplier selection in uncertain environment: a fuzzy MCDM approach. In: Mandal, J., Satapathy, S., Sanyal, M., Bhateja, V. (eds) Proceedings of the First International Conference on Intelligent Computing and Communication, pp. 257–266. Springer, Singapore (2017)
22. Sarkar, S., Pramanik, A., Khatedi, N., Maiti, J.: An investigation of the effects of missing data handling using 'R'-packages. In: Raju, K.S., Senkerik, R., Lanka, S.P., Rajagopal, V. (eds.) Data Engineering and Communication Technology. AISC, vol. 1079, pp. 275–284. Springer, Singapore (2020). https://doi.org/10.1007/978-981-15-1097-7_24
23. Sarkar, S., Pramanik, A., Maiti, J., Reniers, G.: Predicting and analyzing injury severity: a machine learning-based approach using class-imbalanced proactive and reactive data. Saf. Sci. **125**, 104616 (2020)
24. Sarkar, S., Vinay, S., Pateshwari, V., Maiti, J.: Study of optimized SVM for incident prediction of a steel plant in India. In: 2016 IEEE Annual India Conference (INDICON), pp. 1–6. IEEE (2016)
25. Sarkar, S., Vinay, S., Raj, R., Maiti, J., Mitra, P.: Application of optimized machine learning techniques for prediction of occupational accidents. Comput. Oper. Res. **106**, 210–224, e0161501 (2019). https://doi.org/10.1016/j.cor.2018.02.021
26. Vapnik, V., Guyon, I., Hastie, T.: Support vector machines. Mach. Learn. **20**(3), 273–297 (1995)
27. Verma, A., Chatterjee, S., Sarkar, S., Maiti, J.: Data-driven mapping between proactive and reactive measures of occupational safety performance. In: Maiti, J., Ray, P.K. (eds.) Industrial Safety Management. MAC, pp. 53–63. Springer, Singapore (2018). https://doi.org/10.1007/978-981-10-6328-2_5
28. Yan, X., Zhu, H., Luo, J.: A novel kernel-free nonlinear SVM for semi-supervised classification in disease diagnosis. J. Comb. Optim. **42**, 948–965 (2021). https://doi.org/10.1007/s10878-019-00484-0

Recognition Algorithm Models Based on the Selection of Two-Dimensional Preference Threshold Functions

S. N. Ibragimova[1](✉)🆔, S. S. Radjabov[1]🆔, O. N. Mirzaev[1,2]🆔,
S. A. Tavboyev[3]🆔, and G. R. Mirzaeva[2]🆔

[1] Research Institute for the Development of Digital Technologies and Artificial
Intelligence, 17A, Buz-2, Mirzo Ulugbek, 100125 Tashkent, Republic of Uzbekistan
snibragimova@mail.ru
[2] Tashkent University of Information Technologies named after Muhammad
al-Khwarizmi, 108, Amir Temur Avenue, 100200 Tashkent, Republic of Uzbekistan
[3] Jizzakh Polytechnic Institute, 4, Islam Karimov Avenue, 130100 Jizzakh,
Republic of Uzbekistan

Abstract. The paper deals with the construction of a model of recognition algorithm (RA) based on the selection of two-dimensional preference threshold functions. The proposed RA model is based on the concept of forming a set of groups formed from tightly coupled features and determining a set of two-dimensional preference threshold functions when constructing an extreme RA within the proposed model. A structural description of the developed RA model is given, presented in the form of a sequence of computational procedures, the main of which are: 1) the definition of support pseudo-objects (SP) in a two-dimensional subspace of representative features; 2) determination of two-dimensional threshold proximity function between the pseudo-object and the object; 3) identification of groups of tightly coupled two-dimensional threshold proximity functions; 4) determination of basic two-dimensional threshold proximity functions. The results of the experimental study showed that the use of the developed RA model provides the possibility of a significant reduction in the computational complexity of the algorithm, which implements the test set in the process of object recognition; tosolve the problem of object recognition, given in the high dimensionality features space, with relatively high accuracy.

Keywords: Model of recognition algorithm · Representative features · Preference features · Threshold function · Preference threshold functions

1 Introduction

It is known [2,18,22,41,42] that in recent years the problem of pattern recognition has been the focus of attention of many specialists in the field of computer data processing systems. This is evidenced by numerous scientific publications

C. Djeddi et al. (Eds.): MedPRAI 2021, CCIS 1543, pp. 354–366, 2022.
https://doi.org/10.1007/978-3-031-04112-9_27

on the topic, the number of which is growing year after year. This is due to the fact that in recent years RA are increasingly used in solving various problems of biometric identification of a person, management of industrial and technological processes, technical and medical diagnostics, and in other areas of human activity [8, 22, 42].

The study of a number of literary sources published to date allows identifying a number of RA models. These include the models based on:

1) the construction of discriminant functions (R-models) [28, 29, 39, 42]. The main idea of these models is to construct various types of hypersurfaces that separate different classes of objects from each other. The most common R-models are linear and piecewise-linear models.

The main advantage of these models is the clarity of mathematical formulation of the recognition problem as an optimization problem. At that, the quality functional of the R-model is associated with the recognition error. The variety of models of this type is explained by the wide range of methods used to search for unknown parameters. The successful application of these models is based on two factors: the parametric form of the discriminant functions and the practical possibility of determining their coefficients;

2) the probability theory and mathematical statistics (C-models). C-models are based on the application of the principles of mathematical statistics in determining the probabilistic characteristics of classes [9, 16, 23, 26, 30, 39, 40]. Methods for constructing C-models are subdivided into parametric and nonparametric ones [16, 40]. When using the parametric approach, it is assumed that the form of the probability distribution functions is given on the basis of the available a priori information. The distribution parameters are determined from the training sample. The problem of determining the parameters can be solved by various methods of mathematical statistics [9, 39, 40]. In the nonparametric approach of the considered recognition models, not only the values of the parameters of the probability distribution function are unknown, but there is no a priori information about the very form of the distribution law. This approach combines recognition algorithms built using nonparametric statistics methods [16, 26, 30]. C-models are based on the principles of mathematical statistics, in particular, on the basis of the Bayesian approach and the minimax principle [9, 39, 40];

3) the method of potential functions (Π-models). The formation of Π-models is based on the so-called potential function, which is an analog of the well-known physical principle [1, 21, 34, 38, 39], and a recurrent procedure, the main idea of which is to determine such a function that corresponds to the cumulative potential determined when constructing an extreme RA.

Currently, there are two types of Π-models: models built on the basis of the potential method, and models based on the potential function method. Although both models are based on the same initial ideas about potential functions, their construction is realized in different ways [1, 21]. It should be noted, however, that choosing the type of potential functions is not an easy task. For example, if they decrease very quickly with increasing distance, then an error-free separation of training samples can be achieved. However, in this case, certain troubles arise when recognizing unidentified objects (the reliability of the decision made decreases, the zone of uncertainty increases). If the potential functions are too "shallow", the number of recognition errors may unreasonably increase, including the errors in training objects;

4) the principle of mathematical logic (L-models) [4, 5, 17, 24, 27, 35, 37]. The main idea used in the construction of the L-model is to search for empirical patterns in the training set and to represent the detected patterns in the form of logical relationships. At that, objects of each class are described in the language of features, and each logical relationship corresponds to a certain area in the feature space. As a result, a certain set of elementary logical classifiers is formed, usually in the form of conjunctions of a number of elementary events. L-models are diverse and include methods of varying complexity and depth of analysis. For dichotomous (boolean) features, the so-called tree-like classifiers, the dead-end test method, the "Kora" algorithm, etc. are popular.

L-models are computationally quite laborious since the selection of conjunctions requires exhaustive enumeration. Therefore, when using these models, high requirements are imposed on the efficient organization of the computing process and computer power. The use of these models gives good results with relatively small dimensions of feature space;

5) the estimates calculation (Γ-models). The Γ-models are based on the voting principle, which consists in assessing the "closeness" between the parts of the descriptions of previously classified objects and the object that needs to be classified [41–43]. Within the framework of Γ-models, the recognition procedure is implemented in the following sequence:

– a system of reference sets of the algorithm is specified, according to which the recognized object is analyzed;
– the concept of the closeness on the set of $\tilde{\omega}$-parts of object descriptions is defined;
– the scheme for calculating the estimation of the closeness of the reference and recognized objects is determined, i.e. a value called an estimate for pairs of objects is calculated;
– the method of forming estimates for each of the classes for a fixed reference set based on estimates for pairs of objects is indicated;
– the method of forming the total score estimate for each of the classes for all reference subsets is determined;
– a decision rule is set, which, based on the estimates for the classes, ensures the assignment of the recognized object to one of the classes or refuses to make a decision.

The theoretical capabilities of Γ-models are not lower than the capabilities of any other pattern recognition algorithm since with these algorithms all conceivable operations with the objects under study can be realized. But, as is usually the case, the expansion of potential opportunities encounters great difficulties in their practical implementation. With high power of the reference set system, the organization of a computational procedure directly from the descriptions of these RA models requires a large number of computing operations.

Another disadvantage of these models is the need for a complete enumeration of the training sample for recognition. The Γ-models are considered in details in [6,7,19,20,33,36,41–43].

Analysis of existing literary sources, in particular [1,2,4,8,9,18–22,24,27,29, 33–35,38–42], shows that the listed RA models are mainly focused on solving problems of object recognition described in the low dimensionality feature space [21,22,25].

In recent years, applied problems related to the study of complex objects are often dealt with in practice. If, earlier, specialists of computer technologies considered simple objects that depend on many parameters of low power (i.e., phenomena or processes of the same physical nature were studied), then with the developed methods and algorithms for analyzing large bulk of data, the increase in the volume of research related to the study of complex objects became possible.

One of the specific features of such objects is their multidimensionality, i.e., a large number of parameters involved in describing similar objects. The problem of recognizing these objects is considered to be a recognition problem in conditions of a high dimensionality of a feature space (HDFS) [11,32]. When solving such problems, the assumption about the independence of the features is often untenable [11,21,25,32]. In such cases, many well-known recognition algorithms do not work correctly [21]. Therefore, the issues of developing new and improving the existing RA models for solving the problem in the conditions of the HDFS are relevant.

The main aim of the study is to develop a RA model of the intentional type based on the construction of threshold proximity functions (TPF) in the representative features (RF) space. The developed RA model is based on the concept of forming a set of groups formed from homogeneous TPF, and determining a set of two-dimensional preference TPF when constructing an extreme RA within the framework of the proposed model.

2   Statement of the Problem

Consider some set of feasible objects $\mathbb{S}$. It is assumed that the set $\mathbb{S}$ consists of l subsets (classes) $\mathcal{C}_1, ..., \mathcal{C}_j, ..., \mathcal{C}_l$ [21,41,42]:

$$\mathbb{S} = \bigcup_{j=1}^{l} \mathcal{C}_j, \quad \mathcal{C}_i \cap \mathcal{C}_j, \quad i \neq j \, (1 \leq i, j \leq l). \tag{1}$$

Moreover, partition (1) is not defined for all objects $\mathbb{S}$, but only for some bounded part of it. Based on that part of the set of objects $\mathbb{S}$, in which the partition (1) is defined, initial information about the classes $\mathcal{C}_1, ..., \mathcal{C}_j, ..., \mathcal{C}_l$ is formed. Note that the initial information is specified as some set $\mathbb{I}_0$:

$$\mathbb{I}_0 = \{ \, < S_1, \overline{\alpha}(S_1) >, \ldots, < S_i, \overline{\alpha}(S_i) >, \ldots, < S_m, \overline{\alpha}(S_m) > \, \}, \tag{2}$$

$$S_i \in \mathbb{S} \, (i = \overline{1, m}), \, \overline{\alpha}(S_i) = (\alpha_{i1}, \ldots, \alpha_{ij}, \ldots, \alpha_{il}).$$

Each component of the information vector $\overline{a}(S_i)$ is specified as predicate $P_j(S_i)$: $\alpha_{ij} = P_j(S_i)$, where $\alpha_{ij} = 0$, if the object S_i does not belong to class $\mathcal{C}_j$, and $\alpha_{ij} = 1$, if the object S_i belongs to class $\mathcal{C}_j$.

It is assumed that each feasible object S ($S \in S$) in space $\mathbb{X}$ corresponds to an n-dimensional numerical characteristic of object $\mathfrak{d}(S)$, which is called the n-dimensional vector of the object S description [42]:

$$\mathfrak{d}(S) = (a_1, \ldots, a_i, \ldots, a_n).$$

Thus, each feasible object S in space $\mathbb{X}$ corresponds to an n-dimensional vector. Therefore, we will not distinguish an object from its description since when it is said that object S is set, then its description is also set:

$$S = (a_1, \ldots, a_i, \ldots, a_n).$$

It is assumed that the set of objects S is specified in the space of interconnected features, which is a characteristic feature of many applied problems of multidimensional data analysis.

Let there be given m objects belonging to set S: $\widetilde{S}^m = \{S_1, \ldots, S_u, \ldots, S_m\}$ in the feature space $\mathbb{X}$. The problem is to construct a RA $\mathcal{A}$, that determines the values of the predicate $P_j(S_i)$ $(P_j(S_i) = "S_i \in \mathcal{C}_j")$ for all objects $\widetilde{S}^m$ according to the initial information (2):

$$\mathcal{A}(\mathbb{I}_0) = \|\beta_{ij}\|_{m \times n}, \quad \beta_{ij} = P_j(S_i).$$

Here β_{ij} is interpreted as in the study of Academician Yu.I. Zhuravlev [41,42]:

$$\beta_{ij} = \begin{cases} 0, & \text{if the object } S_i \text{ belongs to class } \mathcal{C}_j; \\ 1, & \text{if the object } S_i \text{ doesn't belong to class } \mathcal{C}_j; \\ \Delta, & \text{if the model does not calculate the values of predicate } P_j(S_i). \end{cases}$$

3   Method of Solution

To solve the formulated problem, a new approach is proposed, the main concept of which is the formation of a set of support pseudo-objects (SP) and the construction of two-dimensional TPF in the RF space. The main idea of the proposed RA model is to select a set of SP and use them in constructing two-dimensional preference TPF. Consider an arbitrary feasible object S ($S \in S$), defined in the n-dimensional feature space $\mathbb{X}$. Let $\overline{\omega}S$ mean that the object S is described by the $\overline{\omega}$-part of $\mathbb{X}$. Moreover, an n-dimensional Boolean vector $\overline{\omega}$, where $\overline{\omega} = (\omega_1, \ldots, \omega_i, \ldots, \omega_n)$ corresponds to each n-dimensional space $\mathbb{X}$:

$$\omega_i = \begin{cases} 1, & \text{if the } i\text{-th feature is included in } \overline{\omega}; \\ 0, & \text{otherwise.} \end{cases}$$

Thus, $\overline{\omega}S$ is not an object of S, but consists of its $\overline{\omega}$-part. In what follows, the $\overline{\omega}$-part of an object will be called a pseudo-object. It should be noted that the main meaning of undefined concepts and designations used in this study could be found in [20, 21, 41, 42].

Let us consider the main stages of the proposed RA model in more detail.

1. Detection of groups of tightly coupled features. As a result of this stage, a system is distinguished, which consists of n' groups of tightly coupled features (GTCF). Issues related to the definition of GTCF are discussed in detail in [11, 32].

2. Selection of a set of RF. At this stage, an n-dimensional Boolean vector $\bar{\tau}$ ($n' = |\bar{\tau}|$) is formed, and issues related to the definition of RF are discussed in detail in [14, 15].

3. Determination of the difference function in the two-dimensional subspace of RF. At this stage, a two-parameter function that characterizes the similarity of objects is determined. Issues related to the parametric representation of this function and the determination of its parameters are considered in [11, 12, 22]. It should be noted that parameter $\tilde{\gamma}_\tau, \tilde{\gamma}_\tau = (\gamma_{\tau_1}, \gamma_{\tau_2})$ is determined at this stage.

4. Selection of groups of tightly coupled pseudo-objects in the two-dimensional subspace of RF. At this stage, m' groups of tightly coupled pseudo-objects are formed using a two-dimensional difference function. The issues related to the formation of these groups are discussed in [10, 31].

5. Definition of SP in the two-dimensional subspace of RF. At this stage, a set of SP is determined, each of which is a typical representative (E_q^τ) of its own group of pseudo-objects. The components of the SP E_q^τ in each group of $\mathfrak{B}_q$ ($q = \overline{1, m'}$) can be calculated as the average value over all its elements:

$$b_{qi}^\tau = \frac{1}{|\mathfrak{B}_q|} \sum_{a_{ui} \in \mathfrak{B}_q} a_{ui}, \quad i = \overline{1, 2}.$$

Thus, at this stage, m' of SP are determined as: $\mathbb{E}^\tau = \{E_1^\tau, \dots, E_q^\tau, \dots, E_{m'}^\tau\}$. Each of them is specified as a two-dimensional vector, i.e. $E_q^\tau = (b_{qi_1}^\tau, b_{qi_2}^\tau)$. The set of SP calculated for each $\mathfrak{B}_q$ is denoted by $\mathfrak{b}_q$.

6. Determination of two-dimensional TPF $d_\tau(E_q^\tau, S)$ between SP E_q^τ and object S. At this stage, the two-dimensional TPF is determined between the SP E_q^τ and an arbitrary object S in the two-dimensional subspace of the RF:

$$t_\tau(E_q^\tau, S) = \begin{cases} 1, & \text{if } d_\tau(E_q^\tau, S) \leq \varepsilon_\tau; \\ 0, & \text{otherwise}, \end{cases}$$

$$d_\tau(E_q^\tau, S) = \sum_{i=1}^{2} \varrho_{\tau_i}(b_{q\tau_i} - a_{\tau_i}),$$

where $\varepsilon_\tau, \varrho_{\tau_i}$ is a parameter of the algorithm, $\varrho_\tau = (\varepsilon_\tau, \varrho_{\tau_1}, \varrho_{\tau_2})$.

7. Selection of groups of tightly coupled two-dimensional TPF. At this stage, the $\mathfrak{M}_A$ systems of "independent" groups of two-dimensional TPF are determined. Let each proximity function $\mathfrak{H}_u$ correspond to a numerical matrix $\mathfrak{H}_\tau\left(\mathbb{E}^\tau, \widetilde{S}^m\right) = \left\|\mathfrak{h}_{ij}^{(\tau)}\right\|_{m \times m'}$ and $\mathfrak{H}$ be a set of two-dimensional TPF: $\mathfrak{H} = \{\mathfrak{H}_1, \ldots, \mathfrak{H}_n\}$. We assume that some function $\eta(\mathfrak{H}_u, \mathfrak{H}_v)$ is given, which estimates the measure of proximity between pairs of elements $\mathfrak{H}$. Generally, the function $\eta(\mathfrak{H}_u, \mathfrak{H}_v)$ is specified as the distance between two points in space of $m \times m'$-dimensional numerical matrices. At that, the distance between two groups of two-dimensional TPF is defined as the distance between two subsets of points in space of $m \times m'$-dimensional numerical matrices.

As a result of performing this stage, we obtain $\mathfrak{n}'$ groups of two-dimensional TPF in each two-dimensional subspace of RF.

8. Determination of basic two-dimensional TPF. At this stage, basic two-dimensional TPF are selected and a set $\mathfrak{B}$ is formed, which consists of $\mathfrak{n}'$ two-dimensional TPF. The main idea of selecting basic two-dimensional TPF is to eliminate $N_p - 1$ $(p = \overline{1, \mathfrak{n}'})$ of two-dimensional TPF, which give almost the same results when calculating the membership estimates from the selected group of two-dimensional TPF W_p. As a result of performing this stage, we obtain $\mathfrak{n}'$ two-dimensional TPF, which is much less than the initial one, i.e., $\mathfrak{n}' < \mathfrak{n}$. It should be noted that an n-dimensional Boolean vector $\widetilde{\mathfrak{h}}$ $\left(\widetilde{\mathfrak{h}} = (\mathfrak{h}_1, \ldots, \mathfrak{h}_i, \ldots, \mathfrak{h}_n), \mathfrak{n}' = \left|\widetilde{\mathfrak{h}}\right|\right)$ is determined at this stage.

9. Determination of two-dimensional preference TPF. Let a set of basic two-dimensional TPF be given. The search for a two-dimensional preference SFP on a given set is performed using the method of dominance estimation [15,21]:

$$T_i = (e_i + \bar{e}_i/m,$$

$$e_i = \sum_{j=1}^{l} \sum_{S_u \in \widetilde{C}_j} \sum_{S \in \widetilde{C}_j} f_i(S_u, S), \quad \bar{e}_i = \sum_{j=1}^{l} \sum_{S_u \in \widetilde{D}_j} \sum_{S_u \in \widetilde{C}_j} \overline{f}_i(S_u, S),$$

$$f_i(S_u, S) = \begin{cases} 1, & \text{if } \sum_{v=1}^{2} \gamma_{i_v}\left(a_{u_{i_v}} - a_{i_v}\right) \le 1; \\ 0, & \text{otherwise}, \end{cases}$$

$$\overline{f}_i(S_u, S) = \begin{cases} 1, & \text{if } f_i(S_u, S) = 0; \\ 0, & \text{otherwise}, \end{cases}$$

It is known [10,11,13,21], that the greater the value of T_i, the more preference is given to the i-th two-dimensional TPF. As a result of performing this stage, we obtain $\mathfrak{n}''$ two-dimensional preference TPF.

10. Synthesis of an integral recognition operator based on support functions of proximity. At this stage, the integral recognizing operator B is determined by the selected two-dimensional preference TPF:

$$B(\mathcal{C}_j, S) = \sum_{u=1}^{\mathfrak{n}''} \vartheta_u \mathfrak{H}_u(\mathcal{C}_j, S),$$

where ϑ_u is the parameter of the integral recognition operator B; $\mathfrak{n}''$ is the number of selected and preferred two-dimensional TPF.

11. Decision rule. The decision is made element by element [21,42], i.e.

$$\beta_{ij} = C\left(B(\mathcal{C}_j, S)\right) = \begin{cases} 0, & \text{if } B(\mathcal{C}_j, S) < c_1; \\ 1, & \text{if } B(\mathcal{C}_j, S) > c_1; \\ \varDelta, & \text{if } c_1 \le B(\mathcal{C}_j, S) \le c_1, \end{cases}$$

where c_1, c_2 are the algorithm parameters.

Thus, we have defined a RA model of intentional type, built on the basis of the TPF. An arbitrary RA within this model is one-to-one by specifying $\tilde{\pi}$ parameters: $\tilde{\pi} = \left(n', \bar{\mathfrak{r}}, \{\tilde{\gamma}_\tau\}, m', \{\tilde{b}_q\}, \{\tilde{\varrho}_\tau\}, \mathfrak{n}', \{\tilde{\mathfrak{h}}\}, \mathfrak{n}'', \{\vartheta_u\}, c_1, c_2\right)$. The search for the best RA in the framework of the model considered is performed in the space of parameters $\tilde{\pi}$ [14,15,21].

4   Performance Estimate of the Proposed RA Model

In order to conduct experimental studies to assess the performance of the proposed RA model in the C++ programming language, a software package was developed, which includes a software implementation of this model and of the model used for comparative analysis of results.

4.1   Experiments

To conduct an experimental check on the developed RA estimation, a model task was formed. The initial data for this task were generated in the space of interconnected features. As a result of generating the initial data, m ($m = 500$) objects were obtained in the n-dimensional feature space ($n = 400$). In this case, the number of classes is l ($l = 2$), and the number of groups of tightly coupled features is n' ($n' = 3$).

The following RA models were compared:

1) the classical RA model based on potential functions ($\mathfrak{A}_1$-model) [9];
2) the proposed RA model ($\mathfrak{A}_2$-model).

A comparative analysis of the above RA models in problem solution was conducted according to the following criteria: errors in the training set of objects recognition; time spent on constructing the extreme RA; errors in the test set of objects recognition using the extreme RA; time spent by the extreme RA on the test set of objects recognition.

In order to exclude a successful (or unsuccessful) partition of the generated objects into training set and test set, we used the cross-validation method [3].

The initial sample of objects was randomly divided into 10 disjoint blocks, each containing 50 objects. It was required that in all blocks the proportion by the number of objects belonging to different classes was preserved. The process of cross-validation over these blocks includes several steps. At each step, 9 out of 10 blocks are selected as a training sample, and on this sample, the RA was trained with the given parameters. The RA trained in this way is checked on the rest of 1 block (of the test sample). As a result of each check, a quality assessment of the AR is determined and recorded according to the specified criteria. When performing each next step, to assess the quality of the RA, one block is selected from the test and training samples and swapped. In order to exclude the reuse of the objects of the test sample, the corresponding blocks are marked, and they are not involved in the selection of candidates for inclusion in the test sample. After completing the cross-validation procedure, recognition errors and time indicators were determined as averages. The experiments were conducted on a Pentium IV Dual Core 2.2 GHz computer with 1 Gb of RAM.

4.2   Results

In the course of this experimental study, the following main results were obtained:

1) the class of all GTCF was determined;
2) a set of RF was identified;
3) a TPF was constructed between objects in the two-dimensional subspace of the RF;
4) based on the definition of unknown parameters $\widetilde{\pi}$, the extreme recognition algorithm was constructed.

The results of solving this problem using $\mathfrak{A}_1$ and $\mathfrak{A}_2$ are shown in Table 1 (numerical characteristics of the RA calculated during the training set processing) and in Table 2 (numerical characteristics of the RA calculated during the test set processing).

Table 1. Results of training RA models

RA models	Time spent on constructing the extreme RA (in sec.)	Errors in object recognition (in %)
$\mathfrak{A}_1$	8.0162	6.73
$\mathfrak{A}_2$	14.1129	4.91

Table 2. Results of test set of object recognition

RA models	Time spent on constructing the extreme RA (in sec.)	Errors in object recognition (in %)
$\mathfrak{A}_1$	0.0870	14.30
$\mathfrak{A}_2$	0.0042	6.59

A comparative analysis of the results obtained in the course of behavioral experimental studies shows that the proposed model $\mathfrak{A}_2$ more accurately solves the problem of object recognition. At that, recognition errors using the $\mathfrak{A}_1$ model are 7% less than the same index using the $\mathfrak{A}_1$ model. However, the $\mathfrak{A}_2$ model spends more time training than $\mathfrak{A}_1$. The reason is that the procedures for determining some of the parameters of $\mathfrak{A}_2$ are difficult to compute. When recognizing the objects from test set, the rate (the speed of operation) index $\mathfrak{A}_2$ is higher than that of $\mathfrak{A}_1$ since the number of computational operations is less in the process of membership estimation of the test set objects than the number of operations used in the process of model parameters estimation.

4.3 Discussion

The results of the presented experimental study show that the proposed model allows solving the problem of pattern recognition more accurately under the conditions of high dimensionality of a feature space (HDFS). At the same time, the indicator of time spent on object recognition is much less than the same indicators $\mathfrak{A}_1$ and $\mathfrak{A}_2$. This is due to the fact that in the proposed RA for object recognition, only preferred threshold proximity functions (TPF) are used, which led to an increase in the speed of object recognition. Therefore, this model can be used in the development of real-time recognition systems. At that, it should be noted that the time spent on training the algorithm has increased since to construct an optimal RA, it is required to optimize a larger number of parameters than using the traditional model, in particular $\mathfrak{A}_1$.

5 Conclusion

A new approach is proposed based on the formation of a set of two-dimensional RP within the training set. The implementation of the proposed approach makes it possible to pass from the original HDFS to the RF space, which has a significantly lower dimension. Based on this approach, a RA model was developed based on two-dimensional preference threshold functions. The main concept of the proposed model is to select independent subsets of interconnected features and the corresponding set of RF. A distinctive feature of this RA model lies in the determination of the two-dimensional preference TPF when constructing the extreme RA within the framework of the proposed model. The results of solving the model recognition problem using the proposed RA model showed that this model increases the accuracy and significantly reduces computational operations when recognizing an unknown object specified in the HDFS. At that, time spent on model training increased. This circumstance is explained by the fact that more complex optimization procedures are used for its training as compared with training the traditional RA model.

References

1. Ayzerman, M.A., Braverman, E.M., Rozonoer, L.I.: Method of potential functions in the theory of machine learning. Nauka (1970)
2. Beyerer, J., Richter, M., Nagel, M.: Pattern Recognition: Introduction, Features, Classifiers and Principles. De Gruyter Oldenbourg (2017). https://doi.org/10.1515/9783110537949
3. Braga-Neto, U.M., Dougherty, E.R.: Error Estimation for Pattern Recognition. Wiley (2015). https://doi.org/10.1002/9781119079507
4. Djukova, E.V., Masliakov, G.O., Prokofyev, P.A.: Logical classification of partially ordered data. CoRR abs/1907.08962 (2019). https://doi.org/10.1007/978-3-030-30763-9_10, http://arxiv.org/abs/1907.08962
5. Djukova, E.V., Zhuravlev, Y.I., Prokofjev, P.A.: Logical correctors in the problem of classification by precedents. Comput. Math. Math. Phys. **57**(11), 1866–1886 (2017). https://doi.org/10.1134/S0965542517110057
6. D'yakonov, A.G.: Theory of equivalence systems for describing the algebraic closures of a generalized estimation model. Comput. Math. Math. Phys. **50**(2), 369–381 (2010). https://doi.org/10.1134/S0965542510020181
7. D'yakonov, A.G.: Theory of equivalence systems for describing the algebraic closures of a generalized estimation model II. Comput. Math. Math. Phys. **51**(3), 490–504 (2011). https://doi.org/10.1134/S0965542511030067
8. Fazilov, S.K., Khamdamov, R.K., Mirzaeva, G.R., Gulyamova, D.R., Mirzaev, N.M.: Models of recognition algorithms based on linear threshold functions. J. Phys. Conf. Ser. (2020). https://doi.org/10.1088/1742-6596/1441/1/012138
9. Fazilov, S.K., Lutfullayev, R.A., Mirzaev, N.M., Mukhamadiyev, A.S.: Statistical approach to building a model of recognition operators under conditions of high dimensionality of a feature space. J. Phys. Conf. Ser. **1333**(3), 032017 (2019). https://doi.org/10.1088/1742-6596/1333/3/032017
10. Fazilov, S.K., Mirzaev, N.M., Mirzaev, O.N.: Building of recognition operators in condition of features correlations. Radio Electron. Comput. Sci. Control 1, 58–63 (2016)
11. Fazilov, S.K., Mirzaev, N.M., Mirzaeva, G.R.: Modified recognition algorithms based on the construction of models of elementary transformations. Procedia Comput. Sci. **150**, 671–678 (2019)
12. Fazilov, S.K., Mirzaev, N.M., Mirzaeva, G.R., Tashmetov, S.E.: Construction of recognition algorithms based on the two-dimensional functions. In: Santosh, K.C., Hegadi, R.S. (eds.) RTIP2R 2018. CCIS, vol. 1035, pp. 474–483. Springer, Singapore (2019). https://doi.org/10.1007/978-981-13-9181-1_42
13. Fazilov, S.K., Mirzaev, N.M., Nurmukhamedov, T.R., Ibragimova, K.A., Ibragimova, S.N.: Model of recognition operators based on the formation of representative objects. Int. J. Innov. Technol. Exploring Eng. **9**(1), 4503–4507 (2019). 10/35940/ijitee.A4592.119119
14. Fazilov, S.K., Mirzaev, N.M., Radjabov, S.S., Mirzaev, O.N.: Determining of parameters in the construction of recognition operators in conditions of features correlations. In: Proceedings of the School-Seminar on Optimization Problems and their Applications, pp. 118–133 (2018)
15. Fazilov, S.K., Mirzaev, N.M., Radjabov, S.S., Mirzaeva, G.R.: Determination of representative features when building an extreme recognition algorithm. J. Phys. Conf. Ser. **1260**, 1–8 (2019)

16. Fukunaga, K.: Introduction to Statistical Pattern Recognition. Academic Press (1990)

17. Gómez, J.P., Hernández Montero, F.E., Gómez Mancilla, J.C.: Variable selection for journal bearing faults diagnostic through logical combinatorial pattern recognition. In: Hernández Heredia, Y., Milián Núñez, V., Ruiz Shulcloper, J. (eds.) IWAIPR 2018. LNCS, vol. 11047, pp. 299–306. Springer, Cham (2018). https://doi.org/10.1007/978-3-030-01132-1_34

18. Homenda, W., Pedrycz, W.: Pattern Recognition: A Quality of Data Perspective. Wiley (2018)

19. Ignat'ev, O.A.: Construction of a correct combination of estimation algorithms adjusted using the cross validation technique. Comput. Math. Math. Phys. **55**(12), 2094–2099 (2015). https://doi.org/10.1134/S0965542515120064

20. Kamilov, M.M., Fazilov, S.K., Mirzaev, N.M., Radjabov, S.S.: Algorithm of calculation of estimates in condition of features' correlations. In: 3rd International Conference on Problems of Cybernetics and Informatics, vol. 1, pp. 278–281. IEEE (2010)

21. Kamilov, M.M., Fazilov, S.K., Mirzaev, N.M., Radjabov, S.S.: Models of recognition algorithms based on the assessment of the interconnectedness of features. Science and technology (2020)

22. Kamilov, M.M., Fazilov, S.K., Mirzaeva, G.R., Gulyamova, D.R., Mirzaev, N.M.: Building a model of recognizing operators based on the definition of basic reference objects. J. Phys. Conf. Ser. **1441**(1), 012142 (2020). https://doi.org/10.1088/1742-6596/1441/1/012142

23. Kroese, D.P., Botev, Z.I., Taimre, T., Vaisman, R.: Data Science and Machine Learning: Mathematical and Statistical Methods. Chapman and Hall/CRC (2019)

24. Kudryavtsev, V.B., Andreev, A.E., Gasanov, E.E.: Theory of test recognition. Fizmatlit (2007)

25. Lantz, B.: Machine Learning with R: Expert techniques for predictive modeling. Packt (2019)

26. Lapko, A.V., Lapko, V.A.: Nonparametric models and algorithms for information processing. SibGAU (2010)

27. Lbov, G.S., Startseva, N.G.: Logical decision functions and questions of statistical stability of decisions. IM SB RAS (1999)

28. Li, Y., Liu, B., Yu, Y., Li, H., Sun, J., Cui, J.: 3e-lda: Three enhancements to linear discriminant analysis. ACM Trans. Knowl. Discov. Data **15**(4), 1–20 (2021). https://doi.org/10.1145/3442347

29. McLachlan, G.J.: Discriminant Analysis and Statistical Pattern Recognition. Wiley (2004)

30. Merkov, A.B.: Pattern Recognition: An Introduction to Statistical Learning Methods. URSS (2019)

31. Mirzaev, N.M., Khaydarova, M.Y., Mirzaeva, G.R., Ibragimova, S.N.: Models of recognition operators defined in the space of large dimension attributes. J. Phys. Conf. Ser. **1260**(10), 102009 (2019). https://doi.org/10.1088/1742-6596/1260/10/102009

32. Mirzaev, N.M., Saliev, E.A.: Recognition algorithms based on radial functions. In: 3rd Russian-Pacific Conference on Computer Technology and Applications (RPC), pp. 1–6 (2018). https://doi.org/10.1109/RPC.2018.8482213

33. Nishanov, A.K., Djurayev, G.P., Khasanova, M.A.: Improved algorithms for calculating evaluations in processing medical data. COMPUSOFT Int. J. Adv. Comput. Technol. **8**(6), 3158–3165 (2019)

34. Oliveri, P.: Potential function methods: efficient probabilistic approaches to model complex data distributions. NIR News **28**(4), 14–15, 102009 (2017). https://doi.org/10.1177/0960336017703253

35. Povhan, I.F.: Logical recognition tree construction on the basis of a step-to-step elementary attribute selection. Radio Electron. Comput. Sci. Control **2**, 95–105 (2020). https://doi.org/10.15588/1607-3274-2020-2-10

36. Sargsyan, D.S.: On effective implementation of recognition algorithms for calculating estimates. Reports Natl. Acad. Sci. Armenia **119**(1), 7–15, 102009 (2019)

37. Subbotin, S.A.: Construction of decision trees for the case of low-information features. Radio Electron. Comput. Sci. Control **1**, 121–130, 102009 (2019)

38. Sulewski, P.: Recognizing distributions using method of potential functions. Communications in Statistics - Simulation Comput., 1–17 (2021). https://doi.org/10.1080/03610918.2021.1908561

39. Tou, J.T., Gonzalez, R.C.: Pattern recognition principles. Addison-Wesley Pub, Co (1974)

40. Webb, A.R., Copsey, K.D.: Statistical Pattern Recognition. Wiley (2011)

41. Zhuravlev, Y.I.: An algebraic approach to solving problems of recognition or classification. Pattern Recogn. Image Anal. **8**(1), 59–100, 102009 (1998)

42. Zhuravlev, Y.I.: Selected Scientic Works. Magister (1998)

43. Zhuravlev, Y.I., Kamilov, M.M., Tulyaganov, S.E.: Algorithms for calculating estimates and application. Fan (1974)

Using Keytyping as a Biomarker for Cognitive Decline Diagnostics: The Convolutional Neural Network Based Approach

Lucas Salvador Barnardo, Robertas Damasevicius$^{(\boxtimes)}$ ⓘ, and Rytis Maskeliunas ⓘ

Faculty of Informatics, Kaunas University of Technology, Studentu 50, Kaunas, Lithuania

lucas.salvador@ktu.edu, {robertas.damasevicius,rytis.maskeliunas}@ktu.lt

Abstract. Parkinson's disease (PD) can cause many motor impairments in humans such as muscle rigidity/stiffness, hand tremors, etc., causing difficulty when interacting with computer input devices. The purpose of this work was to classify signals obtained from keytyping using wavelet features and deep learning. We proposed a unique technique for diagnosing PD utilizing data-derived scalograms and categorizing them using a custom 10-layer CNN model. The scalograms are created using the wavelet coefficients at different scales. The classification of PD vs. healthy subjects produced results equivalent to most cutting-edge methods, with an accuracy of 93.30%. Our method, which is based on the study of temporal patterns from ordinary interactions with electronic devices, allows us to objectively detect motor impairment in PD patients while they type on a computer at home or at work.

Keywords: Keytyping · Parkinson's disease · Digital health · Scalogram · Convolutional neural network · Pattern recognition

1 Introduction

Parkinson's disease (PD) is causing a difficulty for an increasing number of people as the world population's average age rises. The number of PD sufferers is expected to reach 10 million by 2020. PD is a chronic nervous system condition that mostly affects the motor system. The "pill-rolling" hand tremor (ranging 4 Hz 6 Hz) and muscular rigidity/stiffness are the most prevalent symptoms, while other symptoms include gait [1] and speech [2,3] abnormalities. As a result, fine motor actions (such as grasping objects and pressing keys) are often difficult for Parkinson's sufferers. Interacting with computer keyboards and touchscreen devices is a significant problem for PD patients.

Typing (defined as the act of pressing and releasing keys) can be characterized as a habit in the pathophysiology of PD [4]. In PD, habits are more impacted

© Springer Nature Switzerland AG 2022
C. Djeddi et al. (Eds.): MedPRAI 2021, CCIS 1543, pp. 367–381, 2022.
https://doi.org/10.1007/978-3-031-04112-9_28

than goal-directed activities because the basal ganglia exerts greater control over them. We chose HT from among the many keystroke dynamics because, in addition to being independent of typing abilities, it is essentially uncontrollable.

Currently, there is no commonly acknowledged and conclusive biomarker of PD. Bradykinesia is a symptom of PD that refers to the sluggishness of movement initiation with gradual loss in amplitude and speed of repeated movements The Movement Disorder Society Unified Parkinson's Disease Rating Scale (MDS-UPDRS) component III (motor score) is frequently used to measure bradykinesia [5]. Though MDS-UPDRS-III is a thorough evaluation, the discrete scale makes it difficult to identify small motor changes and is prone to significant variability. As a result, objective and reliable techniques of evaluating motor dysfunction are required.

There is an urgent need to discover early diagnostic biomarkers for two reasons: (1) to act at illness start and (2) to evaluate the progress of treatment therapies that may delay or stop the progression of the disease. One of the promises of personalized medicine in the context of disease development is the capacity to anticipate, on an individual basis, variables contributing to the susceptibility to the development of a specific disease [6].

The motivation behind this study is the observation that the PD group had previously exhibited slower reactions in a keypressing task [7]. In remote evaluations of PD, reliable and precise measurements of stiffness have remained problematic. This has significantly hampered the use of telemedicine [8] in the care and treatment of patients with PD. We investigate a method that translates key hold duration (the time necessary to press and release a key) during regular computer operation to a PD motor index without requiring any hardware changes. This is accomplished by automatically detecting patterns in time series of key hold periods using a deep learning technique.

Scalograms have been used before to transform ECG signals to images for deep learning [9]. By transforming the signal from the time domain to the frequency domain using the wavelet, the 1-D signal becomes a 2-D image matrix, and it could be used for training a deep convolutional neural network (CNN). When a 1-D signal is transformed from time to frequency domain using a wavelet, it creates a 2-D matrix that may be examined at several resolutions. This technique, however, results in morphologically complicated signal analysis. This means that basic classifiers may perform poorly. We explored utilizing the scalogram as input to CNN, which had the best performance for picture classification.

The contribution of this paper with respect to the previous works in this research field is:

- a method for converting the keypress signal into scalogram image;
- a custom convolutional neural network architecture for performing PD recognition from scalogram images;
- performance evaluation using a large number of performance measures.

2   Related Works

The purpose of study [10] was to validate the discriminative features of key typing and finger typing timed performance tests for evaluating bradykinesia in PD. The Halstead-Reitan battery's key tapping subtest, the Purdue Pegboard test, and the Bradykinesia-Akinesia Incoordination (BRAIN) exam were all administered. The findings allowed for an independent examination of individual bradykinesia components, revealing that the decrease in amplitude and maximum opening velocity are significant discriminators between PD patients and normal group.

In Adams et al. [11], keystroke timing data was gathered from 103 participants (32 with mild PD severity level and the remaining healthy controls) while they wrote on a computer keyboard over a lengthy period of time. To identify the individuals' illness state, an unique technique was utilized that included a combination of several keystroke characteristics that were analyzed by an ensemble of classifiers. When used to two independent participant groups, the method had an AUC of 0.98 for correctly discriminating between early-PD individuals and controls.

Ulinskas et al. [12] using keystroke dynamics data investigated the topic of fatigue recognition. The timing data of key typing events is provided by keystroke dynamics (press-release, release-press, and press-press, and release-release time). To distinguish between distinct successive key typing sessions, we suggest utilizing statistical characteristics and a k-Nearest Neighbor (KNN) classifier. With a 91% accuracy, the provided method identifies the stage of increasing fatigue (using key release-release data).

To capture PD motor symptoms, Arroyo-Gallego et al. [13] presented touchscreen typing characteristics based on statistical (skewness, and kurtosis, and covariance) analysis of the finger-tapping data's timing information. The alternating finger-tapping test findings indicate that it might be utilized for a home-based routine typing on touchscreens for PD symptom monitoring.

Arroyo-Gallego et al. [14] analyzed the classification ability of the neuro-QWERTY index introduced by Giancardo et al. [4] using the result of a computational program that detects signs of PD motor impairment and separates healthy subjects from an early PD population by using patterns identified in the sequences of key hold times, the time between pressing and releasing each key on a physical keyboard. The hold time signal is divided into 90-second windows that are evaluated as separate typing units and fed into an ensemble model composed of support vector regressors (SVR).

Shribman et al. [15] adopted the BRAIN test, which is an online keyboard-tapping test that has previously been validated as a sensitive instrument for identifying symptoms of PD, was examined. The study's goal was to see if the BRAIN test might detect cognitive impairment. The kinesia scores (the number of key taps in 30 s), akinesia times (the average dwell time on each key), and incoordination scores (the variation of travel time between keys) were computed and associated with the Expanded Disability Status Scale (EDSS) scores.

Iakovakis et al. [16] offered a technique for identifying fine motor skill deterioration in individuals with early PD by analyzing patterns generated by finger interaction with touchscreen cellphones during natural typing. Our method is based on low-/high-order statistical characteristics of keystroke timing and pressure variables derived from brief typing sessions. Features are input into a two-stage classification workflow, which determines the subject's state (PD/normal) by fusing prediction probabilities derived from typing sessions and keypress characteristics. The AUC for this technique was 0.92.

Subjects in the study of Pham et al. [17] push one or two buttons on a device such as an iPhone as quickly as they can for a brief amount of time. Pham and his colleagues evaluated the data using fuzzy recurrence plots, which take numerous short-time series data points and convert them into two-dimensional grey-scale pictures of texture. Related data points show as a dense grey in the picture, whereas more distant data points become fuzzier. The fuzzy recurrence plot algorithm learns how data points link and can assist reveal differences and similarities in subject groups such as those with early PD and those who do not.

In [18], the researchers examined the temporal metrics of the repetitive alternating finger tapping task with the UPDRS III, bradykinesia, arrhythmicity, etc., and concluded that 30 s of alternating finger tapping on a portable keyboard could be used for diagnostics of PD in telehealth settings.

Abayomi et al. [19] advocated combining machine learning and data augmentation to enhance early diagnosis of PD in extremely small datasets. To produce synthetic data instances, they employed Spline interpolation and Piecewise Cubic Hermite Interpolating Polynomial (Pchip) interpolation techniques. They utilized a deep learning network called Bidirectional LSTM (BiLSTM) for categorization. They used the Oxford Parkinson illness dataset for experimental validation and achieved 97.1% accuracy.

Peachap et al. [20] used Daubechies, discrete Laguerre and biorthogonal wavelets to extract some features from finger typing movements on keyboard. They used Hold time, latency time and flight time as features. The authors reported classification accuracy in the range of 93.5–100%.

In [21], an LSTM model was created to predict early-stage PD based on the subject's keyboard typing time series information. The area under the ROC curve (AUC) is 0.82, the accuracy rate (ACC) is 0.84, the precision (PRE) is 0.85, the recall rate (REC) is 0.98, and the F1 score is 0.90, according to the training and test data.

In [22], novel Distal Bradykinesia Tapping (DBT) test was devised to measure distal upper-limb function in PD patients. The test's kinetic characteristics include kinesia score (KS20, key taps lasting more than 20 s), akinesia time (AT20, average dwell time), and incoordination score (IS20, variance of travel time between key presses). The aggregation of the DBT and BRAIN tests increased discrimination (AUC = 0.91), indicating that the DBT test might be used to detect distal motor impairment in PD, potentially allowing for longitudinal surveillance of PD motor difficulties.

In [23], the typing features created by users with and without PD were identified and compared. The study discovered that users with PD made far more
insertion, omission, and replacement mistakes than young individuals.

Summarising, the keytyping task remains an important diagnostic test for
PD disease, while classification of keytyping features remains a difficult task due
to high variability of subjects and the lack of standard data collection methods.

3   Methodology

3.1   Continouos Wavelet Transform

The continuous wavelet transform (CWT) is calculated by varying the size of
the analysis window, moving the window in time, multiplying by the signal, and
integrating across all times. It is basically a correlation measurement between a
signal and several wavelets deriving from a base wavelet.

Let $d_Z(a, b)$ be the wavelet coefficient of the continuous variable $Z =
\{Z(t), t \in \mathbb{R}\}$ for the scale a and the shift b, with

$$d_Z(a, b) = \frac{1}{\sqrt{a}} \int_{\mathbb{R}} \psi(\frac{t}{a} - b)Z(t)dt = < \psi_\lambda, Z >_{L^2(\mathbb{R})} .$$

For a discrete time series rather than a continuous process, a Riemann sum can
be used for calculating a discretized wavelet coefficient $e_Z(a, b)$. The function ψ
must satisfy $M \in \int e^*$ leading to ,

$$\int_{\mathbb{R}} t^m \psi(t)dt = 0 \text{ for all } m \in \{0, 1, \ldots, M\}. \tag{1}$$

The continuous wavelet transform (CWT) of a signal, $x(t)$, is given by

$$W(\lambda, t) = \int_{-\infty}^{\infty} x(\tau)\psi_{\lambda,t}^*(\tau)d\tau. \tag{2}$$

$W(\lambda, t)$ are called the wavelet coefficients, while

$$\psi_{\lambda,t}(\tau) = \frac{1}{\sqrt{\lambda}}\psi\left(\frac{\tau - t}{\lambda}\right) \tag{3}$$

where $\psi(t)$ is the functional form of the mother wavelet, and the asterisk indicates the complex conjugate. λ is the scale, which changes the frequency being
measured by a given wavelet (larger scale measures lower frequency components).

This is transformed into a filtering process in Discrete Wavelet Transform
(DWT) by a succession of high-pass (HP) and low-pass (LP) filters with varying
cut-off frequencies to examine the signal at different scales. The signal is routed
via a succession of HP and LP filters. Filtering a signal is the convolution of a
signal with the impulse response of a filter. The DWT is calculated by dividing
signals at different frequency bands with varying resolutions into approximation

and detail components. The decomposition is accomplished by filtering the time domain signal with consecutive HP and LP filters.

The approximation and detail components are iteratively convolved using the same LP and HP filters until they reach a specific level, as seen below:

$$ca_{j,k}[x(t)] = DS[\sum x(t) \, g_j^*(t - 2^j k)] \tag{4}$$

$$cd_{j,k}[x(t)] = DS[\sum x(t) \, h_j^*(t - 2^j k)] \tag{5}$$

where the coefficients $ca_{j,k}$ and $cd_{j,k}$ specify approximation and detail components returned by the $g(n)$ LP and $h(n)$ HP responses, respectively, and the DS operator downsamples by a factor of 2.

The 1D decomposition is applied to an image (2D matrix) first in the row-direction and then in the column-direction. In step one, we first convolve the image's rows using LP and HP filters, then discard the odd-numbered columns (downsample) of the two resultant arrays (Fig. 1).

The columns of each of the $N/2$-by-N arrays are then convolved with LP and HP filters and the odd numbered rows are discarded. The result is the four $N/2$-by-$N/2$ subimages which are coarse-coarse (LL), coarse-detail (LH), detail-coarse (HL), and detail-detail (HH) components. The process of the decomposition of an image is shown in Fig. 1.

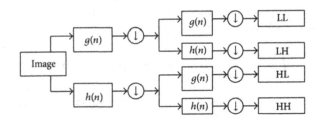

Fig. 1. 2D discrete wavelet decomposition.

The acquired approximation pictures may be dissected again to get 2nd-level detail and approximation images, and the procedure can be repeated for finer analysis by doubling the image scale with each iteration. The picture is rebuilt in the reconstruction step by combining approximation and detail components. Under the reconstruction method, the modified coefficients are returned to the original signal. The approximation component is convolved with a LP filter at each level, while the detail component is convolved with a HP filter. Following filtering, each portion is oversampled by a factor of 2 and combined to provide an approximation signal of the next higher level. The results of this process is the scalogram image which shows the percentage of energy for each coefficient of DWT.

3.2 Convolutional Neural Network (CNN)

As a standard approach, simple CNN was tested. It has an input layer, three convolutional layers, two max-pooling layers, and one fully connected layer. An input layer takes $31 \times 31 \times 3$ image in the first layer. The neighbourhood of each image pixel contributes to the output signal through a set of weights structured as a **filter** aka **kernel** or **mask**. The filter is typically fixed for the specified network layer, and the output is generated via a 2D convolution operator:

$$U = \text{conv2d}\,(X, W) \qquad (6)$$

where X is an input image to the layer, U is the output image, and W is a 2D **filter** or **weight matrix**.

The convolution is a linear operator thatreplaces operation $\mathbf{u}_n^{(k)} = W^{(k)} \cdot \hat{\mathbf{x}}_n^{(k)}$.

In a 2D case, that is, a 2D 3×3 filter W is applied to an image X using a convolution operation. For each pixel x_{mn} and its 8 neighbouring pixels the m, n neuron calculates u_{mn} as a sum of products of corresponding image pixel and mask values:

$$U = W \star X \qquad (7)$$

In addition to the linear part of a layer U, a non-linear function σ is added, so that the output is computed as:

$$z_{mn} = \sigma(u_{mn} + b), \text{ or } \quad Z = \sigma(W \star X + B) \qquad (8)$$

where σ is an activation function d such as ReLU, B being the bias for the layer, Z is a **feature map**.

In a 2D image case, we have a feature map X of size $R \times C$:

$$R \; \begin{array}{c} C \\ \boxed{ X } \end{array} \; = \begin{bmatrix} \mathbf{x}_1 \\ \vdots \\ \mathbf{x}_R \end{bmatrix} \text{ and a mask } W \text{ of size } r \times c\colon \quad r \; \begin{array}{c} c \\ \boxed{ W } \end{array} .$$

For each p, q pixel, the convolution of X and W is computed as:

$$U_{p,q} = (W \star X)_{p,q} = \sum_{m=0}^{r-1} \sum_{n=0}^{c-1} W_{m,n} X_{p-m,q-n} \qquad (9)$$

In this study, we used a custom 10-layer CNN, which has the structure summarized in Fig. 2. It uses scalogram defined in the previous subsection as an input and is trained to output a binary classification decision (PD vs normal).

3.3 Performance Evaluation

For performance evaluation, we use the confusion matrix for binary classification that is defined as follows (Table 1): TP is the number of true positive examples, TN is the number of true negative examples, FP is the number of false positive

↑	Name	Type	Activations	Learnables		Total Learnables
1	imageinput 31×31×3 images with 'zerocenter' normalization	Image Input	31×31×3	-		0
2	conv_1 20 5×5×3 convolutions with stride [1 1] and padding [0 0 0 0]	Convolution	27×27×20	Weights 5×5×3×20 Bias 1×1×20		1520
3	batchnorm_1 Batch normalization with 20 channels	Batch Normalization	27×27×20	Offset 1×1×20 Scale 1×1×20		40
4	relu_1 ReLU	ReLU	27×27×20	-		0
5	conv_2 9 3×3×20 convolutions with stride [1 1] and padding [0 0 0 0]	Convolution	25×25×9	Weights 3×3×20×9 Bias 1×1×9		1629
6	batchnorm_2 Batch normalization with 9 channels	Batch Normalization	25×25×9	Offset 1×1×9 Scale 1×1×9		18
7	relu_2 ReLU	ReLU	25×25×9	-		0
8	fc 2 fully connected layer	Fully Connected	1×1×2	Weights 2×5625 Bias 2×1		11252
9	softmax softmax	Softmax	1×1×2	-		0
10	classoutput crossentropyex with classes 'Healthy' and 'Park'	Classification Output	-	-		0

Fig. 2. Architecture of custom CNN used in this study.

Table 1. Confusion matrix for binary classification.

True class		
Prediction	+1	−1
+1	TP	FP
−1	FN	TN

examples and FN is the number of false negative examples. Various performance measures can be derived from the confusion matrix as follows.

Sensitivity is the ration of correctly categorized positive observations.

Specificity is the ratio of correctly categorized negative observations.

The predicted ratio of the number of erroneous positive classifications (false discoveries) to the total number of positive classifications is referred to as the false discovery rate (FDR). The total number of null rejections includes both false positives (FP) and true positives (TP), i.e., $FDR = FP/(FP + TP)$.

The Misclassification Rate (MCR) is a performance metric that tells you the fraction of the predictions that were wrong, without distinguishing between positive and negative predictions.

Balanced accuracy (BA) is a superior tool for evaluating models trained on data with highly unbalanced target variables. BA is defined as half the sum of the true positive and true negative ratios (TNR).

The F1-Score is a metric used to evaluate the performance of a binary classifier as the harmonic mean of precision (PPV) and recall (TPR).

The Geometric Mean (G-Mean) is a statistic that compares classification performance on both minority and majority classes. A low G-Mean value shows poor performance in classifying positive instances, even if negative cases are accurately identified as such.

The Matthews Correlation Coefficient (MCC) is widely considered as one of the finest indicators for evaluating class predictions in a binary environment even when there is a significant class imbalance. The MCC is essentially a correlation coefficient between anticipated and true values.

Kappa (K) is a measure of agreement between observed and anticipated or inferred classes for instances in a testing dataset.

The receiver operating characteristics (ROC) curve depicts the sensitivity vs specificity when the threshold value is adjusted throughout the whole range of potential values. A classifier with a random prediction of the result will produce a ROC curve that hugs the top left corner, whereas a perfect classifier will produce a ROC curve that hugs the top left corner.

The area under the ROC curve is the AUC score. It has a value between 0 and 1, with a greater value indicating a stronger classifier. An AUC of 1 indicates that all observations were properly categorized. The AUC score is useful for evaluating the performance of different classifiers since it takes into account all potential threshold values.

For statistical analysis and evaluation, The findings from each type setting were analyzed using the Mann-Whitney U test to reject the null hypothesis that the normal and Parkinson's data samples were from the same data distribution.

4   Data and Results

4.1   Dataset and Data Analysis

We used the $MIT\_CS1PDdataset$ [4] which contains typing information from a population sample of sample of 54 subjects, 30 healthy controls and 24 Parkinson's disease (PD) patients. The participants were drawn from two movement disorder centers in Madrid (Spain). The example of the keypress signal acquired from the subjects is given in Fig. 3a. It's histogram is represented in Fig. 3b shows that the keypress values do not follow a Gaussian distribution and the signal is highly skewed. The analysis of average values and standard deviation values presented in Fig. 4 which shows that typical statistical features can not be used for discrimination of Healthy and PD classes, thus motivating the need for a neural network based classifier, which acys as feature extractor. An example of the scalogram obtained from the keypress signal using DWT is shown in Fig. 5. Such scalograms are used as an input to the CNN model for classification.

4.2   Experimental Settings

We used 650 scalogram images generated from the dataset, which were split into 70% images used for training, and 30% images used for testing. For training the network, we used the Adam optimizer with an initial learning rate of 0.0003, squared gradient decay factor of 0.99, and a minibatch size of 32. The training was performed for 20 epochs. The process and results of training is illustrated in Fig. 6.

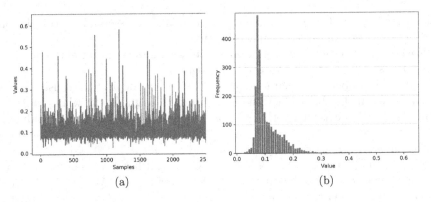

Fig. 3. Example of (a) keypress signal and (b) histogram a keypress signal

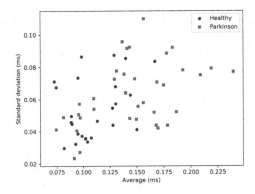

Fig. 4. Distribution of average and standard deviation values between healthy and Parkinson subjects.

4.3   Results

The algorithms were implemented using MATLAB (MathWorks, Inc.) ver. R2020b.

To better represent the performance characteristics of the classifier model, we used many performance measures such as accuracy, balanced accuracy, sensitivity, specificity, F-score, and MCC. The results of performance evaluation with their corresponding 95% confidence limits, and statistical testing are summarized in Table 2. We also visualize the classification performance using confusion matrix in Fig. 7 and roc plot in Fig. 8. To summarize the performance of the classifier using several metrics, we also used the area plot, which is given in Fig. 9.

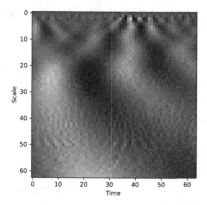

Fig. 5. Iliustration of a scalogram of a keypress signal.

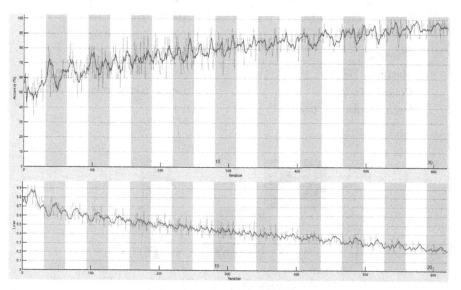

Fig. 6. Accuracy and loss during the training process of the network.

4.4   Comparison with Related Work

Several previous works considered using the keytyping data bor binary classification of PD vs Healty (Normal) subjects. The methods used and the accuracy achieved is summarized in Table 3.

The limitation of this work is that the dataset used is small (54 subjects), so there is a possibility of over-fitting while training the classifier, which may distort the final accuracy result.

Table 2. Summary of performance measures

Metric	Value	Confidence limits
Sensitivity	0.8745	0.8520–0.8942
False Negative rate (FNR)	0.1255	0.1059–0.1479
Specificity	0.9959	0.9888–0.9991
False Positive rate (FPR)	0.0041	0.0014–0.0107
Precision	0.9956	0.9885–0.9989
False discovery rate (FDR)	0.0044	0.0015–0.0111
Negative Predictive Value (NPV)	0.8807	0.8586–0.8999
Accuracy (ACC)	0.9330	0.9152–0.9474
Misclassification Rate (MCR)	0.0670	0.0527–0.0847
Balanced Accuracy (BA)	0.9352	0.9176–0.9494
Balanced Misclassification Rate (BMCR)	0.0670	0.0527–0.0847
F1-measure	0.9311	0.9132–0.9458
G-measure	0.9331	0.9153–0.9475
Matthews (MCC)	0.8733	0.8508–0.8931
Cohen's Kappa:	0.8664	0.8355–0.8973
Mann-Whitney U test	0.0048	–

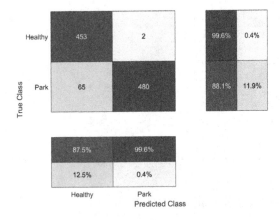

Fig. 7. Confusion matrix of classification results (Parkinson's vs Healthy).

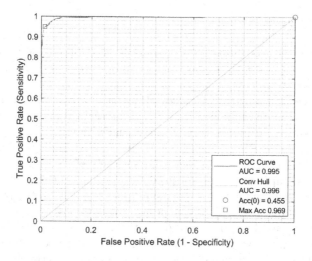

Fig. 8. The ROC plot of the classification results.

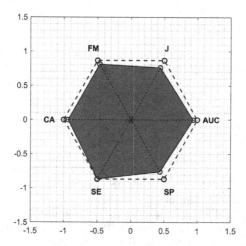

Fig. 9. Visualization of the performance metrics of the classifier (CA - accuracy, SP - specificity, SE-sensitivity, K - Kappa, FM - F-measure).

Table 3. Comparison of results with previous works

Ref.	Year	Methods	Accuracy (%)
[14]	2018	neuroQWERTY algorithm	0.76 (AUC)
[17]	2019	LSTM with Fuzzy Recurrence Plots	72.00
[20]	2020	Wavelet features and machine learning classifiers (KNN, SVM, ANN, Logistic regression)	93.5–100
This study	2021	Scalogram and custom 10-layer CNN	93.30

5 Conclusion

Our approach, which is based on the analysis of temporal patterns acquired from daily interactions with digitak devices, allows to objectively detect motor impairment in PD subjects. The goal of this study was to use wavelets characteristics and deep learning to categorize PD signals derived from keytyping. We presented a novel method for detecting PD using scalograms derived from data and categorized them using a custom CNN model with ten-fold cross-validation. The categorization of PD vs Healthy subjects yielded findings comparable to most cutting-edge techniques, achieving an accuracy of 93.30%.

The suggested approach does not need any specialized equipment or attachments, does not require medical supervision, does not rely on the practitioner's expertise and competence, and may be performed in the patient's home or workplace environment as they do theyr daily activities on a computer.

In our future work, we want to create an app that detects PD using scalograms derived from user typing data and uses deep neural networks for analysis.

References

1. Priya, S.J., Rani, A.J., Subathra, M.S.P., Mohammed, M.A., Damaševičius, R., Ubendran, N.: Local pattern transformation based feature extraction for recognition of Parkinson's disease based on gait signals. Diagnostics 11(8), 1395 (2021)
2. Guimaraes, M.T., et al.: An optimized approach to Huntington's disease detecting via audio signals processing with dimensionality reduction. In: International Joint Conference on Neural Networks (2020)
3. Lauraitis, A., Maskeliunas, R., Damaševičius, R., Krilavičius, T.: Detection of speech impairments using cepstrum, auditory spectrogram and wavelet time scattering domain features. IEEE Access 8, 96 162–96 172 (2020)
4. Giancardo, L., et al.: Computer keyboard interaction as an indicator of early Parkinson's disease. Sci. Rep. 6(1), 1–10 (2016)
5. Goetz, C.G., et al.: Movement disorder society-sponsored revision of the unified Parkinson's disease rating scale (MDS-UPDRS): scale presentation and clinimetric testing results. Mov. Disord. 23(15), 2129–2170 (2008)
6. Miller, D.B., O'Callaghan, J.P.: Biomarkers of Parkinson's disease: present and future. Metabolism 64(3), S40–S46 (2015)
7. Crawford, T., Goodrich, S., Henderson, L., Kennard, C.: Predictive responses in Parkinson's disease: Manual keypresses and saccadic eye movements to regular stimulus events. J. Neurol. Neurosurg. Psychiatry 52(9), 1033–1042 (1989)
8. Vanagas, G., Engelbrecht, R., Damaševičius, R., Suomi, R., Solanas, A.: Ehealth solutions for the integrated healthcare. J. Healthcare Eng. vol. 2018 (2018)
9. Byeon, Y.-H., Pan, S.-B., Kwak, K.-C.: Intelligent deep models based on scalograms of electrocardiogram signals for biometrics. Sensors 19(4), 935 (2019)
10. Růžička, E., Krupička, R., Zárubová, K., Rusz, J., Jech, R., Szabó, Z.: Tests of manual dexterity and speed in Parkinson's disease: not all measure the same. Parkinsonism Rel. Disord. 28, 118–123 (2016)
11. Adams, W.R.: High-accuracy detection of early Parkinson's disease using multiple characteristics of finger movement while typing. PLoS ONE 12(11), 12 (2017)

12. Ulinskas, M., Woźniak, M., Damaševičius, R.: Analysis of keystroke dynamics for fatigue recognition. In: Gervasi, O., et al. (eds.) ICCSA 2017. LNCS, vol. 10408, pp. 235–247. Springer, Cham (2017). https://doi.org/10.1007/978-3-319-62404-4_18

13. Arroyo-Gallego, T., et al.: Detection of motor impairment in Parkinson's disease via mobile touchscreen typing. IEEE Trans. Biomed. Eng. $64(9)$, 1994–2002 (2017)

14. Arroyo-Gallego, T., et al.: Detecting motor impairment in early Parkinson's disease via natural typing interaction with keyboards: validation of the neuroqwerty approach in an uncontrolled at-home setting". J. Med. Internet Res. $20(3)$, e9462 (2018)

15. Shribman, S., Hasan, H., Hadavi, S., Giovannoni, G., Noyce, A.J.: The brain test: a keyboard-tapping test to assess disability and clinical features of multiple sclerosis. J. Neurol. $265(2)$, 285–290 (2018)

16. Iakovakis, D., Hadjidimitriou, S., Charisis, V., Bostantzopoulou, S., Katsarou, Z., Hadjileontiadis, L.J.: Touchscreen typing-pattern analysis for detecting fine motor skills decline in early-stage Parkinson's disease. Sci. Rep. $8(1)$, 1–13 (2018)

17. Pham, T.D., Wardell, K., Eklund, A., Salerud, G.: Classification of short time series in early Parkinson's disease with deep learning of fuzzy recurrence plots. IEEE/CAA J. Automatica Sinica $6(6)$, 1306–1317 (2019)

18. Trager, M.H., Wilkins, K.B., Koop, M.M., Bronte-Stewart, H.: A validated measure of rigidity in Parkinson's disease using alternating finger tapping on an engineered keyboard. Parkinsonism Relat. Disord. 81, 161–164 (2020)

19. Abayomi-Alli, O.O., Damasevicius, R., Maskeliunas, R., Abayomi-Alli, A.: Bilstm with data augmentation using interpolation methods to improve early detection of Parkinson disease. In: Federated Conference on Computer Science and Information Systems, FedCSIS 2020, pp. 371–380 (2020)

20. Peachap, A.B., Tchiotsop, D., Louis-Dorr, V., Wolf, D.: Detection of early Parkinson's disease with wavelet features using finger typing movements on a keyboard. SN Appl. Sci. $2(10)$, 1–8 (2020)

21. Min, O., Wei, Z., Nian, Z., Su, X.: An application of LSTM prediction model based on keystroke data. In: ACM International Conference Proceeding Series (2020)

22. Akram, N., et al.: Developing and validating a new web-based tapping test for measuring distal bradykinesia in Parkinson's disease' (2020)

23. Wang, Y., et al.: Facilitating text entry on smartphones with qwerty keyboard for users with Parkinson's disease. In: Conference on Human Factors in Computing Systems (2021)

Author Index

in the United States
& Taylor Publisher Services